The Morphology of Chinese

This innovative study dispels the common belief that Chinese 'doesn't have words' but instead 'has characters'. Jerome Packard's book provides a comprehensive discussion of the linguistic and cognitive nature of Chinese words. It shows that Chinese, far from being 'morphologically impoverished', has a different morphological system because it selects different 'settings' on parameters shared by all languages. The analysis of Chinese word formation therefore enhances our understanding of word universals. Packard describes the intimate relationship between words and their components, including how the identities of Chinese morphemes are word-driven, and offers new insights into the evolution of morphemes based on Chinese data. Models are offered for how Chinese words are stored in the mental lexicon and processed in natural speech, showing that much of what native speakers know about words occurs innately in the form of a hard-wired, specifically linguistic 'program' in the brain.

Jerome L. Packard is Professor of Chinese in the Departments of East Asian Languages and Cultures and of Linguistics at the University of Illinois. He has also taught Chinese and Linguistics at Cornell University and the University of Pennsylvania, and has been a Fulbright Research Scholar in China. He is the author of two previous books: *A Linguistic Analysis of Aphasic Chinese Speech* (1993) and *New Approaches to Chinese Word Formation: Morphology, phonology and the lexicon in modern and ancient Chinese* (1997).

构词法

The Morphology of Chinese
A Linguistic and Cognitive Approach

JEROME L. PACKARD

CAMBRIDGE UNIVERSITY PRESS
Cambridge, New York, Melbourne, Madrid, Cape Town, Singapore, São Paulo

Cambridge University Press
The Edinburgh Building, Cambridge CB2 2RU, UK

Published in the United States of America by Cambridge University Press, New York

www.cambridge.org
Information on this title: www.cambridge.org/9780521771122

© Jerome L. Packard, 2000

This publication is in copyright. Subject to statutory exception
and to the provisions of relevant collective licensing agreements,
no reproduction of any part may take place without
the written permission of Cambridge University Press.

First published 2000
This digitally printed first paperback version 2006

A catalogue record for this publication is available from the British Library

ISBN-13 978-0-521-77112-2 hardback
ISBN-10 0-521-77112-9 hardback

ISBN-13 978-0-521-02610-9 paperback
ISBN-10 0-521-02610-5 paperback

Dedicated to the memory of
Nicholas C. Bodman, Jim McCawley and Ron Walton

All past experience has taught that . . . we must be prepared for new facts, of an entirely different character from those of our former experience . . . that in reality new orders of experience do exist, and that we may expect to meet them continually.

PERCY BRIDGMAN (1927)

Is it really any wonder that the price of significant scientific advance is a commitment that runs the risk of being wrong?

THOMAS KUHN (1962)

For what it's worth, it was worth all the while.

BILLIE JOE ARMSTRONG (1997)

Contents

List of figures *xiii*
List of tables *xiv*
List of abbreviations *xvi*

1 Introduction *1*
    1.1 Rationale: why investigate Chinese words? *1*
    1.2 The scope of this work *4*

2 Defining the word in Chinese *7*
    2.1 What *is* a 'word'?: different views *7*
        2.1.1 Orthographic word *7*
        2.1.2 Sociological word *8*
        2.1.3 Lexical word *8*
        2.1.4 Semantic word *9*
        2.1.5 Phonological word *10*
        2.1.6 Morphological word *11*
        2.1.7 Syntactic word *12*
        2.1.8 Psycholinguistic word *13*
    2.2 The Chinese concept of 'word' *14*
        2.2.1 The reality of the 'word' in Chinese *16*
    2.3 How we will define 'word' in Chinese *18*

3 Chinese word components *21*
    3.1 Describing the components *21*
        3.1.1 Possible descriptions *21*
            3.1.1.1 Relational description *21*
            3.1.1.2 Modification structure description *22*
            3.1.1.3 Semantic description *25*

            3.1.1.4   *Syntactic description*   27
            3.1.1.5   *Form class description*   32

3.2   **Form classes of the components**   34

  3.2.1   Form class identities within words   36

3.3   **Criteria for determining form class of Chinese word components**   64

3.4   **Morphological analysis of Chinese word components**   67

  3.4.1   Distinguishing 'free' and 'bound'   67
  3.4.2   Distinguishing 'content' and 'function'   69
  3.4.3   Morpheme types   69
            3.4.3.1   *Two types of affix*   70
            3.4.3.2   *Word-forming affixes vs. bound roots*   71
  3.4.4   Summary and some test cases   73
            3.4.4.1   *Determiners, classifiers and numerals*   74
            3.4.4.2   *Location morphemes*   75

3.5   **The nature of the components**   76

  3.5.1   Affixes as word components   76
  3.5.2   Bound roots as word components   77
  3.5.3   Free ('root') words as word components   78

4   Gestalt Chinese words   80

4.1   **Word types**   80

4.2   **Nouns**   82

  4.2.1   Noun types   82
            4.2.1.1   *Noun compound words*   82
            4.2.1.2   *Noun bound root words*   83
            4.2.1.3   *Noun derived words*   84
            4.2.1.4   *Noun grammatical words*   85
  4.2.2 N_1–N_2 words: kinds of relations   85

4.3   **Verbs**   89

  4.3.1   Verb types   89
            4.3.1.1   *Verb compound words*   90
            4.3.1.2   *Verb bound root words*   90

     4.3.1.3 *Verb derived words* *92*
     4.3.1.4 *Verb grammatical words* *93*
  4.3.2 V₁–V₂: kinds of relations *93*
  4.3.3 Resultative verbs *95*
     4.3.3.1 *Three classes of resultatives* *98*
     4.3.3.2 *Lexical resultatives vs. syntactic extent resultatives* *100*
     4.3.3.3 *Other properties of resultatives* *101*
  4.3.4 Verb–Object words *106*
     4.3.4.1 *The problem* *107*
     4.3.4.2 *Previous analyses* *109*
     4.3.4.3 *A proposed solution* *115*
        4.3.4.3.1 The underlying lexical identity of V–O forms *115*
        4.3.4.3.2 Lexicalization and phrase criteria *118*
           4.3.4.3.2.1 Construal as *either* word *or* phrase *123*

 4.4 Nouns and verbs by component form class: statistical tendencies *125*

 4.5 Chinese words: special properties *129*

  4.5.1 Other word properties: Y.R. Chao's insights *132*
     4.5.1.1 *Versatile–restricted* *132*
     4.5.1.2 *Positionally free or bound* *132*

5 X-bar analysis of Chinese words *134*

 5.1 Basic X-bar properties *134*

 5.2 X-bar properties applied to words *135*

  5.2.1 Expectations regarding 'X-bar' notation applied to words *135*

 5.3 X-bar morphology: previous proposals *136*

  5.3.1 Selkirk *136*
  5.3.2 Sadock *144*
  5.3.3 Other proposals *148*

x   CONTENTS

              5.3.3.1   *Scalise*   *148*
              5.3.3.2   *Di Sciullo and Williams*   *149*
    5.3.4   Discussion of Selkirk and Sadock   *149*
              5.3.4.1   *Problems with the Selkirk proposal*   *153*
                      5.3.4.1.1   The limited role of X^{-1} *153*
                      5.3.4.1.2   Lexical listing of predictable information   *156*
    5.3.5   Previous X-bar analyses of Chinese words   *157*
              5.3.5.1   *Tang*   *158*
              5.3.5.2   *Sproat and Shih*   *163*

5.4   **An alternative proposal for Chinese X-bar morphology**   *163*
    5.4.1   Classification of primitives   *165*
             5.4.1.1   *Properties of word components*   *165*
              5.4.1.2   *Why list 'bound' and 'free' in the lexicon?*   *166*
    5.4.2   Rules of word formation   *168*
    5.4.3   Limiting lexical productivity: X^{-0} as the sole recursive node   *168*
              5.4.3.1   *A note on universals*   *169*
    5.4.4   Predicted word forms   *170*
    5.4.5   Single and multiple branching structures   *173*
              5.4.5.1   *Single branching*   *175*
              5.4.5.2   *Multiple branching*   *177*
                      5.4.5.2.1   Right branching   *177*
                      5.4.5.2.2   Left branching   *183*
                      5.4.5.2.3   Some examples of multiple embedding   *192*

5.5   **The concept of 'head' applied to Chinese words**   *194*
    5.5.1   'Canonical head' vs. 'virtual head'   *194*
    5.5.2   'Semantic head' vs. 'structural head'   *195*
    5.5.3   Headless words   *196*

5.6   **The proposed analysis applied to English**   *196*
    5.6.1   Single branching   *200*
    5.6.2   Right branching   *202*
    5.6.3   Left branching   *207*

6 Lexicalization and Chinese words 216

6.1 Lexicalization and the relation between word and constituent 217

6.1.1 Semantic and grammatical reduction in lexicalization 217
6.1.2 Categories of lexicalization 219

- 6.1.2.1 *Conventional lexicalization* 219
- 6.1.2.2 *Metaphorical lexicalization* 220
- 6.1.2.3 *Asemantic lexicalization* 221
- 6.1.2.4 *Agrammatical lexicalization* 221
- 6.1.2.5 *Complete lexicalization* 222
- 6.1.2.6 *Validity of 'degree of lexicalization'* 223
- 6.1.2.7 *Categories of lexicalization and lexical strata* 223

6.1.3 Explaining exceptions to the Headedness Principle 225

- 6.1.3.1 *Systematic exceptions* 230
  - 6.1.3.1.1 Phonetic loans 230
  - 6.1.3.1.2 Neologisms 231
  - 6.1.3.1.3 Left-modified verbs 233
  - 6.1.3.1.4 Zero-derived complex nouns 234
  - 6.1.3.1.5 Induced constituent reanalysis 235
- 6.1.3.2 *Other exceptions* 236

6.2 Lexicalization and the availability of word-internal information 237

6.2.1 Phonological information 238
6.2.2 Morphological information 245
6.2.3 Syntactic information: theta roles in complex verbs 250

- 6.2.3.1 *Availability of resultative V_2 argument structure* 250
- 6.2.3.2 *Availability of 'object' theta roles to [V–O]v verbs* 258
- 6.2.3.3 *A note on non-head opacity* 260

6.2.4 Semantic information 260

6.3 Lexicalization and grammaticalization 262

6.4 Lexicalization and the formation of new words 265

6.4.1 Historical factors 265
6.4.2 The modern language 267

- 6.4.2.1 *Abbreviation and combination ('compounding')* 268

6.4.3 The creation of new morphemes in Chinese 275
    6.4.3.1 *Most new Chinese morphemes are bound roots* 280

7 Chinese words and the lexicon 284
  7.1 What is 'the lexicon'? 284
  7.2 The lexicon and lexical access 285
  7.3 Lexical access in Chinese 286
    7.3.1 Chinese speech comprehension and the lexicon 287
    7.3.2 Chinese speech production and the lexicon 292
    7.3.3 Experimental evidence demonstrating whole-word processing 294
  7.4 The Chinese lexicon: what is 'listed'? 296
    7.4.1 What is 'listed'?: a proposal 299
  7.5 Chinese characters and the lexicon 304
    7.5.1 Character sound and meaning come from the natural speech lexicon 304
    7.5.2 How do characters access the lexicon? 305
    7.5.3 Is Chinese writing 'ideographic'? 309

8 Chinese words: conclusions 310
  8.1 What have we discovered about words? 310
  8.2 The reality of the 'word' 316

References 318
Index 328

Figures

1. Prosodic hierarchy *11*
2. Syntax–Morphology interface *147*
3. Sadock and Selkirk systems compared *152*
4. A model of the Chinese lexicon *303*
5. Relation between lexical entry and orthography *306*

Tables

1. Relational descriptions of Chinese words 22
2. 'Syntactic' descriptions of Chinese words 28
3. Words containing *zhǐ* 'paper' 38–9
4. Words containing *zǒu* 'walk, go' 40–1
5. Words containing *huà* 43–5
6. Words containing *pái* 47–9
7. Words containing *shí* 51–3
8. Words containing *zhù* 54–5
9. Words containing *zhèng* 58–9
10. Words containing *zhī* 61–2
11. Example of *-zhě* and *-yuán* 72
12. Five morpheme types 74
13. Chinese word types 81
14. Noun word types by form class 82
15. Verb word types by form class 90
16. Resultative types 103–4
17. Verb–Object forms 121–2
18. Complex noun and verb structures 127
19. Bound root combinations in English 153
20. Classification of morphemes 165
21. Word component properties 166
22. Possible Chinese word forms 170
23. Predicted and actual Mandarin word types 171
24. Noun word structures 172
25. Verb word structures 173
26. Mandarin word-forming affixes 174
27. English bound roots 198
28. English word-forming affixes 199
29. Categories of lexicalization 222
30. Lexicalization categories and lexical strata 224
31. Other exceptions to the Headedness Principle 236
32. Meaning transparency in neutral-toned words 240–3
33. Internally affixed words 247–8
34. Thematic roles 251

TABLES

35　Semantic opacity and metaphor in lexicalized words   *261*
36　Modern Mandarin abbreviations   *271–2*
37　Function words formed through combination   *273*
38　Combined content words in modern Chinese   *274–5*
39　Creation of bound roots   *281–2*
40　Lexically listed elements in Chinese   *300*

Abbreviations

AAM	Augmented Addressed Morphology
Adj	adjective
Adv	adverb
AFF	affix
ASP	aspect marker
Aux	auxiliary
BA	direct object marker *ba*
CL	classifier
Conj	conjunction
DE	modification marker *de*
EXTENT	marker of extent
FLH	Full Listing Hypothesis
LE	aspect marker *le*
LIH	Lexical Integrity Hypothesis
Mod	marker of modification
N	noun
NOM	nominalizing suffix
NUM	number
O	object
PL	plural
PSC	Phrase Structure Condition
SEN	sentential
SV	stative verb
V	verb
VRB	verbalizing suffix

1 | Introduction

1.1 Rationale: why investigate Chinese words?

Why is Chinese morphology worth investigating? To many, the very posing of this question will seem to suggest an ironic lack of relevance, due to the common belief that Chinese 'doesn't have words' but instead has 'characters', or that Chinese 'has no morphology' and so is 'morphologically impoverished'. The powerful influence that characters have over conceptions of the Chinese language has led many investigators (e.g., Hoosain 1992, Xu 1997) to doubt the existence of words in Chinese. My goal is to demonstrate that speakers of Chinese compose and understand sentences just as speakers of any language do, by manipulating sentence constituents using rules of syntax, and that the smallest representatives of those constituents have the size, feel, shape and properties of words. And while Chinese may not have word forms that undergo morphological alternations such as *give*, *gave*, *giving* and *given*, Chinese does indeed have 'morphology', and the morphology that it has is of a most intriguing and enlightening sort.

Understanding how Chinese words are constructed and used is critical for a full understanding of how the Chinese language operates. Chinese native speakers possess implicit knowledge about the structure and use of words. For example, a native speaker knows that you can change *shuìjiào* 睡觉 sleep-sleep 'sleep' to *shuìguojiào* 睡过觉 sleep-ASP-sleep 'have slept' or *tiàowǔ* 跳舞 jump-dance 'dance' to *tiàoguowǔ* 跳过舞 jump-ASP-dance 'have danced', but that you can't in the same way change *jiějué* 解决 undo-decide 'decide' / *chūbǎn* 出版 emit-edition 'publish' to get **jiěguojué* *解过决 undo-ASP-decide 'have decided' or **chūguobǎn* *出过版 emit-ASP-edition 'have published'. By the same token, the native speaker knows that it is fine to say *tiàodegāo* 跳得高 jump-EXTENT-tall 'can jump high' but not **tuīdeguǎng* *推得广 push-EXTENT-wide 'can push wide'. In this book, I will explain how the native speaker knows these facts about words by describing the form that this knowledge takes. I do this by proposing generalizations that explain the regularities in the creation and use of words, and then offering principled explanations for the exceptions to those generalizations. Following current trends in cognitive science, I shall argue that much of what native speakers know about words and their structure occurs innately in the form of a hard-wired, specifically linguistic 'program' in the brain, and that such hard-wired word structure information is realized in surface form upon exposure to linguistic data.

Following that line of reasoning, Chinese words are worth investigating because they have the potential to tell us a great deal about the universal properties of words in natural language. Chinese words traditionally have been considered uninteresting as objects of morphological investigation because they do not manifest characteristics thought critical to the concept 'morphology' (such as grammatical agreement or morphophonemic and paradigmatic alternation). In the pages that follow I will show that Chinese words are particularly suitable for asking different but equally interesting questions about words – for example, how words evolve, how they come into being via lexicalization, abbreviation or borrowing, and how they pass out of existence through reduction or grammaticalization. Chinese is particularly suited to answer these questions because Chinese word components are relatively easy to isolate, identify and track over time.

Chinese words exhibit other properties that must be understood if we wish to claim a universal characterization of words. For example, to what extent is the concept of 'bound root' – which is important in Chinese (see 3.4) – relevant in other languages? Since Chinese is the world's most widely spoken language, it is clear that any account of language that aspires to a claim of universality – including universals of word structure – must take the Chinese data into account. Chinese words have a story to tell about the degree to which words are susceptible to the algorithms of syntax, and whether there is a definition of *word* that works reasonably well across languages. Using Chinese to address these questions is bound to increase our understanding of universal word properties.

I will demonstrate how the structure I propose for Chinese words goes a long way toward explaining how these words have come to have the shape they now have, resulting in the present designation of Chinese as a language of 'compounds'. If we want to know how Chinese words evolved to take their present shape, it is important to understand how word components evolve to take on the identity they have, and how that identity shifts over time as new words are created and old ones discarded. It would be a mistake to overrely on contemporary data in addressing historical factors, but a good understanding of what is happening in the language now can offer a possible window into the past.

Another important issue this study addresses is the relationship between words and characters in Chinese. Time and again, when I tell people that I work in Chinese linguistics, I get a response like: 'Oh, Chinese makes sentences by putting characters together, right?', as if, unlike the rest of the world's languages, Chinese enables spoken communication by the oral exchange of little visual icons. People for the most part do not really think that Chinese speech communication occurs via 'characters', but many *do* believe that the spoken language unit represented by the character – the morpheme – is the unit that is used to create and understand Chinese sentences. This may seem more reasonable than the notion of little visual icons flying through the air among speakers, but it is quite nearly as untenable, as we shall see in 7.2.

This widely accepted belief that the morpheme is the unit of spoken language lexical access has coloured the attitudes of many who work in the psycholinguistics of Chinese language processing. For this reason, Chinese language perception and production studies have tended to focus on properties of Chinese orthography.[1] Chinese orthography is valuable because its special characteristics enable us to ask questions about the nature of reading that cannot be asked using other orthographies. But if we want to gain insight into the psycholinguistic properties of Chinese we must also focus on the perception and production of spoken Chinese. To do that requires a precise description of Chinese words and their structure. Some who work in Chinese psycholinguistics assume that words in Chinese cannot be defined easily, or that the concept *word* is somehow not relevant for Chinese. But Chinese forms phrases and sentences as do all natural languages, by using rules of syntax to string together words that are retrieved from a mental lexicon. In order to investigate sentence processing in Chinese, we must be able to identify those words and have an understanding of their properties. Only then can we ask how the on-line natural language processing or the first- and second-language acquisition of spoken Chinese occurs.

[1] A notable exception to this is the work of Xiaolin Zhou and William Marslen-Wilson (e.g., Zhou and Marslen-Wilson 1994, 1995).

1.2 The scope of this work

This volume is a combination of descriptive and theoretical approaches. Following this introductory chapter, I provide criteria for identifying Chinese words in chapter 2, and in chapter 3 I explain why word structure is optimally described in terms of the form class identity of word components and how that may be accomplished. Then I offer a morphological analysis of Chinese words in chapter 4, followed by a universal ('X-bar') analysis in chapter 5 that abstracts the morphological properties of words over different form class categories. In chapter 6, I discuss the phenomenon of lexicalization, including why it explains how the relation between the gestalt word and its constituents varies, and why this is an important factor in understanding how Chinese words have evolved into their present form. The nature of the Chinese mental lexicon is discussed in chapter 7, including how lexical access occurs in speaking, hearing and reading Chinese. Finally, in chapter 8 I offer a summary and some concluding remarks.

The working hypothesis of this book is that the entity 'word' is a real cognitive construct that is also a linguistic primitive in natural language, and that word properties and word-forming algorithms like those proposed for Chinese arise due to universal principles and constraints that apply to all languages, serving to circumscribe the range of possible word types that may occur. This critically involves the notion of lexical primitives (X^{-0}, X^{-1} etc., see chapter 5),[2] the existence and combination of which I propose constitute the universal character of word structure. It is proposed that words in all human natural languages are analysable into these lexical primitives and their concatenation, subject to limited parametric variation.

I shall be referring in all cases to Mandarin Chinese, transcribed using the pinyin system of phonetic romanization and represented using simplified Chinese characters. Also, I'll be dealing for the most part with only two-syllable words. There are many words of three, four and more syllables in Chinese, but I feel better able to investigate

---

[2] For the purposes of this study, the terms X^{-0} and X^0 (with negative and non-negative superscripts respectively) may be considered the same. I generally follow the convention of using negative superscripts for morphological objects as a notational device to distinguish them from syntactic objects.

INTRODUCTION 5

the various aspects of word formation in depth by restricting the data base at present to words consisting of two syllables. To further restrict my data base, in this study I deal for the most part only with complex words formed from noun and verb elements.

I would like to thank for helpful comments or references (in more-or-less chronological order) Yingxing Yin, Joan Bybee, Isabel Wong, Michael Sawer, Dick Anderson, Bill Nagy, Yu-chiao Jade Longenecker, Yu Shen, Yabing Wang, Xiaolin Hu, Tianwei Xie, Carl Pollard, Jim Dew, Vivian Ling, Mike Wright, Taiyuan Tseng, Richard Sproat, Kevin Miller, Chiung-chu Wang, Gary Feng, Shiou-yuan Chen, Bob Good, Chih-ping Sobelman, Jerry Morgan, Georgia Green, Jennifer Cole, Dan Silverman, Hans Hock, Adele Goldberg, Elabbas Benmamoun, Chin Woo Kim, James Tai, Yung-li Chang, James Myers, Jane Tsai, Shou-hsin Teng, C-C. Cheng, Benjamin Tsou, Liejiong Xu, Derek Herforth, Marcus Taft, Xiaolin Zhou, Tongqiang Xu, Charles N. Li, Tsu-lin Mei, Elizabeth Traugott, Wen-yu Chiang, Yuancheng Tu, Si-qing Chen, David Chen, Yan Chen, Shenghang Huang, Yu-min Ku, Kazue Hara, Shu-fen Chen, Gary Dell, Carol Packard, Jose Hualde, Jenn-Yeu Chen, James Yoon, Victor Mair and Stanley Starosta. I would especially like to thank my friend Shengli Feng, two anonymous Cambridge University Press reviewers and two additional anonymous reviewers for giving me valuable detailed feedback on draft versions of the manuscript. Special thanks also to Alain Peyraube for detailed comments on the manuscript and for many valuable references to complex word formation in earlier stages of the Chinese language. Thanks also to Christine Bartels and Kate Brett for having faith in my work, to Citi Potts for excellent copy editing, and to Barbara Cohen for making the index. I would like to thank the University of Illinois at Urbana-Champaign for granting the sabbatical leave allowing me to work on this book, and the UIUC Research Board for awarding the grant that enabled me to complete the project. Finally, I want to thank my fellow family members Carol, Errol, Sam and Eric, whose patience as I worked on this book was always appreciated (though it may not have seemed so at times), and whose dinner conversations have provided an endless font of linguistic and conceptual creativity as well as comic relief.

As the reader goes through this work, in many places it will become evident that I have remained overly simplistic, choosing to sidestep many questions of interest. In some cases I have remained at that level intentionally, because to do otherwise would have resulted in great delays as I tackled problems of detail, and also because the resulting exposition has allowed me to make the points and address the issues I wish to focus on. There are also likely to be logical lacunae and analytical abysses in the interplay of ideas that I have forged in putting this work together. I invite the reader to point these out, and to offer suggestions and criticism.

2 | Defining the word in Chinese

2.1 What *is* a 'word'?: different views

For speakers of some languages, the 'word' is a robustly intuitive notion. But it seems that no matter what the language, we have a hard time providing an exact definition that encompasses all and only those entities that our intuition tells us are words (see, e.g., Anderson 1985b: 153–4). This means that the concept 'word' is nothing if not elusive, and suggests that perhaps there is no concept of word that is universally applicable. Indeed, if there is no cross-linguistic, or universal psycholinguistic evidence for the existence of the word, then we may well doubt the validity of the word as a primitive natural language construct. It could a priori be the case that there is really no such thing in absolute terms as the 'word', and that it is just an artifactual linguistic construct that happens to coincide with salient units intermediate between morphemes and phrases that happen to appear in many of the world's languages.

There is another reason why the possibility that the 'word' is a derived rather than primitive construct may occur to us: words are definable using several disparate linguistic criteria. For some of these criteria considered in isolation, the label 'word' seems strangely inappropriate, since words so defined seem overly abstract, with nothing very 'word-like' about them. Let us take a look at these criteria to see if any of them are closer than others in providing an accurate portrayal of 'word'.

2.1.1 Orthographic word

Probably the most popular conception of the word (especially in languages such as English) is that of the 'orthographic word', that is, the word as defined by writing conventions. It is easy for an English speaker (or a pigeon, for that matter) to segment a written English text into words strictly by the visual appearance of the text, i.e., by picking out the written material that occurs between the spaces. Speakers of English therefore have a strong 'intuition' as to what is and is not a word in spoken language, partly as an effect learned through experience with orthography: in producing written English the speaker/writer must put the spaces in their proper place. This, of course, raises the question of what criteria are used to decide where the spaces go in the first place. It turns out that the criterion that is closest to the orthographic word in English is remarkably close to that of the 'syntactic word' (see 2.1.7 below).

In deciding for the purposes of this study what are words in Chinese, we could safely eliminate the orthographic word for reasons having little to do with Chinese per se – namely, that orthographic words are usually defined using non-orthographic criteria. That is, items are usually selected for membership in the 'orthographic word' category based upon linguistic properties other than the nature of the orthography. In any case, the orthographic word has no relevance specifically for Chinese, since Chinese orthography segments written texts into characters, which generally represent morphemes rather than 'words'.[1]

2.1.2 Sociological word

The term 'sociological word' may be attributed to Chao (1968: 136), and describes a concept that native speakers use to refer to linguistic units of a certain size. Chao defines it as 'that type of unit, intermediate in size between a phoneme and a sentence, which the general, non-linguistic public is conscious of, talks about, has an everyday term for, and is practically concerned with in various ways' (Chao 1968: 136–8). The sociological word is the familiar 'word' in English, and in Chinese, it is the *zì* 字, meaning either the Chinese written character or the Chinese spoken morpheme. The concept of the sociological word will be further discussed in 2.2.

2.1.3 Lexical word

Another common conception of 'word' we might call the *lexical word* (termed the *listeme* by Di Sciullo and Williams 1987: 1), which incorporates the 'listedness' characteristic of lexical items. That is, the lexicon is traditionally seen as that component of the grammar that contains

---

[1] Of course the orthographic definition of 'word' does work, albeit tautologically, for romanized Chinese, since in romanized Chinese the goal is generally to put spaces between words rather than between morphemes.

all that is not predictable, and must therefore be stored in a memorized list. To that extent, 'words' are those idiosyncratic, arbitrary pairings of sound and meaning that cannot be generated by rule 'on line' that we file away in memory for use in the performance of a speech act.

The 'listedness' criterion is neither sufficient nor necessary to define 'word', because it is common to have both 'listed' items that are not words (e.g., idiomatic phrases or 'listed syntactic objects', Di Sciullo and Williams 1987: 5) and words that are not 'listed' (e.g., large numbers of complex words in languages such as Turkish or Italian that are productively constructed using members of affixation paradigms, and are not likely to be stored away as 'listemes'). The concept of the lexical word is popular because it most closely comports with the idea of 'listing as a dictionary entry' that is popularly taken to be a defining criterion for 'word', and because it overlaps almost completely with the orthographic word discussed above.

The lexical definition of 'word' is not useful as a defining concept in our investigation of Chinese for just this reason: the 'listedness' criterion fails to include many Chinese words created by rule (see 7.4.1) and improperly includes many things approximating Di Sciullo and Williams' 'listed syntactic objects'. So while it will be interesting to keep this notion in mind – especially when it comes to the time to consider the structure of the Chinese lexicon – for the time being we will set aside the concept of lexical word.

2.1.4 Semantic word

A definition using semantic criteria is one of the most traditional ways of characterizing the notion of 'word'. The *semantic word* is sometimes equated with the idea of a 'unitary concept'. Sapir (1921/1949: 25) portrayed the word as 'the outward sign of a specific idea, whether of a single concept or image or of a number of such concepts or images definitely connected into a whole'. Baxter and Sagart (1997; citing Dowty, Wall and Peters 1981) characterize the semantic word as the 'basic expression' of formal semantics, a form with a semantic value such that such expressions may combine to form complex expressions, but may not be further decomposed into subexpressions (Baxter and Sagart 1997).

The semantic definition of word is one that strongly appeals to intuition – many people probably feel they have an idea of what a 'basic concept' might be, even if it is not uniquely definable either within or among speakers. However, the notion of semantic word is only minimally useful, because reducing concepts to their semantic primitives is a notoriously difficult exercise. Even if it were possible to come up with a list of such semantic primitives, examining them independently of their phonological form actually gets us no closer to defining 'word', since the concept of 'word' crucially requires reference to phonetic form. And once we relate those semantic primitives to phonological forms, what we get is a minimal pairing of form and meaning – an entity that is closer to the traditional morpheme than to the word.[2]

2.1.5 Phonological word

The *phonological word* is a 'word-sized' entity that is defined using phonological criteria. Chao (1968: 153–4) considers the existence of potential pauses – the places in a sentence where it is possible to pause naturally – to be a phonological criterion for the definition of word boundaries in Chinese (for a more general application of the concept, see Anderson 1985b: 150–2). But 'word' as defined by the phonological criterion of potential pause turns out to be of little use, since, like the orthographic and lexical definitions of 'word', this criterion turns out largely to be based upon other (i.e., syntactic, morphological or prosodic phonological) criteria. That is, the reason 'pauses' cannot go where a speaker feels it is inappropriate to place them is because their placement would violate the constituency of a syntactic, a morphological or a (otherwise defined) phonological word.

More recently the phonological definition of word has been based upon the domain of phonological rule application, or the output of a phonological rule. Dai (1997) gives examples of phonological word boundaries, defined by the application of a phonological rule. Baxter and Sagart (1997) give examples of accent (Czech) and sandhi (Sanskrit) phenomena, as well as stress units in Swahili, Polish and ancient Greek conditioned by independently defined word boundaries. The phonological word has also been characterized in prosodic terms, with Duanmu (1997) using phonological tone and stress evidence to distinguish words and phrases in modern Chinese.

[2] Thus we do refer to semantics when defining the morpheme, and make use of semantic criteria when we discuss the concept of 'semantic head' in 5.5.2.

Figure 1   Prosodic hierarchy

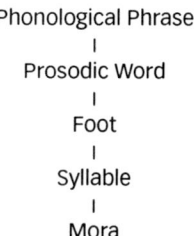

Another characterization of words in prosodic terms – the *prosodic word* – has been defined as an abstract constituent of a given level of prosodic phonological structure, located in the prosodic hierarchy between the phonological foot and the phonological phrase (see figure 1), with the prosodic word overlapping in many cases with the word as independently defined using other criteria (Selkirk 1980; Nespor and Vogel 1982, 1986; Inkelas 1989, 1993; McCarthy and Prince 1993; Feng 1997). In this theory, any instance of prosodic word must contain at least one foot, and every foot must in turn be bimoraic or bisyllabic. Thus, a prosodic word must contain at least two syllables or one bimoraic syllable. Feng (1997) applies this concept of prosodic word to ancient Chinese word formation, arguing that the prosodic word was important in the historical development of bisyllabic Chinese words.

We will not focus on words defined phonologically, because, while phonological structure may indeed be sensitive to and correspond to word-sized entities as independently defined elsewhere, and phonology does provide another important piece of evidence that converges on the construct *word*, nonetheless the other types of evidence correlate better with speakers' intuitions of what words are.

2.1.6 Morphological word

The *morphological word* may be understood as the result or 'output' of a word-formation rule. Di Sciullo and Williams (1987: 1) see morphological words (their term is *morphological objects*) as the set of items comprising morphemes and the output of the rules of morpheme combination. Anderson (1985b: 153) defines morphological word as 'a base together with the expression of the [grammatical] categories appropriate for its part-of-speech class'. Dai (1997: 112) has applied the concept of morphological word to Chinese, meaning 'the maximal domain to which morphological rules may refer' also, 'the domains or outputs of compounding and affixation processes'.

My own definition of morphological word applied to Chinese is the proper output of word-formation rules in the language. Words defined in this way overlap to large extent albeit not completely with the set of wordlike entities defined using other criteria. For example, in the word *māotóuyīng* 猫头鹰 cat-head-hawk 'owl' (with the structure [[N⁰ N⁰]N⁰]N⁰; it is a 'cat-headed hawk' and not a 'hawk-headed cat'), the constituent **māotóu-* 'cat-head' is a morphological word because it is formed from the bona fide Chinese word-creating rule N⁰ → N⁰ N⁰, including the proper bracketing that results from the output of that rule (see 5.4 and table 23), as seen from the existence of words like *huǒshān* 火山 fire-mountain 'volcano', *bīnghé* 冰河 ice-river 'glacier' and *mǎxióng* 马熊 horse-bear 'brown bear'. However, unlike *huǒshān*, *bīnghé* and *mǎxióng*, **māotóu-* may not occur independently in an utterance (i.e., it may be a morphological word but it is not also a 'syntactic word', see 2.1.7 and the discussion of examples in chapter 5).

The morphological word – the 'morphological object' of Di Sciullo and Williams – turns out to be an important construct for Chinese, because there exists a clear, discrete set of word-formation rules in the language, the output of which does not overlap completely with the set of wordlike entities derived using other criteria. That is, all proper outputs of bona fide morphological rules are morphologically legal (and are therefore 'morphological words'), but some entities formed by these rules must be augmented with additional information before they can appear freely in utterances. However, while we will use the concept of morphological word in the analysis of Chinese that follows, it will not constitute our primary point of departure.

2.1.7 Syntactic word

A *syntactic word* is a form that can stand as an independent occupant of a syntactic form class slot, in other words, a syntactically free form, commonly designated in the literature as X^0. This is probably the most common current linguistic characterization of the notion 'word', and seems to serve as the basis for identifying the 'orthographic' and 'lexical' words discussed above (in languages with orthographies and dictionaries so designed, at any rate). In their X-bar analyses of word structure, Sadock (1991: 27) and Selkirk (1982: 6) use the X^0 designation to represent words as the minimal units of syntax, as do Di Sciullo and Williams, who term them 'syntactic atoms' (1987: 1).

Defining a syntactic word presumes that we can identify basic form class categories, and then use native speaker judgments to determine what entities are able to minimally occupy the category slots within utterances. This notion of syntactic word, as we shall see, will be one we crucially rely on in our description of Chinese words.

2.1.8 Psycholinguistic word

I use the term *psycholinguistic word* to refer to a portion of language at roughly the 'word' level of linguistic analysis that is (albeit perhaps not consciously) salient and highly relevant to the operation of the language processor, but does not necessarily match up consistently with any of the notions of *word* defined in traditional linguistic terms: it is a conception of 'word' as described vis-à-vis the operation of the language processor. The construct so defined could be a cognitive compilation of, e.g., phonological/prosodic, semantic, morphological and syntactic knowledge, with the relative proportions of such knowledge at any given point in processing time being dependent upon linguistic task demands or the state of the language processor.[3]

The existence of a psycholinguistic word is plausible from the perspective of psychology, as explained in a discussion of the contents of the lexicon by Henderson, who says that 'the lexicon of linguistics enjoys a different ontological status than psychology' and that 'it is perilous to assume that the boundaries of the linguist's hypothetical "lexicon" are congruent with that of the psychologist' (Henderson 1989: 35). With that as background, it is clear that the psycholinguistic word involves the 'psychological reality' of the linguistic construct 'word',[4] in the sense that it seeks to hold constant that part of 'word' that is the most 'psychologically real' at any given point in language processing.

---

[3] Di Sciullo and Williams (1987: 15–21), in a section entitled 'the psychological lexicon', discuss the storage of lexical items, but seem to equate the concept to that of 'listed object' or 'listeme'. Also, Hu (1985: 68–70) discusses an entity he calls the 'psychological word' (*xīnlǐcí* 心理词), but uses it to refer to the consensus of Chinese adults on the identity of words as extracted from written character texts.

[4] Hoosain (1992) discusses the psychological reality of words in Chinese.

One could imagine, for example, that of the semantic, phonological and grammatical information that composes the 'word', the type of information that is 'most active' at a given, fixed, point in the time course of language production (say, 500 milliseconds prior to onset of articulation) might be semantic, phonological or grammatical, depending upon whether linguistic task demands more heavily implicate the 'message' (roughly corresponding to the meaning; see Garrett 1988 and Levelt 1989), the sound or the syntax. Given this conception, the *psycholinguistic word* would have, e.g., a phonological identity in some contexts and a semantic identity in others, depending on the linguistic task.

The notion of the psycholinguistic word is quite intriguing and may in the end turn out to be quite relevant, but since little research has been done to determine what its properties might be in *any* language – much less Chinese – we are better off delaying its discussion until we have a firmer grasp on the concept *word* as understood based on traditional criteria.

2.2 The Chinese concept of 'word'

The 'word' is a clear and intuitive notion in English, because in the culture of English speakers the concept of the 'word' is particularly salient and robust. For example, there are cross*word* puzzles, English speakers find themselves searching for the right *word*, all writing is divided up into *words*, and what are searched for in dictionaries or databases are usually *words*. This is what Chao called the sociological word (Chao 1968: 136–8; see 2.1.2): the unit that the society and culture takes to be the salient, critical subcomponent of an utterance. For the English language and culture the concept is highly intuitive, and speakers of English might assume that the concept 'word' is universal because it is so salient in the culture and tradition of the English language.

In Chinese, however, the *word* is by no means a clear and intuitive notion. In Chinese language and culture, the clear and intuitive notion – the *sociological word* – is the *zì* 字. The term *zì* actually has two distinct meanings in popular usage: it can mean either a morpheme in the spoken language, or it can mean a written Chinese character (Hoosain

1992: 112).⁵ But most speakers of Chinese do not distinguish between these two meanings of *zì* when they use the term: to these speakers, the *zì* as morpheme and the *zì* as written character are *one and the same thing*. This is due to the tacit assumption that the spoken *zì* (morpheme) can always be visually rendered with a written *zì* (character).

The status of the *zì* as the 'sociological word' in Chinese is just as salient as the status of the 'word' as the 'sociological word' in English. For example, in Chinese there are *zì* puzzles, Chinese speakers find themselves searching for the right *zì*, all writing is divided up into *zì*, and what are searched for in dictionaries or databases are usually *zì*. In the linguistic study of the Chinese language, the *zì* was considered to be the basic, primary unit of linguistic analysis as late as the 1920s (see Duanmu 1997; Packard 1997b). Further evidence of the salience of the *zì* as the sociological word is seen from the fact that Chinese speakers will often use the term *zì* to refer to a single two-character (two-syllable or two-morpheme) form, running counter to the usual equation of *zì* with 'character'.

There is a term in Chinese for 'word' as distinct from character, namely, *cí* 词. This term – which is used mostly as a technical term by specialists in language and linguistics – may be considered the 'syntactic word' in Chinese. For example, *hóngniǎo* 红鸟 red-bird 'red bird' consists of two characters and two morphemes, and it is also two *cí*, a noun and a modifying adjective. This is evident because of the generalizability and productivity of the two constituents: we can substitute virtually any adjective and any noun and it still retains its compositional meaning. In contrast, the term *hónghuā* 红花 red-flower 'safflower (a Chinese medicinal term)' consists of two characters and two morphemes, but it is one *cí*⁶ because of its lack of compositionality: we cannot substitute another adjective for *hóng* or another noun for *huā* without losing the idiomatic meaning (example from Zhang 1985: 64).

Chinese scholars have written a great deal on how to distinguish *cí* from the smaller *zì* and the larger 'word groups' (*cízǔ* 词组) or phrases (*duǎnyǔ* 短语 or *lèyǔ* 仂语), most often basing their decisions on

---

[5] There are, in addition, technical terms for morpheme: *císù* 词素 'word-element' and *yǔsù* 语素 'language-element'.

[6] The string *hóng huā* may also be considered two *cí* (meaning 'red flower'), and so it has both idiomatized and non-idiomatized readings, as with the English *black bird* and *blackbird*.

semantic or syntactic criteria. Wang (1953; citing Shuxiang Lü), for example, in addition to using semantic criteria (generally corresponding to 'basic unit of meaning'), defines a *cí* in Chinese as the 'smallest independently useable part of language' or 'that part of the sentence that can be used independently'.[7]

This issue of identifying the word arises as a practical problem in China because of the need to segment *pinyin* alphabetic phonetic writing into discrete orthographic units. *Pinyin* orthography is not written as an unsegmented string of letters nor is it segmented according to the syllable (as with the character orthography). Rather, scholarly authorities in China in principle define the unit of orthographic parsing to be the *cí* (Committee on Chinese Phonetic Orthography 1985). But in fact, the *cí* as defined for purposes of segmenting *pinyin* orthography and the *cí* as defined using grammatical principles are not the same thing. The former is termed the 'formal word' (or 'orthographic word') and the latter the 'theoretical word' (Zhang 1985: 62; citing Shuxiang Lü). The difference between the two is that the 'theoretical word' is, in essence, the *cí*, while the 'formal word' is based on the *cí* but undergoes further subjective redefinition based on length, conventional usage etc., focussing on ease of popular use (Zhang 1985: 62). This means, for example, that there is a de facto length constraint on the 'formal word' that does not apply to the 'theoretical word'.

The way I define the Chinese 'word' in the present work closely comports with the notion 'theoretical word' discussed above. The implication is that the notion of word presented here will have relatively little bearing on proposals such as those presented for orthography as seen in *Basic Rules of Chinese Phonetic Writing Orthography* (Committee 1985), because the latter is concerned with issues such as ease of use. The proposals in the present work could however be relevant to the parsing of texts into words as performed by computer algorithm, since, as we shall see, the present work is rule based, and depends on the identities and properties of constituent morphemes.

2.2.1 The reality of the 'word' in Chinese

The possibility that the 'word' is merely an artificial construct or epiphenomenon certainly occurs to speakers of Chinese, since –

[7] 词是'语言的最小的独立运用的单位'；词是'句子所由组成的各个可以独立运用的部分' Wang (1953: 3).

metalinguistically speaking – the 'word' in Chinese does not appear to be a particularly intuitive notion. Knowledge of the Chinese language, along with the 'culture of language' that accompanies that knowledge, suggests to Chinese speakers that the notion 'word' is a concept that comes from the West and so is based on the structure of western-type languages. Therefore, the intuition of many a Chinese speaker is that words simply do not exist in Chinese, and that the hearer simply 'gets the meaning' of an utterance as it unfolds, without it necessarily being parsed into word-sized units. This is suggested by some investigators in Chinese psycholinguistics as well, with Hoosain, for example, saying that 'a greater proportion of multimorphemic words in Chinese (compared with English) is not necessarily listed in the lexicon but instead have meanings *arrived at in the course of language use*' (Hoosain 1992: 126; my italics). Hoosain (1992: 126–8) also expresses doubt about whether Chinese speakers in fact possess an inherent conception of what a word is. Hoosain claims that a 'fluidity' of the word–morpheme boundary exists in the minds of Chinese speakers (1992: 118–20), and gives several reasons why this is true in Chinese more than in other languages.

Firstly, Hoosain says that the knowledge of classical Chinese language (in which many morphemes that are now bound were originally free) is variable among the native speaker population, and may affect speakers' judgments about what is and is not a word. Secondly, there is great variation among Chinese speakers in their knowledge of other Chinese dialects, which is important because, according to Hoosain, the bound–free status of morphemes differs across dialects. Thirdly, there is great variation in the bound–free status of morphemes according to context. Finally, Hoosain says that morphemes are more versatile in Chinese than in other languages, implying that morphemes may be inherently more indeterminate with respect to their bound–free status in Chinese.

All of these reasons that Hoosain uses to explain the fluidity of the word–morpheme boundary in the mind of the Chinese native speaker involve within- and among-speaker variation on the bound–free status of certain morphemes caused by various factors (see also Tang 1995: 196–8). However, the only thing this really suggests is that such speakers may be uncertain in their *metalinguistic judgment* about the status of certain morphemes. Metalinguistic judgments about one's language and how the language actually 'works' are two different things. In particular, while speakers may be uncertain in making metalinguistic judgments about certain words and morphemes, it is unlikely that such speakers would be uncertain about the proper *use* of such forms. This becomes clear once we recognize that for a single morpheme to have both bound and free usages means that such a morpheme actually requires two separate entries in the mental lexicon: one as a free morpheme and one as a bound morpheme. Especially under these circumstances, native speakers may be uncertain when confronted with a metalinguistic choice, but will be totally clear on proper usage within a given context (see further discussion in 3.4.1).

Hoosain also cites several experiments purporting to show that the word is not a perceptual gestalt, and therefore not a psychologically real entity for native Chinese speakers. However, those results conflict with those of several more recent studies (Zhang and Peng 1992; Zhou and Marslen-Wilson 1994, 1995; Liu and Peng 1997; Taft and Zhu 1997), all of which suggest that two-morpheme words are indeed stored, retrieved and perceived as gestalt units. Also, Chinese characters were the experimental stimuli used in the studies cited by Hoosain to infer the properties of words. As we shall see in 7.5, it is likely that such results are confounded by the perceptual characteristics of Chinese characters as distinct from the words and morphemes those characters represent in the natural speech lexicon.

2.3 How we will define 'word' in Chinese

In this work, the syntactic definition of word will be used as the basis for analysing Chinese words. We begin with the syntactic definition as a first step in isolating wordlike units for analysis, for several reasons.

First, the syntactic definition is the one that most closely comports with the intuitive notion of 'word' among native speakers of Chinese, as evidenced by the fact that the Chinese technical term for 'word' (*cí* 词) is very close to the notion as defined using the syntactic definition. Also, aside from expressions which derive from Classical Chinese and different registers of use (such as literary vs. colloquial, standard vs. local dialect, individual variation, etc.), there is a surprising degree of unanimity among Chinese native speakers as to which entities are able to occupy a syntactic form class slot independently (see, e.g., Hu 1985: 69, who cites a study that found over 85 per cent agreement on word boundaries). Where there is less than complete unanimity, it is likely that there are in fact two independent identities that coexist separately on a continuum in transition between, e.g., 'bound and free' or 'word and phrase' (see 4.3.4.3.2.1).

Second, the syntactic definition of 'word' motivates the concept in most other languages. It is the concept that Anderson refers to when speaking of the intuition of 'something real about the organization of the sentence' (1985b: 150), and says that sentences seem to be composed of such independent isolable entities. Third, some of the criteria for defining word discussed above – for example, the orthographic and lexical definitions, and the potential pause – are based upon the syntactic word. Finally, it will make sense for us to give a basic characterization of words using the syntactic definition because, as we shall see below, in Chinese the internal components of words are best understood and analyzed within a framework that complements the notion of 'syntactic word' as a basic defining concept.

The assumption of the existence of the syntactic word follows a universalist argument, which assumes that the word is biologically hard-wired and psychologically real, and has a tendency in natural language to 'weaken' the status of individual component morphemes, undermining their ability to function as free forms (see 6.1.1 and 6.2.2). Since it is generally recognized that sentence syntax contains the rules by which we produce and comprehend meaningful language, we must presume that utterances are segmented into minimal units that the syntax can manipulate. The constituents that are moved about by rules of syntax are nouns, verbs, etc., and the smallest occupant of one of those constituent slots is what we are theoretically defining as a 'word'. In the case of Chinese, these constituents cannot be morphemes, because morphemes are in no sense the units that are manipulated by syntactic rules to produce a comprehensible sentence or utterance (see discussion in 7.3.1 and 7.3.2). The *zì* or morpheme serves as a subpart of those entities that are the smallest things that can occupy a syntactic slot. Sometimes the *zì* can occupy it alone, but sometimes – indeed most of the time – the *zì* cannot occupy that slot by itself. But there are things that can minimally occupy those slots, and we have given them a name: they are called *words*.

To summarize, this work critically assumes that the linguistic construct of the syntactic 'word', rather than being an artifact of western linguistic analysis, is real and fundamental to the nature of language, and therefore exists as a real linguistic construct universally used in producing and understanding utterances. To believe otherwise for Chinese, we would have to assume that the Chinese language is not so much 'word-based' as based on something else, with the most viable candidate being the morpheme. As we shall see in 7.3, such an assumption finds little empirical support.

3 | Chinese word components

3.1 Describing the components

3.1.1 Possible descriptions

Having decided to use the 'syntactic' definition as our means of isolating Chinese words as units of analysis in this study, let us now consider how to understand the inner constituents of those words. We must determine which properties of word constituents will give us the greatest insight into Chinese words, and especially into the relationship between words' inner and outer properties. The characteristics of gestalt Chinese words are, as we shall see, related to the characteristics of the components that make them up. The question is: Of the many ways to characterize word components, which will give us the best insight into the properties of the gestalt word? Some of these characterizations apply poorly or inconsistently, and so provide an inadequate understanding of word components and their relation to the words they compose.[1] Let us consider some of the ways that have been used to describe Chinese word component morphemes.

3.1.1.1 Relational description

Chinese words can be characterized by the general type of relationship that obtains between the two morphemes that make up the word. An example of this type of approach is Xia (1946) *Methods of Composing Two-character Words* (Pan, Yip and Han 1993: 38). Xia uses 'meaning limiting' (*xiànyì* 限义) to describe two-morpheme nouns whose reference is 'limited' by having the first morpheme be a modifier of the noun morpheme on its right. He uses the term 'oppositional' (*fǎnduì* 反对) to describe words composed of opposing concepts. 'Modificational' (*fùzhuàng* 副状) describes a general relationship of modification between the two word constituents. Finally, Xia uses the term 'cause-effect'

---

[1] Note that the question of how word components may be characterized is orthogonal to the discussion in 2.1 of how words themselves are to be defined. For example, it is conceivable that words are defineable using syntactic criteria (see 2.1.7) but that the components of words are best described using a semantic analysis.

Table 1 Relational descriptions of Chinese words

type	examples*	Chinese characters	English gloss	meaning
'meaning limiting' (xiànyì)	máobǐ yáolán	毛笔 摇篮	hair-pen sway-basket	'writing brush' 'cradle'
'oppositional' (fǎnduì)	mǎimài shìfēi	买卖 是非	buy-sell right-wrong	'business' 'right and wrong'
'modificational' (fùzhuàng)	guóyíng zuòshì	国营 坐视	country-operate sit-watch	'state-run' 'sit by and watch'
'cause–effect' (yīnguǒ)	dǎdǎo tuīfān	打倒 推翻	hit-fall push-turn:over	'overthrow' 'topple'

* Xia's examples taken as cited in Pan, Yip and Han (1993: 38)

(*yīnguǒ* 因果) to describe words in which the first morpheme indicates a 'cause' and the second indicates its 'effect' (many of these would fall into the class of 'resultative verbs'; see 4.3.3). Some examples of these word categories are seen in table 1.

One reason the relational description method falls short is because it is inconsistent in characterizing the relationships it describes. For example, it is not clear that there is a real difference between the descriptive categories 'meaning limiting' and 'modificational'. Also, while this method may provide a reasonably good way of describing word types in general terms, it has little linguistic or psycholinguistic value beyond the surface description. That is, it tells us little about the underlying speaker knowledge that native speakers exercise in creating and using these words.

3.1.1.2 Modification structure description

Chinese words may also be characterized in terms of the type of modification relationship that obtains between morphemes, or, in other words, 'what modifies what'. The modification structure can take a juxtapositional, 'flat' form, in which the two morphemes are structurally 'parallel' and neither modifies, or is subordinate to, the other; or it can take a hierarchical form, with one constituent modified by and therefore structurally 'dominating' the other.

Examples of words of the former type, with a 'parallel' modification structure are: *shùmù* 树木 tree-wood 'trees' [[shù][mù]], *qiángbì* 墙壁

wall-wall 'wall' [[qiáng][bì]], *jiějué* 解决 undo-decide 'solve' [[jiě][jué]] and *xuǎnzé* 选择 select-pick 'choose' [[xuǎn][zé]]. In these words, the placement of modifying brackets indicates that neither constituent has a modifying or subordinate relation to the other. The same is seen in the structure of the trees illustrating the modification, seen in (1), in which the constituents of the words above are represented as being on the same structural 'level', with neither constituent being in a position of 'dominance' over the other.

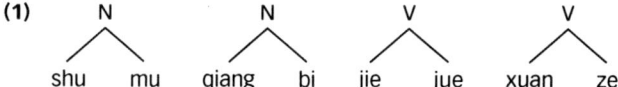

Examples of words with a 'hierarchical' modification structure are: *qiānbǐ* 铅笔 lead-writing:tool 'pencil' [qiān[bǐ]], *diànnǎo* 电脑 electricity-brain 'computer' [diàn[nǎo]], *suǒxiě* 索写 contract-write 'abbreviate' [suǒ[xiě]] and *chuàngzuò* 创作 begin-make 'create' [chuàng[zuò]]. The bracket placement in these examples and the tree structures in (2) represent the element on the right as being higher in the structural tree than, and therefore dominating, the element on the left.

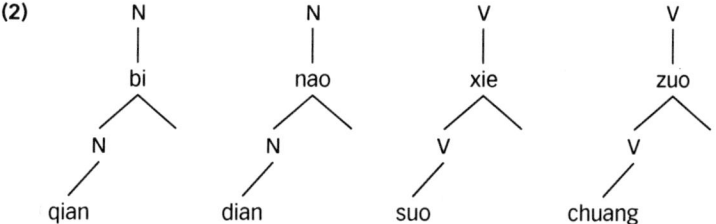

In words with a hierarchical modification structure, the modifier limits the scope of the modified element. So the example *qiānbǐ* lead-writing:tool 'pencil' can be conceived of as 'the subset of writing tools that are made of "lead",[2] and *suǒxiě* contract-write 'abbreviate' can be thought of as 'a subset of writing activity that contracts'. This type of 'scope delimitation' does not occur in words with a 'parallel' structure. That is, the example *shùmù* 树木 tree-wood 'trees' in no sense refers

---

[2] See Li and Thompson 1981: 49–53 for a fuller discussion of the many types of semantic relations that occur between the modifying and modified elements within complex noun words.

to a subset of 'wood' that is 'trees' (or vice-versa), and *jiějué* undo-decide 'solve' does not refer to a subset of those actions of 'deciding' in which 'undoing' takes place (or vice versa).

One problem with characterizing words by their modification structure is that in the case of hierarchical modification, even when there is unmistakably a dominance relation between the two constituents, very often the *direction* of that relationship is indeterminate or arbitrary. That is, it is often possible a priori to assign the roles of 'modifier' and 'modified' arbitrarily to either constituent. To give an example: in the case of *qiānbǐ* lead-writing:tool 'pencil', in terms of modification structure arguably there may be no reason a priori to view it as 'that portion of writing tools that are made of "lead"', rather than 'that portion of the material "lead" that is used to make writing tools'. By the same token, there is arguably no reason to consider *suǒxiě* contract-write 'abbreviate' to be 'a type of writing activity that contracts that which is written' rather than considering it to be 'those instances of contracting that apply to writing'. It may well be that the former rather than the latter interpretations are correct for the examples *qiānbǐ* and *suǒxiě* above, but looking solely at the possible types of modification structure that exist offers us no explanation for why one rather than the other might be correct. Semantically, either one is possible (see discussion in 4.2 and n. 3 to chapter 4).

Another problem with relying on a word's modificational structure as a primary means of word description or categorization is that explanations like 'x modifies and therefore is dominated by y', or 'x and y have a coordinate structure and therefore neither dominates the other' may be true as far as they go, but they offer nothing further than surface descriptive accuracy. In other words, these descriptions tell us little about what goes on in the mind of native speakers when words of this type are known, used or created. For example, knowing that the modificational structure of the word for 'pencil' is 'writing implements that use lead' does not explain *why* the native speaker knows that it is 'writing implements that use lead' instead of 'the lead that is used in the making of writing implements', and does not account for *how* that knowledge comes about or is represented within the language system.

The modification structure approach is indeed useful as a description supplementary to other types of analysis, because once we have found a good way of representing the knowledge speakers have when they know words, it is indeed useful to know what the modification relations are within the word.

3.1.1.3 Semantic description

Words can be described solely in semantic terms, that is, by describing how the meaning of the whole word is built up from the meanings of its parts. Using such a semantic description, the meaning of the word is related to its component meanings by a sort of fortuitous match, rather than being set forth in a determinate fashion.

As an example, in the word *diànnǎo* 电脑 electricity-brain 'computer', the speaker perceives the meaning to be 'electric brain' or 'brain that is composed of electric circuits' – an entirely reasonable semantic interpretation that also happens to conform to the general modification structure of Mandarin: the modifier virtually always precedes that which is modified. On the other hand, the meaning of the word *kǒuàn* 口岸 mouth-coast 'harbour' is counterintuitive when interpreted in accordance with Mandarin modification structure: such an interpretation would yield 'a mouth's coast' or 'a coast that takes the form of a mouth'. The semantic criterion, on the other hand, perfectly well describes speakers' knowledge that the word is in fact interpreted as 'a coast's mouth' or 'mouth of a coast'; a meaning that a native speaker readily perceives as sensible, even in the face of contradictory grammatical information (viz., that of the left member being the modifier and the right being the head).

This semantic criterion focusses on the 'centre of meaning' of a word, or what the word's most basic or salient component of meaning is perceived to be by the native speaker (Longenecker 1995). Here, the focus is on the imagery or feeling engendered by the overall semantic 'weight' of the word. Longenecker cites hundreds of further examples similar to *kǒuàn* above – such as *shùhǎi* 树海 tree-ocean 'trees', *shìlín* 士林 scholar-woods 'intellectuals' and *liǎndàn* 脸蛋 face-egg 'face, cheeks' – in which the overall meaning of nouns seems to be more closely related to the left rather than the right word component.

Such a purely semantic mode of description has the advantage of allowing for a variable relation between the meaning of a word and its components, permitting the proper semantic interpretation of words that do not conform to the general modifier–modified structure of Mandarin words. Semantic description also plays a role in defining the notion of 'semantic head' (see 5.5.2 below), and goes a longer way than sentential syntactic description (see 3.1.1.4) in accounting for the use or knowledge of words in the minds of native speakers.

However, semantic description cannot be the primary criterion that we rely upon in characterizing native speakers' knowledge of words. This is because while semantic description may often be descriptively adequate and provide the correct interpretation when the semantic and modification criteria fail to match, the lack of predictability and the arbitrariness inherent in the semantic criterion make it unsuitable for representing whatever systematic knowledge the native speaker does have about the structure and formation of words. To put it another way: if children used semantics as a primary way of acquiring their knowledge of words and their usage, in essence their basic hypothesis or operating principle would be 'choose the most semantically plausible interpretation', a proposition that is much too open-ended – given the possible states of the world they would have encountered by that time – unless it is constrained in some way.

Furthermore, using solely semantic criteria, the outer identity of the word cannot be seen in any sense as 'driving' or determining the identity of word components, independently of grammatical structure: the identity of a gestalt word as a noun or verb often results in the right- or left-hand members being reanalysed as nouns or verbs respectively (see also 6.1.3.1.5). But it is usually not the case that a word-internal morpheme is reanalysed semantically to take on the meaning of the gestalt word: such reanalysis is driven by grammatical structural criteria.

To give an example, the word *xiǎobiàn* 小便 'to urinate' may be grammatically described as [[*xiǎo*]Adj [*biàn*]N]v, that is, it is a verb composed of an adjective and a noun (*xiǎobiàn* was originally a noun, and was converted to a verb through 'zero derivation'). This has resulted in the adjective *xiǎo* 'small' being reanalysed as a verb, by analogy with verb–object verbal word forms (i.e., [[ ]v[ ]N]v), as seen in (3):

(3) tā   xiǎole   èrshí   fēnzhōng   de   biàn
    他   小了   二十   分钟   的   便
    he   small-ASP   20   minutes   MOD   convenience
    'He urinated for 20 minutes' (lit. 'He smalled 20 minutes of convenience')

In this example (from Huang 1984), the stative verb *xiǎo* 小 'small' has been reanalysed as an active, transitive verb (as evidence by its occurrence in the verbal slot followed by an object and its affixation by the aspect marker *le*), determined or 'driven' by the verbal form class identity of the gestalt word. The opposite never occurs in Mandarin: the identity of a gestalt word never (to my knowledge) results in a word component being reanalysed in a manner that does not also conform to the word's grammatical structure. In other words, the identity of a gestalt word as a noun never results in its *left*-hand member being reanalysed as a noun, and the identity of a gestalt word as a verb never results in the *right*-hand member being reanalysed as a verb. Such reanalysis of internal word constituents 'driven' by the identity of the gestalt words always strictly follows word-headedness principles (to be discussed in 3.2.1).

This phenomenon of word component reanalysis is not adequately explained on semantic grounds: it is a grammatical form class phenomenon; that is, the reanalysis occurs because of native speaker knowledge or analysis of the form class of word constituents and not because of their knowledge of the 'meaning' of the components per se.

3.1.1.4 Syntactic description

There are two ways to conceive of the 'syntactic' analysis of the internal structure of Chinese words. One is to view word constituents as possessing the same identities as the 'surface' syntactic constituents (such as subject and object) that make up a sentence, and the other is to view word-internal constituent structure in terms of 'deeper' syntactic structural principles. The latter implies a system of underlying rules and principles akin to those posited for sentence syntax, and assumes the concomitant existence of entities such as null operators, movement rules, barriers and so forth. Here I use the term 'syntactic description' in the former sense, using the nomenclature of sentence syntax to provide a description of word components in terms of apparent, 'surface' syntactic properties. The latter sense, i.e., the one based on the theory that word formation exploits the set of universal principles posited for syntactic structure, will be discussed in 5.3.3.

The first uses of a 'surface syntactic' description to account for word structure were by Xia (1946) and Liao (1946), but the idea was more fully developed by Chao (1948) and Lu (1964), and greatly expanded in Chao 1968. The examples in table 2 are from Chao 1947 (42–4) and 1968 (368, 416, 435); and Li and Thompson 1981 (70–3). In these examples, the word constituents seem to have the same syntactic relationship as that which exists among the parts of a sentence. So, in a 'subject–predicate' word such as *xīnténg*, *xīn* 心 'heart' and *téng* 疼 'ache' seem

Table 2 'Syntactic' descriptions of Chinese words

syntactic description	example (pinyin)	example (characters)	gloss
subject–predicate	xīnténg	心疼	heart-hurt 'to grudge'
	qìchuǎn	气喘	breath-pant 'asthma'
	dǎnxiǎo	胆小	gall-small 'cowardly'
	liǎnhóng	脸红	face-red 'embarrassed'
verb–object	diǎnxīn	点心	dot-heart 'refreshment'
	kāiduān	开端	open-end 'set a precedent'
	shāngfēng	伤风	hurt-wind 'catch cold'
verb–complement	chībǎo	吃饱	eat-full 'to be full'
	kèfú	克服	conquer-submission 'to subdue'

to function respectively as the subject and predicate of a sentence, while in *diǎnxīn*, *diǎn* 点 'dot' and *xīn* 心 'heart' would appear to have a 'verb–object' relationship.

The syntactic description method has great appeal at first blush, because it adequately describes (at some level) the relation between the two morphemes, since word parts often mimic surface syntactic relationships. Another reason for the appeal of the syntactic method is that it often accounts for the origins of words, that is, it shows that some words were once (and in many cases still are) phrases in sentence syntax that have simply become lexicalized (see 6.4.1). However, although syntactic description may be a convenient heuristic that provides a useful surface description and a certain degree of diachronic insight, as an aid to understanding the properties of words and their use by native speakers, it has surprisingly little to offer.

First of all, using sentence syntax to explain word structures carries with it an implicit expectation that such word structures will exhibit the collocation properties that apply in syntax – an expectation that is generally not fulfilled. For example, subject–predicate words (such as *dǎnxiǎo* 胆小 gall-small 'cowardly') generally do not have the properties of their subject–predicate sentential counterparts (e.g., they cannot directly negate the 'predicate', they cannot form A-not-A questions by reduplicating the 'predicate', time adverbials may not modify the 'predicate' and so forth; Li and Thompson 1981: 70). If we adopt a syntactic analysis for a subject–predicate word such as *dǎnxiǎo*

CHINESE WORD COMPONENTS

gall-small 'cowardly', for example, there is no immediate explanation for why the predicate *xiǎo* cannot be preceded by adverbial modifiers such as *hěn* 'very' or *bù* 'not' as in (6) and (7), following normal syntactic and word order principles shown in (8) and (9) respectively.

(4) tā   hěn   dǎnxiǎo
    他   很   胆小
    he   very   gall-small
    'He is very cowardly'

(5) tā   bù   dǎnxiǎo
    他   不   胆小
    he   not   gall-small
    'He is not cowardly'

(6) *tā   (de)   dǎn   hěn   xiǎo
    他   的   胆   很   小
    he   (MOD) gall   very   small

(7) *tā   (de)   dǎn   bù   xiǎo
    他   的   胆   不   小
    he   (MOD) gall   not   small

(8) tā   (de)   tuǐ   hěn   cháng
    他   的   腿   很   长
    he   (MOD) leg   very   long
    'His legs are long'

(9) tā   (de)   tuǐ   bù   cháng
    他   的   腿   不   长
    he   (MOD) leg   not   long
    'His legs are not long'

Thus, the syntactic explanation of word structures carries with it the implication that simple syntactic generalizations apply to such forms, which is not usually the case.

Second, syntactic analysis of words usually reveals little about the use or knowledge of such words by native speakers. In other words, to note that, e.g., *tā hěn liǎnhóng* 'He is very embarrassed' in (10) is in some sense (i.e., metaphorically) equivalent to *tā (de) liǎn hěn hóng* 'His face is very red' in (11) does little more than point out that a (metaphorical) sentential paraphrase of *liǎnhóng* can be constructed using lexical items that correspond to the morphemes used in the word, and does little to explain the word's use or structure.

(10) tā   hěn   liǎnhóng
     他   很   脸红
     he   very   face-red
     'He is very embarrassed'

(11) tā   (de)   liǎn   hěn   hóng
     他   的   脸   很   红
     he   (MOD)   face   very   red
     (literally) 'His face is very red'
     (metaphorically) 'He is very embarrassed'

The syntactic analysis of *liǎnhóng* does not elucidate the fact that *liǎnhóng* is a bona fide lexical item with the form class distribution of a stative verb, and that it has given up the lion's share of its syntactic identity and characteristics following lexicalization.

Third, although a syntactic description may provide some information about the diachronic origins of a word, it does so at the expense of accurately portraying synchronic meaning and function. The origin of *liǎnhóng* undoubtedly arises from the usage seen in (11), but simply that a syntactic form fortuitously indicates a word's diachronic origins is no basis for attributing a syntactic structural identity to that word.

Fourth, describing words using syntax implies a syntactic-type productivity for words that is not justified. So, for example, it is possible that someday the use of a phrase such as *tuǐcháng* 'legs are long' repeated as (12) could come to be lexicalized as **tuǐcháng* leg-long as in (13), acquiring some sort of idiomatized meaning such as 'able to make great strides; be a pioneer' on analogy with 'subject-predicate' forms *dǎnxiǎo* 胆小 gall-small 'cowardly', *shǒujǐn* 手紧 hand-tight 'stingy', *zuǐyìng* 嘴硬 mouth-hard 'argumentative', *yǎnhóng* 眼红 eye-red 'covetous' or *shǒuruǎn* 手软 hand-soft 'softhearted'.

(12) tā   (de)   tuǐ   hěn   cháng
     他   的   腿   很   长
     he   (MOD)   leg   very   long
     'His legs are very long'

(13) *tā   hěn   tuǐcháng
     他   很   腿长
     he   very   leg-long
     'He is quite a pioneer'

However, *tuīcháng* as a word in fact does not exist, and so while a pattern called 'subject–predicate' may point out the potential acceptability of such word types, it does not predict their actual acceptability and use.

Fifth, for all of its appeal in reflecting surface syntactic properties, even at that level the syntactic approach often lacks a basic descriptive adequacy. For example, Chao (1968: 373) says that verbs such as *yīkào* 依靠 follow-lean:on 'rely on' or *shībài* 失败 lose-defeat 'fail' are in a 'coordinate construction'. The coordinate verbal structure posited by Chao for these forms (i.e., [[ ]v[ ]v]v) belies the fact that there is nothing about them that mimics a 'coordinate verb structure' in syntax. That is, labeling them 'coordinate verb' structured words introduces the expectation that the words so termed will in some sense exhibit the syntactic properties of that structure, which is not the case. Another example of basic descriptive adequacy failure is the interpretation of a modifier–head word such as *kǒuàn* 口岸 mouth-coast 'harbour'. The semantics of the word *kǒuàn* perfectly well reveal the fact that it is a 'coast's mouth' or 'mouth of a coast', a mouth-type break along a coastline – a meaning that a native speaker can readily perceive as sensible and relevant. Using a strictly syntactic modification relation, however, the meaning is nonsensical and counterintuitive: *kǒu de àn* 口的岸 [mouth MOD coast] only has a strictly syntactic meaning if we allow quite a metaphorical stretch – 'a mouthed coast' – implying 'a subset of coastlines that take the form of mouths' (as discussed in 3.1.1.3).

Finally, and most importantly, the syntactic approach to word structure ignores the fact that such entities have passed (however completely) into the realm of wordhood, and therefore are subject to a host of different principles and constraints. For example, they are the X^0 entities that are stored away for potential insertion into lexical slots. When all is said and done, the storing away of syntactic phrasal entities for use in lexical slots is a relatively unusual occurrence. Also, words are subject to properties that correlate with 'degree of lexicalization' (to be discussed in chapter 6; see also Craig 1991: 467), as well as idiomatization and conventionalization of meaning. While it is true that phrasal entities also sometimes exhibit these properties (see, e.g., Nunberg, Sag and Wasow 1994), this is clearly the exception rather than the rule. Also, words, and not phrases, are subject to the Lexical Integrity Hypothesis (Jackendoff 1972), which states that syntactic rules may not refer to the internal structure of words.

In the end, the syntactic descriptions of word structure boil down to the fact that certain word components may have a 'subject-like', an 'object-like' or a 'complement-like' identity, but do not take us much further than that. Although the study of syntax is able to tell us a great deal about the knowledge and use of language, what syntax can tell us does not apply or applies in very limited ways to word structure. We gain very little by looking at words in terms of a surface syntactic description, to the extent that by focussing on syntax we miss critical insights available to us regarding the properties of words.

3.1.1.5 Form class description

A word's component morphemes can also be viewed in terms of their form class identity, or 'part of speech'. So a word like *qìchē* 汽车 gas-vehicle 'automobile' may be analysed as a noun [ ]N composed of, in this case, two noun elements [N N]N 'gas' and 'vehicle', and the word *chūbǎn* 出版 emit-edition 'to publish' is analysed as a verb [ ]V composed of a verb and a noun: 'emit' and 'edition' respectively ([V N]V). This is the method used by Lu (1964) in his analysis of complex Chinese words. What is there to recommend this method of word component analysis, and how does it avoid the pitfalls of the previously described methods?

If we view a word's component morphemes in terms of their form class identities, it allows us to account for different types of systematic knowledge that native speakers possess regarding the composition of words. For example, the fact that the form class of the gestalt Chinese word usually matches the form class of at least one of the members on the inside of the word (i.e., [**V** N]**v**) is not an accidental fact under this type of analysis, but rather represents systematic knowledge that a native speaker brings to the task of learning and using the language. This knowledge reflects native speaker awareness of the structures and properties of words based on the identity of a word and the identities of its components. It affects the use of these words and the knowledge of their properties in the minds of native speakers.

The form class approach avoids the inconsistencies of 'relational' descriptions outlined in 3.1.1.1 because all relationships between inner and outer identities are either consistent or their inconsistencies are predicted and explained using an independent set of principles (to be outlined in chapter 6). The form class approach avoids the arbitrariness of the 'modification structure' descriptions outlined in 3.1.1.2, because it provides a method of determining modification direction that is based on values inherent in the system, with deviations also accounted for systematically. It also avoids the indeterminacy described for this approach as outlined in the 'pencil' example in 3.1.1.2, by assigning default values, and giving a set of principles predicting departures from those default values (to be discussed in chapter 6).

The lack of systematicity inherent in the semantic approach to describing word-component structure is not a problem in the form class approach, because the form class approach, as we shall see, is nothing if not highly systematic. It relies upon systematic, determinate algorithms, which account for and even predict knowledge of word properties by native speakers. Furthermore, the form class approach explains why the outer identity of the word determines or 'drives' the identity of word components, as demonstrated in example (3) (see also 6.1.3.1.5).

The problems with using the syntactic descriptions of word structure outlined in 3.1.1.4 are avoided by the form class approach because, generally speaking, all of the predictions and expectations engendered by the syntactic approach either do not exist or are accounted for under the form class approach. For example, expectation of collocation, knowledge of identity and distributional characteristics of components, accurate portrayal of synchronic word characteristics, overstatement of productivity and so forth fail to arise on the form class approach. Another advantage of looking at Mandarin word components by their form class identity is that they are easily categorized by form class. In 3.3 we outline a procedure for assigning a form class identity to morphemes as they occur within words.

Adopting the syntactic form class criterion allows for the fact that the forms of words are in many cases diachronically related to, or derived from, syntactic structure. This approach does not suggest that words are formed using rules and principles of syntax, but rather that words have come to have the structure and form that they have partly due to the lexicalization of words in syntactic phrases (see 6.3). In other words, the maxim 'today's morphology is yesterday's syntax' (Givón 1971: 413) applies to Chinese just as it does to other languages.

Another argument in favour of this 'form class' method of word component analysis is that, as seen in 2.3, we are using the syntactic definition of 'word' – that is, 'word' as the minimal syntactic unit – as our means of defining what words are. So those minimal syntactic units ('syntactic atoms') – by hypothesis – must all have syntactic form class identities. This being the case, we can observe how and to what extent those 'outer' form class identities that isolate and identify basic word units are related to the 'inner' form class identities of the word constituents. A natural working hypothesis would be that the outer form class identities are critically related to the inner form class identities. Not only is this method of analysis a convenient heuristic approach – being descriptively simple and elegant – but, as we shall see, it is easily incorporated into a larger framework that offers the possibility of great explanatory power.

The heuristic benefit of the form class approach is that the larger entities in the system (words) are composed of smaller items (morphemes, word components) that possess equivalent identities. This is no coincidence or descriptive convenience – scientifically speaking, it makes sense to define properties of larger system entities in terms of related smaller ones. While such a reductionist approach is not a required system property or even necessarily a desideratum, it does provide the system with a certain appeal that, if not constituting a solution to our analytical problem, at least provides us with a methodologically clear starting point.

Of course, the form class approach is going to present its own set of problems that must be dealt with if we are going to claim that it is a viable and insightful indicator of how and why native speakers know what they know about the properties of words. For example, is it possible to assign word components a clear form class identity? What criteria do we use to assign form class identity to bound morphemes, for example, since the most obvious criterion – the free occurrence of an item in a syntactic form class slot – may be irrelevant in the case of bound morphemes? This and other problems will be addressed in the sections that follow.

3.2 Form classes of the components

Having decided to view word components by their grammatical form class identities, it is important for us to consider at the outset what that approach will entail. This is an important step because assigning form class identities to Chinese morphemes is traditionally considered to be a difficult process – one that is potentially rife with indeterminacy.

To demonstrate, it is well known that in Chinese (as in many languages), individual words or morphemes can belong to more than one form class category. For example, the words *bīng* 冰 and *diàn* 电 are usually thought of as nouns by default ('ice' and 'electricity' respectively), as seen in (14) and (16), but can also act as verbs ('to ice' and 'to get an electric shock') as seen in (15) and (17).

(14) Lùshang   jiézhe   bīng
     路上   结著   冰
     road-top congeal-ASP   ice
     'Ice has formed on the road'

(15) Qǐng   bǎ   nàpíng   píjiǔ   bīngshang
     请   把   那瓶   啤酒   冰上
     please BA   that:CL   beer   ice-attain
     'Please ice that beer'

(16) Tíng   diàn   le
     停   电   了
     stop   electricity   ASP
     'The electricity has gone off'

(17) Wǒ   diànle   yíxiàr
     我   电了   一下儿
     I   electricity-ASP   a little
     'I got a shock'

Conversely, the morpheme *dī* (滴) is usually a verb ('drip') as in (18), but can also be a noun ('drop'), as seen in (19).

(18) yóu   wàng   xià   dī
     油   往   下   滴
     oil   toward   down   drip
     'The oil dripped down'

(19) Wǒ   lián   yì   dī   dōu   méi   hē
     我   连   一   滴   都   没   喝
     I   even   one   drop   all   not   drink
     'I didn't even drink a drop'

Words such as *bīng*, *diàn* and *dī* are not a problem, because native speakers generally feel that there is a primary, 'default' value for these words, and that when they are used as members of a different form class, this constitutes a derived, marked or 'secondary' usage.

But in the case of many morphemes, it is not as clear that one is necessarily the 'default' and the other is the 'secondary' form class value. Consider for example the words *huà* (画 'draw, paint, picture, drawing') and *pái* (排 'arrange, row, discharge, push, platoon, perform/ rehearse'). The form class of *huà* may be a verb as in (20), or a noun as in (21). The same is true for *pái*, which in (22) is used as a verb and in (23) is used as a noun.

(20) Tā xǐhuān huà tú
他 喜欢 画 图
he like draw picture
'He likes to draw pictures'

(21) Tā yǒu sānzhāng huà
他 有 三张 画
he have three:CL picture
'He has three pictures'

(22) Qǐng nǐmen pái duì
请 你们 排 队
please you-PL arrange group
'Please line up'

(23) Nǐ zuò zài qián pái
你 坐 在 前 排
you sit at front row
'You sit in the front row'

Although the words *huà* and *pái* may be used as either nouns or verbs, and native speakers may not agree as to their 'default' form class identities, note that in any given context there is no ambiguity regarding their part of speech: the syntactic context makes clear what the form class identity of the word is to be. Therefore, we can say that if a word has W^N form class identities, one of those identities – W^X – is 'selected for' or 'designated' by the syntactic context. The syntactic distributional characteristics of a word in Chinese are called its *cíxìng* 词性 'wordness' (word-characteristic; often translated 'part of speech').

3.2.1 Form class identities within words

Deciding the form class of a morpheme by its *cíxìng* works fine for morphemes as they appear in syntactic contexts, i.e., when they are

CHINESE WORD COMPONENTS

used as free words. But how useful is the construct *cíxìng* in determining the form class identity of morphemes as they occur outside of syntactic contexts and *within* words?

To address this question, we select morphemes that have unambiguous form class identities, and note whether these identities undergo modification when they occur within words. For this purpose, we use two dictionaries: *A Chinese–English Dictionary* (Wu 1988) and the *Concise Chinese Reverse-Order Dictionary* (Chen, He and Xu 1986). We use the reverse-order dictionary in addition to the standard-order dictionary in order to consider all entries that contain the morpheme of interest, whether it be the first or second morpheme in the word. As examples of words that have unambiguous form class, we use *zhǐ* 纸 'paper' as an example of an unambiguous noun and *zǒu* 走 'walk, go' as an example of an unambiguous verb. According to all modern sources, *zhǐ* is never used as a verb and *zǒu* is never used as a noun.

Note that some of the items are in fact listed as phrases in the *Modern Chinese Dictionary*[3] (Chinese Academy of Social Sciences 1988) and in Chen, He and Xu 1986 rather than as words, but are not discarded from the analysis for the sake of completeness and so as not to prejudge the issue of word status (even though I do provide criteria in 4.3.4.3 for distinguishing V–O words from V–O phrases, by which most of the items in question would indeed be phrases). Note also that the part of speech of the English gloss for an entry will not always agree with the part of speech indicated for Chinese. This is because the part of speech a word best translates as in English is often different from its form class as indicated by its use in Chinese. We permit this surface discrepancy in order to allow form class to be determined by the distribution and use of the morphemes in Chinese, rather than having it be influenced by English translation. The English glosses are from Wu (1988) or are provided by the author.

First, consider the unambiguous noun *zhǐ* 纸 'paper', seen in table 3. We see in this table that the form class of the unambiguous noun *zhǐ* does not change within a word: it remains a noun in all word-internal contexts, whether it serves as the left- or right-hand member of the word. We also note that, without exception, there is a match between word form class and word component identity: all these complex nouns have nouns as their right-hand members.

[3] The *Modern Chinese Dictionary* is used as a V–O phrase authority since Wu 1982 and Chen, He and Xu 1986 do not indicate V–O phrases.

Table 3 Words containing *zhǐ* 'paper'

word	English gloss	form class of word	form class of zhǐ	form class of C₂	word	English gloss	form class of word	form class of C₁	form class of zhǐ
zhǐbǎn 纸板 paper-plank	cardboard	N	N	N	bàozhǐ 报纸 report-paper	newspaper	N	N	N
zhǐbǎn 纸版 paper-edition	paper mould	N	N	N	cǎozhǐ 草纸 straw-paper	straw paper	N	N	N
zhǐbì 纸币 paper-currency	paper currency	N	N	N	fǎngzhǐ 仿纸 imitate-paper	practising paper	N	V	N
zhǐhuā 纸花 paper-flower	paper flower	N	N	N	gǎozhǐ 稿纸 draft-paper	draft paper	N	N	N
zhǐjiāng 纸浆 paper-liquid	paper pulp	N	N	N	jiǎnzhǐ 剪纸 cut-paper	paper cutting	V	V	N
zhǐniǎn 纸捻 paper-twisted:thing	paper spill	N	N	N	qìzhǐ 契纸 agreement-paper	contract paper	N	N	N
zhǐpái 纸牌 paper-sign	playing cards	N	N	N	shāozhǐ 烧纸 burn-paper	burn paper (as an offering)	P*	V	N
zhǐqián 纸钱 paper-money	paper money	N	N	N	túzhǐ 图纸 chart-paper	drawing	N	N	N
zhǐshéng 纸绳 paper-string	paper string	N	N	N	xīzhǐ 锡纸 tin-paper	tin foil	N	N	N
zhǐxíng 纸型 paper-form	paper mould	N	N	N	xìnzhǐ 信纸 letter-paper	stationery	N	N	N
zhǐyān 纸烟 paper-smoke	cigarette	N	N	N	xuānzhǐ 宣纸 name-paper	a type of calligraphy paper	N	N	N
zhǐyú 纸鱼 paper-fish	silverfish	N	N	N	zhézhǐ 折纸 fold-paper	paper folding	V	V	N

Table 3 (cont'd)

word	English gloss	form class of word	form class of zhǐ	form class of C2	word	English gloss	form class of word	form class of C1	form class of zhǐ
zhǐyuān 纸鸢 paper-bird	paper bird	N	N	N	zhuàngzhǐ 状纸 complaint-paper	official lawsuit form	N	N	N
zhǐzhāng 纸张 paper-sheet	paper	N	N	N	zìzhǐ 字纸 character-paper	waste paper (with characters)	N	N	N
zhènzhǐ 镇纸 press-paper	paperweight	N	V	N					

* listed in the cited reference dictionary as phrases, not words

Now let us consider the unambiguous verb *zǒu*, seen in table 4. We see that, as with words formed with the noun *zhǐ*, the verb *zǒu* steadfastly maintains its form class identity in all words in which it appears. Also, in all verbs formed with *zǒu*, the constituent on the left is a verb.

So far, it seems to we can make two generalizations based on this limited data. The first is that words with unambiguous form class identities tend to retain their form class identities when they appear within words. The second is that noun words have nominal constituents on the right and verb words have verbal constituents on the left. This latter generalization we shall term the *Headedness Principle*, and is presented here as (24).

> (24) Headedness Principle: (bisyllabic) noun words have nominal constituents on the right and verb words have verbal constituents on the left

We also note in passing that so far there does not seem to be any real problem or controversy in assigning form class identities to morphemes within words. This seems true for these morphemes *zhǐ* and *zǒu* that were selected because they are unambiguous representatives of their form class categories. Now, what about words with multiple form class identities – that is, words that can commonly appear as either nouns or verbs?

Table 4 Words containing *zǒu* 'walk, go'

word	English gloss	form class of word	form class of *zǒu*	form class of C₂	word	English gloss	form class of word	form class of C₁	form class of *zǒu*
zǒubǐ 走笔 walk-pen	write rapidly	V	V	N	bēnzǒu 奔走 flee-walk	run	V	V	V
zǒubù 走步 walk-step	to travel (basketball)	V	V	N	chūzǒu 出走 exit-walk	flee	V	V	V
zǒudào 走道 walk-path	sidewalk	N	V	N	gǎnzǒu 赶走 rush-walk	expel	V	V	V
zǒudàor 走道儿 walk-path	to walk	P*	V	N	jìngzǒu 竞走 compete-walk	walking race	V⁴	V	V
zǒudiàor 走调 go-melody	out of tune	P*	V	N	táozǒu 逃走 flee-walk	flee	V	V	V
zǒudòng 走动 walk-move	walk about	V	V	V	tuìzǒu 退走 retreat-walk	to retreat	V	V	V
zǒudú 走读 walk-study	attend day school	V	V	V	xíngzǒu 行走 walk-walk	to walk	V	V	V
zǒufǎng 走访 walk-interview	to interview	V	V	V					
zǒufēng 走风 go-wind	divulge a secret	P*	V	N					
zǒugǒu 走狗 walk-dog	lackey	N	V	N					
zǒuhuǒ 走火 go-fire	to spark	P*	V	N					
zǒulòu 走漏 go-leak	divulge	V	V	V					
zǒulù 走路 walk-road	walk	P*	V	N					
zǒumǎ 走马 walk-horse	gallop on horseback	V	V	N					

4 Note that *jìngzǒu* is a verb, despite the facts that (a) it is often used in nominalized form, and (b) it has been translated using a nominalized form ('walking race').

Table 4 (cont'd)

word	English gloss	form class of word	form class of zǒu	form class of C₂
zǒuqín 走禽 walk-bird	cursorial birds	N	V	N
zǒushǎi 走色 go-colour	fade	V	V	N
zǒushéng 走绳 walk-rope	tightrope walk	P*	V	N
zǒushī 走失 go-lose	to be missing	V	V	V
zǒushí 走时 walk-time	have good luck	V	V	N
zǒushòu 走兽 walk-amimal	quadruped	N	V	N
zǒushuǐ 走水 go-water	be on fire	V	V	N
zǒusī 走私 walk-illicit	smuggle	P*	V	O
zǒuwèi 走味 go-taste	lose flavour	P*	V	N
zǒuxiàng 走向 walk-direction	trend, run	N	V	N
zǒuyàng 走样 go-form	lose shape	P*	V	N
zǒuyùn 走运 walk-luck	be in luck	P*	V	N
zǒuzú 走卒 walk-pawn	lackey	N	V	N
zǒuzuǐ 走嘴 go-mouth	make a slip of the tongue	P*	V	N

* listed in the cited reference dictionary as phrases, not words

We know that the words *huà* (画 'draw, paint, picture, drawing') and *pái* (排 'arrange, row, discharge, push, platoon, perform/rehearse') have variable form class identities, as we saw in examples (20)–(23) above. Let us therefore consider the form class identities of *huà* and *pái* within all two-syllable words listed, as we did for *zhǐ* and *zǒu*. Following that procedure, we obtain data for *huà* as seen in table 5. *Huà* may appear either as a verb or as a noun when it occurs within words, just as when it occurs as a free morpheme. Also, as is the case with words formed using *zǒu* and *zhǐ* above, all gestalt words formed with *huà* follow the Headedness Principle: all verbs have a verb on the left, and all nouns have a noun on the right.

When *huà* occurs in a word-internal position in which it could be interpreted structurally as either a noun or verb (that is, when *huà* occurs as the left-hand member of a two-morpheme noun[5]), the interpretation it receives is the one that is consistent with its role in the gestalt word. To determine the proper interpretation, we may ask: within the gestalt noun, does the left-hand morpheme *huà* entail the act of painting? If so, then *huà* is a verb. Conversely, if *huà* directly entails the notion of a picture or a drawing, then it is a noun.

To illustrate, in *huàjù* 画具 paint-utensil 'painter's paraphernalia', it is clear that *huà* means the verb 'to paint' and not the noun 'picture/painting'. This is because the meaning of the head noun *-jù* 'utensil' that is modified or 'delimited' by *huà* is more closely related to the *act* of painting than to *the painted item as a finished product*. Likewise in *huàcè* 画册 picture-book 'picture album', the meaning of the head noun *-cè* 'book' has more to do with the *finished products* than with the *act of producing them* per se, and so it is clear that *huà* in this example refers to the noun 'picture/painting'. But in the example *huàpíng* ('painted screen'), *huà* could reasonably entail either the verb 'to paint' ('screen that has been painted') or the noun 'painting' ('screen that has paintings on it'). In cases like *huàpíng*, since either a noun or verb may occur in that position to modify the nominal head, and since *huà* lexically is able to be either a noun or verb, the form class identity of *huà* is left 'free to vary'. This being the case, it remains a matter of interpretation whether, at a given time in the mind of a

---

[5] This example anticipates one of many distributional facts to be introduced later on, namely that the left-hand position of a complex noun word in general modifies the head on the right, and so is considered a general modification position whether is it occupied by a noun, verb, etc.

CHINESE WORD COMPONENTS

Table 5 Words containing *huà*

word	English gloss	form class of word	form class of huà	form class of C₂
huàbǎn 画板 draw-board	drawing board	N	V	N
huàbào 画报 picture-paper	pictorial	N	N	N
huàbǐ 画笔 paint-pen	painting brush	N	V	N
huàbù 画布 picture-cloth	canvas	N	V	N
huàcè 画册 picture-book	picture album	N	N	N
huàfǎ 画法 paint-way	technique of painting	N	V	N
huàfǎng 画舫 paint-boat	gaily-painted pleasure boat	N	V	N
huàfú 画幅 picture-painting	painting	N	N	N
huàgǎo 画稿 picture-draft	rough sketch (painting)	N	N	N
huàjiā 画家 picture-specialist	artist	N	N	N
huàjià 画架 paint-frame	easel	N	V	N
huàjiàng 画匠 picture-artisan	artisan-painter	N	N	N

word	English gloss	form class of word	form class of C₁	form class of huà
bǐhuà 比画 compare-draw	to gesture	V	V	V
bǐhuà 笔画 pen-stroke	stroke	N	N	N
bòhuà 擘画 split-draw	arrange	V	V	V
fēihuà 扉画 door:leaf-picture	frontispiece	N	N	N
gōuhuà 勾画 draw-draw	to sketch	V	V	V
guóhuà 国画 country-picture	traditional Chinese painting	N	N	N
huìhuà 绘画 paint-picture	painting	N	V	N
kèhuà 刻画 carve-draw	depict	V	V	V
miáohuà 描画 copy-draw	draw, depict	V	V	V
rùhuà 入画 enter-picture	picturesque	Adv	V	N
shūhuà 书画 book-picture	painting and calligraphy	N	N	N
túhuà 图画 chart-picture	picture	N	N	N

Table 5 (cont'd)

word	English gloss	form class of word	form class of huà	form class of C_2	word	English gloss	form class of word	form class of C_1	form class of huà
huàjǐng 画景 picture-scene	picturesque scene	N	N	N	zhǐhuà 指画 point-draw	point at	V	V	V
huàjù 画具 paint-utensil	painter's paraphernalia	N	V	N	zìhuà 字画 character-picture	calligraphy and painting	N	N	N
huàjuǎn 画卷 picture-scroll	picture scroll	N	N	N					
huàjuàn 画绢 paint-silk	drawing silk	N	V	N					
huàkān 画刊 picture-periodical	pictorial	N	N	N					
huàláng 画廊 paint-hall	painted corridor	N	V	N					
huàláng 画廊 picture-hall	gallery	N	N	N					
huàméi 画眉 picture-eyebrow	a kind of thrush	N	N	N					
huàmiàn 画面 picture-face	tableau, frame	N	N	N					
huàpí 画皮 picture-skin	disguise	N	N	N					
huàpiàn 画片 picture-slip	miniature painting	N	N	N					
huàpíng 画屏 picture-screen	painted screen	N	N	N					
huàpǔ 画谱 paint-manual	book on painting	N	V	N					
huàpǔ 画谱 picture-manual	book of paintings	N	N	N					

Table 5 (cont'd)

word	English gloss	form class of word	form class of huà	form class of C₂
huàshī 画师 picture-specialist	painter	N	N	N
huàshì 画室 paint-room	studio	N	V	N
huàtiè 画帖 picture-model	book of paintings	N	N	N
huàtú 画图 paint-chart	to draw designs	P*	V	N
huàtú 画图 picture-chart	picture	N	N	N
huàxiàng 画像 paint-likeness	to draw a portrait	P*	V	N
huàxiàng 画像 picture-likeness	portrait	N	N	N
huàyā 画押 draw-signature	to sign	P*	V	N
huàyè 画页 picture-page	plate	N	N	N
huàyuàn 画院 picture-academy	art academy	N	N	N
huàzhǎn 画展 picture-exhibition	art exhibition	N	N	N
huàzhóu 画轴 picture-spool	painted scroll	N	N	N

* listed in the cited reference dictionary as phrases, not words

given native speaker, the nature of the modification is more 'verb-like' or 'noun-like'.[6] The fact that the left-hand constituent is 'free to vary' is also nicely demonstrated by the dual lexical entry for *huàpǔ* 画谱 in table 5, in which one entry selects the 'verb' interpretation of *huà* ('book on painting'), and the other entry selects the 'noun' interpretation ('book of paintings').

Note that while the left-hand members of nouns such as *huàpíng* and *huàpǔ* are free to vary, the identities of the *right*-hand members are not in question: they are all nouns, as predicted by the Headedness Principle given the nominal form class identity of the gestalt word.

Let us now consider the word-internal form class distribution of our other word selected because of its variable form class identity, *pái*, presented in table 6. As we saw with *huà*, *pái* may be either a noun or verb within a word (the same as when it is used as a free morpheme) depending on context: so, for example, in *páiwěi* (row-tail 'last person in row') it is a noun, and in *páiyǎn* (perform-perform 'rehearse') it is a verb. Furthermore, as with all previous examples, gestalt verbs containing *pái* generally have a verb on the left, and those that are nouns generally have a noun on the right. But now we begin to see exceptions to the Headedness Principle emerge. For example, some nouns are composed of two verbs and therefore do not have a noun on the right: ([V V]N) *páibǐ* arrange-compare 'parallelism' and *páiguàn* drain-irrigate 'drainage and irrigation'. Also, *cǎipái* colour-rehearse 'to dress rehearse' is a verb that has a noun rather than a verb on the left ([N V]v).

The [V V]N (*páibǐ*, *páiguàn*) examples are cases of form class category change via 'zero derivation': a shift in form class with no consequent grammatical marking. For example, *pái* with the lexical meaning of 'drain' is never used as a noun (in other words, *pái* is never used as a free lexical item to mean the lexical noun 'drain'), and neither is *guàn*, but when they combine to form a word, that word undergoes zero derivation to form a noun (like the more common example *mǎimài* buy-sell 'buying and selling'; i.e., 'business').

As for the [N V]v word *cǎipái* (colour-rehearse 'to dress rehearse'), this is a verb that has a noun (-*cǎi*- 'colour') rather than a verb on the left, and therefore is an exception to the Headedness Principle. Such

---

[6] In an informal poll of native Mandarin speakers over the Internet (the Kenyon College Chinese language bulletin board), ten out of twelve respondents said that the *huà* in *huàpíng* is a noun, and two said it is a verb.

Table 6 Words containing *pái*

word	English gloss	form class of word	form class of pái	form class of C₂
páibǎn 排板 arrange-plank	typeset	P*	V	N
páibǐ 排比 arrange-compare	parallelism	N	V	V
páibǐ 排笔 row-brush	broad brush	N	N	N
páichǎng 排场 arrange-field	ostentation	N	V	N
páichì 排斥 discharge-expel	exclude	V	V	V
páichú 排除 discharge-remove	eliminate	V	V	V
páidǎng 排档 row-gear	(vehicle) gears	N	N	N
páiduì 排队 arrange-group	line up	P*	V	N
páigǔ 排骨 row-bone	spare ribs	N	N	N
páiguàn 排灌 remove-irrigate	drainage and irrigation	N	V	V
páiháng 排行 arrange-line	seniority among siblings	V	V	N
páijǐ 排挤 arrange-squeeze	push aside	V	V	V

word	English gloss	form class of word	form class of C₁	form class of pái
ānpái 安排 arrange-arrange	arrange	V	V	V
biānpái 编排 arrange-arrange	arrange	V	V	V
bīngpái 冰排 ice-row	ice floe	N	N	N
bìngpái 并排 equally-arrange	side by side	Adv	Adv	V
cǎipái 彩排 colour-perform	dress rehearse	V	N	V
fāpái 发排 emit-arrange	send to be typeset	V	V	V
fùpái 付排 submit-arrange	send to be typeset	V	V	V
mùpái 木排 wood-row	raft	N	N	N
niúpái 牛排 cow-row	beefsteak	N	N	N
pūpái 铺排 spread-arrange	arrange	V	V	V
zhūpái 猪排 pig-row	pork steak	N	N	N

Table 6 (cont'd)

word	English gloss	form class of word	form class of pái	form class of C_2
páijiě 排解 arrange-resolve	mediate	V	V	V
páilào 排涝 remove-water	drain waterlogged fields	P*	V	N
páiléi 排雷 remove-mine	minesweep	P*	V	N
páiliàn 排练 perform-practise	rehearse	V	V	V
páiliè 排列 arrange-arrange	arrange	V	V	V
páiluǎn 排卵 discharge-egg	ovulate	P*	V	N
páiniào 排尿 discharge-urine	urinate	P*	V	N
páipào 排炮 row-cannon	salvo (of gunfire)	N	N	N
páiqì 排气 discharge-gas	exhaust gas	P*	V	N
páiqiǎn 排遣 remove-dispel	alleviate (boredom)	V	V	V
páiqiāng 排枪 row-gun	volley (of gunfire)	N	N	N
páiqiú 排球 push-ball	volleyball	N	V	N

CHINESE WORD COMPONENTS 49

Table 6   (cont'd)

word	English gloss	form class of word	form class of pái	form class of C_2
páishēng 排笙 row-reed:pipe	reed pipe instrument with keyboard	N	N	N
páishuǐ 排水 discharge-water	drain water	P*	V	N
páitóu 排头 row-head	file leader	N	N	N
páiwài 排外 remove-outside	expel outsiders	V	V	N
páiwěi 排尾 row-tail	last person in row	N	N	N
páixiè 排泄 remove-discharge	drain, excrete	V	V	V
páiyǎn 排演 perform-perform	rehearse	V	V	V
páiyìn 排印 arrange-print	typeset and print	V	V	V
páizhǎng 排长 platoon-leader	platoon leader	N	N	N
páizhōng 排钟 row-bell	chimes	N	N	N
páizì 排字 arrange-character	typesetting	P*	V	N

* listed in the cited reference dictionary as phrases, not words

words are permitted to exist by rule (see section 5.3.5), but they are predicted to behave exceptionally in the grammar. Although there is a verbal constituent (*pái*) within this complex verb word, I will argue in 5.5.1 that this is a 'virtual' rather than real head – 'virtual' because it does not possess the predicted properties of a 'real' verb head.

We have seen from the examples and discussion pertaining to table 5 and table 6 that the *cíxìng* (syntactic form class distribution) of a free morpheme appears to determine the form class of that morpheme within a word, and that the form class of the free morpheme as determined by its *cíxìng* tends not to be overridden by the form class of the gestalt word.

But what about bound morphemes? The majority of morphemes in Chinese are indeed bound (they are 'bound roots'; see 3.4), and so technically could be argued not to possess a syntactic form class distribution, or '*cíxìng*'. This being the case, let us consider the form class distribution within words of some morphemes that are bound but nonetheless have unambiguous form class identities, and see what happens to their form class identities in word-internal environments. Do their form classes remain 'unambiguous', as was found to be the case in general for the free words *zhǐ, zǒu, huà* and *pái* above, or do they change as dictated by the identity of the gestalt word?

For this purpose, we use the morphemes-*shí*- 石 'rock, stone' and -*zhù*- 助 'to help' to represent unambiguous members of the form classes 'noun' and 'verb' respectively, since they are bound morphemes listed in *New China Dictionary* (Commercial Press 1988) as possessing only the identities of noun and verb respectively. Using the same dictionary listing procedure as outlined for *zhǐ, zǒu, huà* and *pái* above, the data for -*shí*-, is listed in table 7, and for -*zhù*- in table 8.

In table 7 we see that the identity of the unambiguous noun-*shí*- does not undergo change in word-internal environments – it is a noun in all contexts. Whether acting as the right or left constituent of the word, it is always a noun (and, as it turns out, always occurs within words that are also nouns). When on the left, it acts as a modifier of the other noun on its right, and when on the right, it serves as the head noun modified by the noun or verb to its left.

Also, we see that, for the most part, gestalt words that are nouns have a noun on the right. There is, however, an exception to this – the noun *shídiāo* 石雕 stone-carve 'stone carving' has a verb ('carve') on the right ([N V]N): *diāo* is listed in no dictionary entries as being anything

Table 7 Words containing *shí*

word	English gloss	form class of word	form class of *shí*	form class of C₂	word	English gloss	form class of word	form class of C₁	form class of *shí*
shíbǎn 石板 stone-plank	flagstone	N	N	N	bǎoshí 宝石 gem-stone	gem	N	N	N
shíbǎn 石板 stone-plank	stone plate	N	N	N	huàshí 化石 change-stone	fossil	N	V	N
shíbēi 石碑 stone-tablet	stone tablet	N	N	N	jīshí 基石 base-stone	cornerstone	N	N	N
shíbǐ 石笔 stone-pen	slate pencil	N	N	N	jiāoshí 礁石 reef-stone	reef	N	N	N
shíbì 石壁 stone-wall	cliff	N	N	N	jièshí 界石 boundary-stone	boundary stone	N	N	N
shídàn 石担 stone-load	stone barbell	N	N	N	jīnshí 金石 metal-stone	symbol of durability	N	N	N
shídiāo 石雕 stone-carve	stone carving	N	N	V	kuàngshí 矿石 mine-stone	ore	N	N	N
shídūn 石墩 stone-mound	stone seat	N	N	N	pánshí 磐石 boulder-stone	boulder	N	N	N
shífāng 石方 stone-metre	cubic metre of stone	N	N	N	yánshí 岩石 rock-stone	rock	N	N	N
shígāo 石膏 stone-paste	gypsum	N	N	N	yǔnshí 陨石 fall: from: sky-stone	stony meteorite	N	N	N
shígōng 石工 stone-work	masonry	N	N	N	zhùshí 柱石 pillar-stone	pillar	N	N	N
shíhuī 石灰 stone-ash	lime	N	N	N	zuànshí 钻石 diamond-stone	diamond	N	N	N
shíjī 石鸡 stone-chicken	chukar	N	N	N					

Table 7 (cont'd)

word	English gloss	form class of word	form class of shí	form class of C₂
shíjiàng 石匠 stone-artisan	mason	N	N	N
shíkè 石刻 stone-carving	carved stone	N	N	N
shíkū 石窟 stone-hole	rock cave	N	N	N
shíkuài 石块 stone-chunk	stone	N	N	N
shílà 石蜡 stone-wax	paraffin wax	N	N	N
shílì 石栗 stone-chestnut	candlenut tree	N	N	N
shíliú 石榴 stone-pomegranate	pomegranate	N	N	N
shílǜ 石绿 stone-green	mineral green	N	N	N
shíméi 石煤 stone-coal	bone coal	N	N	N
shímián 石棉 stone-cotton	asbestos	N	N	N
shímò 石墨 stone-ink	graphite	N	N	N
shímò 石磨 stone-mill	stone mill	N	N	N
shínán 石楠 stone-tree	Chinese Photinia	N	N	N
shínǚ 石女 stone-woman	barren woman	N	N	N

Table 7 (cont'd)

word	English gloss	form class of word	form class of shí	form class of C2
shíqì 石器 stone-utensil	stone artifact	N	N	N
shíqīng 石青 stone-green	azurite	N	N	N
shíruǐ 石蕊 stone-stamen	reindeer moss	N	N	N
shísuàn 石蒜 stone-garlic	short-tube lycoris	N	N	N
shísǔn 石笋 stone-bamboo	stalagmite	N	N	N
shísuǒ 石锁 stone-lock	stone dumbbell	N	N	N
shítou 石头 stone-AFF	rock	N	N	N
shíyáng 石羊 stone-sheep	blue sheep	N	N	N
shíyìn 石印 stone-print	lithography	N	N	N
shíyīng 石英 stone-hero	quartz	N	N	N
shíyóu 石油 stone-oil	petroleum	N	N	N
shízhú 石竹 stone-bamboo	China pink (kind of plant)	N	N	N
shízǐ 石子 stone-pebble	cobblestone	N	N	N

Table 8 Words containing *zhù*

word	English gloss	form class of word	form class of *zhù*	form class of C_2	word	English gloss	form class of word	form class of C_1	form class of *zhù*
zhùcí 助词 help-word	auxiliary word	N	V	N	bāngzhù 帮助 help-help	help	V	V	V
zhùgōng 助攻 help-attack	secondary attack	V	V	V	bìzhù* 臂助 arm-help	help	V	N	V
zhùjì 助剂 help-potion	auxiliary	N	V	N	bìzhù* 臂助 arm-help	helper	N	N	V
zhùjiào 助教 help-teaching	teaching assistant	N	V	N	bǔzhù 补助 mend-help	subsidize	V	V	V
zhùlǐ 助理 help-manage	assistant	N	V	V	fúzhù 扶助 support-help	help	V	V	V
zhùpǎo 助跑 help-run	run-up (sports)	V	V	V	fǔzhù 辅助 help-help	assist	V	V	V
zhùrán 助燃 help-burn	combustion-supporting	V	V	V	hùzhù 互助 mutual-help	help each other	V	Adv	V
zhùshǒu 助手 help-hand	assistant	N	V	N	jièzhù 借助 borrow-help	to have the aid of; to use	V	V	V
zhùwēi 助威 help-awe	cheer for	P*	V	N	jiùzhù 救助 save-help	to relieve	V	V	V
zhùxìng 助兴 help-happy	liven things up	P*	V	N	juānzhù 捐助 contribute-help	contribute	V	V	V
zhùzhàn 助战 help-fight	assist in fighting	P*	V	N	nèizhù 内助 inside-help	wife	N	N	V
zhùzhǎng 助长 help-grow	foment	V	V	V	qiúzhù 求助 implore-help	to seek help	V	V	N

Table 8 (cont'd)

word	English gloss	form class of word	form class of C_1	form class of zhù
tánzhù 谈助 chat-help	topic of conversation	N	V	V
xiāngzhù 襄助 help-help	assist	V	V	V
xiézhù 协助 help-help	assist	V	V	V
yuánzhù 援助 help-help	help	V	V	V
zànzhù 赞助 praise-help	support	V	V	V
zīzhù 资助 money-help	subsidize	V	V	V

* listed in the cited reference dictionary as phrases, not words

other than a verb. Here, we may argue that the putative verb *diāo* is actually a noun that has undergone reanalysis because it occupies the right-hand side of the gestalt noun *shídiāo*. Further evidence of this is that we can find other examples of complex nouns with *diāo* in right-hand position: *bèidiāo* 贝雕 shell-carve 'shell carving', *fúdiāo* 浮雕 float-carve 'relief sculpture', *qīdiāo* 漆雕 carve-paint 'carved laquer-ware' and *yádiāo* 牙雕 ivory-carve 'ivory carving'.

Given this apparently productive use of *diāo* as a noun in this way in so many words, it is reasonable to presume that, despite its listing as a verb in dictionaries, it should be listed as a noun as well (albeit only when used as a bound morpheme at this point in its linguistic history). Lexicons are not always up to date either regarding the freeness and boundness of their morpheme entries, or whether the morphemes are considered nouns or verbs. This V → N reanalysis of *diāo* represents a kind of gestalt word 'dominance' over word-internal constituents, since *diāo* is a lexical verb that has acquired a noun form class interpretation because it is the right-hand member of a gestalt noun. In other words, the verb form class of *diāo* as determined by its verbal *cíxìng* appears to have been 'overridden' by the noun form class of gestalt nouns such as *shídiāo*. In sum, we see the following facts regarding the unambiguous noun *-shí-* 'stone' when it is used within words: it retains its nominal identity in either right- or left-hand position, and also participates in the nominalization of the verb *diāo* as the right-hand member of the gestalt noun *shídiāo*.

Now let us consider the unambiguous verbal morpheme *-zhù-* 'help' as seen in table 8. *-zhù-* is a verb in most cases, but, like the verb *diāo*, *-zhù-* 'gives up' its form class identity in certain contexts, changing from a verb to a noun when it appears as the right-hand constituent in certain words: *qiúzhù* seek-help 'to seek help', *tánzhù* chat-help 'topic of conversation' and *nèizhù* inside-help 'wife'. In *qiúzhù*, *-zhù-* has been nominalized as the object of a bound V–O verb, while in *tánzhù* and *nèizhù*, *-zhù-* receives a noun interpretation because it serves as the head noun of these gestalt nouns. In each of these examples, a noun form class interpretation is 'forced' upon *-zhù-* by the form class identity of the gestalt word.

In words formed with *-zhù-*, we see apparent exceptions to the Headedness Principle in (24). For nouns, the apparent exceptions are *zhùlǐ* help-manage 'assistant' ([V V]n), *nèizhù* inside-help 'wife' ([N V]n), *tánzhù* chat-help 'topic of conversation' ([V V]n) and *bìzhù* arm-help 'helper' ([N V]n). *zhùlǐ* would appear to be a noun composed of two verbs,[7] but in actuality *-lǐ* 理 'run, manage' can be considered to have undergone nominalization like the verbal forms *diāo* and *-zhù-* above. The evidence for this is that there are other complex nouns that have *-lǐ* as their right-hand morpheme, such as *jīnglǐ* 经理 manage-manage 'manager' and *zǒnglǐ* 总理 chief-manage 'premier'. Thus, it would appear that in the synchronic grammar of Mandarin word formation, *-lǐ* has begun to take on a nominal identity (as a bound morpheme, at least), with the meaning of 'one in charge; manager'. In *tánzhù* and *nèizhù*, *-zhù-* is nominalized as the right-hand constituent in a gestalt noun, and takes on the meaning of 'something/someone that helps'. Finally, *bìzhù* arm-help 'helper' is best analysed as a zero-derived nominalization of the verb *bìzhù* arm-help 'help'.

[7] *zhùlǐ* cannot be considered a zero derived nominal form, because it is never used as a verb.

For gestalt verbs, the apparent exceptions to the Headedness Principle are *bìzhù* arm-help 'help' ([N V]v) and *hùzhù* mutual-help 'help each other' ([Adv V]v). As with *căipái*, these are true exceptions to the Headedness Principle and are therefore predicted to behave exceptionally in the grammar even though they are permitted to exist by rule (see section 5.3.5). I will argue in 5.5.1 that the verbal element on the right is a 'virtual' rather than real head – virtual because it does not possess the predicted properties of a bona fide word head.

When the morpheme *-zhù-* occurs on the left in a word, if the word is [V N]N *-zhù-* is the verbal modifier of the head noun (e.g., *zhùshŏu* 助手 help-hand 'helper' or *zhùjiào* help-instruction 'teaching assistant'). If it is in a [V N]v word structure, *-zhù-* is the verb in a bound V–O word (e.g., *zhùwēi* help-strength 'to cheer on'). In a ([V V]v, left-hand *-zhù-* is a modifying verbal element, modifying the verb to its right.

We have seen that the verbal morpheme *-zhù-* retains its verbal form class identity when it occurs on the left, and appears to be nominalized in many cases when it occurs on the right, namely in words such as *tánzhù*, *nèizhù* and *qiúzhù*. All three of these words represent a form of reanalysis in which a noun identity is 'forced' on the intrinsically verbal *-zhù-*. We see more and more of this 'enforced' word component form class change, as morphemes are reanalysed as having a new form class identity by the force of the dominating gestalt word, no matter what the component's basic form class is represented as, e.g., in lexical dictionary entries. Thus, a principle is beginning to emerge: the form class identity of morphemes is subject to change – in conformity with the Headedness Principle – induced by the properties of the gestalt word within which it occurs. This seems especially true for morphemes that do not have an independent distribution in syntax – a true *cíxìng*.

Now, what about bound morphemes whose form classes are ambiguous, allowing variable interpretation? We might predict that since such morphemes do not have an independent distribution in syntax, and since they allow varying form class interpretation, they would be even more subject to domination by the gestalt word, with their form class identities conforming to the Headedness Principle based on the positions they occupy within the word. To test this, we look at two bound morphemes that, according to their dictionary entries, can possess both noun and verb form class identities: *-zhèng-* 证 'to prove/proof', and *-zhī-* 知 'to know/knowledge'. First let us look at *-zhèng-*, seen in table 9.

Table 9 Words containing *zhèng*

word	English gloss	form class of word	form class of *zhèng*	form class of C₂
zhèngcí 证词 proof-word	testimony	N	N	N
zhèngjiàn 证件 proof-document	credentials	N	N	N
zhèngjù 证据 proof-proof	proof	N	N	N
zhèngmíng 证明 prove-clarify	prove	V	V	V
zhèngquàn 证券 proof-certificate	negotiable securities	N	N	N
zhèngrén 证人 prove-person	witness	N	V	N
zhèngshí 证实 prove-fact	verify	V	V	N
zhèngshū 证书 proof-book	credentials	N	N	N
zhèngwù 证物 proof-thing	exhibit	N	N	N
zhèngyàn 证验 prove-test	verify	V	V	V
zhèngzhāng 证章 proof-badge	badge	N	N	N

word	English gloss	form class of word	form class of C₁	form class of *zhèng*
bǎozhèng 保证 protect-prove	guarantee	V	V	V
biànzhèng 辨证 distinguish-prove	to analyse and verify	V	V	V
cházhèng 查证 investigate-prove	to check	V	V	V
dǎngzhèng 党证 party-proof	party card	N	N	N
duìzhèng 对证 match-prove	check, verify	V	V	V
fǎnzhèng 反证 overturn-proof	counter-evidence	N	V	N
gōngzhèng 公证 public-proof	notarization	N	N	N
jiànzhèng 见证 see-proof	witness	N	V	N
kǎozhèng 考证 test-prove	verify	V	V	V
lìzhèng 例证 example-proof	case in point	N	N	N
lùnzhèng 论证 statement-proof	proof	N	N	N
míngzhèng 明证 clear-proof	clear proof	N	Adj	N
pángzhèng 旁证 side-proof	circumstantial evidence	N	N	N

Table 9 (*cont'd*)

word	English gloss	form class of word	form class of C_1	form class of zhèng
píngzhèng 凭证 proof-proof	proof	N	N	N
qiānzhèng 签证 sign-proof	visa	N	V	N
qiúzhèng 求证 seek-proof	look for proof	V	V	N
rénzhèng 人证 person-proof	human testimony	N	N	N
rènzhèng 认证 identify-proof	authentication	N	V	N
shízhèng 实证 fact-proof	concrete evidence	N	N	N
tiězhèng 铁证 iron-proof	ironclad proof	N	N	N
wùzhèng 物证 material-proof	material evidence	N	N	N
xiǎnzhèng 显证 clear-proof	clear proof	N	Adj	N
yànzhèng 验证 test-prove	test and verify	V	V	V
yǐnzhèng 引证 cite-prove	cite as proof	V	V	V
yìnzhèng 印证 conform-prove	verify	V	V	V
zuìzhèng 罪证 crime-proof	evidence of a crime	N	N	N
zuǒzhèng 左证 left-proof	evidence	N	N	N

Since *-zhèng-* is capable of being either a noun ('proof') or verb ('prove'), we might expect it to be able to shift between its noun and verb identity as dictated by the form class of the gestalt word in which it occurs and its position within that word, with its form class identity left 'free to vary' in other, 'non-dictating', positions. Looking at table 9, this is in fact precisely what we find. When *-zhèng-* is located on the right within a noun, it is always a noun (a modified nominal head). When it is on the right in a verb, it is either the noun object in a lexicalized V–O verb, or the second verb in a V_1–V_2 complex verb. When it is on the left in a verb, it is always itself a verb: it is either the verb in a lexicalized V–O word, or the first verb in a V_1–V_2 complex verb.[8]

Now, *-zhèng-* seems to be a simple, straightforward example. For a more problematic case, let us consider *-zhī-* 知 know/knowledge. *-zhī-* is a morpheme that not only can serve as either a noun or a verb, it also has a highly storied past – it is a word that is important in Chinese philosophy, with very extensive usage and connotation in the classical language. As a salient classical concept with varied uses in different contexts, many of its contemporary uses reflect that classical flavour, inherited from the days when it was a free morpheme (word) capable (like many words in classical Chinese) of acting as either a free noun or free verb. It is not that most other words in the classical language could not do this, it is just that given the seminal role of *-zhī-* in Chinese language and philosophy, it is more likely to have retained elements of its classical usage down to this day. Our choice of the morpheme *-zhī-* will serve to illustrate the difficulty of defining form class in some Chinese words precisely because of properties stemming from their classical usage.

With that in mind, let us take a look at the form class identities of *-zhī-* in contemporary word environments, as seen in table 10. In accordance with the Headedness Principle, when it appears as the left constituent, *-zhī-* is usually a verb, and assumes the identity of noun

---

[8] Admittedly, there are cases where the interpretation of *-zhèng-* appears arbitrary, as for example in the word *rènzhèng* identify-proof 'authentication' in table 9, where I have listed *-zhèng-* as a noun ('proof') when it might just as easily be interpreted as a verb ('prove'). The point is that rather than considering the interpretation of forms such as *-zhèng-* to be arbitrary, since the form class of *-zhèng-* is 'free to vary' in these circumstances, the most likely interpretation will be that determined by the identity of the gestalt word in concert with the Headedness Principle.

Table 10 Words containing *zhī*

word	English gloss	form class of word	form class of *zhī*	form class of C_2	word	English gloss	form class of word	form class of C_1	form class of *zhī*
zhīdào 知道 know-way	know	V	V	N	gǎnzhī 感知 feeling-knowledge	perception	N	N	N
zhīdǐ 知底 know-bottom	know the details	P*	V	N	gùzhī 故知 ancients-knowledge	ancient people	N	N	N
zhījǐ 知己 know-self	intimate	Adj	V	N	huàzhī 画知 stroke-knowledge	acknowledge notification	P*	V	N
zhījiāo 知交 know-relation	good friend	N	V	N	huòzhī 获知 obtain-knowledge	learn	V	V	N
zhījué 知觉 knowledge-perception	consciousness	N	N	N	míngzhī 明知 clear-know	know clearly	V	Adj	V
zhīkè 知客 know-guest	person in charge	N	V	N	qīnzhī 亲知 intimate-knowledge	first-hand knowledge	N	Adj	N
zhīliǎo** 知了 know-finish	cicada	N	V	V	qíngzhī 情知 affection-know	know clearly	V	N	V
zhīmíng 知名 know-name	famous	Adj	V	N	qiúzhī 求知 seek-knowledge	seek knowledge	V	V	N
zhīmǔ** 知母 know-mother	kind of medicine	N	V	N	shúzhī 熟知 close-know	know clearly	V	Adj	V
zhīqíng 知情 know-event	know the facts	V	V	N	tōngzhī 通知 pass-knowledge	notify	V	V	N
zhīqù 知趣 know-interest	tactful	Adj	V	N	wúzhī 无知 not:have-knowledge	ignorance	N	V	N
zhīshi 知识 knowledge-knowledge	knowledge	N	N	N					

Table 10 (cont'd)

word	English gloss	form class of word	form class of zhī	form class of C₂	word	English gloss	form class of word	form class of C₁	form class of zhī
zhīxī 知悉 know-know	know	V	V	V	xiānzhī 先知 first-know	prophet	N	Adv	V
zhīxiǎo 知晓 know-know	know	V	V	V	xiāngzhī 相知 mutual-know	know each other	V	Adv	V
zhīxīn 知心 know-heart	intimate	Adj	V	N	xūzhī 须知 must-knowledge	notice	N	N	N
zhīyīn 知音 know-sound	bosom friend	N	V	N	xūzhī 须知 must-know	should know	V	Aux	V
zhīzhào 知照 know-notify	notify	V	V	V	zhēnzhī 真知 real-knowledge	real knowledge	N	Adj	N
zhīzú 知足 know-enough	be content	Adj	V	N					

* listed in the cited reference dictionary as phrases, not words
** non-compositional, highly lexicalized words

only when the gestalt word is a noun. As with previous examples, its use as a verb on the left takes one of two forms – it is either the verb in a lexicalized V–O word, or the first verb in a V_1–V_2 word. One anomaly involving -zhī- when it appears as the left constituent of a word is the number of adjectives (stative verbs) it may form in verb–noun V–O [V N]$_{SV}$ combinations.

-zhī- occurring on the right is used both as a noun and as a verb. When used as a noun, it is either the nominal head of a gestalt noun or the nominal object in a lexicalized 'Verb–Object' verb. When used as a verb, it is either V_2 in a [V_1 V_2]$_V$ word, or a verb that is modified by an adjective or adverb. In those cases, the gestalt words so formed are usually verbs (e.g., [Adj V]$_V$; [Adv V]$_V$), but there is one instance of a noun formed in this way ([Adv V]$_N$), namely, xiānzhī first-know 'prophet'. These latter examples do not conform to the Headedness Principle, and so are predicted to behave exceptionally in the grammar, i.e., they are predicted not to possess the properties of regular, left-headed verbs.

An example of exceptional behaviour is that most verbs allow a question to be formed by duplicating the head (*xǐhuān* 'like' → *xǐ-bu-xǐhuān* like-not-like 'like or not?'). But this does not generally work for verbs that do not conform to the verb-left convention of the Headedness Principle: e.g., *míngzhī* → *míng-bu-míngzhī. The same is true for the other examples of 'right-headed' verbs we have seen: *hù-bu-hùzhù, *xū-bu-xūzhī, *shú-bu-shúzhī, *qíng-bu-qíngzhī, *cǎi-bu-cǎipái. That is, these words are exceptions to the generalization that verbs in Chinese are overwhelmingly left-headed, with these (apparently) right-headed verbs (i.e., verbs containing a 'virtual' head; see 5.5.1) predicted to behave differently in the grammar.

What has this investigation of form classes within words shown us? To summarize, we found that there is a Headedness Principle in the grammar of Chinese word formation that may be contravened, that is, admit of exceptions such as: [V V]$_N$ (*páibǐ, páiguàn, zhùlǐ*), [X V]$_V$ (where the X is adjective, auxiliary, adverb or noun modifying the verb; *cǎipái, chángpǎo, bìzhù, míngzhī, qíngzhī, shúzhī, xiāngzhī, xūzhī*), [V N]$_{SV}$ (*zhījǐ, zhīmíng, zhīxīn, zhīzú*), [N V]$_N$ (*shídiāo, bìzhù, nèizhù*) and [Adv V]$_N$ (*xiānzhī*). The list of exceptions is relatively small: in general, verbs occur on the left of gestalt verbs, and nouns occur on the right of gestalt nouns (see statistics in table 18 and discussion in 6.1.2.7).

There are a couple of ways to think about this. One is to say that gestalt verbs only use or 'select' verbs as their leftmost elements, and gestalt nouns only 'select' nouns as their rightmost elements. Another way of looking at this is to say that gestalt nouns *nominalize* their rightmost element, and gestalt verbs *verbalize* their leftmost element. That would certainly appear to be true in the case of morphemes with a variable form class identity (e.g., *huà* or *-zhèng-*), as demonstrated above. For, since the form class interpretation in these morphemes is variable, they generally appear as nouns when they occur on the right, and as verbs when they occur on the left.

Since this list of exceptions to the Headedness Principle is small, we can make the following statement regarding the identity of morphemes within words, on analogy with our statement on the identity of words appearing in syntactic structures (3.2): by and large, there is little ambiguity with respect to word-internal morpheme form class – the word context makes clear what the form class identity of the morpheme is. Therefore, we may say that if a morpheme has M^N form class identities, one of those identities – M^X – is 'selected for' or 'designated' by its context within the word. However, the situation with respect to word-internal morphemes is even stronger than this: not only is the morpheme form class 'selected for' or 'designated' by the word context, in most cases it is actually *determined* by the form class identity of the word.

Take the word *huà* 画 ('draw, paint, picture, drawing'), for example. When it is the left-hand member of a word, it may be either a noun or a verb as determined by its interpretation within the word context. The words within which *huà* occurs on the left are all nouns. In these nouns, the left-hand member is free to be either a noun or a verb, and so, accordingly, the left-hand member *huà* modifies the noun on its right either as a noun or a verb. Contrasting the two homographic and homophonic words *huàláng*₁ 画廊 'painted corridor' and *huàláng*₂ 画廊 'art gallery': in *huàláng*₁ 'painted corridor', the *huà* is a verb, because in this word, *-láng* refers to a place in which the act of painting has occurred, and that act of painting is indicated by a verbal reading of *huà*. In the *huàláng*₂ 'gallery' example, on the other hand, *-láng* refers to a place in which paintings are present, and so the *huà* in this case is a noun referring to those paintings.

Turning to *huà* as a right-hand word component, as seen in table 5, *huà* has a verbal identity in some cases and a nominal identity in others. It is a verb when the entire word is a verb, and a noun when the entire word is a noun. This is also generally true for *-zhèng-*, as seen in table 9. When it is the left-hand member of a word it may be noun or verb, and that choice is determined by its interpretation within the word context. When the word is a verb, left-hand *-zhèng-* is a verb. When the word is a noun, the left-hand member is free to be either a noun or a verb (a verb either as V₁ in a V₁–V₂ verb, or as the verbal modifier of a head noun); and so, as in the case of *huà* above, *-zhèng-* takes a noun or a verb interpretation according to the nature of its modifying role.

3.3 Criteria for determining form class of Chinese word components

What do the observations in 3.2.1 mean for our task of determining the form class identities of morphemes within words? We have explicitly posited a form class identity for word constituents based on (a) the form class of the gestalt word, (b) the constituent's role or position within that word and (c) the form classes of constituents as they are listed in authoritative prescriptive sources; e.g., dictionaries. This procedure leaves surprisingly few ambiguous cases, and the ambiguities that do arise end up either being resolvable or are exceptions that are handled specially in the grammar.

We also have discovered what may seem like a trivial and obvious point, but is a crucially important point nonetheless: *the identity of morphemes within words is largely word-driven – the form class identity of the word generally determines the form class identities of its constituents*. In other words, what we found to be true for words in syntactic slots above – namely, that the syntactic context makes the form class identity of words clear – is even truer for the identities of morphemes in word-internal slots: not only does the word-internal context make clear what the form class identity of the word constituent is to be, to a large extent it actually determines or 'drives' the form class identity of word components.[9] So when we say that a morpheme has M^N form class identities with identity M^X determined by word-internal context, we are in effect saying that, e.g., in the case of a complex noun $[X_1 X_2]_N$, the N identity of the word 'confers' an identity upon X_2, yielding $[X_1 N]_N$. So, in $[X_1 X_2]_N$, X_2 is equal to N, while X_1 is left relatively 'free to vary', subject to constraints imposed by the requirements of its position within the word. This is quite different from the situation in syntax, where form class identities of phrases are *determined by* the identities of phrasal heads, by 'percolation' of form class information from the phrasal head to higher phrasal nodes. The difference in the case of word formation is that the 'identity-conferring' power is posited to occur in the 'opposite' direction: the identity of the higher structure – the word – determines the identity of the word head.

This is easily demonstrated by the phenomenon of word-internal morpheme reanalysis. As seen above, the verbs *diāo* 雕 'carve', *-zhù-* 助 'to help' and *-lǐ* 理 'manage' are reanalysed as nouns because they occupy the right-hand side of gestalt $[X X]_N$ nouns (e.g., *shídiāo* 石雕 stone-carve 'stone carving', *qiúzhù* 求助 implore-help 'seek help' and *jīnglǐ* 经理 manage-manage 'manager'). Also, non-verb morphemes are reanalysed as verbs because they occupy the left-hand side of gestalt $[X X]_V$ verbs. For example, the stative verb *dà* 'big' that occurs in the

[9] Note that this is not true for a certain class of words – derived words – whose form classes are determined by word-forming affixes, as we shall see below.

active verb *dàbiàn* 大便 big-convenience 'to move the bowels' (with the structure [SV N]v; a denominal verb, formed by zero derivation from the original noun 'bowel movement' with the structure [SV N]n) may be reanalysed as an active verb (meaning something like 'to do'), allowing it to serve as the active verb V_1 in a [V_1 V_2]v resultative verb compound (see 4.3.3): *dàwánbiàn* 大完便 big(→ do)-finish-convenience 'to finish a bowel movement'. Similar examples involve the words *xiǎobiàn* small-convenience 'to urinate' becoming → *xiǎole èrshí fēnzhōng de biàn* 小了二十分钟的便 small:ed-twenty-minutes-of-convenience 'to urinate for twenty minutes' (as seen in (3)), and *yōumò* 幽默 (a phonetic loan meaning 'humour') reanalysing its first syllable as a verb that may be marked with verbal aspect, as in *yōu-le tā yi mò* 幽了他一默 '*hu*-ed him one -*mour*' as seen in (52) (both examples are from Huang 1984). A final example is the noun *piānjiàn* 偏见 inclined-view/see 'bias' selecting the 'nominal' reading of *jiàn* 'view' over the more common verbal reading 'to see', since the noun *piānjiàn* cannot be used as a verb and *jiàn* occupies the canonical nominal right-hand word slot.

We now have criteria for assigning form class identities to word components. Following the Headedness Principle, in the default case nouns have nouns on the right, and verbs have verbs on the left, with the other word positions left relatively free to vary according to the particular word-structure requirements. For words in which this principle obviously clashes with native speaker intuition (such as *cǎipái* colour-rehearse 'to dress rehearse' [N V]v, and *zhùlǐ* help-manage 'assistant' [V V]n), these words are either only apparent exceptions (i.e., *zhùlǐ* is a noun whose apparent verb in right-hand position has actually been reanalysed as a noun), or are true exceptions, and as such are 'marked', i.e., predicted to behave differently in the grammar of Mandarin.

The issue here is the grammatical form class opacity of word constituents in the minds of native speakers. Specifically, what do native speakers know about the identity of word constituents simply by virtue of their knowing the gestalt word? The answer presented here – by hypothesis – is that native speakers know that a noun will tend to have a noun on the right, and a verb will tend to have a verb on the left. This generalization of course has exceptions, but the words that are exceptional are posited to have special properties (among other things, as I shall argue in 6.2, they are relatively strongly lexicalized).

Thus, we have seen that assigning a form class identity to Chinese word components need not be a difficult and arbitrary process, but rather that it can be a relatively straightforward procedure that nonetheless admits of interesting classes of exceptions. In the next section we take a look at Mandarin word constituents in terms of their morphological identity.

3.4 Morphological analysis of Chinese word components

Now that we have formulated a way to assign the morphemes in a word to part-of-speech categories, let us look at those morphemes in terms of their morphological properties. To analyse word components in a morphological framework, we need criteria for classifying the morphemes. The first two criteria are (a) whether the morpheme is free or bound, and (b) whether the morpheme is a 'function' (grammatical) or 'content' (lexical) morpheme. The combination of these properties gives us four possible morpheme types ([+free, +function], [+free, −function], [−free, +function], [−free, −function]), three of which are relevant to word formation in Chinese.

3.4.1 Distinguishing 'free' and 'bound'

The characteristics 'bound' and 'free' are clearly definable in Chinese, despite claims to the contrary (e.g., Tang 1995: 196–8). The issue arises when a given morpheme appears to be free in certain contexts and bound in others, leading some to conclude that the bound–free status of such a morpheme is indeterminate. The resolution of this indeterminacy lies in the fact that a morpheme that possesses varied characteristics or identities potentially has separate (though undoubtedly related) entries in the mental lexicon for each identity. That being the case, a given characteristic applies unambiguously for any given morpheme as a function of its lexical identity, and the native speaker knows clearly what the usage is for any given entry in the mental lexicon.

To illustrate, take first an example having to do with variation in the *register* of morpheme use. The morpheme *yán* 言 meaning 'speak, speech' may not be used as a free morpheme in modern Mandarin, but it is perfectly acceptable as a free word in the classical Chinese language. The distinction here is clear: whatever the status of this morpheme in the classical language (and whatever its status is in modern sayings that are derived from older stages of the language), *yán* 言 is a bound morpheme in modern Mandarin.[10] The same situation obtains in bidialectal speakers or speakers operating within different registers (such as classical–modern, spoken–written, colloquial–formal, etc.).

In the second type of example, a morpheme is bound in certain of its usages, and free in others. For example, the morpheme *mù* 木 is a bound morpheme when used to mean 'tree' or 'wood', but when it is used to mean 'numb' it is free, as seen from the fact that it can be freely used in the sentence *Wǒ shétou mù le* 我舌头木了 my tongue-NOM numb ASP 'My tongue is numb.'[11] The variable usage here involves two separate lexical entries. It either means one thing or the other, and either it is able independently to fill a syntactic slot with that meaning or it isn't.

The third kind of examples involve polysemy – cases in which a morpheme is bound in one usage but free in another, albeit closely related, usage. For example, as Tang (1995: 197) points out, the morpheme *gōng* 工 means many things ('labour, art, industry, work, job'), and it is bound in certain of those meanings ('labour, art, industry') and free in others ('work, job'). But this does not mean that the bound–free distinction is indeterminate with respect to the morpheme *gōng* 工: it simply means that the mental lexicon will contain separate (albeit related) entries for the different usages. For *gōng* 工, it means that one entry ($gōng_1$) will be used as a bound morpheme (meaning it can't be used as a word in a syntactic slot), and another ($gōng_2$) will be used as a free morpheme (meaning it can be used as a word in a syntactic slot). For productive word formation, it means that the free form, but not the bound form, will be able to function as a recursive node (see 5.4.3).

In sum, a morpheme that seems indeterminate in its bound–free identity either is actually used in different linguistic registers (e.g., classical–modern, spoken–written, colloquial–learned, dialectal, etc.)

---

[10] And of course, it may be used as a free morpheme by those persons (e.g., scholars) who may be able to converse in the classical language.

[11] This is only assuming that $mù_1$ 木 'tree/wood' and $mù_2$ 木 'numb' are the 'same' morpheme, which is in fact somewhat doubtful, as the historical, orthographic and phonological relationships between $mù_1$ and $mù_2$ are not supported by a strong semantic relationship.

or, if used in the same register, will contain separate entries in the mental lexicon for each of its free and bound identities, each controlled with no difficulty or ambiguity by the native speaker.

3.4.2 Distinguishing 'content' and 'function'

The distinction between 'content' and 'function' is a traditional one in linguistics, and has a long history in Chinese linguistics in particular. Morphemes in Chinese traditionally have been divided into content (*shí* 实 'real') and function (*xū* 虚 'empty') morphemes, a distinction that dates back at least to the seventeenth century (Peyraube forthcoming).

Hopper and Traugott define content words as words that are 'used to report or describe things, actions and qualities' (1993: 4). They define function words as words that 'indicate relationship of nominals to each other . . . to link parts of a discourse . . . to indicate whether entities . . . in a discourse are already identified or not . . . and to show whether they are close to the speaker or hearer' (1993: 4). The function–content distinction is not discrete, and indeed there is a continuum upon which the concepts of content and function rest, with most function morphemes finding their historical origins in the grammaticalization of content morphemes (Hopper and Traugott 1993: 6; Bybee, Perkins and Pagliuca 1994: 40–1). Chinese, as we shall see in chapter 6, is no exception.

3.4.3 Morpheme types

Based on these criteria of free–bound and content–function, if the morpheme is a function morpheme and is free ([+free, +function]), it is a *function word*. If it is a content morpheme and is free ([+free, –function]), it is a *root word* (or simply a 'word'). If the morpheme is content and is bound ([–free, –function]), it is a *bound root*. If the morpheme is bound and is grammatical ([–free, +function]), then it is an *affix*.[12] Of these four morpheme types, generally only function words do not freely combine with other morphemes to form larger words. Since function words generally are not very productive word-forming elements in Chinese, we will concentrate on the other three morpheme types.

---

[12] I use this term only advisedly; see 3.5.1 below.

3.4.3.1 Two types of affix

Of the three categories of morpheme relevant to word formation (word, bound root and affix), within the category of affix there are two subcategories: *word-forming affix* and *grammatical affix*. These two 'intuitive' subcategories of affix, it turns out, are surprisingly difficult to characterize with clear criteria that uniquely distinguish them. But a lot of work has been done on the subject, and so I suggest the following.

Word-forming affixes are affixes that:
- *may* change the form class of items to which they attach (for further discussion of this criterion, see discussion of bound roots versus word-forming affixes below)
- apply selectively, to only certain members of a category
- have a meaning across contexts that is relatively variable and unpredictable (Bybee, Perkins and Pagliuca 1994: 22)
- may attach to free words or bound roots

As examples from Mandarin,[13] we have the 'nominalizing' suffixes *-zi* 子, *-tou* 头, *-xìng* 性 and *-dù* 度, the 'verbalizing' suffix *-huà* 化, the negative prefixes *wú-* 无, *wèi-* 未 and *fēi-* 非, the adverbial suffix *-rán* 然 and the agentive suffix *-zhě* 者. While not all of these forms fit all four of the criteria above, most fit two or more.

Note that word-forming affixes are exceptions to the generalization that the gestalt word drives internal constituent form class (see 3.3), because the form class identity of a word-forming affix is usually not reanalysed or determined by the form class of its dominating word. Note also that one other criterion often used to identify this category of affix (Matthews 1991: 36–7; Spencer 1991: 9) is that they make 'new' or 'different' words (or lexemes)[14] out of existing words. The circularity of this criterion (i.e., the fact that it 'forms new words if it is a word-forming affix' and it is a 'word-forming affix if it forms new words') is especially apparent when viewed from the perspective of Mandarin,

---

[13] A more complete list is given in table 26.
[14] The term 'lexeme' refers to the form of a word that abstracts away from all inflectional changes that it may undergo (Matthews 1991: 26; Spencer 1991: 45). For example, if we take the words 'eat', 'eats', 'ate', 'eaten', and so forth, an abstract entity – the lexeme EAT – may be posited which abstracts away from all possible inflected forms of 'eat'. This concept seems to apply only marginally to Chinese, since Chinese does not have copious inflectional paradigms.

CHINESE WORD COMPONENTS 71

since 'new word' is not as straightforward a notion as it might appear to be based upon highly inflecting Indo-European languages.

Grammatical affixes, in contrast, are affixes that:
- are completely general, that is, apply to all members, or at least large subclasses, of a given class (Bybee, Perkins and Pagliuca 1994: 22, 39)
- have a constant, predictable meaning across contexts (Bybee, Perkins and Pagliuca 1994: 22)
- *must* attach to free words
- *never* change the form class of the words to which they attach

Examples from Mandarin are the verbal aspect markers -*le* 了, -*zhe* 著 and -*guo* 过; the resultative potential 'infixes' -*de* 得 and *bu*- 不 and the human noun plural suffix -*men* 们. These morphemes are general because they apply to all members of a given form class, or large subclasses of that form class (-*le* 了, -*zhe* 著 and -*guo* 过 apply to virtually any active verb; -*de* 得 and *bu*- 不 apply to the head of any resultative verb; -*men* 们 applies to virtually any human noun; see 4.2.1.4), they are extremely stable in meaning, none of them attaches to anything other than free words, and none of them ever causes a word to change its form class.

3.4.3.2 Word-forming affixes vs. bound roots

Based on the above criteria, the distinction between word-forming affixes and inflectional affixes seems clear. However, the distinction between bound roots and word-forming affixes may seem less so. For example, we may ask: why are *fēi*- 非 'not, non-' and *wèi*- 未 'not, not yet' listed as word-forming affixes rather than bound roots, and not *fǎn*- 反 'anti-' (table 26)? Likewise, why are -*mín* 民 'people' and -*yuán* 员 'person' listed as bound roots rather than word-forming affixes, and not -*zhě* 者 'one who does/is X' (table 26)? Since both bound roots and word-forming affixes are bound morphemes, in the proposed system the difference between the two must lie in whether the morphemes in question are considered 'grammatical' or 'lexical'. While admitting that the distinction between 'grammatical' and 'lexical' exists on a continuous rather than dichotomous scale (as noted in 3.4.2), it is nonetheless possible to draw a distinction between the two, as I will demonstrate using the bound root -*yuán* 员 and the word-forming affix -*zhě* 者 as examples.

Table 11 Examples of -zhě and -yuán

word	word + -zhě	word	word + -yuán
bǐ 笔 'pen'	bǐzhě 笔者 'the author'	chuán 船 'boat'	chuányuán 船员 'crew member'
dà 大 'big'	dàzhě 大者 'the big one'	jiāo 教 'teach'	jiàoyuán 教员 'teacher'
dú 读 'read'	dúzhě 读者 'the reader'	xué 学 'study'	xuéyuán 学员 'student'
lǎo 老 'old'	lǎozhě 老者 'old man'	bàomù 报幕 'announce'	bàomùyuán 报幕员 'announcer'
qiáng 强 'strong'	qiángzhě 强者 'the strong'	bǎoyù 保育 'child care'	bǎoyùyuán 保育员 'child-care worker'
xué 学 'study'	xuézhě 学者 'scholar'	cǎigòu 采购 'purchase'	cǎigòuyuán 采购员 'purchasing agent'
láodòng 劳动 'work'	láodòngzhě 劳动者 'worker'	chūnà 出纳 'receive and pay out'	chūnàyuán 出纳员 'cashier'
shènglì 胜利 'win'	shènglìzhě 胜利者 'victor'	yánjiū 研究 'research'	yánjiūyuán 研究员 'research worker'
yánjiū 研究 'research'	yánjiūzhě 研究者 'researcher'	yùndòng 运动 'sport, activity'	yùndòngyuán 运动员 'athlete'
zìyuàn 自愿 'voluntarily'	zìyuànzhě 自愿者 'volunteer'	zhídǎo 指导 'guide, advise'	zhídǎoyuán 指导员 'adviser'
fúhébiāozhǔn 符合标准 'up to standard'	fúhébiāozhǔnzhě 符合标准者 'one who is up to standard'	zhíxīng 值星 'be on duty for a week'	zhíxīngyuán 值星员 'person on duty'

The first criterion is the generality and abstractness of the morphemes involved, with grammatical items tending to be more general and abstract. The bound root -yuán means 'person whose job/position is X', while the word-forming affix -zhě means 'one who does/is X'. Some examples are seen in table 11. Since the meaning of -yuán ('person whose job is X') entails the meaning of -zhě ('one who does/is X') while the meaning of -zhě does not entail the meaning of -yuán, the word-forming affix -zhě has the more general meaning. Despite some surface similarities in their meanings, a careful examination of the data in table 11 reveals that -*zhě* and -*yuán* are qualitatively different. Also, words formed with -*yuán* tend to have meanings that are more 'fixed' and 'lexicalized', while words formed with *zhě* have more the sense of being derivationally related to the words to which they are attached.

Secondly, word-forming affixes are more productive than bound roots. So for example in the *Reverse Order Modern Chinese Dictionary* (Chinese Academy of Social Sciences 1986), there are many entries ending in -*yuán* (n = ^{c}76), but far fewer ending in -*zhě* (n = ^{c}26). This indicates the productivity of -*zhě*, since the vast number of forms which may take -*zhě* as an ending precludes their being exhaustively listed.[15]

Finally, addition of word-forming affixes involves a grammatical change that, in general, is on a par with that caused by a logical operator (identity, negation, alternation, iteration and so forth) or a change in thematic role (see, e.g., Barker 1998 for a discussion of thematic roles in derivational morphology). For verbs it is the shift to 'agent', 'patient' or 'having/conferring the property of'; for nouns it is the shift to 'having/conferring the property of'; for adjectives it is the shift to 'having/conferring the property of', 'agent' or 'extent of the property of'. -*zhě* for example, affixes to adjectives, noun and verbs to indicate the characteristics of agency or property, much the same as the nominative or genitive cases respectively mark such characteristics in languages with overt case marking. So in other words, if the morpheme (a) asserts, (b) negates or (c) iterates the occurrence, existence, possession or properties contained in the form it is bound to, or if it causes a shift in grammatical role to something like 'agent' (e.g., 'employer') or 'patient' (e.g., 'employee'), it is defined as a 'function' morpheme, and considered a word-forming affix. Otherwise, it is a 'content' morpheme, and considered a bound root.

3.4.4 Summary and some test cases

To summarize, then, these morpheme categories are illustrated in table 12. In Chinese, the four morpheme types – root word, bound root, word-forming affix and grammatical affix – freely combine to

---

[15] A better way to estimate productivity is to count the single token occurrences of a given productive form in a text (see Sproat and Shih 1996). If *zhě* is more productive, then such a count would find a greater number of single token occurrences of words containing -*zhě* than words containing -*yuán*.

Table 12 Five morpheme types

is it free or bound?	is it content or function?	then it is a	examples
free	function	**function word**	*de* 的 Mod *le* 了 SEN ASP *hé* 和 Conj
free	content	**(root) word**	*bīng* 冰 'ice'
bound	content	**bound root**	*-fáng-* 房 'house'
bound	function	**affix**	
	does the affix change form class, apply selectively, etc.?	then it is a	examples
	yes	**word-forming affix**	*wú-* 无 not *wèi-* 未 not *-zi* 子 NOM *-zhě* 者 'one who' *-huà* 化 VRB *-tou* 头 NOM etc.
	no	**grammatical affix**	*-le* 了 V ASP *-men* 们 PL *-zhe* 著 V ASP *-guo* 过 V ASP

form words (subject to the rules and constraints in 5.3.5), except that affixes cannot combine with one another to form words. There are many questions we can ask about the identity of Chinese morphemes, now that criteria have been set out. In what follows, we try out some potentially problematic test cases to see how they respond to the morphological analysis presented above.

3.4.4.1 Determiners, classifiers and numerals

How do we analyse classifiers like *-ge* 个, *-zhāng* 张 and *-běn* 本 and determiners like *zhè* 这 and *nà* 那? What about numerals like *yī-* 一 'one', *sān-* 三 'three' and *wǔ-* 五 'five'? Let us take a look at these interesting cases.

First, are the morphemes mentioned above bound or free? The answer is fairly straightforward: classifiers are obviously bound, numerals are bound (they must occur with classifiers)[16] and determiners are free (you can say *zhè shì wǒde, nà shi tāde* 这是我的, 那是他的 'This is mine, that is his'). That means determiners are words, and since numerals and classifiers are bound, they must be either bound roots or some sort of affix. Numerals fit the criteria for bound root, because they are clearly content and not function. That leaves classifiers: since they are clearly function rather than content morphemes, they must be a kind of affix. Using our criteria, we see that they must be word-forming affixes because they may attach to other than free words (e.g., they attach to numerals, which we have just classified as bound roots: *wǒ yǒu sānge* 我有三个 'I have three').

To sum up, determiners are words, numerals are bound roots and classifiers are word-forming affixes. To complete the analysis, the combination 'number-classifier' (e.g., *sānge* 三个 three-classifier 'three') is a word, because it can occur in a 'noun' syntactic slot (*wǒ yǒu sānge* 我有三个 'I have three'). The combination of determiner and classifier may also be a word, because it too can occur in a 'noun' slot (*wǒ yǒu zhège* 我有这个 'I have this'). Finally, the combination of determiner, number and classifier is also a word, because it can also occur in a 'noun' slot: *wǒ yǒu (zhè) sānge* 我有(这)三个 'I have these three.' Note that the combination of 'determiner-number' is not a word, because it cannot freely occur in a syntactic slot (*zhè sān shì wǒde *这三是我的).

3.4.4.2 Location morphemes

The morphemes typically used to indicate location (*-lǐ-* 里 'in', *-wài-* 外 'out', *-shàng-* 上 'on/top', *-xià-* 下 'under/beneath' *-qián-* 前 'front/ahead' and *-hòu-* 后 'back/behind') are classified as bound roots, because they are bound and may occur with either words, bound roots or word-forming affixes. These morphemes freely occur with words, as in *zhèli* 这里 here-in 'here', *chēwài* 车外 car-out 'outside the car', *lùshang* 路上 road-on 'on the road', *shàngcéng* 上层 top-level 'upper level', *wàirén* 外人 out-person 'stranger', *qiánrén* 前人 ahead-person 'predecessors' and *xiàshuǐ* 下水 under-water 'downriver'. They are more restricted in occuring with bound roots, but somewhat productive when used in this way nonetheless. Some examples are *zhuōshàng* 桌上

---

[16] The only time numerals might be considered 'free' is in the specialized context of serial counting.

table-on 'on the table', *shìshàng* 世上 world-on 'on the earth', *wūlǐ* 屋里 room-in 'in the room', *lǐwū* 里屋 in-room 'inner room', *shàngyī* 上衣 top-clothes 'overcoat' and *xiàshēn* 下身 under-body 'lower body'. Finally, all the location morphemes may occur (albeit with varying degrees of frequency) with the word-forming affix -*tou* 头 (e.g., *lǐtou* 里头 in-AFF 'inside', *shàngtou* 上头 top-AFF 'top', etc.).[17]

3.5 The nature of the components

3.5.1 Affixes as word components

I have opted to use the term *affix* even though it is traditionally associated with many properties that are not relevant to Chinese word formation, and thus arguably not valid for a universal characterization of the concept. Although affixes are an important aspect of word formation in many languages, their role in Chinese, while arguably not marginal, is clearly different. We saw in 3.4.3 that Chinese does contain a nontrivial number of affixes, but they possess only a subset of the properties that we usually associate with that term.

Usually the term *affix* carries with it the ideas of *agreement, paradigmaticity* and *morphophonemic alternation*. These properties cooccur with affixation in many of the languages of the world, and therefore would appear to be an intrinsic part of the notion *affix*. However, many languages, including Chinese, simply do not have grammatical agreement, morphological paradigms and morphophonemic alternation. From our perspective, the term *affix* stands for a set of properties and relations common to all the world's languages. These universal properties critically include *boundness* and *grammatical function*, but do not necessarily include the phenomena of agreement, paradigmaticity and morphophonemic alternation. Therefore, I use the term *affix* only advisedly, for convenience, as a label indicating bound word-formation elements possessing a grammatical function, and intend for the term to be devoid of the traditional associations with non-universal properties such as agreement, paradigmatic alternation and morphophonemic alternation. It turns out that Mandarin and

---

[17] These location morphemes appear to be slowly undergoing grammaticalization, and so could be moving in the direction of becoming word-forming affixes or case markers. A. Li (1990) argues that these are indeed case markers.

English are strikingly similar in the structure of their words (see 5.4 and 5.6), but they differ inasmuch as in English certain word subparts (grammatical affixes) must 'pay attention to' other parts of the sentence, i.e., those subparts are required to match the 'number' or 'person' characteristics of other members of the sentence. It is quite fascinating that Mandarin and English may in fact be quite similar in the formation and structure of their words, with one difference being that grammatical agreement or paradigmaticity are relevant for English but irrelevant for Mandarin.

Note that within the category 'affix', 'grammatical affix' seems similar to the traditional 'inflectional affixation', and 'word forming affix' bears a strong resemblance to 'derivational affixation'. These categories may indeed be universal in word formation at a certain level of abstraction, with the caveat that not all the world's languages possess the properties (such as agreement, paradigms and morphophonemic alternation) that are often associated with these affix categories.[18]

3.5.2 Bound roots as word components

Bound roots are the largest class of morpheme type in Chinese. Much as in Italian, bound roots are morphemes with lexical rather than grammatical identity that cannot occur in a syntactic form class category slot until they are supplemented with additional morphological material that causes them to be 'completed' as words. This is also true for the so-called 'latinate' stems in English (*anti-*, *-itis*, *-osis*, *-ectomy*, etc.; see 5.6), that are also bound and productive but lexical rather than grammatical. But unlike in Italian, in Mandarin bound roots may, and in fact usually do, form words by combining with other bound roots. Also unlike bound roots in both Italian and English, Mandarin bound roots generally are less positionally restricted, i.e., they may in general occur as either the first or second constituent of a word (see the discussion of 'positionally free or bound' in 4.5.1.2), whereas in English and Italian a given bound root generally is restricted to occurring as either a left- or right-hand word constituent, but not both.

[18] See Packard (1996), in which I argue that a universal distinction between inflectional and derivational affixation does exist, but that they are distinguished by properties such as order of affixation, productivity and degree of boundness, and not properties such as obligatoriness, configurationality and extrinsic definition.

We might ask: why are most complex words in Chinese formed by combining bound roots? There are several possible explanations. One is that even though these words in many cases find their origins in the lexicalization of juxtaposed free words, when this lexicalization occurs, the tendency is for the components of the new word, over time, to cease being free words. Another explanation is that many new words were formed by abbreviating combinations of longer words that were themselves composed of bound roots. A third possibility is that there are linguistic forces that 'conspire' to make morphemes non-free, either universally or in Chinese. These possibilities are discussed further in 6.4.3.1.

3.5.3 Free ('root') words as word components

Free words may serve as word components in Chinese just as they may in most other languages. Words composed in this way are defined in western linguistics as 'true compounds'. If we follow this definition, then, strictly speaking, the majority of bisyllabic words in Chinese should not be called 'compounds' because one or both of the constituents of most complex Chinese words are bound roots rather than free words (see Duanmu 1997 and Starosta et al. 1997).

Why has there been confusion on this issue of 'compound' in Chinese linguistics? It is largely a matter of conflicting terminology. In Chinese, the early label for 'two-syllable words' was *fùhé cí* 复合词 compound-word 'compounded word', because they were indeed words that were formed through the combination of morphemes as implied by the term *fùhé* 'compound'. This term lent itself rather nicely to the English translation 'compound word', even though strictly speaking (at least according to the definition common in western linguistics) the term 'compound' is restricted to words formed from two free words.[19] This, then, is the reason for the terminological confusion: if compounds are indeed to be defined as words that are composed from other words, then most Chinese '*fùhé cí*' are not compounds: they are, rather, 'bound root words' (see 4.1).

---

[19] Chao (1968: 359) used a looser definition of compound, not requiring constituents of a compound to be free, but requiring only that they not be affixes and not be submorphemic.

Having presented a morphological analysis of Chinese word components, we now move on to the identity of Chinese gestalt words considered in terms of the form class identities of those components as discussed in 3.3. Regarding the morphological analysis of the components just presented, we will use that information in the following chapter, and use it even more fully when we discuss the abstract properties of Mandarin morphemes in chapter 5.

4 | Gestalt Chinese words

Now that we have a framework for classifying Chinese word component morphemes and a procedure for assigning them form class identities, in this chapter we take a look at the range of complex noun and verb words viewed by the form class and morphological identities of their constituents.

Why is gestalt word identity important? Following the discussion in 2.3, we proceed from the assumption that the operation of the language does indeed revolve around the *word* as a fundamental construct, with all the properties and grammatical identities that this implies. The grammatical identity of the word is what marks it for availability and selection for use in a syntactic slot. In terms of native speaker awareness, a word has a definite – if often implicit – form class identity. The grammatical identity of the word constitutes an important aspect of what the native speaker knows about its properties and distribution. Also, as argued in 3.3, knowledge of gestalt word identity provides the native speaker with implicit knowledge of word structure.

4.1 Word types

First of all, let us consider gestalt words in terms of what types of morphemes compose them. We may consider all two-syllable complex Mandarin words to be combinations of the four morpheme types – root words, bound roots, word-forming affixes and grammatical affixes – presented in 3.4. This yields four types of complex word in Mandarin: *compound word, bound root word, derived word* and *grammatical word*.[1]

A compound word is composed of two root words; a bound root word is composed of a root word plus bound root, or two bound roots;

---

[1] This particular taxonomy of word type does not reveal anything very profound about Chinese word formation or syntax. From the perspective of syntax, a word is a word is a word: if it carries the identity of X^0, then it can occupy a word slot and the syntax doesn't much care about how the X^0 came to be an X^0 (with the possible exception of grammatical words, which are posited to be more closely related to syntactic processes; see, e.g., Anderson 1992: 101).

Table 13 Chinese word types

combine what?	= word type	examples
two root words	compound word	bīngshān 冰山 ice-mountain 'iceberg' mǎlù 马路 horse-road 'street' zǒujìn 走进 walk-in 'walk in'[2] jìnqu 进去 go-in 'go in'
root word plus bound root, or two bound roots	bound root word	diànnǎo 电脑 electric-brain 'computer' xiàngpí 橡皮 rubber-skin 'rubber' tīngjiàn 听见 hear-perceive 'hear' chūbǎn 出版 emit-edition 'to publish' pǎoguò 跑过 run-pass 'to run past'
bound root or root word plus word-forming affix	derived word	fángzi 房子 house-AFF 'house' chātou 插头 insert-AFF 'plug' diànhuà 电化 electricity-AFF 'electrify'
word plus grammatical affix	grammatical word	zǒule 走了 go-ASP 'went' wǒmen 我们 me-PL 'us' zǒubujìn 走不进 walk-AFF-enter 'unable to go in' jìndequ 进得去 walk-AFF-enter 'able to go in'

a derived word is composed of a bound root or root word plus a word-forming affix; and a grammatical word is composed of a root word plus a grammatical affix. Examples of these four word types are given in table 13. It is important to note that, as seen in table 13, any of the four word types can consist of any form class. For example, a bound root word can be either a noun or a verb. This tells us something interesting about the nature of Chinese words: namely, that words of the same type but a different form class nonetheless share properties at a certain level of abstraction. Those shared properties are the types of rules that were used to put those words together.

Let us now look at an inventory of noun and verb word structures, starting with nouns.

---

[2] An anonymous reviewer asks why zǒujìn is considered a word since '-jìn can follow any verb of movement. I doubt whether there is any dictionary that treats zǒujìn as a separate entry'. The fact that few dictionaries would list zǒujìn does not affect its status as a word. It is a word – albeit one that is composed of a free word (zǒu) combined with another (extremely productive) free word (jìn).

Table 14 Noun word types by form class

	nouns
N N	*zhuōqiú* 桌球 table-ball 'table tennis', *diànnǎo* 电脑 electricity-brain 'computer', *mùgōng* 木工 wood-labor 'carpenter', *niúròu* 牛肉 cow-meat 'beef'
N V	*wàiyù* 外遇 outside-encounter 'extra-marital affair', *zhǔgù* 主顾 master-care:for 'customer', *qiūfēn* 秋分 autumn-divide 'autumn', *bìzhù* 臂助 arm-help 'helper'
V N	*lǐngshì* 领事 lead-event 'consul', *pǎojiē* 跑街 run-street 'messenger', *tiánfáng* 填房 fill-house 'second wife', *wòchē* 卧车 sleep-car '(train) sleeper', *tí'àn* 提案 raise-case 'proposal'
V V	*dòngzuò* 动作 move-do 'activity', *cānmóu* 参谋 refer-consult 'staff officer', *juésài* 决赛 decide-compete 'final competition', *zhuǎnzhé* 转折 turn-bend 'a turn'

4.2 Nouns

Some examples of specific noun structures are seen in table 14, arranged by the form classes of the constituents. Below we give examples of complex nouns by word type.

4.2.1 Noun types

4.2.1.1 Noun compound words

These are nouns composed of two words. Following the Headedness Principle, we might expect most of these nouns to have nouns on the right; and while there are exceptions, this is largely correct, as we shall see in the statistical breakdown in 4.4.

noun word + noun word *mǎxióng* 马熊 horse-bear 'brown bear', *bīngshān* 冰山 ice-mountain 'iceberg', *huǒshān* 火山 fire-mountain 'volcano', *xióngmāo* 熊猫 bear-cat 'panda', *shuǐtǔ* 水土 water-earth 'climate', *huāniǎo* 花鸟 flower-bird 'painting containing flowers and birds'

verb word + noun word *lǐngshì* 领事 lead-affair 'consul', *tóushǒu* 投手 throw-hand 'pitcher', *yáogǔ* 摇鼓 shake-drum 'drum toy', *chuándào*

传道 transmit-doctrine 'preacher', *dǐngzhēn* 顶针 push-needle 'thimble', *chuánpiào* 传票 transmit-ticket 'subpoena', *táohé* 淘河 dredge-river 'pelican'

noun word + verb word *zhǔgù* 主顾 master-care:for 'client'; *shìbiàn* 事变 thing-change 'incident', *xīndé* 心得 heart-obtain 'what one has learned through study', *guōtiē* 锅贴 post-stick 'fried dumpling', *bǐxǐ* 笔洗 pen-wash 'writing brush washer'

verb word + verb word *dòngzuò* 动作 move-do 'activity', *mǎibàn* 买办 buy-manage 'comprador', *mǎimài* 买卖 buy-sell 'business', *cāoshǒu* 操守 operate-preserve 'integrity', *chuándòng* 传动 transmit-move '(vehicle) transmission'

4.2.1.2 Noun bound root words

These are nouns composed of a word and a bound root, or two bound roots.

noun word + noun bound root *diànnǎo* 电脑 electricity-brain 'computer', *chēhuò* 车祸 vehicle-misfortune '(vehicle) accident', *hàomǎ* 号码 number-code 'number', *biǎodài* 表带 watch-strip 'watchband', *jiājù* 家具 home-utensil 'furniture', '*dìcí* 地磁 earth-magnet 'geomagnetism', *qiúmí* 球迷 ball-fan '(sports) fan'

noun bound root + noun word *zúqiú* 足球 foot-ball 'soccer', *xiàngpí* 橡皮 rubber-skin 'rubber'; *dírén* 敌人 enemy-person 'enemy'

noun bound root + noun bound root *mùbǎn* 木板 wood-plank 'board', *dànjiā* 弹夹 bullet-clip 'bullet clip', *quánlì* 权力 authority-power 'authority', *mǔxiào* 母校 mother-school 'alma mater', *jīqì* 机器 machine-utensil 'machine', *mùcái* 木材 wood-material 'lumber', *lǚlì* 履历 shoe-history 'resumé', *guāngnǎo* 光脑 light-brain 'photon computer'

verb word + noun bound root *màmíng* 骂名 curse-name 'infamy', *zūjīn* 租金 rent-money 'rental money', *dǔjù* 赌具 gamble-utensil 'gambling equipment', *gùnóng* 雇农 hire-farm 'farmhand', *chuàngjiàn* 创见 create-viewpoint 'original idea', *zhùfáng* 住房 live-house 'residence', *zhǐshù* 指数 point-number 'index', *yáoyǐ* 摇椅 rock-chair 'rocking chair', *fēijī* 飞机 fly-machine 'airplane'

verb bound root + noun word *zhùshǒu* 助手 help-hand 'helper', *chùjiǎo* 触角 touch-horn '(insect) antenna', *píngfēng* 屏风 screen-wind 'screen'

verb bound root + noun bound root *nàilì* 耐力 bear-strength 'stamina', *dǎodàn* 导弹 guide-bullet 'guided missile', *zhùjiào* 助教

assist-instruction 'teaching assistant', *hùěr* 护耳 protect-ear 'earmuffs', *hùshì* 护士 protect-person 'nurse', *suíyuán* 随员 follow-person 'entourage member'

noun bound root + verb word *zhíshǒu* 职守 job-defend 'duty', *bǎncā(r)* 板擦 board-rub 'eraser', *bìguà* 壁挂 wall-hang 'wall hanging', *shídiāo* 石雕 stone-carve 'stone carving', *ěrwā* 耳挖 ear-dig 'ear pick'

noun word + verb bound root *jiézòu* 节奏 section-play 'rhythm', *diànshì* 电视 electricity-see 'television'

noun bound root + verb bound root *qiūjué* 秋决 autumn-decide 'autumn execution'

verb bound root + verb word *gòuzào* 构造 compose-create 'structure'

verb word + verb word *zhùlǐ* 助理 help-manage 'assistant', *jīnglǐ* 经理 manage-manage 'manager', *dǎoyóu* 导遊 guide-travel 'guide'

verb word + verb bound root *xuéjiū* 学究 study-research 'pedant', *páiguàn* 排灌 drain-irrigate 'drainage and irrigation'

verb bound root + verb bound root no examples found

4.2.1.3 Noun derived words

These are nouns composed of a word or bound root, plus a word-forming affix

noun bound root + word-forming affix *fángzi* 房子 house-AFF 'house', *bízi* 鼻子 nose-AFF 'nose', *mùtou* 木头 wood-AFF 'wood', *mǎtou* 码头 number-AFF 'wharf', *mǎzi* 码子 number-AFF 'numeral', *shítou* 石头 stone-AFF 'stone', *jīzi* 机子 machine-AFF 'machine', *dànzi* 弹子 bullet-AFF 'bullet', *tiězi* 帖子 invitation-AFF 'invitation', *shàozi* 哨子 whistle-AFF 'whistle', *zhàotou* 兆头 sign-AFF 'omen'

noun word + word-forming affix *pízi* 皮子 skin-AFF 'skin', *pír* 皮儿 skin-AFF 'skin', *rénxìng* 人性 person-AFF 'reason', *diàotou* 调头/ *diàozi* 调子 tune-AFF 'tune', *yānzi* 烟子 smoke-AFF 'soot'

verb word + word-forming affix *kòuzi* 扣子 button-AFF 'button', *piànzi* 骗子 deceive-AFF 'swindler', *tànzi* 探子 seek-AFF 'a probe', *xiǎngtou* 想头 think-AFF 'idea', *zhuàntou*(r) 赚头 earn-AFF 'profit', *zhézi* 折子 fold-AFF 'folder', *shuōtou* 说头 talk-AFF 'something to talk about', *tánxìng* 弹性 bounce-AFF 'elasticity', *chǎotou* 吵头 argue-AFF 'reason for argument', *kàozi* 靠子 rely-AFF 'something to lean on'

verb bound root + word-forming affix *wùxìng* 悟性 realize-AFF 'power of understanding'

word-forming affix + noun bound root *āguó* 阿国 AFF-country 'state-run enterprise', *āwù* 阿物 AFF-thing 'dummy', *āxiāng* 阿乡 AFF-village 'village-run enterprise'
word-forming affix + noun word *āgē* 阿哥 AFF-brother 'brother'
word-forming affix + verb bound root no examples found
word-forming affix + verb word *āfēi* 阿飞 AFF-fly 'juvenile delinquent', *āhùn* 阿混 AFF-muddle 'muddle-head'

4.2.1.4 Noun grammatical words

These are nouns composed of a word plus a grammatical affix.

noun word + grammatical affix *wǒmen* 我们 I-AFF 'we', *rénmen* 人们 person-AFF 'people', *gēmenr* 哥们儿 brother-AFF 'brothers', *tóngzhìmen* 同志们 comrade-AFF 'comrades', *gūniángjiā* 姑娘家 lady-AFF 'ladies', *háizijiā* 孩子家 child-AFF 'children', *línjūmen* 邻居们 neighbour-AFF 'neighbours', *liúmángmen* 流氓们 ruffian-AFF 'ruffians', *xiǎojiàngmen* 小将们 general-AFF 'generals'

4.2.2 N₁–N₂ words: kinds of relations

It is clear that there are many types of complex two-syllable nouns, but as we shall see (table 18), the majority (more than 54%) are composed of two nouns, that is, are of the type [N₁ N₂]ₙ.

When complex noun lexical items take the form of [N₁ N₂]ₙ, the relation between the N₁ and N₂ can be a hierarchical 'modifier–modified' relation, or it can be a non-hierarchical, 'parallel' relation. When the relationship is hierarchical, the type of relationship between the modifying and modified elements is nearly without limit, constrained only by pragmatic, 'real world' considerations (Li and Thompson 1981). Indeed, the examples below are virtually an arbitrary subset of the types of modification relation that exist between N₁ and N₂. However, one principle that remains consistent in all 'modifier–modified' [N₁ N₂]ₙ forms is that N₁ always specifies a property or characteristic of N₂ (this of course is true virtually by definition, since these words are defined as having a modifier–modified structure). The following contains examples of the kinds of hierarchical relations that obtain, including examples from Chao (1968) and Li and Thompson (1981). All the examples below are either compound or bound root words.

N_1 is the place where N_2 operates or is located:

yǎnjìng	眼镜	eye-lens	'glasses'
hǎitān	海滩	sea-beach	'beach'
lùjūn	陆军	land-troops	'army'
shǒubiǎo	手表	hand-watch	'wristwatch'

N_2 indicates a medical condition of N_1:

fèiyán	肺炎	lung-inflammation	'pneumonia'
pízhěn	皮疹	skin-rash	'rash'
xīnbìng	心病	heart-disease	'mental disorder'
wèiái	胃癌	stomach-cancer	'stomach cancer'

N_1 depicts the form of N_2:

shātáng	砂糖	sand-sugar	'granulated sugar'
piànjì	片剂	tablet-medicine	'medicine pill'
kuàiméi	块煤	chunk-coal	'lump coal'
zhuānchá	砖茶	brick-tea	'brick tea'

N_2 depicts the form of N_1:[3]

xuěhuā	雪花	snow-flower	'snowflake'
bīngkuài	冰块	ice-piece	'ice cube'
yàofěn	药粉	medicine-powder	'medicine powder'
cházhuān	茶砖	tea-brick	'brick tea'

N_2 is used for N_1:

càidāo	菜刀	vegetable-knife	'cleaver'
jīchǎng	机场	machine-field	'airport'
yāndǒu	烟斗	tobacco-cup	'pipe'
qiúpāi	球拍	ball-paddle	'racket'

[3] Examples such as *xuěhuā* 雪花 snow-flower 'snowflake', which show N_2 in the form of N_1, seem to run counter to the structural generalization that 'N_1 specifies some characteristic of N_2'. Grammatically speaking, this is still interpreted structurally as 'N_2 composed of N_1', e.g., *xuěhuā* is grammatically construed as 'a flower (shaped thing) composed of snow'. Examples such as these serve to point out that while semantics is important, form class grammatical modification structure is the primary criterion. This is because if children learned language using semantics as the primary criterion, they would face the Herculean task of determining the correct interpretation using the semantic hypothesis 'choose the meaning that makes semantic sense' – a much more open-ended proposition than the highly constraining structural hypothesis 'N_1 specifies some characteristic of N_2'.

N_1 is the habitat of N_2:

shuǐniǎo	水鸟	water-bird	'aquatic bird'
bìhǔ	壁虎	wall-tiger	'gecko'
hǎiniú	海牛	sea-cow	'manatee'
sōngshǔ	松鼠	pine-rat	'squirrel'

N_2 is caused by N_1:

shuǐzāi	水灾	water-disaster	'flood'
lèihén	泪痕	tear-stain	'tear stains'
chēhuò	车祸	vehicle-misfortune	'vehicle accident'
xuèyìn	血印	blood-stamp	'blood stain'

N_2 is a container for N_1:

chábēi	茶杯	tea-cup	'teacup'
fànwǎn	饭碗	rice-bowl	'rice bowl'
jiǔpíng	酒瓶	wine-bottle	'wine bottle'
shūbāo	书包	book-bag	'bookbag'

N_2 is produced by N_1:

jīdàn	鸡蛋	chicken-egg	'(chicken) egg'
niúnǎi	牛奶	cow-milk	'(cow's) milk'
cánsī	蚕丝	silkworm-silk	'silk'
yúluǎn	鱼卵	fish-egg	'roe'

N_2 is made from or composed of N_1:

píxié	皮鞋	leather-shoe	'leather shoes'
tiělù	铁路	iron-road	'railroad'
zhūròu	猪肉	pig-meat	'pork'
mùcái	木材	wood-material	'lumber'

N_1 is a type or subclass of N_2:

lánhuā	兰花	orchid-flower	'orchid'
píngguǒ	苹果	apple-fruit	'apple'
xīnzàng	心脏	heart-organ	'heart'
sōngshù	松树	pine-tree	'pine tree'

N₁ is a metaphorical description of N₂:

yínháng	银行	silver-business	'bank'
tuóniǎo	鸵鸟	camel-bird	'ostrich'
huǒchē	火车	fire-vehicle	'train'
cháiyóu	柴油	firewood-oil	'diesel fuel'

N₂ is a source of N₁:

diànchí	电池	electricity-pool	'battery'
yóujǐng	油井	oil-well	'oil well'
guǒyuán	果园	fruit-garden	'orchard'
méikuàng	煤矿	coal-mine	'coal mine'

N₁ is a source of N₂:

hǎiyán	海盐	sea-salt	'sea salt'
dìcí	地磁	earth-magnetism	'geomagnetism'
hénní	河泥	river-mud	'river silt'
huāfěn	花粉	flower-powder	'pollen'

N₂ is something that N₁ has or contains:

chētiáo	车条	vehicle-strip	'wheel spoke'
fángdǐng	房顶	house-top	'roof'
shǒuzhǎng	手掌	hand-palm	'palm'
piàogēn	票根	ticket-root	'ticket stub'

N₁ is something that N₂ has or contains:

míngpiàn	名片	name-strip	'name card'
bānmǎ	斑马	stripe-horse	'zebra'
cèsuǒ	厕所	toilet-place	'lavatory'
xiàngpiàn	相片	appearance-strip	'photograph'

When the [N₁ N₂]ɴ are in a non-hierarchical relation, the relationship between N₁ and N₂ can either be one of synonymy, in which both elements are more or less semantically equivalent to each other and to the gestalt noun they combine to form, or it can be one in which the N₁ and N₂ are semantically disparate items. In the latter case, the meaning of the gestalt noun is usually a superordinate class that includes both N₁ and N₂.

The following are examples in which N₁ and N₂ are virtually synonymous (in the modern language), both possessing meanings more or less equivalent to the gestalt noun they compose:

dàozéi	盗贼	thief-thief	'thief'
fángwū	房屋	house-house	'house'
gēqǔ	歌曲	song-song	'song'
pífū	皮肤	skin-skin	'skin'
qiángbì	墙壁	wall-wall	'wall'
sēnlín	森林	forest-forest	'forest'
shēngyīn	声音	sound-sound	'sound'
yǎnjīng	眼睛	eye-eye	'eye'
yīshang	衣裳	clothing-clothing	'clothing'
zhīfáng	脂肪	fat-fat	'fat'

The following are examples in which the formed gestalt noun refers to a superordinate class to which N1 and N2 both belong. Since these gestalt words represent superordinate categories, they are usually more general and abstract than the [N1 N2]N examples above.

dāoqiāng	刀枪	knife-gun	'weapons'
dēnghuǒ	灯火	light-fire	'lights'
fēngshuǐ	风水	wind-water	'geomancy'
jiēdào	街道	street-road	'neighbourhood'
qínshòu	禽兽	bird-quadruped	'animals'
shānshuǐ	山水	mountain-water	'scenery'
shūkān	书刊	book-periodical	'reading materials'
shuǐtǔ	水土	water-earth	'natural environment'
túhuà	图画	chart-picture	'picture'
tǔmù	土木	earth-wood	'building, construction'

So we see that [N1 N2]N nouns have a number of interesting characteristics, including different types of modification relations. Next we look at the forms of verbs.

4.3 Verbs

In table 15 we see examples of specific verb structures listed by form class. Of the various types of complex two-syllable verbs, the largest category (more than 44.6 per cent of all verbs; see table 18) is that of verbs composed of two verbs, or [V1 V2]V.

4.3.1 Verb types

In this section we list complex verbs by word type, with examples of each possible type of word.

Table 15 Verb word types by form class

	verbs
V V	*jiějué* 解决 dissect-decide 'solve', *xuéxí* 学习 study-practice 'study', *shùixǐng* 睡醒 sleep-awaken 'wake up', *kànwán* 看完 read-finish 'to finish reading', *shùimián* 睡眠 sleep-sleep 'sleep' *shǔnxī* 吮吸 suck-suck 'suck', *fānxiū* 翻修 overturn-fix 'rebuild'
V N	*yíxīn* 疑心 doubt-heart 'to doubt', *jiùyào* 救药 save-drug 'medicine', *chūbǎn* 出版 emit-edition 'publish', *bìyè* 毕业 end-profession 'graduate', *qiúzhèng* 求证 seek-proof 'to look for proof', *xǐzǎo* 洗澡 wash-bath 'take a bath'
N V	*tǐtiē* 体贴 body-stick 'show consideration for', *shēnshòu* 身受 body-receive 'to experience', *jiǎotī* 脚踢 foot-kick 'to kick', *jiǎocǎi* 脚踩 foot-step 'to pedal'
N N	*wùsè* 物色 thing-color 'hunt for', *zuǒyòu* 左右 left-right 'to influence'

4.3.1.1 Verb compound words

These are verbs composed of two words. Following the Headedness Principle, we would expect most of these verbs to have verbs on the left, and while there are exceptions, this is generally the case, as we shall see in table 23.

verb word + verb word *jièyòng* 借用 borrow-use 'borrow', *guòwèn* 过问 pass-ask 'concern oneself with', *chuánjiàn* 传见 transmit-see 'call someone for a meeting', *suōxiě* 缩写 reduce-write 'to abbreviate', *gōuxiě* 勾写 sketch-write 'to sketch', *dēngjì* 登记 post-mark 'register', *hūxī* 呼吸 exhale-suck:in 'breathe'

verb word + noun word *nàoguǐ* 闹鬼 make:noise-ghost 'haunt', *màjiē* 骂街 curse-street 'call people names in public', *chuàngshù* 创树 create-tree 'to establish'[4]

noun word + verb word *dúshā* 毒杀 poison-kill 'kill with poison', *guāfēn* 瓜分 melon-divide 'to partition', *fēnghuà* 风化 wind-change 'to erode', *yóuzhá* 油炸 oil-fry 'fry in oil'

noun word + noun word no examples found

4.3.1.2 Verb bound root words

These are verbs composed of a word plus bound root, or of two bound roots.

---

[4] Chinese Academy of Social Sciences 1992: 79.

GESTALT CHINESE WORDS

verb word + verb bound root *jiéshù* 结束 conclude-bind 'conclude', *bāngzhù* 帮助 help-help 'help', *sǐwáng* 死亡 die-die 'die', *pīpíng* 批评 criticize-criticize 'criticize', *tiáozhěng* 调整 adjust-rectify 'adjust', *jiēchù* 接触 touch-contact 'contact', *tīnghòu* 听候 listen-wait 'to wait for', *lǐngdǎo* 领导 lead-guide 'to lead'

verb bound root + verb word *xiǎngshòu* 享受 enjoy-accept 'enjoy', *jiéshěng* 节省 save-save 'save', *gòumǎi* 购买 buy-buy 'buy', *jùpà* 惧怕 fear-fear 'fear', *sōují* 搜集 collect-collect 'collect', *jìniàn* 纪念 remember-commemorate 'commemorate', *jiūchán* 纠缠 tangle-tangle 'to nag', *cháoxiào* 嘲笑 ridicule-laugh 'to ridicule'

verb bound root + verb bound root *biànbié* 辨别 distinguish-differentiate 'differentiate', *biànlùn* 辩论 debate-discuss 'debate', *yǔnxǔ* 允许 permit-permit 'permit', *tǎolùn* 讨论 discuss-discuss 'discuss', *jiějué* 解决 untie-resolve 'solve', *jièshào* 介绍 interpose-continue 'introduce', *chǔlǐ* 处理 do-order 'handle', *xiézhù* 协助 help-help 'to help', *jiěcháo* 解嘲 undo-ridicule 'to explain away ridicule'

verb word + noun bound root *chūbǎn* 出版 emit-edition 'publish', *kāidāo* 开刀 open-knife 'operate', *mièdǐng* 灭顶 extinguish-head 'to be drowned', *duānxiáng* 端详 hold:out-details 'look someone over', *dòngyuán* 动员 move-person 'mobilize', *qǔyàng* 取样 get-type 'to sample', *qǔqīn* 取亲 get-intimacy 'to marry (a wife)', *qiúhūn* 求婚 request-marriage 'to propose marriage', *xǐzǎo* 洗澡 wash-bath 'to wash', *shuìjiào* 睡觉 sleep-sleep 'sleep', *zàoyáo* 造谣 create-rumour 'spread rumours', *tiàoshéng* 跳绳 jump-rope 'to jumprope', *gàozhuàng* 告状 accuse-complaint 'to sue', *jiètí* 借提 'have a pretext', *chūxí* 出席 exit-seat 'be present', *liúyì* 留意 leave-meaning 'be careful', *bàoyuàn* 抱怨 embrace-enmity 'complain', *shuōméi* 说媒 speak-medium 'act as a go-between'

verb bound root + noun word *jiěshǒu* 解手 relieve-hand 'to relieve oneself', *yíxīn* 疑心 doubt-heart 'to suspect', *chōngdiàn* 充电 fill-electricity 'recharge', *shùshǒu* 束手 bind-hand 'tie one's hands', *gémìng* 革命 remove-mandate 'carry out revolution', *nàfú* 纳福 enjoy-happiness 'enjoy oneself', *shīshì* 失事 lose-event 'have an accident', *dānxīn* 担心 carry-heart 'worry'

verb bound root + noun bound root *zhímín* 殖民 breed-people 'colonize', *juécè* 决策 decide-policy 'make policy', *jiūpiān* 纠偏 correct-bias 'rectify an error', *shìwēi* 示威 show-strength 'to demonstrate', *yímín* 移民 move-people 'immigrate', *jígé* 及格 attain-standard 'to pass', *shīzōng* 失踪 lose-steps 'to be lost', *xiàofǎ* 效法 imitate-method 'imitate', *xiàoláo* 效劳 devote-work 'work for', *xíwǔ* 习武 practice-weapon-person 'practice martial arts'

noun bound root + verb word *tǐtiē* 体贴 body-stick 'show consideration', *gōutōng* 沟通 ditch-connect 'communicate', *guīdìng* 规定 rule-determine 'regulate', *wǔdǎ* 武打 weapon-hit 'to fight in acrobatic style', *tǐchá* 体察 body-investigate 'experience and observe', *cǎipái* 彩排 colour-rehearse 'dress-rehearse'

noun word + verb bound root *qiāngbì* 枪毙 gun-kill 'execute by gunfire'

noun bound root + verb bound root *tǐxiàn* 体现 body-manifest 'embody', *bùxíng* 步行 footstep-go 'go on foot', *tǐyàn* 体验 body-experience 'to learn through experience', *bìzhù* 臂助 arm-help 'to help'

noun bound root + noun word no examples found

noun word + noun bound root no examples found

noun bound root + noun bound root *wùsè* 物色 thing-colour 'hunt for', *zuǒyòu* 左右 left-right 'to influence'

4.3.1.3 Verb derived words

These are verbs composed of a word or bound root, plus a word-forming affix.

word-forming affix + verb word *fùfā* 复发 AFF-occur 'to relapse', *fùchá* 复查 AFF-investigate 'reinvestigate', *fùhuó* 复活 AFF-live 'to come back to life'

word-forming affix + verb bound root *kělián* 可怜 AFF-pity 'to pity', *wúshì* 无视 AFF-see 'disregard', *fùxí* 复习 AFF-study 'study, review', *fùxiàn* 复现 AFF-appear 'to reappear'

word-forming affix + noun word *kějiǎo* 可脚 AFF-foot 'to fit one's feet'

word-forming affix + noun bound root *kětǐ* 可体 AFF-body 'to fit'

verb word + word-forming affix[5] *kāihuà* 开化 open-AFF 'civilize', *tuìhuà* 退化 retreat-AFF 'to degenerate', *fūhuà* 孵化 hatch-AFF 'incubate', *tuìhuà* 蜕化 moult-AFF 'to moult; to degenerate', *láodònghuà* 劳动化 work-AFF 'to integrate oneself with the working people', *quànhuà* 劝化 persuade-AFF 'to convert', *shāohuà* 烧化 burn-AFF 'burn'

---

[5] The morpheme *huà* 化 attached to verbs in the examples given in some cases may seem like the free verb *huà* 化 meaning 'change' rather than the morpheme ordinarily used as a word-forming affix. However, this is not the case with other examples, e.g., *láodònghuà*.

GESTALT CHINESE WORDS 93

verb bound root + word-forming affix *guīhuà* 归化 return-AFF 'to naturalize', *gǎnhuà* 感化 feel-AFF 'to sensitize', *mùhuà* 募化 raise: money-AFF 'to beg for money'
noun word + word-forming affix *dúhuà* 毒化 poison-AFF 'to poison', *qìhuà* 汽化 vapour-AFF 'vapourize', *qìhuà* 气化 gas-AFF 'gassify', *yǎnghuà* 氧化 oxygen-AFF 'oxidize'
noun bound root + word-forming affix *ōuhuà* 欧化 Europe-AFF 'Europeanize', *shíhuà* 石化 stone-AFF 'petrify', *gānghuà* 钢化 steel-AFF 'to temper (glass)', *yǔhuà* 羽化 feather-AFF '(of an adult insect) emerge', *gǔhuà* 骨化 bone-AFF 'ossify'

4.3.1.4 Verb grammatical words

verb word + grammatical affix *zǒule* 走了 walk-AFF 'walked', *chīzhe* 吃著 eat-AFF 'eating', *zǒubujìn* 走不进 walk-AFF-enter 'unable to walk in', *kànguo* 看过 see-AFF 'have seen'

4.3.2 V₁–V₂: kinds of relations

As we saw in the case of the N₁–N₂ nouns in 4.2.2, verbs with a structure of [V₁ V₂]ᵥ may occur in either a hierarchical or non-hierarchical relation. Unlike nouns, however, cases in which V₁ and V₂ combine to form a verb that represents a superordinate class are relatively uncommon. Rather, when V₁ and V₂ are semantically disparate, the relationship is more likely to be a kind of semantic coordination, with the meaning of the gestalt verb generally containing both of the meanings of each of the component verbs.

The following are examples in which V₁ and V₂ are virtually synonymous, with the gestalt verb representing that one synonymous meaning.

dàoqiè	盗窃	steal-steal	'steal'
dìjiāo	递交	pass:over-transfer	'submit'
diūshī	丢失	lose-lose	'lose'
dǔsè	堵塞	stop:up-plug	'stop up'
duǒbì	躲避	hide/avoid-hide/avoid	'hide, avoid'
guànchuān	贯穿	pierce-penetrate	'penetrate'
guàngài	灌溉	irrigate-irrigate	'irrigate'
tǎolùn	讨论	discuss-discuss	'discuss'
yuèdú	阅读	read-read	'read'
zhǐdǎo	指导	point:out-guide	'direct, guide'

94   THE MORPHOLOGY OF CHINESE

The following are examples in which V₁ and V₂ possess disparate meanings. Note that the meaning of the gestalt verb in these examples is one that includes both activities of V₁ and V₂ as relatively discrete, independent activities, and does not refer to a superordinate class of verb activity of which the V₁ and V₂ may be considered subactivities, as we saw in 4.2.2 is often the case with nouns possessing the same type of [X₁ X₂]ₓ structure. In these examples, the gestalt verb is not obviously a superordinate activity that includes both V₁ and V₂.

fángchú	防除	defend-eliminate	'prevent and kill off'
gēchú	割除	cut-eliminate	'cut out'
guānchá	观察	observe-investigate	'investigate'
jiàoxǐng	叫醒	call-wake:up	'awaken by calling'
qiǎnggòu	抢购	seize-buy	'rush to buy'
shuōfú	说服	speak-convince	'convince'
zhuīqiú	追求	pursue-seek	'seek and pursue'

There are examples of V₁–V₂ verbs that represent a larger, superordinate verbal category that includes the two verbs V₁ and V₂ (rather than representing a combination of the two activities), but verbs that possess this characteristic are somewhat uncommon.

fànyùn	贩运	buy:to:sell-transport	'to traffic in'
hūxī	呼吸	inhale-exhale	'breathe'
jiějué	解决	undo-decide	'solve'

There are also [V₁ V₂]ᵥ forms in which V₁ and V₂ occur in a hierarchical modification structure. In this structure, the modified verb retains its general characteristics but takes on the attributes of the modifying verb, since the modified verb is the more general activity. For example, it makes more sense to refer to *fēixíng* 飞行 fly-go 'fly' in terms of the modifying verb 'fly' (or 'go by flying'), since 'go' gives no information beyond the meaning of the general activity represented by the modified verb V₂.

The following are examples in which V₁ modifies V₂. In these examples, the gestalt verb is a kind, or subclass, of V₂.

diàodòng	调动	transfer-move	'transfer'
dìnggòu	定购	order-buy	'(buy by) order'
dǒudòng	抖动	shake-move	'shake'
duīfàng	堆放	stack-put	'stack'
duóqǔ	夺取	seize-obtain	'(obtain by) seizure'

fǎngzào	仿造	imitate-make	'make in imitation'
fēixíng	飞行	fly-go	'fly'
hǎnjiào	喊叫	shout-call	'shout'
hùsòng	护送	protect-send:off	'escort'
tànwèn	探问	explore-ask	'make inquiries'

The following are examples in which the opposite modification relation occurs, with V₂ modifying V₁, a relatively uncommon occurrence. In these examples the gestalt verb is a kind, or subclass, of V₁:

fēiwǔ	飞舞	fly-dance	'flutter'
tàntǎo	探讨	explore-discuss	'inquire into'

The default modification relation between V₁ and V₂ (i.e., the fact that V₁ usually modifies V₂) would seem to contradict the headedness of verbs as implied by the Headedness Principle because the V₁ modifying V₂ implies a right head. The resolution of this contradiction lies in the fact that in cases of V₁ modifying V₂, the semantic head of the verb is indeed on the right, but the structural head – the head responsible for determining the grammatical rather than semantic characteristics of the word – is on the left. The difference between semantic head and structural head is discussed in 5.5.2.

4.3.3 Resultative verbs

A well-known type of [V₁ V₂]ᵥ word is the 'resultative' complex verb, in which V₂ indicates the result of the head V₁, with that V₁ head often taking the *-de-/-bu-* 'potential affix' as a special type of grammatical marking. There have been many descriptions and analyses of resultative verbs, often with very different explanations depending on the focus of the investigator. Although resultative verbs seem to form a coherent class of grammatical objects that share certain properties, the members of the class often resist generalizations that might be made about them. Some of these generalizations are: (a) whether or not they always take the *-de-/-bu-* potential affix; (b) their productivity and concomitant predictability of meaning; and (c) the ability of various verb types to occur as either V₁ or V₂, and the consequent properties of the complex verb.

The V₁ of resultative verbs (*chī, pǎo* and *kàn* in (25), (26) and (27) respectively) represents in general the open set of Mandarin transitive verbs, and V₂ (*bǎo, shang* and *dao* in (25), (26) and (27) respectively) is a member of a class of usually non-transitive, often stative verbs that indicates the result of the predication of V_1. V_1 is virtually always a free morpheme[6] (i.e. a root word; see 4.1), while V_2 is under no such restriction.[7]

(25) chī-bǎo
吃饱
eat-full
'eat until full'

(26) pǎo-shang
跑上
run-ascend
'run up'

(27) kàn-dao
看到
look-arrive
'see'

Resultative verbs are considered special among Chinese complex words because they possess a host of distinctive properties. The most notable is that, as mentioned above, they allow a special type of grammatical marking (the -de-/-bu- 'potential affix') word internally, that is, on the V_1 head (leftmost member) of the complex verb. As seen in (28)–(31), the morphemes -de-/-bu- (meaning 'able to' and 'not able to' respectively) are affixed to the head of the complex verb (i.e., V_1), indicating the ability or inability of the predication expressed by the complex verb to take place.

(28) chī-de-bǎo
吃得饱
eat-able-full
'able to eat until full'

(29) chī-bu-bǎo
吃不饱
eat-unable-full
'unable to eat until full'

[6] At least one exception to this is *yùjiàn* 遇见 meet-perceive 'meet, run into', since *yù-* does not occur as a free word (Thompson 1973: 379).
[7] Verb₂ may be a root word or a bound root, but may not be a word-forming affix, and may not be a grammatical affix, with the exception of *-deliǎo, -buliǎo, -deqǐ* and *-buqǐ*.

(30) pǎo-de-shàng
跑得上
run-able-ascend
'able to run up'

(31) pǎo-bu-shàng
跑不上
run-unable-ascend
'unable to run up'

(32) kàn-de-dao
看得到
look-able-arrive
'able to see'

(33) kàn-bu-dao
看不到
look-unable-arrive
'unable to see'

(34) Wǒmen   yào   tuīguǎng   Hànyǔ   pīnyīn
     我们   要   推广   汉语   拼音
     We   want   promote-broad   Chinese spell-sound
     'we should popularize Chinese alphabetic writing'

(35) *Wǒmen   tuīdeguǎng   Hànyǔ   pīnyīn
     我们   推得广   汉语   拼音
     we   promote-able-broad   Chinese spell-sound

(36) *Wǒmen   tuībuguǎng   Hànyǔ   pīnyīn
     我们   推不广   汉语   拼音
     we   promote-not-broad   Chinese spell-sound

As seen in (34)–(36), the 'potential affix' operation cannot be performed on 'ordinary' [V₁ V₂]ᵥ words, even when V₂ may reasonably be considered a result of V₁ (as is the case with *tuīguǎng* in (34)).

How the argument structure of the complex verb derives from the independent argument structures of V₁ and V₂ is a subject of considerable interest (Y. Li 1990, Ross 1990, Chang 1989, 1997). In general, the thematic structure of V₁–V₂ resultative verbs reflects the combined thematic structures of V₁ and V₂, but there are interesting exceptions that we will have more to say about below. It is also interesting to consider the different types of completion, direction, accomplishment and achievement relations that obtain between V₁ and V₂, discussed by Lu (1977) and Ross (1990). Resultative verbs are also unusual in that, unlike other complex verbs, they do not allow reduplicative question-forming processes to operate on the head, or V₁, of the verb (Thompson 1973, Packard 1990) – the only head operation allowed is the *-de-/-bu-* potential affixation operation. Finally, the individual constituents of resultative verbs are not available for syntactic operations (such as embedding, movement, deletion, insertion and anaphora), and thus conform to the Lexical Integrity Hypothesis (Jackendoff 1972). Resultative verbs are discussed in Chao (1968), Thompson (1973), Lu (1977), Li and Thompson (1981), Y. Li (1990), Ross (1990), Chang (1997) and Starosta et al. (1997).

4.3.3.1 Three classes of resultatives

Resultatives may be divided into three general classes based on the nature of V₂. The first is a large class we may call 'stative' resultatives (e.g., (25), (28), (29)), in which V₂ is a stative verb (an open and infinitely large class of verbs) that indicates the result of the predication of V₁. Note that, as pointed out by Ross (1990: 66), the stative verb V₂ of this type of resultative indicates the result of the activity of V₁ upon one of its arguments. To state this in terms of theta role percolation, stative resultative verbs must take as an argument one of the arguments of the V₂ stative ending. In other words, the arguments of the V₂ in stative resultatives are required to percolate to the gestalt verb.[8]

The second class may be called 'directional' resultatives (e.g., (26), (30), (31)), and are those in which V₁ is any verb of motion and V₂ is a verb of directional motion – a small, closed set consisting of *jìn* 进 'enter', *chū* 出 'exit', *guò* 过 'pass over', *shàng* 上 'ascend', *xià* 下 descend' and *huí* 回 'return'. The V₂ verbs of directional motion indicate the result (i.e., the direction and successful completion) of the V₁ motion vis-à-vis a target (usually the locative prepositional 'object' of V₂), and may be followed by *-lai* 来 'come' and *-qu* 去 'go'. As we saw is the case with stative resultatives above, the arguments of the V₂ verbs of directional motion are also required to percolate to the level of the gestalt verb.

The third class we may call 'attainment' resultatives (e.g., (27), (32) and (33)). Attainment resultatives have a rather large, but nonetheless

---

[8] There are exceptions to this generalization. For example, in the stative resultative verb *zhuājǐn* 抓紧 grab-tight 'to hold tight', the stative verb *jǐn* does not percolate its 'theme' theta role to the gestalt verb, but rather 'modifies' the verb *zhuā* (see (279)).

closed, class of V₂ endings, including: -*dào* 到 'arrive, attain', -*wán* 完 'finish', -*zhù* 住 'firmly stay', -*jiàn* 见 'perceive', -*guò* 过 'pass, exceed', -*dé* 得 'obtain', -*kāi* 开 'open', -*diào* 掉 'fall, go away', -*zháo* 著 'attain, reach', *dǒng* 懂 'understand', *huì* 会 'able to', *dòng* 动 'move', -*lái* 来 'come', -*chéng* 成 'turn into' and -*guàn* 惯 'be accustomed to'.⁹ An interesting thing to note about attainment resultatives is that, unlike with stative and directional resultatives, the arguments of the V₂ of attainment resultatives do not always percolate to the gestalt verb: e.g., in *kàndao*, although -*dao* is lexically listed as a verb that possesses an argument structure, those arguments do not appear as arguments of the gestalt verb *kàndao*. This fact will be relevant to our discussion of theta role transparency in lexicalization in 6.2.3.

Each of these three classes has an 'open' subset (those that are productively created and have predictable meanings) and a 'closed' subset (those that fit the grammatical criteria but are listed in the lexicon due to semantic unpredictability) as noted in Thompson (1973). As examples of listed forms, there are the stative resultatives *zuòmǎn* 坐满 sit-full 'seated to capacity' and *fàngdà* 放大 put-big 'to magnify'; the directional resultatives *zuòxià* 坐下 sit-descend 'to seat' or *kànchū* 看出 look-exit 'to figure out by looking'; and the attainment resultatives *wènzhu* 问住 ask-stay 'to stump' and *pèngjiàn* 碰见 bump-perceive 'to meet (casually)'.

Regarding the non-occurrence of some resultative forms generated by rule, Thompson (1973) says these restrictions are due to the properties of our contemporary environment. Thompson argues that such generated forms are 'grammatical', if not sensible, given the state of the world, and that changes in, e.g., technology could make formerly unacceptable forms acceptable. The potential -*de*-/-*bu*- affixation operation may be performed on any resultative verb, as long as it 'makes sense' (Chao 1968: 452).

The argument structures of resultative verbs are not generally predictable from the independent argument structures of the head

---

⁹ Some scholars have considered the endings -*deqǐ* 'can afford to', -*buqǐ* 'can't afford to', -*deliǎo* 'able to', -*buliǎo* 'unable to', -*dejí* 'to have time to' and -*bují* 'to not have time to' to constitute a special class of resultatives in which the potential operation is obligatory, since they never appear without the -*de*-/-*bu*- inflectional marking. While these endings are historically derived from lexical resultatives, they must now be considered lexically frozen non-decomposable verb suffixes, because they have a consistent meaning and may suffix to virtually any verb.

or ending separately, but rather are generally determined by the head and ending in combination (Chang 1989, Li 1990, Ross 1990). The head and ending assign identical theta roles to identical referents in the case of overlap (termed 'theta identification' by Y. Li 1990), and there is more than one possible reading of the resultative verb in cases where the theta roles of the head and ending are the same but do not corefer.

4.3.3.2 Lexical resultatives vs. syntactic extent resultatives

It is worthwhile pointing out that there is sometimes confusion, but a clear distinction nonetheless, between the resultatives we have been discussing here, namely, the 'lexical' resultatives, and what might be termed 'phrasal' resultatives formed using syntactic rules. There is sometimes surface ambiguity between the lexical resultative reading and the phrasal resultative reading, especially when V₂ in the complex verbal form is a 'stative' resultative (see (25), (28) and (29) above and also, e.g., Lu 1977: 280–1).

For example, the string *zuò hǎo* 做好, composed of *zuò* 'do' and the stative verb *hǎo* 'good, well', is semantically unambiguous and means 'to do well'. It is, however, structurally ambiguous: it can be either a resultative verb, with the *hǎo* acting as a resultative suffix, as seen in (37), or a phrase, with the *hǎo* acting as an adverb modifying the verb *zuò*, as seen in (38).

(37) zuò-hǎo
做好
do-good
'to do well'

(38) zuò hǎo
做好
do good
'to do well'

But when the form *de* 得 is added, they remain homophonous although both the structure and the meaning become different. Thus, (39) and (40), while completely homophonous, are lexical 'potential' and phrasal 'extent' respectively, with (39) meaning 'able to do well' and (40) meaning 'to do well'.

(39) zuò-de-hǎo
做得好
do-able-good
'able to do well'

(40) zuò-de hǎo
做得好
do-ADV good
'to do well'

The '*de*' in 39 is the lexical 'potential' -*de*, while the '*de*' in (40) is the syntactic 'extent' *de* (Lu 1977: 308–9 n. 10). Thus, the two *de* are analogous but functionally distinct, even though they are completely homophonous and are represented orthographically using the same Chinese character.

The lexical 'potential' resultative and the syntactic 'extent' resultative are clearly distinguished by how they accommodate negation (Lu 1977: 308–9 n. 10). As we saw in (29), (31) and (33) above, the lexical resultative forms the negative by the use of the -*bu*- affix on the verb head, as seen in (41). The phrasal extent resultative, on the other hand, forms the negative by using the negative *bu* to modify syntactically the word *hǎo* 'good', as seen in (42).

(41) zuò-bu-hǎo
做不好
do-able-good
'not able to do well'

(42) zuò-de   bu   hǎo
做得   不   好
do-ADV   not   good
'to do poorly'

The meanings of the two different forms are clearly different, with the negated potential lexical resultative in (41) meaning 'not able to do well' and the negated extent syntactic resultative in (42) meaning 'to do poorly'.

4.3.3.3 Other properties of resultatives

In terms of the framework presented in 4.1, resultative V₁ elements are root words: virtually all V₁ members of resultative verbs can occur as free verbs, as can the V₂ elements of stative and directional resultative verbs. Attainment resultative V₂ elements, on the other hand, may be either root words or bound roots. Consequently, stative and directional resultative verbs are classified as compounds, while attainment resultatives may be either compounds (when V₂ is a root word) or bound root words (when V₂ is a bound root). Finally, the 'potential' *-de/bu-* 得/不 'able/unable' grammatical marking that occurs on the left-hand member of these V₁–V₂ verbs falls into the category of grammatical affix, because it is bound and clearly a function rather than content morpheme according to the criteria in 3.4.3.1 (since it describes a completely regular semantic and grammatical relation between V₁ and V₂, viz., the ability (*-de-* 得) or inability (*-bu-* 不) of the V₂ result to come about following the occurrence of V₁). Therefore, any resultative verb is classified as a grammatical word when it contains the *-de-/-bu-* potential grammatical affix marking.

The stative and directional V₂ members are considered root words because they can be used as free syntactic words with the same meaning that they carry when they are used as resultative endings. This is certainly true, as seen in table 16, for the V₂ of stative resultatives (e.g., the *jǐn* of *zhuādejǐn* 'able to grasp tightly') and directional resultatives (e.g., the *xià* of *zǒudexià* 'able to walk down'). Attainment resultative endings can also be root words, since their meanings when used as lexical items may be synonymous with their use as resultative endings (as seen in attainment resultative V₂ morphemes *dǒng* 懂 'understand' and *dòng* 动 'move' in table 16).

Many attainment resultative endings, however, must be considered bound roots, because they cannot be used as free words with the same meaning that they possess when used as resultative endings. For example, as seen in table 16, the resultative *-jiàn* 见 has a meaning of 'perceive' while the lexical verb *jiàn* 见 has a meaning of 'see' or 'meet'. This means that the resultative and lexical variants of what might appear to be the same morpheme (*jiàn* 见) are actually two different morphemes.

This is quite clear in the case of *jiàn* 见, because resultative *-jiàn* 'perceive' is historically derived from the lexical *jiàn* 'see', with the meaning and function having diverged enough that they can clearly be considered different morphemes. They are also phonologically different – *jiàn* as a resultative ending often occurs with a reduced, 'neutral' tone, while *jiàn* as a lexical verb always occurs with a full

Table 16 Resultative types

resultative form	type of resultative (see 4.3.3)	meaning of V₂ as lexical item	meaning of V₂ as resultative ending	'same' or 'different' morpheme?
zhuādejǐn 抓得紧 grasp-able-tight 'able to grasp tightly'	stative	tight	tight	same
zhànbuwěn 站不稳 stand-unable-steady 'unable to stand steadily'	stative	steady	steady	same
zǒudexià 走得下 walk-able-descend 'able to walk down'	directional	descend	descend	same
pǎobushàng 跑不上 run-unable-ascend 'unable to run up'	directional	ascend	ascend	same
kàndejiàn 看得见 look-able-perceive 'able to see'	attainment	see	perceive	different
tīngbujiàn 听不见 hear-unable-perceive 'unable to hear'	attainment	see	perceive	different
jìdezhù 记得住 remember-able-fixed 'able to remember'	attainment	stop, live	firm	different
guǎnbuzhù 管不住 control-unable-firm 'unable to control well'	attainment	stop, live	firm	different

Table 16   (cont'd)

resultative form	type of resultative (see 4.3.3)	meaning of V₂ as lexical item	meaning of V₂ as resultative ending	'same' or 'different' morpheme?
kànbudǒng 看不懂 see-unable-understand 'unable to understand (what one sees)'	attainment	understand	understand	same
tīngdedǒng 听得懂 hear-able-understand 'able to understand (what one hears)'	attainment	understand	understand	same
nádedòng 拿得动 take-able-move 'able to pick up and move'	attainment	move	move	same
zǒubudòng 走不动 walk-unable-move 'unable to walk'	attainment	move	move	same

lexical tone. It is especially clear that lexical *jiàn* and resultative *-jiàn* may be considered 'different' morphemes when compared with, e.g., the lexical and resultative variants of *dǒng* 懂 'understand', which are absolutely identical both in meaning and phonological form, as seen in table 16.

Different morphemes must also be posited in the case of the word *zhù* 住 'stop, live' and the resultative ending *-zhù* 住 'firm, fixed' (see table 16). The word *zhù* 'stop, live' and the resultative ending *-zhù* 'firm, fixed' have identical phonological (and orthographic) forms. They are also semantically related, as 'firmness' or 'fixedness' (*-zhù*) implies the cessation (*zhù*) of activity. And of course they are historically related, with *-zhù* 'firm, fixed' having derived from *zhù* 'stop'. But phonological and orthographic similarity notwithstanding, *zhù* 'stop' and *-zhù* 'firm' must still be considered 'different' morphemes, because of the clear semantic difference that corresponds completely with their different functions.

This interesting question of 'same' versus 'different' morphemes once again involves the issue of polysemy – the occurrence of identical linguistic forms with different but related meanings (see Hopper and Traugott 1993: 69–72). Usually, if two morphemes have related meanings and are phonologically identical, they are considered polysemous variants of the 'same' morpheme (especially if the two are historically related). An example of polysemy in English is the auxiliary verb *will*, which (among its various senses) has the meanings of simple futurity ('They will appear later'), likelihood or certainty ('You will regret this') and willingness ('Will you help me with this package?'; *American Heritage Dictionary* 1992). The *will* meaning 'future' and the *will* meaning 'likelihood' are not considered different words, but rather are considered polysemous variants of the same word because they are phonologically (and orthographically) identical, historically related, semantically similar and functionally identical (both are auxiliary verbs).

Chinese word and resultative ending pairs like *zhù* 'stop' and *-zhù* 'firm' must be considered different morphemes rather than polysemous variants of the same morpheme, because the difference in their meanings corresponds completely with their different functions. This is exactly analogous to the status of the English morphemes *full* and *-ful* (as in 'wonderful', 'playful', 'useful' or 'masterful') – the two morphemes are phonologically identical and historically related (*-ful* comes from *full*), and their meanings are close enough for them to be considered polysemous (e.g., 'containing all that is normal or possible' for *full*, and 'full of, characterized by' for '-ful'; *American Heritage Dictionary* 1992). However, they are still considered different morphemes because their difference in function (*-ful* being a suffix and *full* being a word) corresponds completely with their difference in meaning (and their orthographic forms, of course, follow suit).

The positing of different morphemes because meaning differences correspond with function differences also applies to words other than resultatives. For example, *mù* 木 means 'wood' in the word *sōngmù* 松木 pine-tree 'pine wood' and 'tree' in the word *guǒmù* 果木 fruit-tree 'fruit tree', but the two *mù* are considered polysemous variants of the same morpheme (and therefore have the different meanings listed under a singular dictionary entry; e.g., *New China Dictionary*

(Commercial Press 1988: 323)), because the different meanings of *mù* do not correspond to differences in pronunciation or function.[10]

On the other hand, the two different senses of *fù* 复 seen in *fùshì* 复视 double-see 'double vision' and *fùfā* 复发 repeat-occur 'relapse' could be considered two different morphemes, despite their phonological identity and historical relatedness, because one is used as an adjective ('double') and the other is used as a verbal affix ('repeat').[11] In fact, they are indeed considered different morphemes by many speakers of Mandarin, as demonstrated by the different orthographic forms used to represent them: in Taiwan and Hong Kong, the character 複 is used for 'double' and 復 is used for 'repeat'. The meaning difference can be seen most clearly in the minimal pair *fùhé* 複合 double-unite 'compound' (Liang 1992: 1228) and *fùhé* 復合 repeat-unite 'reunite' (Liang 1992: 413).

We see that the proposed morphological framework helps determine to what extent meaning and functional differences yield 'different' morphemes rather than polysemous variants of the 'same' morpheme in Chinese. This, as we shall see, is very useful in determining the evolution of morphemes in Chinese; especially their lexicalization and grammaticalization.

4.3.4 Verb–Object words

Another type of Chinese complex verbs – V– O forms – are considered an interesting problem in Chinese complex word formation, because they represent a textbook case of apparent indeterminacy between morphology and syntax. The problem is not specific to the Chinese language, nor is it specific to V–O structures in Chinese (it applies in some cases to the resultatives discussed in 4.3.3; see also, e.g., Dai 1997 and Duanmu 1997 for discussion of other types of word–phrase indeterminacy in Chinese).

A given V–O form in Chinese may be considered a word (a morphologically complex verb), rather than a syntactic phrase, if certain criteria

---

[10] Although see Chao 1968: 443, which gives an example of *mù* 木 used as a free adjective meaning 'dense, stupid'.

[11] See Jiang (1989: 31–2), who argues that mere differences in syntactic function (i.e., form class) do not yield different words or morphemes. In Jiang's example, the verb *mù* 目 'see' and the noun *mù* 目 'eye' should be considered two polysemous variants of the same word.

GESTALT CHINESE WORDS

are met. These criteria include: lexicality or specialization of meaning, the inability of the verb and object to be moved or separated, the 'bound' status of the verb or object, neutral tone in the object, the V–O construction as a whole being exocentric and the V–O structure allowing an additional, 'external', object.

4.3.4.1 The problem

The problem is that some V–O forms appear to be both words and phrases. This is because the defining criteria listed above are often in conflict, and so paradoxically seem to identify certain V–O constructions as having both word and phrase identities. Note that there is no problem when the V–O combination consists of free words that are straightforwardly generated in a syntactic structure with no hint of idiomatic or specialized meaning. So in (43) and (44) the verb *xǐ* and the object *yīfu* possess the precise meanings of 'wash' and 'clothes' respectively, and so clearly constitute a V–O sequence in phrasal syntax. Furthermore, in (44) we see that the object *yīfu* may undergo topicalization – a syntactic operation – with no difficulty.

(43) Wǒ wǎnshang qù xǐ yīfu
我 晚上 去 洗 衣服
I evening go wash clothes
'I'm washing clothes this evening'

(44) Yīfu hái méi xǐ
衣服 还 没 洗
clothes still not wash
'The clothes haven't been washed yet'

The problem arises in the case of V–O forms whose components are, for example, bound morphemes (making the V–O form appear to be a word) but which are nonetheless manipulable by syntactic rules (making the V–O form appear to be a phrase), as seen in (45)–(47) (from Huang 1984: 64–5). The verb *dānxīn* 担心 carry-heart 'worry' in (45) contains the bound verbal morpheme *dān-* 'carry' with the free noun morpheme *xīn* 'heart' as its object. The fact that *dān-* is a bound morpheme would serve to identify *dānxīn* as a word rather than a phrase, because as a bound morpheme *dān-* cannot stand alone in a syntactic 'verb' form class slot. Furthermore, as seen in (45), *dānxīn* may be followed by an object (*zhèijiàn shì* 'this matter'), which also serves to identify *dānxīn* as a word. However, in (46) *dān*- and *xīn* are separated by modifiers, and in (47) the object *xīn* even undergoes topicalization, both suggesting that [*dān* + *xīn*] is a syntactic phrase.

(45) Tā hěn dānxīn zhèijiàn shì
他 很 担心 这件 事
He very worry this matter
'He is very worried about this matter'

(46) Tā dān-le sān nián de xīn
他 担了 三 年 的 心
He carry-LE three year de heart
'He worried for three years'
(lit. 'He wor- ed three years -ry')

(47) Xīn, wǒ xiǎng tā shì huì dān de
心 我 想 他 是 会 担 的
heart I think he be will carry DE
'Worry, I think he will'
(lit. '-ry, I think he will wor-')

Further complicating the V–O paradox is the fact that many common Chinese verbs require an overt object, even though the meaning of V–O structures so formed is the generic, 'objectless' form of the verb, as seen in (48)–(50).

(48) Tā xǐhuān kàn shū, bù xǐhuān kàn bàozhǐ
他 喜欢 看 书 不 喜欢 看 报纸
He like read book not like read newspaper
'He likes to read books, and doesn't like to read newspapers'

(49) Tā xǐhuān kànshū, bù xǐhuān zuòshì
他 喜欢 看书 不 喜欢 做事
He like read-book not like do-thing
'He likes to read, and doesn't like to work'

(50) *Tā xǐhuān kàn, bù xǐhuān zuòshì
他 喜欢 看 不 喜欢 做事
He like read not like do-thing
(intended meaning: 'He likes to read, and doesn't like to work')

In (48), *kàn* 'read' and *shū* 'book' are each independent syntactic words ('syntactic objects'; Di Sciullo and Williams 1987; see 2.1.7), with *kàn* occupying a 'verb' syntactic form class slot and *shū* occupying a 'noun' form class slot as the direct object. In (49), on the other hand, *kànshū* appears to be a single syntactic word, a verb with the generic meaning 'to read'. The verb *kàn* cannot be used without its 'default' object *shū*[12] 'book', as seen by the unacceptability of (50). In addition to *kàn* 'read', many other verbs in Mandarin (such as *hē* 喝 'drink', *jiāo* 教 'teach' and *chàng* 唱 'sing') also cannot be used without objects, which can be compared with, for example, a verb such as *wán* 玩 'play'. Ross (1997: 329) terms these obligatory, semantically weak, objects whose semantic content is entirely predictable from the verb 'cognate objects'.

This fact about certain Chinese verbs requiring a surface object that goes semantically unrealized adds to the V–O paradox because two syntactic words (i.e., *kàn* 'read' and *shū* 'book') that occur in a syntactic V–O combination paradoxically are categorizable as the single verb 'read' on semantic grounds,[13] since the meaning of 'book' carried by the morpheme *shū* is not realized. This also may be considered a case of non-compositionality, since the meaning of, e.g., *kànshū* 'to read' cannot be derived straightforwardly in compositional fashion from the meanings of its components, *kàn* 'read' and *shū* 'book'.

4.3.4.2 Previous analyses

Chao (1968), Li and Thompson (1981), Huang (1984) and Chi (1985) all discuss the problem of V–O words versus phrases, and each offers criteria to distinguish the two. The criteria differ somewhat between the investigators, but generally include compositionality of meaning, whether the verb and object can be separated or otherwise manipulated, and whether the V–O structure can itself take an additional, 'external', object.

Chao (1968: 415–34), in a long and detailed discussion of V–O 'compounds' (words), says a V–O construction is considered a compound under one or more of the following conditions (1968: 415): (a) at least one of the constituents is bound; (b) the object is in neutral tone; (c) the construction as a whole is exocentric; (d) it has lexicality; i.e., the meaning of the constituents in combination is specialized and (e) the constituents are inseparable.

[12] Unless it is in anaphoric, 'zero' form, with a word such as *shū* occurring as a contextual antecedent.

[13] Of course, it is possible that verbs such as these in Chinese and other languages as well possess highly redundant 'understood' objects.

To illustrate his criterion involving bound constituents, Chao gives examples of forms that are free–bound (e.g., *chūchāi* 出差 exit-errand 'to go (out) on an errand'), bound–free (e.g., *tànqì* 叹气 sigh-air 'to sigh') and bound–bound (e.g., *gézhí* 革职 remove-position 'remove from office'). Chao's examples of V–O words defined by neutral tone on the object include *xiūxíng* 修行 cultivate-conduct 'become a Buddhist', *dézuì* 得罪 get-offense 'offend' and *hùshū* 护书 protect-documents 'portfolio', and his examples of exocentric V–O words include transitive verbs[14] (e.g., *zhùyì* 注意 pour-(one's)-mind 'pay attention'), nouns (e.g., *lǐngshì* 领事 lead-affairs 'consul'), adjectives (e.g., *chūmíng* 出名 exit-name 'famous'), adverbs (e.g., *yòngxīn* 用心 use-mind 'carefully') and interjections (e.g., *láojià* 劳驾 bother-carriage 'would you please').

Chao calls this lexicality or specialization of meaning a 'non-structural' criterion, and considers it difficult to apply because it admits of degrees of difference. Chao uses *qīnzuǐ* 亲嘴 caress-mouth 'to kiss', *fācái* 发财 develop-wealth 'get rich' and *suànmìng* 算命 calculate-destiny 'tell fortune', as examples of V–O forms whose meanings must be given as wholes rather than compositionally. Chao also discusses 'frequency of association' as a criterion for determining wordhood, although he does not place it along with the five criteria presented above in his ordered list (1968: 415). In discussing 'frequency of association', Chao's point is simply that V–O forms that occur frequently (e.g., *fàngxīn* 放心 put:down-mind 'relax') tend to lexicalize as words.

On the criterion of the separation of the verb and object in the V–O structure, Chao posits five 'degrees' of separability (1968: 426), with, in general, the V–O forms that are least separable being the most word-like. Going generally from those that are least to those that are most separable, Chao posits (a) 'solid' V–O forms that are 'truly inseparable' (e.g., *yànshì* 厌世 loathe-world 'cynical'); (b) V–O forms that admit suffixes and complements to the verb (e.g., *zǔgé* 组阁 organize-cabinet 'to organize a cabinet' → *zǔ-le-gé* 组了阁 organize-ASP-cabinet 'to have organized a cabinet'); (c) V–O forms that admit modifiers to the object (e.g., *zhùyì* 注意 pour-(one's)-mind 'pay attention' → *zhù-yìdiǎr-yì* 注一点儿意 pour-a-little-(one's-) mind 'pay a little attention'); (d) V–O forms that allow inversion of the verb and object (e.g., *kāixué* 开学 open-school 'to start class' → *xué hái méi kāi* 学还没开 class-still-not

---

[14] Though it is not clear what Chao means by 'exocentric' in this instance, since the V–O form both contains and constitutes a verb, making it by definition endocentric.

start 'class hasn't started yet'; versus *zhùcè* 注册 fix-books 'to register (as a student)' → **cè hái méi zhù* *册还没注) and (e) V–O forms that allow the separation of the verb and object in questions and answers (not a clear or rigorous criterion; Chao uses the example *dǎzì* 打字 strike-characters 'to do typing' → *dǎbudǎzì* 打不打字 strike-not-strike-characters '(are you) typing?', answerable with the single verb element *dǎ* 打 '(yes, I'm) typing').

Li and Thompson (1981: 73–81) generally follow Chao's criteria, except that they exclude Chao's neutral tone criterion, and they explicitly discuss the criterion that V–O words usually do not take direct objects (1981: 76–7). Li and Thompson offer the word *gémìng* 革命 remove-mandate 'revolution' as an example of a form that (a) has a bound morpheme (*gé*); (b) has a meaning not derivable from the meaning of the constituents and (c) allows nothing to intervene between the constituents. Li and Thompson state (1981: 75) that the vast majority of V–O compounds are separable. They suggest *shāngfēng* 伤风 hurt-wind 'catch cold' as an example of a form that is idiomatic and has constituents that are free words but may possess the idiomatic meaning even when separated (e.g., *shāngdàfēng* 伤大风 hurt-big-wind 'catch a bad cold', or *shānglefēng* 伤了风 hurt-ASP-wind 'caught a cold'), though these constituents are not separable to the point where the object *fēng* can be topicalized (e.g., → **fēng, shāng le* 风, 伤了).

Li and Thompson then give examples (1981: 74–6) to show how the separation of the V–O constituents sometimes involves (a) separation by an aspect marker (e.g., *bìyè* 毕业 finish-instruction 'to graduate' → *bìleyè* 毕了业 finish-ASP-instruction 'to have graduated', *lǐfà* 理发 arrange-hair 'have a haircut' → *lǐguofà* 理过发 arrange-ASP-hair 'to have had a haircut'); (b) separation by a measure phrase (*xínglǐ* 行礼 perform-salutation 'to salute' → *xíngle yíge lǐ* 行了一个礼 perform-ASP one-M salutation 'to salute once' and *liūbīng* 溜冰 glide-ice 'to skate' → *liūguo yícì bīng* 溜过一次冰 glide-ASP one-M ice 'to skate once'); (c) separation by other modifiers of the object constituent (*shēngqì* 生气 grow-anger 'be angry' → *shēng tāde qì* 生他的气 grow his/her anger 'be angry with him/her') and (d) moving the object to a position preceding the verb (*shuō huǎng* 说谎 say-lie 'to lie' → *zhèige huǎng wǒmen bu néng shuō* 这个谎我们不能说 this lie we not able say 'This lie we cannot tell'). I note in passing that all above types of 'separation' involve either modification of the verb (i.e., aspect marking) or modification or movement of the object.

Li and Thompson end their discussion with a historical note (1981: 80), saying that since most V–O words come from syntactic phrases, they reflect a gradual process of phrases developing over time into completely fused words that are inseparable and completely idiomatic in meaning. The authors note that since such linguistic processes are gradual rather than abrupt, idiomaticity and separability are not discrete, 'all-or-nothing properties', but rather form a continuum, with idiomaticity and inseparability on one end and compositionality and separability on the other. Li and Thompson note that although the vast majority of V–O compounds are separable, separability and idiomaticity are not predictable and hence must be learned individually.

Huang (1984) and Chi (1985) criticize Chao's five criteria in depth, offering theoretical objections or exceptions to them. Huang reduces all the criteria (with the exception of specialization of meaning) to a single criterion, the Lexical Integrity Hypothesis (LIH: that syntax does not have access to word-internal information; see, e.g., Jackendoff 1972), while Chi takes the position that compositionality of meaning is the only clear criterion for distinguishing words from phrases (1985: 70, 82).

Regarding Chao's criterion that a member of the V–O combination be bound, Huang (1984: 63) argues that this criterion reduces to a special case of criterion (e) involving the separability of compounds. Chi's objection (1985: 73) to Chao's analysis is that it is contradictory to define a morpheme as bound because it cannot be used with a particular meaning as a free morpheme elsewhere, while the form it occurs in is defined as a word because it contains a bound morpheme.

Regarding the neutral tone criterion, Huang says neutral-toned forms are usually bound, and therefore this criterion reduces to a special case of criterion (e) involving the separability of compounds. Chi (1985: 74) says the neutral tone criterion cannot be taken seriously because it is simply not an accurate predictor of V–O wordhood, since in most V–O forms the object cannot occur in neutral tone.

Huang (1984: 63–4) claims that criterion (c) involving exocentricity falls under LIH because endocentricity is a requirement of phrase structure, and therefore is a *phrasal* principle. This, according to Huang, makes an exocentric word structure inaccessible to the phrasal endocentricity requirement under LIH, thus allowing the exocentricity to exist in word form. Chi's (1985: 74–5) argument is that Chao's notion of exocentricity is unclear, because his concepts of 'centre' and 'verb governing the object' upon which exocentricity are based are also unclear.

The inseparability criterion, Huang argues, is 'a special case of the criterion of lexical integrity' without further explanation (1984: 63), implying his position that any grammatical operation that separates word constituents is necessarily a syntactic operation. Chi argues that separability is a corollary of lexicality (1985: 98), and does not change a form's status as a word (1985: 86).

Huang and Chi's area of sharpest disagreement over Chao's criteria comes over criterion (d), compositionality or specialization of meaning. Huang (1984: 62–6) excludes compositionality of meaning outright as a useful criterion for identifying words, since, he argues, there are plenty of examples of phrases whose meaning is idiomatic and therefore not compositional (Huang's example: *guà yáng-tóu, mài gǒu-ròu,* 挂羊头卖狗肉 'hang a goat's head, sell a dog's meat', meaning to 'bait and switch', i.e., to misrepresent what one is selling or offering). Chi, on the other hand, takes the opposite position that lexicality of meaning is the only clear criterion for distinguishing words from phrases (1985: 70, 82), and that context provides the proper identity in the cases where it is possible for a V–O combination to be either a word or a phrase (1985: 82–4).

Huang's (1984: 68–9) solution to the V–O problem is that such forms 'have a dual status, either as words or as phrases ... determined by independent principles of grammar and by the context of its occurrence'. In discussing instantiation of those principles, Huang offers three possibilities. First, V–O structures might be doubly listed in the lexicon as both phrases and words; second, they might be listed as words but reanalysed as phrases when they occur sentence-finally; third, they might all be listed as syntactic phrases and undergo lexicalization when followed by an object.

Huang then settles in favour of the third possibility, taking the position that the primary factor determining wordhood is whether the V–O form is itself followed by object, and that all idiomatic V–O forms are listed as phrases and undergo lexicalization when followed by an object (1984: 69). Huang takes this to be directly due to the Phrase Structure Condition (PSC; Huang 1982, 1984: 54), which states (in simplified form) that a Mandarin verb may be followed by at most one constituent. Thus, when a V–O form is followed by an object, the PSC requires it to be analysed as a V–O word, since if it were a V–O phrase it would violate the PSC by allowing the verb to be followed by two objects. When the V–O form is not followed by an object, the PSC does not apply, in which case it exhibits phrasal properties.

The problem with Huang's analysis is that it relies far too heavily on the PSC as a determining principle, i.e., it places too much emphasis on the presence of a second constituent following the V–O form as a determinant of wordhood. The problem is that although the presence of a second object may indeed determine the identity of a V–O form as a word in most cases, its absence by no means identifies the V–O form as a phrase. That is, there are many sentence-final V–O forms that are words and not phrases.

Huang addresses this problem by stating that 'There is no reason why we cannot insert a V–O... compound as an intransitive verb sentence-finally' (1984: 70). But if that is so, then it greatly reduces the rationale for the PSC as the operative determining principle, since – through parity of reasoning – there should also be 'no reason' why we cannot insert a V–O compound as an intransitive verb in *non*-sentence-final position.

Chi's solution to the V–O problem is to offer three general criteria for identifying a V–O form as being a word versus a phrase (1985: 44): (a) neither component may be an affix;[15] (b) the V–O form must have single-word status either syntactically or semantically and (c) context must be considered. Chi then argues that lexicality of meaning is the only clear criterion for distinguishing words from phrases (1985: 70, 82), and that expandability does not change a form's status as a word (1985: 86), but rather occurs as a corollary of lexicality (1985: 98).

Certain of Chi's criteria are useful but do not go far enough in offering a solution to the V–O problem. Firstly, Chi's criterion that the V–O form 'must show single-word status in either syntactic or semantic terms' provides no real answer, since it merely raises the question we seek to answer in the first place, namely: is a given V–O form a word or not? Secondly, stating that 'context' determines whether a given V–O form is a phrase or a word is true enough (it actually comes closest to the solution that I will offer below), but provides little insight into what 'context' means with respect to the representation of V–O forms

---

[15] Chi includes the 'affix' criterion because, although the main body of his work is on V–O forms, the criteria were intended to apply to complex verbs in general. This criterion does not of course apply to V–O forms, because the object status of the second member effectively rules out affixes.

in the mind of a native speaker. Finally, Chi's asserting that simple lexicality of meaning is the only criterion for determining wordhood is insufficient, because there are simply too many instances of lexicality or specialization of meaning for things that are not words, as Huang's example *guà yáng-tóu, mài gǒu-ròu* 挂羊头卖狗肉 'hang a goat's head, sell a dog's meat' clearly shows.

4.3.4.3 A proposed solution

The following proposed solution attempts to demarcate clearly V–O words and phrases with minimal ambiguity or indeterminacy, adopting some of the criteria proposed by previous investigators to distinguish V–O words from phrases. The present proposal critically assumes that the lexicon and syntax are two separate, autonomous modular linguistic components.

4.3.4.3.1 The underlying lexical identity of V–O forms

My proposal is that idiomatic V–O forms are capable of having a dual status as both words and phrases, as suggested by Huang (1984: 68). But, contrary to Huang, I propose that the underlying identity of all such V–O combinations is as *words* listed in the lexicon, and that once a V–O form attains word status (see Di Sciullo and Williams 1987: 79), it is always listed as a word, even though it may still occur in syntax as a V–O phrase.

The first time a V–O form is used as a word, it is listed in the lexicon – potentially in perpetuity – as a lexical item. At that point, the V–O form normally also continues – perhaps even indefinitely – to exist as a phrase (albeit potentially an idiomatic one) in syntax. If the V–O form retains its identity as a phrase in syntax (that is, if the verb and object are still free morphemes), then of course it remains available for use as a phrase. This is obviously true, for example, in the case of V–O word forms such as *kànshū* 看书 'read books' that are composed of elements that are syntactically free, as seen in examples (48) and (49).

If the V–O form has been lexicalized to the point where the verb or object are not free morphemes (e.g., the verb *dān-* of *dānxīn* in (45), and is therefore technically not available as a syntactic phrase, then that form is still subject to *reanalysis* as a phrase, because virtually any two-syllable verb in Mandarin may be reanalysed as a limited, 'ersatz' V–O syntactic phrasal structure. This is demonstrated by just such a reanalysis of the word for 'tease' *yōumò*, a phonetic borrowing of the English word 'humour', as seen in (51) and (52) (from Huang 1984: 65).

(51) Wǒ   chángcháng   yōumò   tā
     我   常常   幽默   他
     I   often   tease   he
     'I often tease him'

(52) Wǒ   yōu-le   tā   yi   mò
     我   幽了   他   —   默
     I   hu-LE   he   one   -mour
     'I teased him once'
     (lit. 'I hu-ed him one -mour')

In this example, the word *yōumò*, which, as a phonetic loan, technically is morphologically unanalysable, is nonetheless decomposed and reanalysed into ersatz verb and object components, as seen in (52). Examples such as these demonstrate that following V–O word reanalysis as V–O phrases the word components mimic syntactic words – in very limited fashion – on analogy with 'normal' verbs and objects. The evidence that this V–O reanalysis is limited is that nowhere else, i.e., in no other contexts, can the putative 'V–O' constituents that appear syntactically free in this narrow context act as syntactically free words. So, for example, the *yōu* and the *mò* of *yōumò* are never seen anywhere else as free words, despite the fact that the *yōu* and the *mò* can mimic free verbs and nouns respectively, as in (52).

This proposal that V–O forms with dual status underlyingly always carry word status differs from the proposal of Huang (1984: 68–9) that such forms are underlyingly phrases and lexicalize in certain environments (see 4.3.4.2). Huang argues against the 'underlying word' solution, which he likens to Chao's (1968: 160, 426) 'ionization', by saying that it requires all such V–O forms to be obligatorily reanalysed as phrases when they occur sentence-finally, in order to exclude certain resultative sentences properly (1984: 68; Huang's examples (31b–c)) from the application of the *ba* and *bei* syntactic operations.[16]

But this requirement is neither necessary nor desirable. The requirement is not necessary because the resultative sentences that Huang

---

[16] Resultatives are mentioned here because Huang's justification for his choice of underlying phrases undergoing lexicalization is intended also to account for the behaviour of resultatives.

would rule out by this obligatory reanalysis are actually ruled out by another restriction, namely, that true resultative verbs (as opposed to the resultative extent phrases in syntax cited in Huang's example; see (37)–(42), and also Lu 1977: 308–9 n. 10) are incapable of undergoing the *ba* or *bei* syntactic operations. The requirement is not desirable because it incorrectly prohibits V–O forms from occurring as words in sentence-final position.

Now it is true that for a two-syllable form to be reanalysed as a syntactic structure it clearly must be operating in the domain of syntax: forms such as *dānle sān nián de xīn* 'worried for three years' in (46) and *yōu-le tā yi mò* 'teased him once' in (52) must be utilizing phrase structure rules from the syntactic component. But they cannot be phrases underlyingly, because although it is patently obvious that syntactic rules are being used to manipulate the constituents of *dānxīn* when it appears in the form of *dānle sān nián de xīn*,[17] it is just as obvious that this is not the permanent, underlying state of affairs with respect to the reanalysed constituents. This is because those constituents – although temporarily assuming an arrangement based on syntactic structure – have not been enabled to occur in combination with other elements as anything approaching free words in syntax. So even though words such as *dānxīn* may temporarily take on the form of syntactic structure as in *dānle sān nián de xīn*, this cannot be their underlying identity because the constituents of such words are not subsequently able to be freely selected and manipulated by the syntax.

In other words, while there is a great potential for 'limited reanalysis' of two-syllable verbs as V–O syntactic items as I have argued, there is no corresponding potential for 'limited lexicalization' of V–O phrases as implied in Huang's analysis (1984: 70), because once an item is lexicalized it remains so indefinitely. The dictum 'once a word, always a word' applies here – in this diachronic sense of an item becoming lexicalized by a native speaker – as well as in the LIH sense of a word's internal structure being unavailable to syntactic operations. The same statement regarding permanence of representation cannot be made regarding the reanalysis of two-syllable verbs as V–O syntactic items, because the putative 'words' so manipulated by syntax (such as the *dān-* of *dānxīn*, and the *yōu* and *mò* of *yōumò*) generally do not attain the status of free morphemes. Finally, it simply makes no sense to say

---

[17] Chi (1985: 104) makes much the same point.

that a phonetic loan word such as *yōumò* is lexicalized from syntax – a position we are forced to take under Huang's analysis.

4.3.4.3.2 Lexicalization and phrase criteria

I have argued that a V–O form is always primarily a word once it has been lexicalized, but how do we determine when such a form has in fact undergone lexicalization? There are three criteria, any of which is independently sufficient to indicate wordhood: first, when the V–O form may be followed by an object (by Huang's PSC);[18] second, when one of the constituents is a bound morpheme; and third, when the meaning of the V–O form is specialized, that is, when its meaning is not derivable in compositional fashion from the meanings of its parts.

There are also criteria that unambiguously identify a V–O form as a syntactic phrase (whether a limited, 'ersatz' V–O syntactic structure reanalysed from a word, as discussed above, or a 'bona fide' syntactic structure). A given V–O structure is unambiguously syntactic when the object is either modified (e.g., by expressions of time or quantification) or moved (e.g., via topicalization). While modification or movement of the object identifies a given V–O form as syntactic, that syntactic identity may be either a bona fide, generated syntactic structure, or simply a case of reanalysis from an underlying word. The critical variable which distinguishes a lexical item syntacticized via reanalysis from a bona fide syntactic structure is whether the constituents are free morphemes able to occur as syntactic words. When they are, we may consider the syntactic structure to be bona fide, and not just a temporary reanalysis of a lexical item.

It should be clear why these criteria unambiguously indicate a syntactic identity: the modification and movement of the V–O object are elements of Mandarin sentence grammar that properly fall into the domain of syntax, and not word formation. In the grammar of Mandarin word formation, there are no provisions for any type of modification or movement of the V–O object.

Note that I have not included a set of items that some investigators have included as an earmark of syntactic identity – the modification of the V–O verb by aspect makers (such as *-le*, and *-guo*). I have not included these because they are properly considered part of word

---

[18] See also Li and Shi (1997), who argue that the lexicalization of grammaticalized aspect markers in the history of the Chinese language was achieved when such elements could be followed by objects.

formation, specifically that aspect of word formation comprising inflection. These morphemes are considered part of the word formation component rather than part of syntax because they are examples of word-internal inflectional marking that operates on the head of the V–O word, viz., the verb. There is copious theoretical justification for this treatment, with many investigators in theoretical morphology proposing that inflection occurs on the head of the word, both in Chinese (Packard 1990, 1997c) and in other languages (e.g., Selkirk 1982, Di Sciullo and Williams 1987).

The modification and movement of the V–O object and the inflection of the verbal V–O head are demonstrated in (53)–(56) (examples slightly adapted from Li and Thompson 1981: 74).

(53) Shuì yi jiào
睡 一 觉
sleep one sleep
'Take a nap'

(54) Shuìle sānge zhōngtou de jiào
睡了 三个 钟头 的 觉
sleep-ASP three-CL hour DE sleep
'(I) slept for three hours'

(55) Zhèi yi jiào, shuì de zhēn hǎo
这 一 觉 睡 得 真 好
this one sleep sleep ADV real well
'I had a real good sleep'

(56) Wǒ shuìle jiào le
我 睡了 觉 了
I sleep-ASP sleep ASP
'I've slept'

The word *shuìjiào* 睡觉 sleep-sleep 'sleep' is a V–O form meaning 'to sleep', consisting of the verb *shuì* and the bound nominal *-jiào* 'sleep' as the object. According to our criteria given above, *shuìjiào* is a word because it may not be followed by an object, and because *-jiào* is a bound morpheme. In (53) and (54) we see the object *-jiào* modified by a numerical quantifier and a time adverbial respectively, and in (55) we see the object undergo movement to sentence-initial position via topicalization. These examples containing *shuìjiào* are considered to be instances of 'temporary' syntactic structure occurring by virtue of reanalysis. They are syntactic because the object has undergone modification or movement, and reanalysis because the underlying identity of *shuìjiào* is that of word (since it may not be followed by an object, and *-jiào* is a bound morpheme). In (56), on the other hand, *shuìjiào* is a word rather than an instance of reanalysed syntax, because the verbal head *shuì* is inflected by the aspect marker *-le*.

It is now clear that the separation, movement and modification criteria suggested by previous investigators in 4.3.4.2 may be broken down into those processes that modify the verb, and those that modify or move the object – my proposal is that the former identify words, while the latter identify phrases. This is actually not far from Chao's proposal regarding 'separability', as discussed on pp. 110–11. Chao's criteria, moving from least to most separable, are: (a) 'solid' V–O forms → (b) V–O forms that admit suffixes and complements to the verb → (c) V–O forms that admit modifiers to the object → (d) V–O forms that allow inversion of the verb and object. In the present proposal, (c) and (d) indicate syntactic structure (even if only by virtue of reanalysis).

So, is, for example, *shāngfēng* 伤风 hurt-wind 'catch cold' a word or a phrase? The answer is that it is a word – it is a word because it conforms to Mandarin word structure rules (see 4.1 and 5.3.5) and because it is listed in the lexicon with specialized meaning. What about *shānglefēng* hurt-ASP-wind 'caught cold' – is it a word or a phrase? The answer is that it is a word, because the inflection of the word head (*shāng*) by the verbal aspect marker *-le* is a lexical operation. *shāng-dà-fēng* 伤大风 hurt-big-wind 'catch a bad cold' (Li and Thompson 1981: 73), on the other hand is a phrase by virtue of syntactic reanalysis. This is because (a) *shāngfēng* is first and foremost a word and (b) the relation between the verb and object is clearly syntactic, since the object *-fēng* is modified by the adjective/stative verb *dà* 'big' which is not considered a lexical operation in any theory of word formation. The identity of *shāng dà fēng* as a syntactic phrase via reanalysis is further indicated by the fact that *-fēng* is not a free morpheme when used with the meaning it represents in the word *shāngfēng*. That is, *-fēng* is not used as a free syntactic word with the meaning '(a) cold'. And what about *bìyè* – is it a word or a phrase? It is a word and nothing but a word. It is clearly idiomatic, the verb may be inflected by an aspect marker, and the object cannot be modified by anything, nor can it be topicalized or otherwise moved. It is even questionable whether *bìyè* can be reanalysed as a syntactic form. Table 17 lists various V–O forms, along with explanations for why they are considered words, or phrases, or both.

Table 17 Verb–Object forms

V–O form	word?	phrase?	why?
chī miàn 吃面 eat-noodle 'to eat noodles'	no	yes	meaning not idiomatized, may not be followed by object, both morphemes are free
chīfàn 吃饭 eat-rice 'to eat'	yes	no	meaning idiomatized as intransitive verb 'eat'
'to eat rice'	no	yes	meaning not idiomatized, may not be followed by object, both morphemes are free
dúshū 读书 read-book 'to study'	yes	no	meaning idiomatized as intransitive verb 'study'
'to read book(s)'[19]	no	yes	meaning not idiomatized, may not be followed by object, both morphemes are free
dānxīn 担心 carry-heart 'worry'	yes	by reanalysis	meaning idiomatized as 'worry', *dān-* is not free
shāngfēng 伤风 hurt-wind 'catch cold'	yes	by reanalysis	meaning idiomatized as 'catch cold', *-fēng* is not free
fùzé 负责 carry-duty 'to be responsible for'	yes	no (unless by reanalysis)	may be followed by object, *-zé* is not free
yōumò 幽默 remote-silent 'to tease'	yes	by reanalysis	neither morpheme is free

[19] Liang 1992: 1282.

Table 17 (cont'd)

V–O form	word?	phrase?	why?
bìyè 毕业 end-career 'to graduate'	yes	no (unless by reanalysis)	meaning idiomatized as 'graduate', neither morpheme is free
xiǎobiàn[20] 小便 minor-convenience 'to urinate'	yes	by reanalysis	meaning idiomatized as 'urinate'
chūbǎn 出版 emit-edition 'to publish'	yes	no	may be followed by object
jiāgōng 加工 add-work 'to process'	yes	no (unless by reanalysis)	meaning idiomatized as 'process', may be followed by object[21]
guàchǐ 挂齿 hang-teeth 'to mention'	yes	no (unless by reanalysis)	may be followed by object, -chǐ is not free, meaning idiomatized as 'mention'
gémìng 革命 change-mandate 'revolution'	yes	no (unless by reanalysis)	-gé is not free, meaning idiomatized as 'to carry out revolution'
tóuzī 投资 throw-money 'to invest'	yes	no (unless by reanalysis)	-zī is not free, meaning idiomatized as 'to invest', may be followed by object
xǐzǎo 洗澡 wash-bath 'take a bath'	yes	by reanalysis	-zǎo is not free
bōpí 剥皮 peel-skin 'to peel'	no	yes	meaning not idiomatized; may not be followed by object; both morphemes are free

[20] xiǎobiàn is a verb through reanalysis; see (3) on p. 26.
[21] Zhang and Sang 1986: 393.

It follows as a corollary of this analysis that for those V–O forms that have double status as both word and phrase – such as *dúshū* (读书 read-book) as seen in table 17, which as a word means 'to study' and as a phrase means 'to read (books)' – there are actually three possible surface instantiations: (a) *dúshū* as a word – *tā xǐhuān dúshū, bu xǐhuān zuòshì* 他喜欢读书不喜欢做事 he like read book not like do thing 'He likes to study, and doesn't like to work'; (b) *dúshū* as a phrase reanalysed from a word – *wǒ jīntiān dúle liǎng cì shū* 我今天读了两次书 I today read-ASP two-CL book 'I studied twice today'; and (c) *dúshū* as a bona fide, freely generated, non-reanalysed syntactic structure – *tā xǐhuān dú shū, bu xǐhuān dú bàozhǐ* 他喜欢读书不喜欢读报纸 he like read book not like read newspaper 'He likes to read books, and doesn't like to read newspapers.'

Lexical items formed from bound morphemes – like *dānxīn* – on the other hand, only have two possible instantiations: as a word (example (45): *Tā hěn dānxīn zhèijiàn shì* 'He is very worried about this matter') or as a reanalysed syntactic structure (example (46): *Tā dān-le sān nián de xīn* 'He worried for three years'). The use of a word such as *dānxīn* as a bona fide generated, non-reanalysed syntactic structure would be possible only if the component morphemes were to become free, and therefore become able to occur independently in freely generated syntactic structures.

4.3.4.3.2.1 Construal as *either* word *or* phrase

It is worth pointing out that although many Mandarin V–O forms paradoxically seem to possess identities as both words and phrases, these forms are in fact not construed as ambiguous during their on-line natural language processing by native speakers. In other words, only one interpretation – that of word or phrase – is active at any given moment in on-line natural language processing. This means that in the case of speech production, a speaker generates either the lexical or phrase (basic or reanalysed) version for output; and for speech comprehension, it means the hearer will interpret the V–O input form as either word or phrase depending on context and the criteria presented previously in 4.3.4.3.2.

I make this point because V–O forms may be considered to be ordered on a continuous scale, such that 'the behavior of verb–object compounds forms a continuum, with any specific compound falling at some point on the continuum' (Li and Thompson 1981: 80). This should not be taken to mean that a gradient continuum exists between the word and phrase interpretations of individual V–O forms. Whether a form is interpreted as lexical or syntactic is a discrete, all-or-nothing phenomenon, given the hypothesis of the modularity of the syntactic and morphological systems. The gradient continuum property refers to the identity of individual V–O forms, and specifically the degree to which each individual V–O form has been lexicalized. So V–O forms do indeed lie on a continuum with respect to how lexicalized they are.

This construal of a V–O form as either a word or a phrase but not both at a single point in processing time is a property of the system given the modular hypothesis – the assumption that the lexicon and the syntax are autonomous modular components. In the end, whether a V–O form has two or more possible 'paradoxical' interpretations, it is nonetheless construed and used as either a word or a phrase, because, by hypothesis, the lexicon and the syntax exist as two separate, independent, modular components. The V–O 'paradox' – i.e., the perceived contradiction between word and phrase interpretations – occurs only upon native speaker reflection or linguistic analysis. If, upon reflection, it is perceived that a given form conforms to conflicting sets of criteria, then the form may paradoxically seem to possess a dual identity.

Useful analogies of this phenomenon may be seen in the domains of visual perception and natural language processing, where we see 'either–or' effects in which ambiguous stimuli are perceived in mutually exclusive fashion as having either one or another interpretation, but not both simultaneously. An example from visual perception is the famous 'Necker cube', which is perceived as having either an 'upward-tilting' or a 'downward-tilting' three-dimensional (in addition to a flat, two-dimensional) orientation, but is not perceived as having more than one of these orientations at a given instant, nor is it perceived as having a 'graded' quality at intermediate stages between the different orientations. In all of these examples, there is a categorical all-or-nothing 'switch-in switch-out' phenomenon, whereby the stimulus is at any given point perceived as either one or the other, but never perceived as both at once, nor perceived as having a 'graded' or intermediate value between the two interpretations. So it is with the 'ambiguous' V–O forms: a given V–O form may indeed have dual status, 'flipping' or 'toggling' between word and phrase interpretations depending on the state of the native speaker processor. But, computationally speaking, at any given moment in time or with any given state of the processor, there is only one 'active' reading.

Evidence from connectionist modelling of natural speech lexical processing for this 'toggle-in toggle-out' property of ambiguous stimuli comes from Kawamoto (1993), who finds that in the perception of ambiguous words, the system does not represent both of the ambiguous candidate words simultaneously, but rather that at any given point in time, only one of the ambiguous candidates is fully activated.[22] Kawamoto describes the two different representations corresponding to the two senses of the ambiguity as being instantiated over two different sets of activated units. In those relatively unusual circumstances when an ambiguity is actually perceived, the system naturally works toward a resolution of the ambiguity rather than maintaining full activation of both representations. Initially, subsets of units common to both representations are active. Subsequently, only one of the two representations increases in activation while the other decreases (Kawamoto 1993: 510). Although the cited research deals with multiple states within one component (i.e., the lexical component), it should be clear that such an 'either–or' state of ambiguous representations would be even more likely if the two candidate representations belonged to 'different components'.[23]

In terms of the framework presented in 4.1, V–O words are normally bound root words, because the putative object is usually a bound morpheme when it possesses the idiomatized word meaning. When it is reanalysed as a syntactic phrase, the object is still a bound form, but one that has been 'temporarily' taken as a free morpheme in a very limited context, as argued in 4.3.4.3.1.

4.4 Nouns and verbs by component form class: statistical tendencies

Now that we have talked about the composition of nouns and verbs by the form classes of their component parts, let us try to get a handle on how the actual identities of these nouns and verbs break down by preponderance of types of constituents. In other words, I have

---

[22] Thanks to Gary Dell for this reference.
[23] I intend the term 'component' to refer to the degree of functional unity. So, if two representations belong to 'different components', the assumption is that they will be functionally more distant than if they belong to the 'same component' (see discussion in n. 13 to chapter 7).

said that, according to the Headedness Principle, a preponderance of nouns should have nouns on the right and a preponderance of verbs should have verbs on the left. Let us now see how close that is to being true in terms of the actual numbers of words involved.

There are a couple of things to note here. First, we limit our analysis to nouns and verbs, allowing us to focus on the majority (about 88 per cent; see table 18) of Mandarin words. In delimiting our database in this way, we are better able to discover principles and generalizations that may also apply to the rest of the data, left for future research.

Second, we do not consider for componential analysis words that are not morphemically complex, i.e., bisyllabic words that consist of only one morpheme (the items indicated by 'φφ' in table 18). Examples of such words are *galár* 旮旯儿 'nook' *púfú* 匍匐 'to crawl', *tăntè* 忐忑 'perturbed', *bōlí* 玻璃 'glass' and *gāngà* 尴尬 'awkward'. Another class of examples whose components we do not analyse is the set of modern phonetic borrowings such as *shāfā* 沙发 sand-emit 'sofa' and *jítā* 吉他 lucky-him 'guitar'. The syllables of such words simply represent the sounds of the borrowed word and do not represent individual morphemes (even though they are written using Chinese characters that ordinarily stand for morphemes). Like *galár*, such borrowings are bisyllabic, monomorphemic words.

To restate (or make explicit) some points that arose in chapter 3: first, by the Headedness Principle, nouns generally have nominal elements on the right and verbs have verbal elements on the left. Second, as seen in our discussion of modification structures in 3.1.1.2., the possible structures of nouns with nouns on the right is either of the right-hand noun being modified in a 'descriptive' sense by a noun or verb on the left, or of the right-hand noun occurring in parallel with a noun on the left. The possible structures of those verbs with verbs on the left are either that the left verb takes an object on the right or that the left verb occurs in parallel with another verb on the right.

The range of possible Mandarin complex word structures is presented in table 18 (from Huang 1997: 264). As we look at the data, let us pay particular attention to what types of roles the right-hand nouns and left-hand verbs play in nouns and verbs respectively. The question we seek to answer is: to what extent do nouns actually have a noun on the right and verbs actually have a verb on the left? We will see that there is a surprising degree of similarity between nouns and verbs in how much latitude they have in departing from the Headedness Principle.

Table 18 Complex noun and verb structures (data from Huang 1997)

word structure	nouns	verbs	adjectives	total
N N	6,910	21	90	7,021
N V	306	446	72	824
N Adj	168	?	209	377
V V	276	3,730	103	4,109
V N	1,581	2,940	378	4,899
V Adj	?	434	?	434
A N	2,961	?	198	3,159
A V	116	707	173	996
A Adj	163	?	1,609	1,772
φφ*	257	72	66	395
TOTAL	12,738	8,350	2,898	23,986

* φφ indicates unmorphemicizable words, e.g., phonetic loans

The Headedness Principle states that nouns will predominantly have nouns on the right, and verbs will predominantly have verbs on the left. The data in table 18 indicate that this is indeed true. As computed from table 18, 89.9 per cent of all nouns (11,452 out of 12,738) have a noun on the right, and 85 per cent of all verbs (7,104 out of 8,350) have a verb on the left. What do these data tell us about the 'reliability' of the Headedness Principle? Based on frequency alone, knowledge by a native speaker that a complex word is a noun predicts with a high degree of certainty (near 90 per cent) that the right-hand member will be a noun, and knowledge that a complex word is a verb predicts with 85 per cent certainty that the left-hand member will be a verb. I interpret these data as supporting the Headedness Principle, indicating that verbs predictably have verbs on the left, and nouns predictably have nouns on the right.[24]

Given the Headedness Principle, a certain degree of indeterminacy might be expected for words with a [V N] structure, since the structure

---

[24] Huang, the author of the cited study (1997), interprets these data differently, namely as indicating that Chinese is a headless language, under his assumption that a word head must be in a constant position within a word in the language regardless of its form class. This is a reasonable interpretation given his assumption that head position is independent of form class. My proposal, however, is that the headedness value of a word depends upon its form class, with different head positions possible for words with different form class identities.

[V N] fits the Headedness Principle for nouns by having a noun on the right, and also fits the Headedness Principle for verbs by having a verb on the left. At least in terms of frequency, this expectation is confirmed by the data in table 18, which show that out of 4,899 [V N] forms, 2,940 (60 per cent) are verbs and 1,581 (32.2 per cent) are nouns.

However, although the word form [V N] being shared by nouns and verbs suggests potential ambiguity, words with this form are rarely ambiguous in practice. This is because it is knowledge of the form class of the gestalt word that drives the system, and not, in general, knowledge of the form class of the components. This means that a [V N] word is going to be recognized and used appropriately by virtue of its gestalt identity despite its potentially ambiguous internal structure.

This will be true even in cases of actual lexical ambiguity. To demonstrate, consider the form *jìnkǒu* 进口 enter-mouth. *jìnkǒu* has a [V N] composition, and has two homophonous readings – one as a noun ('entrance') and the other as a verb ('to import') – making the gestalt word ambiguous with respect to form class. As is clear from their uses in the following examples, however, information provided by position of the word within the sentence makes confusion unlikely. In (57) *jìnkǒu* can only be construed as a verb because it occupies the position reserved for sentence verb, while in (58) it can only be construed as a noun because it serves as the object of the preposition *wǎng* 往 'toward'.

(57) jìnkǒu   Měiguó   yùmǐ
     进口   美国   玉米
     enter-mouth   USA   corn
     'Import United States corn'

(58) Wǎng   jìnkǒu   zǒu
     往   进口   走
     toward enter-mouth   walk
     'Walk toward the entrance'

Confusion due to V–N ambiguity could occur in cases where the lexical ambiguity is not resolved by linear position, as seen is (59) and (60). The words *tóuzī* 投资 throw-money and *sàichē* 赛车 race-car both have a [V N] composition, and can either be the verbs 'to invest' and 'to race cars' or the nouns 'investment' and 'race car' respectively, as the examples in (59) and (60a) and (60b) indicate.

(59) tóuzī   qǐyè
    投资   企业
    throw-money enterprise
    (a) 'to invest in enterprises'
    (b) 'investment enterprises'

(60) Tā   hěn   xǐhuān   sàichē
    他   很   喜欢   赛车
    he   very like   race car
    (a) 'he likes to race cars'
    (b) 'he likes race cars'

Even in cases such as these, however, the pragmatic context has a disambiguating function. For example, *tóuzī* would likely only be interpreted as a noun in a context in which investment as an enterprise in and of itself were being discussed.

Describing words as being composed of such-and-such form class elements tells us little about the precise nature of their relationship, which varies for any given word type. For example, a noun composed of a verb and a noun [V N]ₙ can be a V–O form, referring to the agent of a V–O action, such as *lǐngshì* 领事 lead-event 'consul', with the presumption here that a 'consul' is someone who 'leads events'. Or, the [V N]ₙ can be any number of noun heads modified by a preceding verb, such as *wòchē* 卧车 sleep-car '(train) sleeper' or *zhèngrén* 证人 prove-person 'witness'. In the same way, the noun structure [N N]ₙ can be either a parallel structure (e.g., *shùmù* 树木 tree-wood 'trees') or a hierarchical, modifier–head, structure (*shùpí* 树皮 tree-skin 'bark').

The point here is that while the internal structure of words is an important and – I am claiming – a predictable entity in the linguistic competence of native Chinese speakers, it is the form class identity of the gestalt word that drives native speaker knowledge about the structures of words rather than vice versa, as is the case with syntactic knowledge (see 3.3).

4.5 Chinese words: special properties

Chinese words and their components exhibit a host of interesting and, arguably, unique properties. First, Chinese word components are almost invariably completely isolatable morphemes consisting of single syllables – the morpheme and the syllable are very nearly coextensive in Mandarin.[25] This is different from most other languages, in which multisyllabic or subsyllabic morphemes are, if not the norm, at least quite common. Second, most word components in Chinese are bound lexical morphemes (bound roots; see 3.4), a statement that – to my knowledge – cannot be made for any other language. Third, there is no morphophonemic[26] or paradigmatic[27] alternation in Mandarin, and there are no grammatical agreement phenomena.[28] In other words, a Chinese grammatical morpheme does not vary its sound shape or substitute for other members of a related set, either to indicate its own grammatical function or to match a grammatical value that inheres somewhere else in the sentence.

To say there is no morphophonemic alternation, paradigmatic alternation or grammatical agreement is not the same thing as to say that the grammatical values and functions that would be marked by such phenomena do not exist in Mandarin. It could be argued

---

[25] As we saw earlier, exceptions to this general principle in Mandarin are phonetic loan words from other languages, and 'one-sided' words (piānyì fùcí 偏义複词). In phonetic loans, the sounds of the borrowed word are represented in writing by characters which, although they have standard meanings, nonetheless contribute no semantic information to the borrowed word. In 'one-sided' words, the complete word has come to take on the meaning of only one of its constituents, effectively losing the meaning of the other constituent. Despite these exceptions, in general it is more difficult in other languages than in Mandarin to divide words unambiguously into morphemes. In English, for example, the element -ceive in words such as receive, conceive and deceive may be considered a morpheme 'by default', because it is possible to assign morphemic status to the rest of the word (re-, con- and de-), and because of its wide distribution and similarity of form across environments (thanks to Dick Anderson for this example). Bill Nagy points out that the notion of meaning in identifying morphemes in a language may be overrated, noting that sometimes it is the distribution of a particular form in the language that results in its morphemic status rather than its containing 'meaning' per se.

[26] Some exceptions are changes in form class of word-internal constituents as a function of tone, which could be argued to constitute a kind of morphophonemic variation. So, for example, the verb jiāo means 'to teach, instruct', but when used word-internally with a nominal meaning (in which case it is a bound root), the pronunciation changes to -jiào-, as in jiàoshì instruction-room 'classroom' or zōngjiào sect-instruction 'religion'.

[27] Paradigmatic alternation apparently existed in Ancient Chinese. For example, pronouns had different phonological and orthographic forms in Ancient Chinese according to differences in, e.g., person, case and number.

[28] The closest thing to grammatical agreement in Mandarin is the fact that classifiers are often selected from a closed set to match various features of the noun they modify, as Richard Sproat points out.

that grammatical case is marked in Mandarin by certain morphemes, but simply does not – transparently at any rate – involve paradigmatic and morphophonemic alternation. For example, there is a set of grammatical morphemes in Mandarin (usually thought of as 'coverbs' occurring after the first nominal argument in the sentence and directly preceding the second nominal argument) that could be argued to 'prefix' to nouns in order to mark them with the following traditional grammatical cases: nominative or agentive (*bèi* 被), locative (*zài* 在), dative (*gěi* 给 or *dào* 到), ablative (*cóng* 从), instrumental (*yòng* 用) and accusative (*bǎ* 把) (see Y.-C. Li 1971). What makes this argument implausible is that these morphemes – even though they usually occur directly in front of the noun they modify – always occur in an absolutely fixed position within the sentence. That fact and the fact that they are free and transparently related to other free lexical items cause us to view them as syntactic constituents of the Mandarin sentence rather than as morphological case markers.

A stronger argument, however, can be made that the function of the bound morphemes *-li* 里 and *-de* 的 when suffixed to nominals is to mark them with locative (see 3.4) and genitive cases respectively, and that the function of the bound morpheme *-men* 们 is to mark [+human] nouns for plural number. These are more plausible than the examples of *bèi*, *zài*, etc. given above because, unlike those grammatical morphemes, *-li*, *-de* and *-men* are bound and their positions within the sentence are unrestricted, the only requirement being that they attach to the right-hand edge of a word.

These properties of monosyllabism, existence of isolated morphemes, preponderance of bound roots, absence of morphophonemic alternation, paradigmatic alternation, grammatical agreement and so forth having been noted, what is unique about Chinese words is that these properties individually are universal and common in the languages of the world, but infrequently occur combined in any one language. In other words, the normal, 'universal' properties of words consist of differing values on a number of universal 'factors', and Chinese is unusual in the sense that that it possesses a unique nexus of values on these universal factors. Chinese is different not because it in some sense contains fundamental properties that no or few other languages have, but rather because the particular combination of factors possessed by Chinese words is not seen with great frequency, and especially not in the world's more commonly investigated languages.

These properties are not commonly observed in one language, but they are part of a reasonable, universal, range of parametric characteristics that languages 'choose' from.

4.5.1 Other word properties: Y.R. Chao's insights

There is still no work of Chinese linguistic analysis that compares with *A Grammar of Spoken Chinese* by Yuen Ren Chao (1968). In particular, Chao devoted large sections of that work to words and their properties, offering many insightful observations regarding the properties of words and morphemes in Chinese.

4.5.1.1 Versatile–restricted

Chao used the terms 'versatile' and 'restricted' (Chao 1968: 155) to refer to whether a particular morpheme needs to be accompanied by other specific items in the lexical context. Limiting our discussion to word formation, the versatile–restricted dichotomy in essence breaks down to whether a given morpheme occurs in a lot of different words. This is closely correlated with but different from productivity, which Chao defines (1968: 155; after Hockett 1968: 307–8) as the ability of a form to be used to coin new words. The difference between the two concepts is that versatile–restricted involves the number of different words within which a morpheme presently occurs: a morpheme is versatile if it occurs in many words in the contemporary lexicon. Productivity, on the other hand, involves how useful a morpheme is in coining new words. The two concepts are highly correlated because in general the greater the number of contemporary words a morpheme occurs in, the more productive it is in the formation of new words. Sproat and Shih (1996) offer a good discussion of productivity as distinct from versatility in Chinese.

4.5.1.2 Positionally free or bound

Chao spoke of morphemes as free or bound – a traditional concept – but included in his discussion the issue of whether morphemes were free or bound with respect to the position they occupy within a two-morpheme word. In this application, Chao used the terms 'start-free', 'start-bound', 'end-free', and 'end-bound'. For example, a morpheme that is 'start-bound' must be preceded by a morpheme in a word while a 'start-free' morpheme need not be, and a morpheme that is 'end-bound' must be followed by another morpheme. The concept is related to the notions 'prefix' and 'suffix': since a 'start-bound' morpheme is bound and must be preceded by another morpheme in a word, it would be considered a 'suffix' in western parlance if it had a grammatical rather than lexical identity.

The property of being 'positionally free or bound' has limited relevance in describing western or Indo-European languages, because in these languages such properties are largely possessed by grammatical morphemes and such morphemes are therefore considered affixes. Furthermore, in these languages bound morphemes are remarkably consistent with respect to the position they occupy within a word (i.e., they usually occur on the right or left of a word, but not both). Critically, these languages by-and-large do not possess what in Chinese constitutes the largest class of morphemes, those that are – as Chao put it (1968: 145) – 'Start-Free or End-Free, but Not Both' (in other words, bound roots that may occur on either the right or the left; see 3.4).[29]

---

[29] One possible example of such a word formative from English is '-*log*-' (meaning 'word' or 'text'), since it is reasonably productive, represents content rather than function information, may occur in either word-initial (logogram, logograph, logotype, logorrhea) or word-final (monolog(ue), dialog(ue), travelog(ue)) position and may not occur as a free word. Another possibility is '-*phyll*-', meaning 'leaf' (*phyll*otaxis and chloro*phyll*).

5 | X-bar analysis of Chinese words

In this chapter I offer an analysis of Chinese word formation that complements the X-bar theory of syntax. In one sense the approach presented here represents a shift to a more abstract level of analysis because it generalizes over form class category. In another sense, however, this chapter simply represents a unification of the two general approaches to morphological analysis already presented – form class and morphemic identity – by presenting a formal proposal for how the properties that determine morphemic identity ('bound/free' and 'content/function') interact with form class to account for speakers' knowledge of word structure.

5.1 Basic X-bar properties

A basic property of X-bar syntactic theory is that a category expands as a lower-bar copy of itself, optionally including other maximal expansions. X-bar syntactic rules have the form seen in (61), where the symbol on the right of the arrow that is the lower-bar copy of the symbol on the left of the arrow is the head of the phrase, and is posited to be the element from which the phrase gets its properties.

(61) $X^n \rightarrow \ldots X^{n-1} \ldots$

The significance of the 'bars' is twofold: first, they represent a property that ranges over form class categories, which means that a category expands as itself plus other 'complements' no matter what its form class – in effect saying that the notion of 'head-plus-complement(s)' is true for all form class categories in a language. This also means that the degrees or 'depths' of phrase complementation are roughly equivalent in a given language no matter what 'part of speech' the phrase is. Second, it accounts for the productivity and recursiveness of syntax, because once rules of this form are proposed for a language, they enable recursion of structure by allowing a 'higher node' maximal projection to be part of the expansion on the right side of the arrow. This recursive property of syntactic structure is what is thought to be universal about all languages and therefore may constitute the innate, abstract capacity for learning languages that children have at birth due to their human genetic endowment.

5.2 X-bar properties applied to words

Note that the categorization system for individual morphemes presented in 3.4.3 is generally valid for both nouns and verbs: either a noun or a verb may be a bound root or a grammatical affix. Likewise, the types of complex words discussed in 4.1 exist no matter from what 'part of speech' they are composed. In other words, the word types 'compound word' and 'bound root word' exist for both verbs and nouns in Chinese. The present chapter argues that it is possible to capture these generalizations about Chinese words and their construction with a framework that operates at the level of those generalizations, viz., the X-bar system, in which word constituents are analysed as having the same general properties and combinatorial possibilities regardless of whether they are nouns or verbs.

This approach is possible because the basic units have been categorized according to: (a) their form class identities; (b) the extent to which they can stand alone as free morphemes; (c) whether they have a 'grammatical' or a 'lexical' identity and (d) the manner in which they combine to form words.

5.2.1 Expectations regarding 'X-bar' notation applied to words

As many colleagues have pointed out, the present proposal arguably has only a notational relation to X-bar syntactic theory, because many of the properties of that theory (such as government, barriers, empty categories and the like) do not emerge here. But this is completely natural, because such properties are not properties of the lexical component: they simply fail to emerge 'at' or 'below' the level of X^0. Another way of thinking about this is to consider the question: since the present proposal is, on the surface, little more than a framework that specifies different ways of concatenating various types of morphemes, what do we lose if it is not presented using X-bar notation?[1]

[1] My thanks to Liejiong Xu for framing the question in this way.

I would offer two answers to that question: (a) we lose the insight that, at a basic level, the primitives that are manipulated (i.e., X^N) and the rules used to manipulate them (i.e., phrase structure rules) are the same as those that account for the properties of syntax, with many of the salient and obvious differences between words and syntax (e.g., productivity) accounted for by trivial differences in (i) the 'numeration' of the primitives and (ii) the forms of the rules; (b) we lose the observation that the proposed system is transparently compatible and fully commensurable with a characterization of the language component that uses X-bar notation. Note that I am by no means breaking new ground in proposing an X-bar notation to account for word formation: Selkirk (1982), Sadock (1988, 1991) and others have done work in this area. Let us now review the work of these investigators.

5.3 X-bar morphology: previous proposals

The X-bar analytical framework yields a somewhat different set of results when it operates at or 'below' the X^0 level. In general, the generative and recursive power that X-bar theory so well accounts for in syntax is not as salient a property of word structure. This is seen in Selkirk's principle (see (62)) which disallows recursion at lower levels. There appears to be a more definite limit on generative productivity and recursion in words, both in terms of their sheer length and in terms of actual structure generation.

Another important point is that word structures are exocentric more often than are structures in syntax: that is, often the form class of a word is not the same as the form classes of its constituents. That fact points out another major difference between morphological and syntactic structure: word structures are much more easily 'lexicalized' than syntactic structures. In other words, it is common for a complex word to 'give up' the semantic and form class identities of its component morphemes to the gestalt word, while it is not even clear what it would mean for, e.g., the coindexed daughter of a syntactic maximal projection to 'give up its identity' to that maximal projection.

5.3.1 Selkirk

Elizabeth O. Selkirk (1982) developed a complete framework of morphology based on X-bar theory specifically to account for the structure of words. Her system takes the form of a 'mixed' context-free phrase structure grammar, with the 'mixed' aspect being that grammatical category symbols (rather than specific morphemes) are allowed as elements of the terminal string, with lexical insertion providing the specific morphemes (1982: 67–8). For English, Selkirk's system formally distinguishes words, roots and affixes as morphological primitives, two types of compounding (native and non-native) and two types of derivational affixation (Class I 'non-neutral' and Class II 'neutral'), but provides no formal distinction between inflectional and derivational affixation.

Selkirk proposes a universal morphological schema to which all languages are posited to conform in constructing their word-formation systems (1982: 8). That schema, seen in (62), proposes that syntax-forming and word-forming rules differ qualitatively in that word-forming rules are much more restricted in their generating power.

(62) $X^n \to \varphi\, Y^m\, \psi$
where $0 \geq n \geq m$

This is well summarized by Selkirk: 'a category may not be written in terms of another category (or categories) higher than itself in the X-bar hierarchy . . . Should the claim . . . in fact hold up, then, it would provide important evidence that the systems of word syntax and phrase syntax are truly distinct' (1982: 8–9). Selkirk is claiming that word formation rules possess limited recursion: 'recursion' because, as we see in the expansion of (62) in (63) (1982: 64–5), the same symbol may appear on both sides of the arrow; and 'limited' because, unlike in syntax, the expansion on the right of the arrow may not include an element that has a 'higher' bar level than the element on the left.

(63) (a) $X^n \to \varphi\, Y^m\, X^{AFF}\, \psi$
(b) $X^n \to \varphi\, Y^{AFF}\, X^m\, \psi$
(c) $X^n \to \varphi\, X^m\, Y^{AFF}\, \psi$
(d) $X^n \to \varphi\, X^{AFF}\, Y^m\, \psi$
where $0 \geq n \geq m$

The rule schemata in (63) mean that complex words are formed by expanding a category 'X' into a category or categories with a bar value equal to or less than that of 'X', with affixes that can be either prefixes or suffixes and that either can be or are not heads. Languages 'choose' among the schemata in (63), with, e.g., suffixing languages choosing (63a) and (c) and prefixing languages choosing (63b) and (d).

For English, Selkirk posits the three morphemic primitives word (X^{-0}), root (X^{-1}) and affix (X^{AFF} or Y^{AFF}). The designation of words as X^{-0} makes their representation as morphological objects the same as the representation of 'syntactic words' (X^0). This provides a natural connection between morphology and syntax, because items designated as fully derived objects in the morphological component have the same formal designation as those designated as occupying a terminal node in syntax.

In Selkirk's system, English (non-compound) words have three possible derivations, consisting of the rules in (64):

(64) $X^0 \rightarrow Y^0, X^{AFF}$
$X^0 \rightarrow Y^{AFF}, X^0$
$X^0 \rightarrow X^{-1}$

while roots have two derivations, of the form seen in (65):

(65) $X^{-1} \rightarrow Y^{-1}, X^{AFF}$
$X^{-1} \rightarrow Y^{AFF}, X^{-1}$

where X^0 is a word, X^{-1} is a root and X^{AFF} or Y^{AFF} stands for the category Affix (elements of the category Affix will either match the category to the left of the arrow, as X^{AFF}, or not, as Y^{AFF}, depending upon their syntactic feature composition). In prose, the rules for X^0 words in (64) mean that words are formed from the combination of a word plus an affix. The rules for X^{-1} roots in (65) mean that roots are formed from the combination of a root plus affix. Roots, as their '–1' X-bar numbering indicates, are the 'next lower category' down from word. The rule $X^0 \rightarrow X^{-1}$ in (64) conveys Selkirk's contention that all words are redundantly roots: in principle, all roots (monomorphemic non-affix morphemes) can be words, and monomorphemic words are redundantly marked as roots (1982: 98).

Note that Selkirk rejects the possibility of words being formed by affixation to roots, as illustrated in (66), in favour of roots being formed by affixation to roots, together with the derivation of words from roots, as seen in (67), with the reasoning that (66) is not motivated by English (1982: 95).

X-BAR ANALYSIS OF CHINESE WORDS

(66) $X^0 \rightarrow Y^{-1} X^{AFF}$

(67) $X^{-1} \rightarrow Y^{-1} X^{AFF}$
$X^0 \rightarrow X^{-1}$

The rules in (64) and (65) indicate that the process of affixation yields as its output both words and roots. The fact that Selkirk gives no rules allowing X^{-n} elements to be formed via the attachment of affixes to elements at a lower bar level (such as $X^{-1} \rightarrow Y^{-2}, X^{AFF}$, or $X^{-0} \rightarrow Y^{-1}, X^{AFF}$) is consistent with her position that there is no formal category (such as 'stem') intermediate between root and word. The rules also indicate that the heads of words (and roots) in English are exclusively on the right (since X never occurs as the left-hand member of the expansion). Therefore English prefixes, in general, cannot serve as the heads of words (or roots).[2]

From the rules in (64) and (65), we see that affixed words (ignoring prefixes) may be generated directly as words, taking the form seen in (68) (generated from the rules in (64)):

(68)

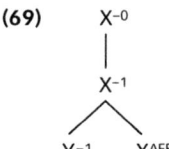

or they may be generated first as stems, taking the form seen in (69) (generated from the rules in (65)).

(69) X^{-0}
           |
           X^{-1}
          /   \
       Y^{-1} X^{AFF}

The difference between (68) and (69) is intended to capture the distinction between words formed via Class II ('neutral' or 'word') derivational affixation ((68); for words such as *sisterhood*, *kindness* and *singer*) and those formed via Class I ('non-neutral' or 'root') derivational affixation ((69); for words such as *sermonette*, *Catholicism* and *employee*). Class I derivational affixes are called 'non-neutral' because they are not

---

[2] Selkirk provides a small list of exceptions, such as *asleep* and *enslave*, and a means for deriving them (1982: 87–9).

neutral with respect to the stress pattern of the words they form (e.g., emplóy → employée), and are called 'root' because they are posited to attach to roots rather than words. Class II derivational affixes attach to words and do not affect the newly formed word's stress pattern (e.g., síng → sínger; see Chomsky and Halle 1968, Siegel 1974 and Scalise 1984: 81–7 for discussion of these two classes of derivational affixes).

The Class I and Class II affixes themselves are not formally different in Selkirk's system – since both are designated X^{AFF} – but their subcategorization (i.e., the specification for what their sister node is required to be) as listed in the lexicon does differ, with Class II derivational affixes subcategorizing for words (X^{-0} or Y^{-0}) and Class I derivational affixes subcategorizing for roots (X^{-1} or Y^{-1}). The rule yielding the Class I derivationally affixed word *employee* is therefore as seen in (70), and that for the Class II derivationally affixed word *singer* is represented as in (71).

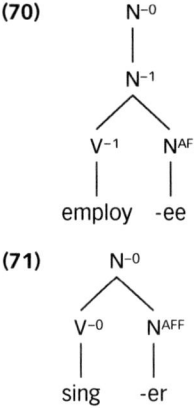

This means that words formed using Class I derivational affixes and those formed using Class II derivational affixes are quite different in Selkirk's system. They differ in structure because the two types of affix take different categories as sisters, but they also structurally differ in that words formed from Class I derivational affixes are initially roots (with a structure such as that seen in [[[employ]$_{V^{-1}}$[ee]$_{N^{AFF}}$]$_{N^{-1}}$]$_{N^{-0}}$), while those formed from Class II derivational affixes are words in the first instance (with a structure like [[sing]$_{V^{-0}}$[er]$_{N^{AFF}}$]$_{N^{-0}}$).

In Selkirk's system, English 'native' compounds (those formed from independent English words) take the form seen in (72) (1982: 53, 55):

X-BAR ANALYSIS OF CHINESE WORDS

(72)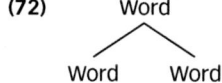

otherwise represented as in (73):

(73)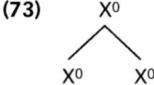

shown in (74) as the structure for the native compound *apron string*:

(74)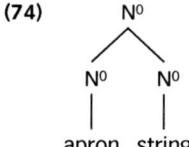

'Non-native' compounds (those formed from, e.g., Greek roots) take the form seen in (75) (1982: 129 n. 18), with the X^{-1} in these examples representing what Selkirk calls *bound roots* (cf my definition of bound root in 3.4 on p. 69).

(75)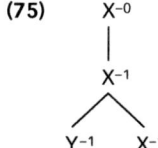

This word structure is seen in (76), demonstrating the derivation of the non-native compound *telescope*.

(76)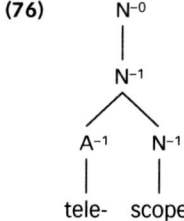

As we saw in the case of Class I derivational affixes versus Class II derivational affixes, native and non-native compounding differ in structure both in terms of their sister constituents and in terms of the identity of non-native compounds as initially roots, and that of native compounds as initially words.

Selkirk claims that non-native compounds such as *telescope* and *erythrocyte* contain bound roots designated X^{-1}, but provides no formal way to distinguish between those X^{-1} that are bound (such as *tele-*), and those that are not (such as any root, as defined in Selkirk's system, that would act as a base for a Class I derivational suffix – like the *employ* in *employee* in (70) above).[3] In this approach, bound roots may only combine with affixes to form roots: they may not combine with anything other than affixes, and they may not combine to form anything other than roots.

It is important to point out that both for compounds (1982: 47–8) and for complex words involving affixation (1982: 82–3), Selkirk says that the set of word formation rules in a given language is restricted to containing the set of specific categories that actually occur in attested words. This of course represents a greatly reduced subset of the set of possible words generated using the rules as they exist in X-bar terms.[4]

Affixes in Selkirk's system are assigned a constant superscript ('AFF' or 'a'; which is to be interpreted as less than zero) rather than an integer, to indicate that the category type 'Affix' falls outside the X-bar system (1982: 123–4). Some other distinguishing properties of affixes are (a) they are necessarily preterminal, in that recursive embeddings of affixes have not been attested; (b) they can dominate neither word nor root; (c) they are always a sister to a non-affix category type and (d) they are not cross-categorial in their subcategorization, that is, they subcategorize for some specific category or categories (1982: 83).

Subcategorization of items in the lexicon (i.e., the specification on a lexical entry that gives the form class and category type of its sister)

---

[3] Selkirk suggests that bound and non-bound roots could be distinguished in the system by, for example, requiring bound roots to have a subcategorization frame (1982: 98–9).

[4] Scalise (1984: 189, citing Drigo 1983) notes that this is a problem, because in restricting language-specific word-formation rules to just those word types that are actually attested in a given language, Selkirk does little more than provide a list of existing combinations rather than positing an actual context-free word generating system, and does not, for example, explain why certain combinations and not others are possible.

plays an important, powerful role in Selkirk's system. Anything but X^{-0} (i.e., X^{-1} and X^{AFF}) may potentially subcategorize. Selkirk suggests that the X^{-1} that are bound roots may subcategorize for either affixes or roots (1982: 98–9), with the ability to subcategorize potentially distinguishing those X^{-1} roots that are bound from those that are not (see n. 3). For X^{AFF}, Selkirk says those X^{AFF} that subcategorize for words (X^{-0}) are either inflectional affixes or Class II derivational affixes, while those X^{AFF} that subcategorize for roots (X^{-1}) are Class I derivational affixes.

It is important to state clearly what it means for Selkirk's system to invest so much information in the subcategorization of lexical entries. It is essentially a tradeoff – allowing information to be an inherent part of the informational structure of the lexical entry rather than having that information be part of the structure-generating word-forming rules. Informally speaking, subcategorization means that a speaker knows a lexical X^{-1} or X^{AFF} morpheme's distributional characteristics due to knowing that particular morpheme, and not due to knowledge of general word-formation principles or knowledge of the general characteristics of system primitives. If the latter were true instead, more of the information about morpheme distribution would reside in system primitives and generative rules rather than in the (subcategorization of the) lexical entry.

For example, according to the Selkirk system, when a speaker knows the lexical entry of the English inflectional plural marker suffix *-s* as: Y^{AFF} [+plural] [subcategorization: N^0 ____]; the speaker knows as a function of knowing *-s* that: (a) it means 'plural'; (b) it is bound; (c) it must cooccur with a noun; (d) that noun must be a word; (e) it must suffix to that noun word; and (f) it is possible for the item *-s* to contain the information (a)–(e) because it has the category type designation of AFF, and therefore 'may subcategorize' for that information. This would be compared to a system in which the inflection marker *-s* is assigned in the lexicon to be: I [+plural] [subcategorization: N]; i.e., as a member of a category I(nflection), but limited subcategorization, and is generated as a word suffix with a separate word-formation rule all its own: $X^0 \rightarrow X^0$, I (or, in prose, words may be formed by the suffixing of an inflectional affix). In a system with these properties, when the speaker knows the lexical entry of the plural suffix *-s*, the speaker still knows (a)–(e) above, but now knows (b), (d) and (e) as completely regular, predictable information (which they are) by rule, rather than as idiosyncratic information (which they are not) stored with the lexical entry.

5.3.2 Sadock

Jerrold M. Sadock proposed an X-bar treatment of morphology as part of his theory of Autolexical Syntax (Sadock 1988, 1991). Sadock developed this theory to account for many types of 'mismatch' that occur between morphology and syntax in natural language, as, for example, in the case of clitics which in a sense belong to both the syntactic and morphological components.

Sadock proposed that the morphological, syntactic and semantic components are autonomous linguistic modules that rely on the lexicon as their interface. The lexicon serves this special transmodular role ('the axis around which the several autonomous modules pivot' (1991: 29)) because knowledge of a lexical item by a native speaker entails knowledge of its meaning, morphology and syntactic distribution and function.

In this theory, the lexicon stores lists of formatives with their syntactic, semantic and lexical specifications, containing 'the basic vocabulary for each of the modules and information as to the structural properties of each lexical item with respect to the several autonomous components' (Sadock 1991: 29). Since it has direct access to all components and all varieties of grammatical information, the lexicon is not 'informationally encapsulated', and therefore not a module in the sense of Fodor (1983) as are the other components (Sadock 1991: 36).

The crux of the theory is that the modular components interact via the lexical interface in a non-hierarchical, 'automodular' manner. So while other theories posit a linear, hierarchical input–output relationship among linguistic components (e.g., phonology → morphology → syntax; or base → lexicon → transformations), Sadock views these components as interacting in a three-dimensional 'autosegmental' type of parallel representation with the lexicon serving as a common, connecting node (cf the 'coanalysed structures' of Di Sciullo and Williams 1987: 88–106).

This non-linear property of the system allows independent mapping to occur among any pair of components, because the information transfer is allowed not merely between fixed pairs as they are hierarchically arranged, but between any of the pairs via the lexical interface. It also means any given module is not dependent upon the output of another module to do its work, since it operates independently.

In Sadock's system, words and formatives stored in the lexicon are connected with their autonomous representations in syntax, semantics and morphology, with principled limits on the degree to which the autonomous representations may differ. The separate outputs of the components 'must pass congruity requirements imposed by the interface', which 'checks to see whether the members of a set of parsings from the individual components fit one another and count as parsings of the same total expression' (Sadock 1991: 20).

Sadock assumes that a context-free phrase structure grammar is sufficient to generate representations in each of the modules (Sadock 1991: 21). This property lends unity to the different representations, because, for example, the notion 'degrees of complementation' is expressed by differences in bar level, with a category expanding as a head plus complement(s) in all three modules.

Sadock's X-bar morphological system begins with stems, designated as X^{-0}. The 'zero' designation of X^{-0} is intended to indicate the fact that the stem is the most basic morphological form. Sadock says that bar levels in morphological structure start 'at the 0-bar level so that a basic lexical form (an uninflectable particle, for example) will have the same representation in both components' (Sadock 1991: 27). Stems may be 'morphologically primitive' (i.e., roots), or they may be 'derived' (i.e., 'regular' stems). Thus, Sadock has no separate designation for roots as distinct from stems – they are both X^{-0} (essentially the same position taken by Selkirk, who calls hers 'roots' and designates them X^{-1}). Sadock's formula for the derivation of 'non-primitive' stems is:

(77) $X^{-0} \rightarrow Y^{-0}, X$

where Y^0 is a stem and X is a derivational morpheme. Implicit in this analysis is the assumption that derivational morphemes are heads of stems. Morphemes that combine with stems to form stems are derivational and those whose presence is obligatory to form an independent word are inflectional. Sadock's derivation of 'compound stems' is:

(78) $X^{-0} \rightarrow X^{-0}, Y^{-0}$

where the X^{-0} to the right of the arrow is the head of the compound. The head of the compound may be on the left of the expansion as in Hebrew (as above), or on the right, as in English (Sadock 1991: 29). 'Fully formed words' (Sadock 1991: 28) are designated X^{-1}. Their derivation is therefore represented as in (79), where the word is X^{-1}, X^{-0} is the stem and Y is the inflection.

(79) $X^{-1} \rightarrow X^{-0}, Y$

In Sadock's system, therefore, stems are the heads of inflected words. Inflectional affixes are not given an X-bar designation, but are rather assigned a subcategorization for the words they inflect in their lexical specification (Sadock 1991: 28, 37). Sadock's representation of a structure formed by cliticization is:

(80) $W^{-2} \rightarrow X^{-n}, Y$

in which W^{-2} is the resulting cliticized structure, Y is the clitic and X^{-n} is the host.

As seen by the designation of affixes as Y, stems as X^{-0}, words as X^{-1} and cliticized structures as W^{-2} (or X^{-2}; Sadock 1988: 274), there is a positive correlation between bar level and structural complexity in Sadock's system. This method of assigning bar values (which differs from the X-bar morphological systems proposed in Selkirk 1982 and the present work, to be discussed in 5.3.4) means that a lexical item's X-bar designation as a syntactic unit (the familiar X-bar designation of a lexical item as X^0) will often not be equivalent (even in absolute value) to its designation as a fully formed morphological unit (Sadock's X^{-1}, or 'fully formed word'). This is counterintuitive under the assumption that the output of the morphological component for lexical insertion should be equivalent in X-bar terms to the value of a syntactic lexical item. However, it is not a problem in Sadock's system – the automodular geometry of the system allows for the lexically inserted morphological item to carry a designation of X^{-1} as a fully derived lexical item.

To illustrate, let us consider the derivation of the complex lexical item *dogs*. The lexical entry for *dog* seen in (81) is represented as a N^{-0} stem in the morphological component (under the assumption that the lexical entry for *dog* is as a stem with a phonological null singular affix;[5] Sadock 1991: 31 n. 5), and N^0 for its representation in the syntactic component.[6]

---

[5] As an alternative to the idea that most words in, e.g., English bear a phonologically null suffix, Sadock suggests that a general rule could be proposed for lightly inflected languages like English that promotes any stem to the status of word (Sadock 1991: 31 n. 5).

[6] The semantic representation is not relevant for our purposes here, and so is ignored.

Figure 2 Syntax–Morphology interface

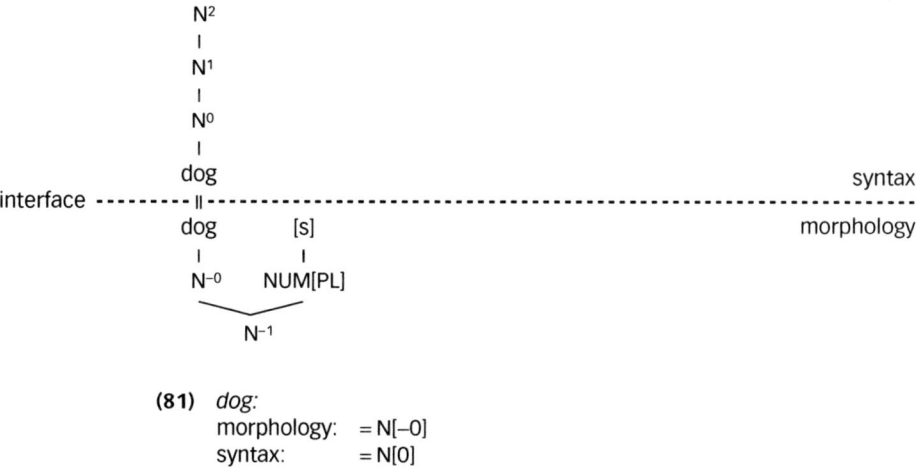

(81) *dog*:
  morphology: = N[–0]
  syntax: = N[0]

Since a N⁻⁰ stem cannot undergo lexical insertion,[7] it must first undergo Morphological Rule 1 as seen in (82) to properly be designated X⁻¹.

(82) Morphological Rule 1:
  X^{-1} → X^{-0}, Y
  i.e., word → stem, affix
  dogs → dog, -s

In figure 2 we see that the appearance of the *morphological* X⁻¹ word filling a *syntactic* X⁰ slot is feasible because it has been properly derived and the geometry of the system allows the properly derived X⁻¹ to be associated with the syntactic lexical form X⁰. In Sadock's system, this lack of a direct association between the two representations is considered a virtue, because it allows for the occurrence of morphosyntactic mismatches while still allowing the 'correct match' to be the default case following general system principles.

Sadock's system would seem to lack parsimony, since the existence of several autonomous modules freely computing structure yields considerable redundancy in the totality of the computational apparatus, especially when elements of computational structure are shared across modules. However, as Sadock argues, parsimony is not necessarily

---

[7] Apparently except for cases such as 'uninflectable particles' (Sadock 1991: 27).

an actual or even desirable property of natural language or any other biological system, since overlap and redundancy may well be an adaptive, necessary feature of the system.

Sadock notes that 'semantically empty lexemes tend not to be morphological stems' (Sadock 1991: 38). This is confirmed by the Chinese data in that, as we saw in 3.4, only root words and bound roots (and not word-forming affixes and grammatical affixes) may serve as stems. However, to propose that monomorphemic words bear a phonologically null singular affix (Sadock 1991: 31 n. 5) is problematic as a universal principle, since it implies that monomorphemic words universally are redundantly stems with a null phonological affix – a questionable assumption, especially when languages with little inflection such as English or Chinese are taken into account.

5.3.3 Other proposals

5.3.3.1 Scalise

Scalise (1984: 186–91), in briefly summarizing Selkirk's X-bar morphology system, offers some suggestions for how that theory might be improved. Scalise notes the fact that the usual X-bar (syntax) condition whereby a category symbol rewrites as an expression that includes itself at one bar level lower, as seen in (61) (repeated here as (83)):

(83) $X^n \rightarrow \ldots X^{n-1} \ldots$

is violated by all of Selkirk's rules (since, as we have noted, Selkirk says that the failure of X-bar morphology rules to take this form is, by hypothesis, one of the critical differences distinguishing the morphological and syntactic generative systems), and suggests instead the levels analysis seen in (84), that would yield the rules in (85) which would preserve the X-bar condition.

(84) Level 1   morphologically complex words
     Level 0   simple words
     Level −1   affixes

(85) $X^1 \rightarrow Y^0 X^{-1}$ (suffixation)
     $X^1 \rightarrow X^{-1} Y^0$ (prefixation)

In preserving the X-bar condition, level 1 morphological categories would be analogous with level 1 syntactic categories because they have a complex internal structure, as in Sadock's proposal. One problem with this approach is that formally it does not actually comply with the condition in (83) because, as seen in (85), X^n (X^1) is in fact not expanded as X^{n-1} (i.e., X^0). Also, on this proposal the morphological term X^1 would be non-distinct from the term X^1 used to designate phrases in syntax.

5.3.3.2 Di Sciullo and Williams

Di Sciullo and Williams (1987) do not actually offer an X-bar theory per se of morphology, but they do broach the subject by saying that words have heads, that suffixes are the heads of words, and belong to the categories N, V and A. Further, they see words ('syntactic atoms') as X^0, and also give the structure of affixation as in (86): affixes being non-distinct from stems except for the fact that they must be bound.

(86)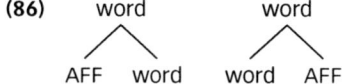

So it seems Di Sciullo and Williams posit at least two categories: that of word and that of stem/affix. Suffixes themselves are heads of words and belong to the categories N, V and A, but are bound and thus cannot surface independent of the stems to which they attach (1987: 25).

However, Di Sciullo and Williams make no commitment to bar-level analysis of any morphological elements 'below' the X^0 level (i.e., in the case of affixation of bound morphemes to form words), and explicitly deny that bar-decrement plays a role in determining the head of a word, as it does, for example, in X-bar syntax.

5.3.4 Discussion of Selkirk and Sadock

The X-bar morphology proposals of Selkirk and Sadock share a commitment to the idea that the morphology and syntax are independent modules, but that the two components nonetheless do have several important properties in common. First, as with syntax, the predictable parts of word formation take the form of rules that represent general knowledge possessed by speakers, rather than being part of the idiosyncratic knowledge associated with individual words or morphemes. Second, these rules are generative – larger structures are derived by combining smaller elements – and recursive, i.e., they build entities that themselves are the building blocks of larger entities. Third, both syntactic and morphological rules allow recursion, but in morphology the recursion is more limited: syntactic rewrite rules allow categories to expand into expressions containing categories of a 'higher' X-bar level, while in morphological rules the expansion contains only equivalent or lower bar levels. Fourth, in both components the primitives are cast in terms of form class identity. Finally, it is just these properties of word formation that allow speakers to create and understand new words, much as rules of syntax allow speakers to create and understand novel sentences.

The Selkirk and Sadock systems share two additional, more specific, properties that have broad implications. The first is that all monomorphemic words are redundantly members of the next 'lower' category in the respective systems: X^{-1} words are redundantly X^{-0} stems in the Sadock system (Sadock 1991: 31 n. 5), and X^{-0} words are redundantly X^{-1} roots in the Selkirk system (1982: 98). Both investigators hold to this property apparently because they assume that the default case in natural language is for words to be inflected, and that a full (monomorphemic) word is a complex concatenation of at least two elements. Anticipating the analysis of Chinese in the sections to follow, it is not at all clear that this should remain a default assumption.

The second property their systems share is that they posit only one intermediate category between full words and affixes, i.e., the traditional distinction between 'root' and 'stem' is collapsed into a single category in both systems ('root' for Selkirk and 'stem' for Sadock). In more abstract terms, both investigators posit the existence of only two bar levels 'below' the level of the complete word.[8] Selkirk and Sadock both assume that the reduced number of morphological system

---

[8] Note that these two properties of monomorphemic words being redundantly members of the next 'lower' category and the collapsing of the categories 'root' and 'stem' contradict rather than entail one another: something is more likely to be redundantly a member of multiple categories if there are more, not fewer, categories in the system. In other words, the existence of redundancy is a reason to posit separate categories, because redundancy is predictable and therefore parcellable into individual primitives. Therefore the redundancy, arguably undesirable in and of itself, seems doubly infelicitous given the reduced number of system categories.

primitives is adequate to account for the range of morphological structures they present for analysis. Sadock states that he 'knows of no compelling evidence that exactly this difference [between root and stem] is relevant to the operation of morphological rules' (Sadock 1991: 28). Selkirk reports (1982: 50–1, 126 n. 8) that she had posited the existence of two intermediate levels (X^{-1} 'stem' to account for English native compounding and X^{-2} 'root' to account for other intermediate morphological phenomena) in earlier work, but in her 1982 work she concludes that 'there is no basis for the category type (inflectional) Stem in English' (p. 57). As I will argue below, there are good reasons why a morphological system of this type should have an intermediate category posited between 'root' and 'affix'.

Aside from these similarities, the systems of Selkirk and Sadock differ in interesting ways, with the major difference being their convention for assigning X-bar superscript ('bar level') numeration. In Selkirk's system, words are designated X^{-0}, the next lower category is designated X^{-1} and the lowest category (affix) is designated X^a. So, in the Selkirk system, an (absolute value) increase in bar level means less structural complexity. Selkirk sees any element capable of occupying a lexical slot as a traditional X^{-0} element, with all words – regardless of their complexity – simply being X^{-0} that may be composed of other elements. In Sadock's system, the number values go in the opposite direction: the more complex a morphological structure is, the greater its (absolute) bar value. This is seen in the X-bar values of stems (X^{-0}), words (X^{-1}) and 'superwords' (X^{-2}, e.g., cliticized elements; Sadock 1988: 274). So in Sadock's system, an increase in bar level means greater structural complexity, parallel to the situation in X-bar syntax.

If these differences in numbering were merely notational variants, then the difference would be trivial and have few consequences for the systems. This might appear to be the case at first glance, since in both systems, regardless of bar level values, items 'below' the level of word possess less structure, are less complex and require 'more morphology' to become words. However, the different numbering systems do represent substantive differences, for two reasons.

First, Sadock's system, and not Selkirk's, allows for a natural representation of cliticized forms (X^{-2}) as elements that possess a more complex morphological structure than stems or words. Second, in both systems it is claimed that X^{-0} represents the lexical item or *word* as it does in syntax (Selkirk 1982: 7; Sadock 1991: 27), but Sadock's system ends up adhering to that claim largely in name only, since in his system most 'full words' as they appear in syntactic slots are actually designated X^{-1}, assuming that all words appear on the surface with affixes, even though the affixes may be phonologically null (Sadock 1991: 31 n. 5). This is actually similar to Selkirk's claim that all X^{-0} words are redundantly X^{-1} roots (1982: 98), but the 'direction' of Selkirk's numbering allows her to maintain that in all cases it is X^{-0} morphological units that occur in X^0 syntactic slots.

In essence, the difference between the two numbering conventions is that the Selkirk system more completely embodies the claim that a syntactic primitive is equivalent to a morphologically complete word, in that (absolute value) increases in bar level represent a sort of 'distance' from complete X^{-0} wordhood, and that movement away from the X^{-0} level makes an entity increasingly less 'structurally able' to occupy a syntactic X^0 slot. In the Sadock system, a morphologically complete word does not constitute input to the syntactic component restricted to the X^0 level, but rather constitutes an item to be associated with potentially different syntactic levels. In the Selkirk system, the lexical and syntactic components are separate, but unified in the sense that they constitute a 'continuum' at which X^0 is the 'point of convergence' (or 'interface'; Selkirk 1982: 2). The difference between the two systems therefore might be visualized as in figure 3.

I ultimately follow a version closer to Selkirk's system (albeit significantly adapted) for my analysis of Chinese presented in 5.3.5, because there seems no compelling reason to have any words – simple or complex – possess a designation different from X^{-0}. This is because all

Figure 3   Sadock and Selkirk systems compared

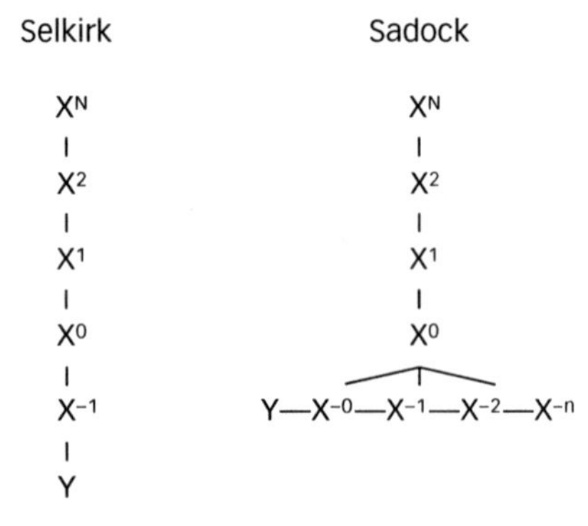

Selkirk:
$$X^N - X^2 - X^1 - X^0 - X^{-1} - Y$$

Sadock:
$$X^N - X^2 - X^1 - X^0$$
$$Y - X^{-0} - X^{-1} - X^{-2} - X^{-n}$$

words, no matter what their complexity, occupy X^0 slots in syntax by definition, and the added complexity of word structure proposed for Sadock's X^{-2} etc. elements has only the advantage of being able formally to represent cliticization as a morphological structure that has greater complexity than that of words. Also, the fact that full words are designated X^{-1} in the Sadock system may offer system-internal elegance from the standpoint of morphology, but does not allow for a smooth interface with syntax, since the syntax presumably would not 'recognize' X^{-1} elements as words.

5.3.4.1 Problems with the Selkirk proposal

My adopting the Selkirk system to account for the Chinese data, however, should not obscure the fact that her system also has several problems, many of which, although apparently specific to her treatment of English, will also be relevant in our analysis of Mandarin.

5.3.4.1.1 The limited role of X^{-1}

The Selkirk proposal fails to consider the fact that English bound roots (X^{-1}) may combine with words as well as with other bound roots to form words, as seen in the examples in table 19. In Selkirk's system, [X^{-1}, X^0] is not a possible expansion (as either a root or a word),

Table 19 Bound root combinations in English

bound root (X^{-1})	bound root + bound root ($X^{-1} + X^{-1}$)	bound root + word ($X^{-1} + X^0$)
bio-	biology	bioethics
inter-	interject	interbreed
micro-	microcosm	microchip
mono-	monologue	monorail
poly-	polygon	polysyllable
pseudo-	pseudonym	pseudoscience
retro-	retrogress	retrofit
sub-	subsume	subacute
tri-	trisect	triangle

making it impossible for the [bound root + word] word types in table 19 to be directly derived. Now, it is of course possible to define as 'roots' just those elements to which the bound roots in question attach, simply because they act as the 'base' for those bound roots. But this is a highly procedural, descriptive definition that does nothing to distinguish between X^{-0} and X^{-1} in formal terms. This was one of Selkirk's intents in proposing that roots are redundantly words ($X^{-0} \rightarrow X^{-1}$), because such a proposal would allow any word to serve as a root when it combines with another root. This proposal, however, fails to provide any substantive distinction between X^{-0} and X^{-1}. This lack of a distinction between words and roots thus incorrectly allows bound roots to be generated as words. To quote Selkirk (1982: 98), 'every monomorphemic non-affix is redundantly a root, and in principle it may also be a word'. This being the case, there is nothing in the system to prevent a bound root in principle from being generated as a free word.

Selkirk does propose a way to distinguish bound roots (e.g., *mono-*) from roots that are not bound (e.g., *sad*; Selkirk 1982: 98) by allowing the former to be assigned subcategorization frames (pp. 98–9). The problem with this is that saying 'bound roots' and 'roots' are of the same form (namely, X^{-1}) implies that these two classes of items have the same properties (excluding the idiosyncratic subcategorization information contained with them in the lexicon, at any rate), which is not the case. The two classes of items have distinctly different privileges of occurrence, with bound roots obviously never able independently to occupy form class slots in syntax. Furthermore, Selkirk's contention that 'the status of an item as a root does not imply that it is bound' (1982: 98) is problematic if it is necessary redundantly to mark roots as both roots and words. Roots have to be considered bound in her framework until they are 'generated' as words. Without such 'word' derivation, they are indeed, structurally, bound.

Selkirk rejects the possibility of *words* being formed by the process of affixation to roots (e.g., $X^0 \rightarrow X^{-1}, X^{AFF}$), in favour of *roots* being formed by affixation to roots (Selkirk 1982: 54 example 2.66; 71 example 3.14; 72 example 3.15; and 95 example 3.30). Selkirk takes this position not simply because she wants to avoid embedded affixes as seen in (87), which her system *does* allow (and which she accounts for; Selkirk 1982: 56–7), but because she believes it is not motivated by English (1982: 95).

(87)

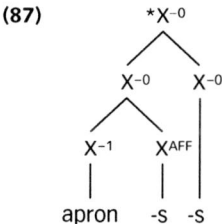

But, as we shall see below, rules such as $X^0 \rightarrow X^{-1}$, X^{AFF} in fact account for a good portion of English word-formation data.

Selkirk's system strongly implies that Class II derivational affixes and inflectional affixes are more similar in kind than are Class I and Class II derivational affixes. This is because although all three are designated X^{AFF}, both Class II derivational affixes and inflectional affixes subcategorize for words (X^{-0}), while Class I derivational affixes subcategorize for roots (X^{-1}). This gives a somewhat elevated status to a distinction that occurs in English but is by no means universal (i.e., the distinction between Class I and II derivational affixation), while ignoring a distinction that has greater claims to universal status (derivational versus inflectional affixation).

To demonstrate, in Selkirk's system inflectional affixation is derived via the rules in (64) (corresponding to the tree in (68)), because inflection subcategorizes for a complete word. This means that the structure for inflectional affixation (as in the plural noun *aprons* example, repeated as (88); 1982: 54–5) clearly is non-distinct from the structure of *singer*, repeated as (89), with both differing from the Class I derivational affixation yielding *employee*, repeated as (90).

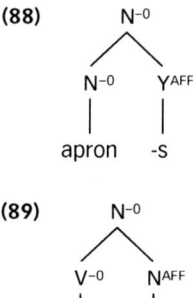

(90)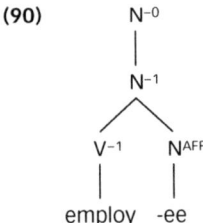

The only difference between inflection in (88) and Class II derivation in (89) is that inflectional affixes such as the -s found in *aprons* possess features like [+plural] number in their lexical entry, while derivational affixes such as the -er in *singer* possess syntactic category features like [+noun] in their lexical entry.

If the distinction between Class I and Class II derivational affixation appeared in the morphologies of many of the world's languages, then a formalism that so powerfully distinguishes the two might be considered a desideratum. But while there may well be no reason to formally distinguish inflection and derivation[9] in the universal scheme of things, we can be reasonably certain that inflection and derivation are 'more' different – either within English or when viewed cross-linguistically – than the Class I/Class II distinction. Intuitively, *aproner* 'one who sells aprons' or 'one who puts aprons on people' and *apronee* 'one who has been aproned' are more similar to each other than *aproner* and *aprons*.

In general, it may be said that the formally powerful distinction between X^{-0} and X^{-1} serves very limited functions in Selkirk's treatment of English. In essence, X^{-1} serves merely to distinguish Class I and Class II derivational affixation (along with inflection) and accounts for non-native compounding.

5.3.4.1.2 Lexical listing of predictable information

A different set of problems in the Selkirk system stems from the fact that it violates the familiar general principle that what is predictable and regular should not be listed in the lexicon (by subcategorization or otherwise), but rather should be incorporated into the rules or primitives of the system (as discussed on p. 143). Selkirk's system runs afoul of this principle by representing the following completely predictable

---

[9] I argue in Packard 1996 that inflection and derivation are in fact universally distinct, but at a level that abstracts away from, e.g., grammatical agreement properties.

aspects of English word formation as idiosyncratic information listed in the lexicon:

- Inflection always suffixes. Selkirk accounts for this fact by having the lexical entry for inflectional affix (X^{AFF}) contain subcategorization information about its position of affixation.
- Inflection always affixes to words, and never to roots or to other affixes. Selkirk accounts for this fact in the lexicon by having inflectional affixes subcategorize for words.
- Inflection always contains grammatical features like number, tense, person or gender. Selkirk accounts for this by having inflectional affixes specified for these as diacritical features in the lexicon.
- Inflectional and derivational affixes are always bound. Selkirk accounts for this fact by the stipulation that affixes 'always have a subcategorization frame' (Selkirk 1982: 64) in the lexicon.

Within Selkirk's system, the fact that X^{-1} serves limited functions, together with the lexical listing of predictable inflectional information, compellingly supports (a) the idea that bound roots (X^{-1}), since they are system primitives, should in general be given a greater share of system load and (b) the need for 'inflectional affix' to be represented by category of its own that possesses in non-idiosyncratic fashion all the predictable properties that were discussed above. Inflection having its own designated category means that there would be two affix-type elements: one to handle inflection with all its special properties and one to account for all other types of affixation.

We will deal with these issues in the system to be proposed in 5.4.

5.3.5 Previous X-bar analyses of Chinese words

Now that we have considered other X-bar approaches to word formation, let us consider X-bar theory as it has been applied to word formation in Chinese. X-bar theory has certainly been applied to Chinese syntax, and is in fact presently the dominant research paradigm in the field. But how does X-bar theory apply to Chinese words?

It has been argued that the same X-bar principles that account for Chinese native speakers' knowledge of syntax also account for their knowledge of words. At first blush, this is a very attractive argument, because a superficial glance at Chinese words and their structure certainly gives the impression that they are constructed using principles that derive from syntax (see 3.1.1.4). However, there are many reasons to believe that they are not one and the same, and that Chinese native speaker knowledge of words and their structure is based on a different set of assumptions and a different underlying data base than that used for the computation and use of syntactic structures. Let us consider, then, the proposal that Chinese syntax and Chinese word formation are, at some level of abstraction, based upon the same underlying principles.

5.3.5.1 Tang

Ting-chi Charles Tang (1993, 1995) offers the most complete theory supporting the notion that syntactic rules and principles extend to the domain of morphology in Chinese, and that therefore Chinese words and syntactic structures are generated using the same set of principles. Tang says 'sentence-syntactic rules and principles extend to apply in the domain of word-syntax . . . in all unmarked cases' (1995: 195), and that 'word-syntax and sentence-syntax are in fact one and the same, since most of the seeming discrepancies between the two can be adequately accounted for by independently motivated principles and parameters of universal grammar' (1995: 196).

The essence of Tang's system is that all word components are identified as stems, or 'X. These stems then serve as the components of words generated using two rules: the Compounding Rule in (91) and the Stem Rule in (92).

(91) 'Compounding Rule'
X → 'X, 'X

(92) 'Stem Rule' (recursive)
'X → 'X, 'X

In prose, the Compounding Rule says that a word can be composed of two stems, and the Stem Rule says that a stem can be composed of two stems. In this system, all word components are uniformly treated as 'X, with no distinction between the properties free and bound,[10] or between affixal and non-affixal elements. This means that there is no formal distinction in the lexicon among such potential word-forming elements as words, stems, roots or affixes.

---

[10] In some of the structure-specific rules given by Tang, word components are specified for the property free or bound (Tang 1995: 199–200). The reference to free and bound however is not a property of the system in general.

Let us take a brief look at how the rules work. Structures for the verb *chūfā* 出发 exit-emit 'to set off' (Tang 1993) and the noun *tiělù* 铁路 iron-road 'railroad' (Tang 1995: 211) are given in (93), and the structure for the noun *yángpízhǐ* 羊皮纸 sheep-skin-paper 'parchment' is given in (94).[11] The structures in (93) are generated using the Compounding Rule in (91), and the structure in (94) is generated using that Compounding Rule and also the Stem Rule in (92).

(93) noun and verb word structures (Tang 1993, 1995: 211)

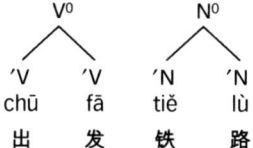

(94) word structure containing a complex stem (Tang 1995: 211)

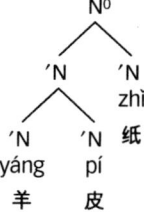

As can be seen from the tree structures, *chūfā* 'to set off' and *tiělù* 'railroad' are each words composed of two simple stems, in accordance with the Compounding Rule. In (94), the word *yángpízhǐ* 'parchment' is also a word composed of two stems: the complex stem *yángpí* 'sheepskin' (formed by the Stem Rule in (92)) and the simple stem *zhǐ* 'paper'.

If left there, the Compounding Rule in (91) would allow any pair of 'X elements ('X₁, 'X₂) to be generated as a word, and the system would overgenerate, predicting the existence of forms that do not appear. But Tang (following Selkirk; see p. 158 and n. 4) provides a comprehensive listing, seen in (95) in simplified form,[12] that delineates the

---

[11] I have taken the liberty of representing the 'word' dominating nodes that Tang represents using V and N as V⁰ and N⁰ respectively.

[12] For ease of reference, the list I provide in (95) is a reduced and simplified representation of Tang's data. Tang's listing includes many more structures, since he distinguishes the free and bound status of some constituents, verb transitivity, and the presence of form class shift within some structures. Also, I have not represented distinctions that exist in the relation between word constituents, e.g., 'coordinative' and 'verb–complement' verb 'compounds', which Tang represents as two different ['X'Y]ᵥ structures.

subset of word types generated from the Compounding Rule that actually appear in Mandarin (A = Adjective; Ad = Adverb).

(95) noun → ['A 'N]ₙ   verb → ['V 'N]ᵥ
            ['V 'N]ₙ   ['V 'V]ᵥ
            ['N 'N]ₙ   ['A 'V]ᵥ
            ['A 'V]ₙ   ['N 'V]ᵥ
            ['V 'N]ₙ   ['Ad 'V]ᵥ
            ['Ad 'V]ₙ   ['N 'A]ᵥ
            ['A 'A]ₙ
            ['Nu 'N]ₙ
            ['M 'N]ₙ
            ['Ad 'N]ₙ
            ['D 'N]ₙ
            ['Cj 'N]ₙ

Tang's system can account for the structures of all bisyllabic Mandarin words by the rules in (91) and (92) and the stem primitives corresponding to 'X (crucially including the subset of allowable word types given in (95)). This provides a 'strong generative capacity', whereby the system gives any extant form its correct structural description, as well as a 'weak generative capacity', whereby the system is able to generate all existent forms (see Selkirk 1982: 67).

The system also accounts for properties of words that involve their status as 'syntactic islands'. This is because all word components are defined as 'X, and the structural requirements for the properties in question are not met by the element 'X. As an example, the well-known properties of word components that they cannot be extracted or serve as antecedents or anaphors, are explained in Tang's proposal by the simple stipulation that movement and referentiality are properties of X⁰ and X¹, and not properties of 'X (Tang 1995: 230–1, 241–2).

However well Tang's system accounts for the structures and island properties of Mandarin words, it suffers from two major problems. The first is failure to account adequately for bound, affix-type word-forming elements like *-tou* 头, *-zi* 子, *-huà* 化, *-zhě* 者, *-xìng* 性, *-le* 了 and *-men* 们. Tang in essence considers these elements to be in the same category as other stems or words, thus leaving the door open for the generation of structures in which, for example, a bisyllabic word may be composed of just *-zi* and *-tou*, or in which *-men* and *-zhě* occur as the left-hand constituents of a word, or in which *-huà* and *-xìng* occur within a morphological structure as recursive nodes.

Tang does defend himself on this point, reasoning that because there exists a certain amount of indeterminacy with respect to the notions bound and free, and affix and stem – indeterminacy that seems magnified by the presence of sociolinguistic and literary–non-literary variation – bound, affix-type elements are therefore not worth considering as part of the generative word-forming system. Tang says that the 'lack of a clear dividing line between free and bound morphemes, or that between compounding and affixation, does not seem to have any significant bearing on investigating and determining the form, structure and function of "possible words" in Chinese' (1995: 198). As a result, Tang subsumes all complex words under compound words for purposes of word formation. The effect of this is essentially to collapse all Chinese affix-type morphemes into the 'higher' category type *word*, merely because there appears to exist variability on some of the cases.

First of all, a framework has been provided to identify affixal elements in 3.4 and 5.3.5. But the existence of that framework notwithstanding, indeterminacy is natural in language at every turn and with all types of linguistic data. The presence of apparent indeterminacy at certain points in the system does not mean that the indeterminacy exists at a given time for a given structure in the mind or linguistic system of a given native speaker, and is not a good reason in and of itself for failing to apply an analytical framework. The structural or linguistic identity posited does not have to be an all-or-none identity for all instances of a form or structure at all times. In fact, most cases are determinate – but even for apparently indeterminate cases, all there needs to be is a fixed identity for a given form or structure at any given moment in the mind or linguistic system of a given native speaker (see more arguments to this effect in 4.3.4.3.2.1).

The second problem with the Tang proposal is that there is nothing in the system that distinguishes the different types of stem, viz., stems that are words versus stems that are not words. To demonstrate, in (93) the word *chūfā* 'to set off' is composed from the stems *chū* 'exit' and *fā* 'emit', each of which are also free words (X^0). Likewise, the other words in (93) and (94) are all composed from stems that are also free words. These stems (*chū* 'exit', *fā* 'emit', *tiě* 'iron', *lù* 'road', *yáng* 'sheep', *pí* 'skin' and *zhǐ* 'paper') must be identified as X^0 words in the lexicon, to allow them to be selected as words for use in normal syntactic slots. But they also must be identified in the lexicon as stems in this system, because otherwise they cannot be selected as components to form words such as those in (93) and (94) (this must be done because Tang's rules only allow words to be composed of stems, and not of words). Contrast this with the word *ěrkǒng* 'earhole' shown in (96), in which the component morphemes -*ěr*- 耳 'ear' and -*kǒng*- 孔 'hole' are bound and therefore not able to serve as free words.

(96) complex noun word structure (bound morphemes; Tang 1995: 200)[13]

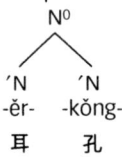

The point is that even though the word *ěrkǒng* is composed of bound morphemes, it is, like *tiělù*, generated via the Compounding Rule in (91). There is in principle no difference in the structure or the node labeling between *tiělù* 'road' in (94) and *ěrkǒng* in (96), because all word component morphemes, whether they are free or bound, are equivalently designated as 'X, and therefore any morpheme, in principle, can occupy an 'X slot. What this means is that the rules in (91) and (92) allow any word or stem in principle to be formed from any two words or stems (in other words, any two morphemes). This yields an extremely powerful system that will wildly overgenerate, creating a virtually unlimited number of forms neither whose structures nor whose specific instances are attested.[14] This point is partially addressed by Tang's inclusion of bound and free information for some of the structure types presented in (95), but since the generative system does allow the productive formation of words from both word stems and non-word stems (see Sproat and Shih 1996 on this point), that capability should be encoded in the rules of the grammar and not listed in the lexicon (see also n. 4).

In summary, Tang's proposal to generate word structure using the rules of syntax by adding two additional rules and then designating all word components as 'X stems does not adequately account for the structures of Mandarin words, because it does not distinguish between free and bound morphemes, allowing virtually any type of word to be generated, and also because it treats affixal elements in

---

[13] I have converted Tang's example from a bracketed structure to a tree structure.
[14] Note that the length of verbs is subject to a constraint limiting them to being composed of at most three morphemes (Tang 1995: 195).

Mandarin as equivalent – in word-formation terms – to all other non-affixal morphemes.

5.3.5.2 Sproat and Shih

Sproat and Shih (1996) do not provide a full X-bar analysis of Chinese words, but nonetheless refer to Chinese words and their formation using enough X-bar terminology and assumptions to be relevant to the present work. The main point of Sproat and Shih's article is that roots (my 'bound roots') combine productively to form complex words (my 'bound root words') in Mandarin. Sproat and Shih thus propose that the grammar of Mandarin word formation 'allows the morphological constructions' seen in (97), in which words are composed of both free words and roots.

(97) Structures of Mandarin root compounds (Sproat and Shih 1996: 50)
 $[N^{root} N^0]_{N^0}$ $[N^0 N^{root}]_{N^0}$ $[N^{root} N^{root}]_{N^0}$

The relevance of the Sproat and Shih article to the present work is twofold. First, Sproat and Shih posit that the Mandarin word-formation system clearly distinguishes the word formatives 'word' and 'root', and does not collapse them into a single category (e.g., 'stem') as does Tang (1993, 1995). Second, the view that roots in Mandarin combine productively to form complex words contrasts with that of Dai (1992: 59–63), who proposes that such words are listed in the lexicon rather than being part of a productive word-formation system (more on this in 7.4).

So although the Sproat and Shih system, because it is restricted to nominal elements, does not represent a complete exegesis of X-bar word formation in Chinese, certain X-bar properties might nonetheless be inferred from their analysis, given their description of nominal root compounds in X-bar terms (see also, for example, n. 8).

5.4 An alternative proposal for Chinese X-bar morphology

The following is a system of morphological analysis based on X-bar principles that is applied to Mandarin Chinese. The proposal in essence consists of assigning X-bar values to the Mandarin morpheme types identified in 3.4, and then combining these X-bar elements into words using word-formation rules that generate complex structures but are limited in their generating power.

My system follows Selkirk's in many respects, notably in having words possess the X-bar identity X^{-0}, and having roots be the 'next lower category' – X^{-1} – in preference to the system proposed by Sadock (see 5.3.2). This is because I agree that words are in some sense the 'interface' between syntax and morphology (Selkirk 1982: 2; Sadock 1991: 36–8), and there is no compelling reason, in my view, to have any words – simple or complex – possess a designation different from X^{-0}. According to this view, complexity of word structure is accounted for not by positing ever more 'bar levels' of X, but by the recursiveness of the rules that allow more complex words to be built up from simplex words or morphemes. Another way of stating this intuition is to say that the less able an element is to stand alone as a free word (i.e., the more 'operations' that must be performed on it or the more morphemes that must be added to it to enable it to stand as a word), the further 'below' X^{-0} (in a negative direction) its bar value will be.

There are, however, some important differences between Selkirk's system and the one I am proposing. Recall I argued in 5.3.4.1 that there were two major flaws in Selkirk's system: first, that roots (X^{-1}) in her system are restricted to functions that do not realize their potential power as system primitives, and second, that there is excessive lexical listing of predictable inflectional information. One important difference between my system and Selkirk's addresses the first problem by proposing that *all* X^{-1} roots are in fact bound, but that they nonetheless are highly active participants in a productive word-formation system. A second major difference addresses the second issue by proposing that there are two 'affix' primitives (versus the single one posited by Selkirk): one for inflection (my 'grammatical affixes') and one for all other kinds of affixation.

Finally, a major difference between the Selkirk system and the proposal offered here is that I propose to limit the generative power of the morphological system by placing universal restrictions on system embedding and recursion, by allowing only one system primitive (namely, X^{-0}) to have those properties. This important characteristic, I shall propose, accounts for a good share of the difference in productivity that exists between morphology and syntax (see 5.4.3).

Table 20 Classification of morphemes

morpheme properties	morpheme type	X-bar value
free, content	root word	X^{-0}
bound, content	bound root	X^{-1}
bound, function (apply selectively, may change form class, etc.; see 3.4.3.1)	word-forming affix	X^W
bound, function (apply broadly, do not change form class, etc.; see 3.4.3.1)	grammatical affix	G

5.4.1 Classification of primitives

The proposed X-bar system for Mandarin has four morphological primitives (X^{-0}, X^{-1}, X^W and G) that correspond to the four morpheme types *root word* (X^{-0}), *bound root* (X^{-1}), *word-forming affix* (X^W) and *grammatical affix* (G)[15] presented for Mandarin in 3.4.3. For word-forming affixes, the fact that the superscript is a letter and not a numeral indicates that these items can never function as word bases, that is, they can never be 'incremented' to the point where they can serve the traditional function of 'stem', i.e., serve as words or roots. For grammatical affixes, the fact that the category designation is 'G' and not 'X' indicates that these items can never function as the heads of words. This is because there are no words of the form *[X^{-0} G]$_G$; that is, there are no complex words that possess the characteristics of 'G' by virtue of the addition of a 'G' suffix. This is a way of formalizing the observation that grammatical affixes can never change the form class of a word to which they affix (see 3.4.3.1). These morpheme types and properties are summarized in table 20.

5.4.1.1 Properties of word components

The proposed X-bar system is posited to be valid for the form class categories noun and verb (limited to those categories for now, at any rate), and captures the following basic descriptive facts: root words may stand alone as free words, may act as stems (with 'stem' defined

---

[15] [+free, +function] function words are not discussed in this presentation.

Table 21 Word component properties

	X-bar designation	may stand alone	may be stems	may be heads
root words	X^{-0}	yes	yes	yes
bound roots	X^{-1}	no	yes	yes
word-forming affixes	X^W	no	no	yes
grammatical affixes	G	no	no	no

as something that may act as the 'base' of a word either independently, or with the inclusion of additional morphological material), and may serve as the heads of words. Bound roots are bound and thus may not stand alone, but they may be stems and may serve as the heads of words. Word-forming affixes are not able to stand alone or act as stems, but they may serve as the heads of words. Finally, grammatical affixes may do none of the above: they may not stand alone, may not be stems and may not serve as word heads. These facts are summarized in table 21.

5.4.1.2 Why list 'bound' and 'free' in the lexicon?

According to this theory, within the lexicon a morpheme will be specified as X^{-0}, X^{-1}, X^W or G, meaning lexical entries are specified as being bound or free and content or function. It may well be asked: why are the particular criteria bound/free and content/function taken here to be privileged, or 'primitive', in categorizing words and their components? In other words, in classifying morpheme and word types, what is it about the 'boundness' of a word's parts and their degree of 'content' that is relevant, in the final analysis, to the characterization of words, such that it should be information that is included as part of the lexical entry?

The most basic reason is that lexical entries operate within the system based upon their specification on this variable, and so this way of classifying lexical entries is directly relevant to their operation or function in the grammar. To give an example, the distinction between 'compound word' and 'bound root word' offered here is salient in the Chinese word data, and may well be a universal characterization of word structure that has been overlooked because it has not been generally recognized in other languages, such as English. Thus, 'compound words' in English may be broken down into 'compounds' and 'bound root words', as suggested by the Chinese data. The compound–bound root word distinction may in turn explain the difference between those words that must recycle back into the lexicon for phonological operations (compounds) and those that do not need to (bound root words). By this analysis, bound root words would be composed before they leave the lexicon (before the last level and before phonological operations), while true compounds, since they are composed of free words, if they are to undergo phonological operations that are germane to their status as compounds, must exit the lexicon and recycle back in order to undergo those phonological operations (see, e.g., Mohanan 1986). To take another example, it may explain differences in behaviour of the so-called 'Latinate prefixes', most of which (e.g., *anti-* *-itis*, *-osis*, *-ectomy*, etc.) may be classified as bound roots (see 5.6).

There is a theory-internal rationale as well, which is that the morphological categorization system proposed earlier (3.4.3) depends upon whether the components in question are or are not independent entities in syntax, and thus have already been defined with respect to the property bound–free following the criteria set up earlier in the theoretical framework.

But probably the most compelling reason to include such information as part of the lexical entry is that the value of a lexical entry on those variables serves to restrict the recursive properties of lexical items in a principled way. The relatively low productivity of word formation as opposed to syntactic structures is posited to be because those components of words that are not words themselves – namely X^{-1}, X^W and G – do not permit the recursive generation of structure, as we shall see in 5.4.3. It is virtually a truism in the science of linguistics that one of the properties that most clearly distinguishes word formation from syntax is that the former is much more restricted in its generative capacity. A morphological system that naturally accounts for this restricted generative capacity based upon the properties of its system primitives is the preferred system, *ceteris paribus*.

5.4.2 Rules of word formation

Given the four primitive morphological elements X^{-0}, X^{-1}, X^W and G, the possible forms of words in Mandarin are captured by the two rules in (98).

(98) Rule 1 $X^{-0} \rightarrow X^{-0,-1,\{W\}}, X^{-0,-1,\{W\}}$
      Rule 2 $X^{-0} \rightarrow X^{-0}, G$

In prose, Rule 1 in (98) means that, irrespective of form class (at least for the form classes noun and verb for now, at any rate), a word may be composed of any combination of bound and free morphemes, with the curly brackets around the W superscript intended to represent the fact that only one X^W element may be selected, or in other words, that X^W may only attach to a root word or a bound root, and may not attach to another X^W. Rule 2 means that a word may also be composed by attaching a grammatical affix to the right of a bona fide word. Note that both rules in (98) conform to Selkirk's schemata in (63) which prohibit the right-hand member of an expansion from having a variable with an X-bar value greater than the symbol on the left.

5.4.3 Limiting lexical productivity: X^{-0} as the sole recursive node

Crucially, note that in the rules presented in (98), X^{-0} is the only term allowed on the left of the expansion symbol ($\rightarrow$), indicating that it is the only morphological system primitive that is allowed to expand. In addition, among the other terms that X^{-0} is allowed to expand into (X^{-1}, X^W, G), it is also allowed to expand into a string that includes itself. This means that X^{-0} is the only term in the system that enables recursion. So the word-formation system proposed here does allow recursion (along with the productivity that it implies), but that recursion is strictly limited (compared, e.g., to the recursion allowed in generated syntactic structures) because, unlike in syntax, there is only one term in the system that allows it. This means that, as we shall see in 5.4.5, a word structure may be a simple structure that has only one level of branching, but it may also show successive branchings – i.e., embedding – so long as the branching term is X^{-0}.

The result of this stipulation is that the word-formation system is limited in its productivity by a property that is imputed to the nature of the formal system primitives. Recall that Selkirk suggested that the limited productivity of word-formation systems may be accounted for by the fact that the expansion of a given term (X^N) may not include a term with an X-bar (absolute) value greater than that of the given term (e.g., $X^N \rightarrow X^{N+1}$; see (63), p. 137). The present proposal conforms to that stipulation (as seen by comparing (63) and (98)), but further restricts it in a natural way by allowing only one system primitive (notably, the *word*, X^{-0}) to generate a structure that includes itself.

5.4.3.1 A note on universals

Since the rule schema given by Selkirk in (63) is proposed as a word-formation universal, and given that the two rules in (98) conform to that schema in (63), we may presume that the rules in (98) are a characterization of Mandarin word structure that is directly based on universal principles. That is, Rule 1 in (98) states in very simple but quite exhaustive terms the very broad and powerful generalization that any two constituents (except G) may occur in either of two word positions,[16] with Rule 2 restricting only the derivation and linear position of grammatical affixes (G). This universal information includes the stipulation that only X^{-0} is allowed to be a branching node.

Even with the system so constrained by universal mechanisms, the schema in (98) is still too powerful in that it generates word forms that do not occur in Mandarin (see table 23). Mandarin thus possesses language-specific information that further constrains the forms of its words. This language-specific information – I shall propose – is precisely the Mandarin Headedness Principle given in (24). The Headedness Principle, it is clear, has nothing of a universal character, but rather derives from structural information specific to Mandarin (in this case, derived from headedness conventions in Mandarin syntax). The point is that in addition to the limitations on the form of word structure provided by universal information such as that in (98), languages also utilize language-specific constraint information (in Mandarin, the Headedness Principle) that has the effect of further limiting its inventory of word structures.

[16] Also part of Rule 1 but not necessarily posited to be universal information is the stipulation that only one X^W element may be selected, or in other words, that X^W may not attach to another X^W. It may well be the case that other languages are not as restricted as Mandarin is on this parameter.

170   THE MORPHOLOGY OF CHINESE

Table 22   Possible Chinese word forms

	word form	made from	word type
$X^{-0} \rightarrow$	X^{-0}, X^{-0}	two words	compound word
	X^{-1}, X^{-1}	two bound roots	bound root word
	X^{-0}, X^{-1}	word + bound root	bound root word
	X^{-1}, X^{-0}	bound root + word	bound root word
	X^{-0}, X^{W}	word + word-forming affix	derived word
	X^{-1}, X^{W}	bound root + word-forming affix	derived word
	X^{W}, X^{-0}	word-forming affix + word	derived word
	X^{W}, X^{-1}	word-forming affix + bound root	derived word
	X^{-0}, G	word + grammatical affix	grammatical word

5.4.4 Predicted word forms

If we freely substitute all possible values for the 'X' terms in the two rules in (98), we get the nine possible word forms seen in table 22. Substituting noun and verb values for the X and G terms in table 22 yields the theoretically predicted values for Mandarin words containing noun and verb elements in table 23. The values that actually occur in Mandarin, obtained from the data in 4.2.1 and 4.3.1, contain check marks in the columns labeled 'actually occur'.

The interesting observation to make regarding the data in table 23 is that with the sole exception of the missing cell for the predicted $[N^{W} V^{-1}]_N$ form, the predicted word types that have empty cells either violate the Headedness Principle – i.e., they are either verbs that have no verb on the left or nouns that have no noun on the right – or their absence is predicted by the reasonable assumptions that (a) the form class of the word-forming affix determines the form class of the word (i.e., there are no verbs formed with noun-forming N^{W} elements or nouns formed with verb-forming V^{W} elements) and (b) there are no instances of $[N^{0} G]$ verbs or $[V^{0} G]$ nouns.

The absence of $[N^{W} V^{-1}]_N$ examples is probably an 'accidental gap' (or, as I suspect, there are one or more of these floating around out

Table 23 Predicted and actual Mandarin word types

X-bar	predicted	actually occur nouns	verbs	X-bar	predicted	actually occur nouns	verbs
$X^{-0}X^{-0}$	$N^{-0}N^{-0}$	✔		$X^{-0}X^W$	$N^{-0}N^W$	✔	
	$V^{-0}V^{-0}$	✔	✔		$V^{-0}V^W$		✔
	$N^{-0}V^{-0}$	✔	✔		$N^{-0}V^W$		✔
	$V^{-0}N^{-0}$	✔	✔		$V^{-0}N^W$	✔	
$X^{-1}X^{-1}$	$N^{-1}N^{-1}$	✔	✔	$X^{-1}X^W$	$N^{-1}N^W$	✔	
	$V^{-1}V^{-1}$		✔		$V^{-1}V^W$		✔
	$N^{-1}V^{-1}$	✔	✔		$N^{-1}V^W$		✔
	$V^{-1}N^{-1}$	✔	✔		$V^{-1}N^W$	✔	
$X^{-0}X^{-1}$	$N^{-0}N^{-1}$	✔		$X^W X^{-0}$	$N^W N^{-0}$	✔	
	$V^{-0}V^{-1}$	✔	✔		$V^W V^{-0}$		✔
	$N^{-0}V^{-1}$	✔	✔		$N^W V^{-0}$	✔	
	$V^{-0}N^{-1}$	✔	✔		$V^W N^{-0}$		✔
$X^{-1}X^{-0}$	$N^{-1}N^{-0}$	✔		$X^W X^{-1}$	$N^W N^{-1}$	✔	
	$V^{-1}V^{-0}$	✔	✔		$V^W V^{-1}$		✔
	$N^{-1}V^{-0}$	✔	✔		$N^W V^{-1}$		
	$V^{-1}N^{-0}$	✔	✔		$V^W N^{-1}$		✔
				$X^{-0}G$	$V^{-0}G$		✔
					$N^{-0}G$	✔	

there somewhere), since there is nothing else that would predict its absence, given the otherwise relative completeness of the set of occurring forms. The fact that the rest of the missing items correspond to forms that are predicted by universal rule but fail to conform to the Headedness Principle indicates that the said principle has a significant degree of (albeit non-universal) power. That the principle is not an absolute prohibition, however, is seen in the existence of many forms in table 23 in violation of that principle, i.e., there are instances

Table 24 Noun word structures

nouns	examples	nouns	examples
$N^{-0} N^{-0}$	*mǎlù* 马路 horse-road 'street'	$V^{-1} V^{-0}$	*gòuzào* 构造 compose-create 'structure'
$V^{-0} V^{-0}$	*mǎimài* 买卖 buy-sell 'business'	$N^{-1} V^{-0}$	*bìguà* 壁挂 wall-hang 'wall hanging'
$N^{-0} V^{-0}$	*guōtiē* 锅贴 pot-stick 'fried dumpling'	$V^{-1} N^{-0}$	*chùjiǎo* 触角 touch-horn '(insect) antenna'
$V^{-0} N^{-0}$	*chuánpiào* 传票 send-slip 'subpoena'	$N^W N^{-0}$	*āgē* 阿哥 AFF-brother 'brother'
$N^{-1} N^{-1}$	*mùbǎn* 木板 wood-plank 'board'	$N^W V^{-0}$	*āhùn* 阿混 AFF-muddle 'muddle-head'
$N^{-1} V^{-1}$	*qiūjué* 秋决 autumn-decide 'autumn execution'	$N^W N^{-1}$	*āguó* 阿国 AFF-country 'state-run enterprise'
$N^{-0} N^{-1}$	*diànnǎo* 电脑 electric-brain 'computer'	$N^{-0} N^W$	*pízi* 皮子 skin-AFF 'skin'
$V^{-0} V^{-1}$	*xuéjiū* 学究 study-research 'pedant'	$V^{-0} N^W$	*piànzi* 骗子 deceive-AFF 'swindler'
$N^{-0} V^{-1}$	*jiézòu* 节奏 section-play 'rhythm'	$N^{-1} N^W$	*fángzi* 房子 house-AFF 'house'
$V^{-0} N^{-1}$	*dǔjù* 赌具 gamble-utensil 'gambling equipment'	$V^{-1} N^W$	*niàntou* 念头 think-AFF 'idea'
$N^{-1} N^{-0}$	*xiàngpí* 橡皮 rubber-skin 'rubber'	$N^{-0} G$	*wǒmen* 我们 I-AFF 'we'

of nouns without a noun on the right, and verbs without a verb on the left. Examples of the noun and verb structures that actually occur in Mandarin (corresponding to the checked boxes in table 23) are seen in table 24 and table 25 respectively.

It is proposed that this framework generates all permissible complex noun and verb word structures in Mandarin, while ruling out the impermissible structures. The following is a demonstration of the power of the rules in (98), and of how they are implemented to form Chinese words in general terms, abstracting over the form classes noun and verb.

Table 25 Verb word structures

verbs	examples	verbs	examples
$V^{-0}\,V^{-0}$	jièyòng 借用 borrow-use 'borrow'	$N^{-1}\,V^{-0}$	wǔdòu 武斗 weapon-struggle 'resort to violence'
$N^{-0}\,V^{-0}$	guāfēn 瓜分 melon-divide 'partition'	$V^{-1}\,N^{-0}$	gémìng 革命 remove-mandate 'carry out revolution'
$V^{-0}\,N^{-0}$	nàoguǐ 闹鬼 make:noise-ghost 'haunt'	$V^{-0}\,V^{w}$	kāihuà 开化 open-AFF 'civilize'
$N^{-1}\,N^{-1}$	wùsè 物色 thing-colour 'hunt for'	$N^{-0}\,V^{w}$	dúhuà 毒化 poison-AFF 'poison'
$V^{-1}\,V^{-1}$	tǎolùn 讨论 discuss-discuss 'discuss'	$V^{-1}\,V^{w}$	guīhuà 归化 return-AFF 'naturalize'
$N^{-1}\,V^{-1}$	bùxíng 步行 footstep-go 'go on foot'	$N^{-1}\,V^{w}$	gānghuà 钢化 steel-AFF 'temper'
$V^{-1}\,N^{-1}$	bìyè 毕业 end-profession 'graduate'	$V^{w}\,V^{-0}$	fùfā 复发 AFF-occur 'relapse'
$V^{-0}\,V^{-1}$	bāngzhù 帮助 help-help 'help'	$V^{w}\,N^{-0}$	kějiǎo 可脚 AFF-foot 'fit one's feet'
$N^{-0}\,V^{-1}$	qiāngbì 枪毙 gun-kill 'execute by gunfire'	$V^{w}\,V^{-1}$	wúshì 无视 AFF-see 'disregard'
$V^{-0}\,N^{-1}$	chūbǎn 出版 emit-edition 'publish'	$V^{w}\,N^{-1}$	kětǐ 可体 AFF-body 'fit'
$V^{-1}\,V^{-0}$	gòumǎi 购买 buy-buy 'buy'	$V^{-0}\,G$	zǒule 走了 go-AFF 'went'

5.4.5 Single and multiple branching structures

The following subsections give examples of all the types of X-bar structures generated by the rules in (98), without respect to specific form class. I will first show simple, single-level binary branching structures, and then embedding – i.e., multi-level binary branching structures – generated by the same rules.

The primitives of the system are words (X^{-0}), bound roots (X^{-1}), word-forming affixes (X^{W}) and grammatical affixes (G), as discussed above. Word primitives of course are not listed, since the set in principle includes any free word. Bound roots are also not listed since this set

Table 26 Mandarin word-forming affixes

prefix	gloss	suffix	gloss
dì- (第)	'ordinalizer'	-dù (度)	'degree'
fēi- (非)	'not'	-huà (化)	'-ize/-ify'
fù- (复)	'again'	-ér (儿)	'nominalizer'
kě- (可)	'may'	-rán (然)	'as'
wú- (无)	'without'	-tou (头)	'nominalizer'
wèi- (未)	'not yet'	-xìng (性)	'nature'
zài- (再)	'again'	-zhě (者)	'one who'
		-zi (子)	'nominalizer'

is also virtually open in Mandarin (the criteria for bound roots are discussed in 3.4.3; especially 3.4.3.1). A selection of Mandarin word-forming affixes (X^w) is seen in table 26 (see criteria in 3.4.3.1). There are notoriously few grammatical affixes in Mandarin, and they include the human plural marker -*men* (们), the verbal aspect markers -*le* (了), -*zhe* (著) and -*guo* (过) and the resultative potential markers -*bu*- (不) and -*de*- (得).

There are several things to note regarding the forms presented below. First, only X^{-0} may expand, which is the formal mechanism primarily responsible for restricting the productivity of the morphological component, as discussed in 5.4.3. Second, we abstract over all form class values of X. In other words, while the structures below are depicted with the correct bar value of X, no attempt has been made to list exhaustively all possible form class values of X. Such a proposal would naturally contain even more gaps than will be seen below, predicting forms that do not occur. In view of this, I would propose ultimately constraining the system as Selkirk does (1982: 15–18): by listing the subset of category names that actually instantiate rules referring to specific occurrences of form classes within a given language. Third, in some cases I could find no examples for the multiple branching structures, in which case I wrote 'not observed'. Finally, many forms that are listed as having the form X^{-0} when they occur internal to a larger word (such as *hūnshēng*- in (129) and many other examples) do not actually occur as free X^{-0} forms. The natural implication is that

X-BAR ANALYSIS OF CHINESE WORDS 175

they are bound, i.e., X⁻¹, and that this presents a problem since X⁻¹ forms are not supposed to branch. My analysis suggests that these are *morphological words* (see discussion of *māotóuyīng* 猫头鹰 cat-head-hawk 'owl' in 2.1.6), and that their use and acceptability as potential free words is predicted.[17]

Structures that show how the generalized X-bar rules in table 22 form Chinese words are seen in (99)–(175). In 5.4.5.1 we see single-branching structures ((99)–(107)), and in 5.4.5.2 we see structures in which one more level of branching occurs, from either the right ((108)–(34)) or the left ((135)–(70)). That is, for the sake of simplicity I do not give exhaustive examples of embedded structures that branch from both the right and left.

5.4.5.1 Single branching

Single-branching structures are simply all possible instantiations of the rules in (98), i.e., all possible binary combinations of X⁻⁰, X⁻¹ and Xᵂ, in addition to X⁻⁰ plus G.

(99)

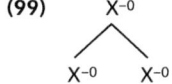

măxióng 马熊 horse-bear 'brown bear', *bīngshān* 冰山 ice-mountain 'iceberg', *jièyòng* 借用 borrow-use 'borrow'

(100)

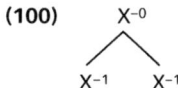

mùbăn 木板 wood-plank 'board', *dànjiā* 弹夹 bullet-clip 'bullet clip', *quánlì* 权力 authority-power 'authority', *biànbié* 辨别 distinguish-differentiate 'differentiate', *biànlùn* 辩论 debate-discuss 'debate', *tăolùn* 讨论 discuss-discuss 'discuss', *wŭjīn* 五金 five-metal 'hardware', *yóumín* 游民 travel-person 'vagrant'

(101)

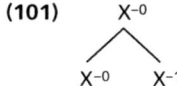

---

[17] My thanks to Derek Herforth for helpful discussion of this issue.

diànnǎo 电脑 electricity-brain 'computer', *chēhuò* 车祸 vehicle-misfortune '(vehicle) accident', *jiéshù* 结束 conclude-bind 'conclude', *bāngzhù* 帮助 help-help 'help', *sǐwáng* 死亡 die-die 'die', *yǒujī* 有机 have-organic 'organic', *yǒumíng* 有名 have-name 'famous', *yǒuxiào* 有效 have-effect 'valid, effective'

(102)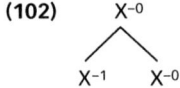

zúqiú 足球 foot-ball 'soccer', *xiàngpí* 橡皮 rubber-skin 'rubber'; *xiǎngshòu* 享受 enjoy-accept 'enjoy', *xiǎngyǒu* 享有 enjoy-possess 'enjoy', *jiéshěng* 节省 save-save 'save', *wēibō* 微波 tiny-wave 'microwave'

(103)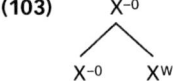

pízi 皮子 skin-AFF 'skin', *rénxìng* 人性 person-AFF 'reason', *diàotou* 调头 *diàozi* 调子 tune-AFF 'tune', *kòuzi* 扣子 button-AFF 'button', *piànzi* 骗子 deceive-AFF 'swindler', *tànzi* 探子 seek-AFF 'a probe', *tiāozi* 挑子 carry-AFF 'load', *xiǎngtou* 想头 think-AFF 'idea', *hónghuà* 红化 red-AFF 'to redden', *gōngtour* 工头 work-AFF 'labourer', *tiānrán* 天然 sky-AFF 'natural', *yóurán* 油然 oil-AFF 'spontaneous'

(104)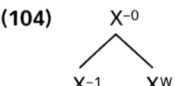

fángzi 房子 house-AFF 'house', *bízi* 鼻子 nose-AFF 'nose', *mùtou* 木头 wood-AFF 'wood', *zhítou* 指头 finger-AFF 'finger', *huànzhě* 患者 suffer-AFF 'patient', *zàohuà* 皂化 soap-AFF 'saponify', *mùrán* 木然 wood-AFF 'stupefy', *guànxìng* 惯性 get:used:to-AFF 'inertia'

(105)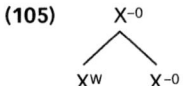

fùchá 复查 AFF-investigate 'reinvestigate', *fùhuó* 复活 AFF-live 'to come back to life', *fùshěn* 复审 AFF-investigate 'reinvestigate', *zàijiàoyù*[18] 再教育 AFF-education 're-educate', *fùfā* 复发 AFF-occur 'to relapse', *kěxiào* 可笑 AFF-laugh 'funny', *fùxīng* 复兴 AFF-begin 'revive', *fùchū* 复出 AFF-exit 'reappear', *wúrén* 无人 AFF-person 'unmanned', *wúxìng* 无性 AFF-sex 'asexual', *wèifā* 未发 AFF-issue 'unissued'

(106)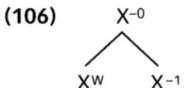

fēifǎ 非法 AFF-law 'illegal', *fùxí* 复习 AFF-study 'study, review', *fùxiàn* 复现 AFF-appear 'to reappear', *wújī* 无机 AFF-organic 'inorganic', *wúmíng* 无名 AFF-name 'nameless', *wúshēng* 无声 AFF-noise 'noiseless', *wúshù* 无数 AFF-numeral 'countless', *wúshì* 无视 AFF-see 'disregard', *kětǐ* 可体 AFF-body 'fit', *wúguī* 无规 AFF-rule 'random', *wúguǐ* 无轨 AFF-track 'trackless', *wèihūn* 未婚 AFF-marry 'unmarried', *wèijué* 未决 AFF-decide 'undecided', *kělián* 可怜 AFF-pity 'to pity'

(107)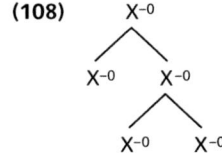

zǒule 走了 walk-AFF 'walked', *tāmen* 他们 he-AFF 'they', *jiànguo* 见过 see-AFF 'saw', *rénmen* 人们 person-AFF 'people'

5.4.5.2 Multiple branching

The multiple-branching word-formation structures of Mandarin shown here are all possible single binary expansions of the X^{-0} nodes that are generated by the structures in (99)–(107).

5.4.5.2.1 Right branching

(108)

---

[18] Zhang and Sang 1986: 390.

tiěfànwǎn 铁饭碗 iron-rice-bowl 'secure job', *suānzhòngdú* 酸中毒 acid-hit-poison 'acidosis'

(109)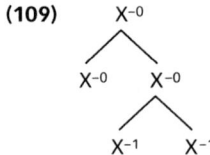

shǒuliúdàn 手榴弹 hand-pomegranate-bomb 'hand grenade',

(110)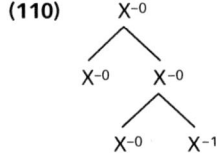

shǒudiàntǒng 手电筒 hand-electric-barrel 'flashlight'

(111)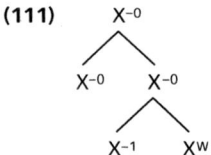

bìnggēnzi 病根子 sickness-root-AFF 'chronic disease'

(112)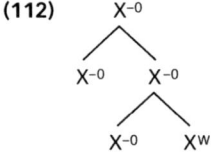

huìyóuzi 会油子 meeting-oil-AFF 'person who likes to have meetings', *diànchātou* 电插头 electricity-insert-AFF 'wire plug', *yóudiǎnzi* 油点子 oil-dot-AFF 'oil drops'

(113)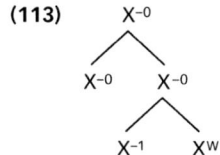

tuǐdùzi 腿肚子 leg-stomach-AFF 'calf', *tiěcíxìng* 铁磁性 iron-magnet-AFF 'ferromagnetism', *ménhuánzi* 门环子 door-ring-AFF 'knocker', *rénfànzi* 人贩子 people-sell-AFF 'trafficker in people'

(114)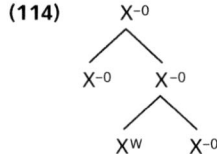

not observed

(115)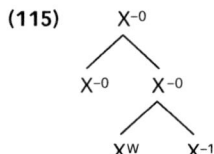

not observed

(116)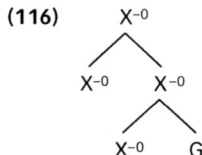

not observed

(117)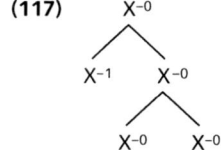

yángdǎgōng 洋打工 foreign-hit-work 'foreign worker', *wēixuèguǎn* 微血管 small-blood-tube 'capillaries'

(118)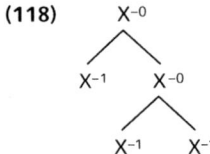

héwǔqì 核武器 nuclear-weapon-artifact 'nuclear weapon'

(119)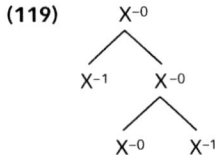

wēidiànnǎo 微电脑 small-electricity-brain 'microcomputer', *wēishēngwù* 微生物 small-live-material 'microbe', *cíliútǐ* 磁流体 magnet-flow-body 'magnetic fluid'

(120)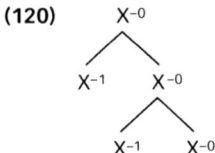

not observed

(121)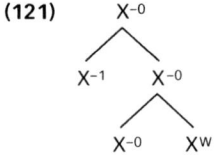

yángxuézi 洋学子 foreign-study-AFF 'foreign student'

(122)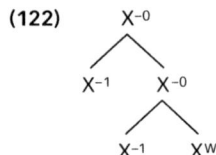

shílázi 石砬子 stone-boulder-AFF 'boulder'

(123)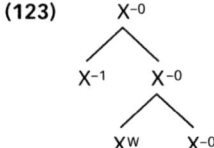

not observed

(124)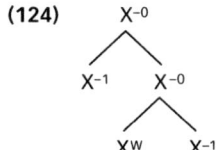

not observed

(125)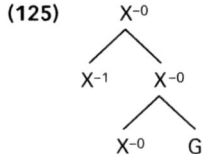

not observed

(126)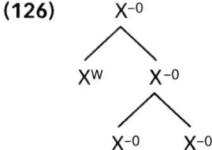

wèifēnpèi 未分配 AFF-divide-distribute 'unallocated', *wèidǐyā* 未抵押 AFF-mortgage-mortgage 'unmortgaged', *ābīnggē* 阿兵哥 AFF-soldier-brother 'big brother soldier'

(127)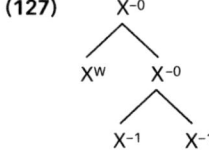

wúyuánzé 无原则 AFF-basic-principle 'unprincipled', *wúguójí* 无国籍 AFF-country-nationality 'stateless', *āmùlín* 阿木林 AFF-tree-forest 'dumb guy', *wúzhǔjiàn* 无主见 AFF-main-view 'indecisive', *wúyìshì* 无意识 AFF-meaning-recognize 'unconscious', *wèishíxiàn* 未实现 AFF-real-appear 'unrealized', *fēidǎotǐ* 非导体 AFF-lead-body 'non-conductor', *fēizhèngshì* 非正式 AFF-correct-form 'informal'

(128)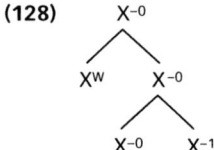

wújìmíng 无记名 AFF-mark-name 'secret (vote)', *wúzhònglì* 无重力 AFF-heavy-force 'agravic', *wèitānxiāo* 未摊销 AFF-spread-expense 'unamortized', *wèigǎiliáng* 未改良 AFF-change-good 'unimproved', *wèiwánchéng* 未完成 AFF-finish-complete 'unfinished', *fēibìngyuán* 非病原 AFF-sickness-origin 'non-pathogenic', *fēiféizào* 非肥皂 AFF-fat-soap 'detergent', *fēimàipǐn* 非卖品 AFF-sell-product '(articles) not for sale'

(129)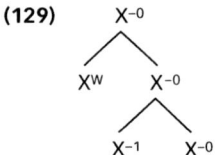

wèichéngrén 未成人 AFF-complete-person 'a minor', *fēilěijī* 非累积 AFF-accumulate-collect 'non-cumulative', *fēihūnshēng* 非婚生 AFF-marry-born 'illegitimate (child)'

(130)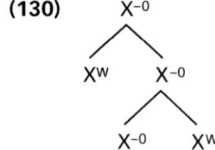

fēijūnshìhuà 非军事化 AFF-military-affair-AFF 'to demilitarize'

X-BAR ANALYSIS OF CHINESE WORDS

(131)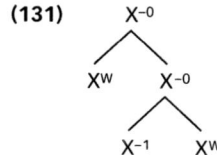

not observed

(132)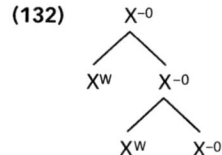

not observed

(133)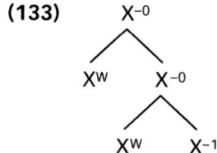

wèikězhī 未可知 AFF-AFF-know 'not yet knowable'

(134)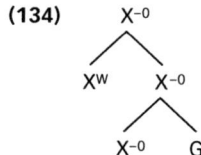

not observed

5.4.5.2.2 Left branching

(135)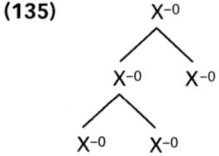

bìngdúbìng 病毒病 sickness-poison-sickness 'virosis', *shǒutuīchē* 手推车 hand-push-car 'wheelbarrow', *shǒutíbāo* 手提包 hand-carry-bag 'handbag', *hūxīdào* 呼吸道 exhale-inhale-passage 'respiratory tract', *māotóuyīng* 猫头鹰 cat-head-hawk 'owl'

(136)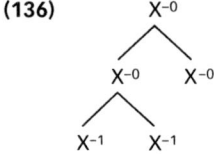

wǔjīnháng 五金行 five-metal-shop 'hardware store', *húntúntāng* 馄饨汤 wonton-wonton soup 'wonton soup'

(137)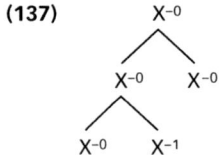

shēngchǎnbù 生产部 produce-product-department 'production department', *diànshídēng* 电石灯 electricity-rock-light 'acetylene lamp'

(138)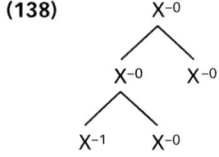

shégēnyīn 舌根音 tongue-root-sound 'velar sound', *bàngqiúduì* 棒球队 stick-ball-team 'baseball team', *wēibōlú* 微型炉 small-wave-oven 'microwave oven'

(139)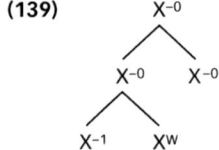

X-BAR ANALYSIS OF CHINESE WORDS

suānxìngyǔ 酸性雨 acid-AFF-rain 'acid rain'

(140)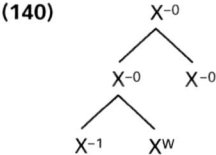

yǐzituǐ 椅子腿 chair-AFF-leg 'chair leg', *mǎtoushuì* 码头税 code-AFF-tax 'pier dues', *mènzichē* 闷子车 sealed-AFF-car 'boxcar'

(141)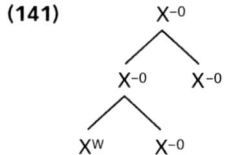

wúxiàndiàn 无线电 AFF-wire-electricity 'radio', *wúdǐdòng* 无底洞 AFF-bottom-hole 'bottomless pit', *wúdúshé* 无毒蛇 AFF-poison-snake 'non-poisonous snake', *wúyānméi* 无烟煤 AFF-smoke-coal 'anthracite coal', *wúhuāguǒ* 无花果 AFF-flower-fruit 'fig', *wèiláipài* 未来派 AFF-come-sect 'futurists'

(142)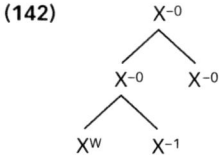

wúhéqū 无核区 AFF-nuclear-district 'nuclear-free zone', *wúyìniǎo* 无翼鸟 AFF-wing-bird 'kiwi', *wèizhīliàng* 未知量 AFF-know-quantity 'unknown quantity', *wèiwángrén* 未亡人 AFF-die-person 'widow'

(143)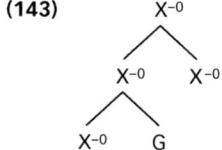

dēngleji 登了记 post-AFF-mark 'registered',[19] *kànbudǒng* 看不懂 see-AFF-understand 'not understand what one sees', *zǒudedòng* 走得动 walk-AFF-move 'able to walk'

(144)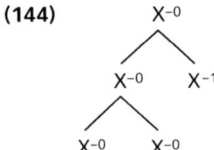

shǒugōngyè 手工业 hand-work-industry 'handicraft industry', *shuǐmìtáo* 水蜜桃 water-honey-peach 'sweet peach'

(145)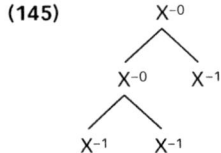

xiūzhǐfú 休止符 rest-stop-symbol '(musical) rest', *lǐliáojī* 理疗机 principle-cure-machine 'therapy machine', *yàoshiér* 钥匙儿 key-spoon-child 'latchkey child'

(146)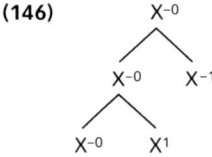

bìngyuántǐ 病原体 sickness-origin-body 'virus', *zàobìchǎng* 造币厂 make-currency-factory 'a mint', *shēngchǎnlì* 生产力 produce-product-strength 'productivity'

(147)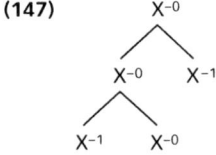

---

[19] Zhang and Sang 1986: 510.

zàoxǐjī 皂洗机 soap-wash-machine 'a soaper', *wēifēnxué* 微分学 small-divide-study 'differential calculus', *yěxīnjiā* 野心家 wild-heart-AFF 'careerist'

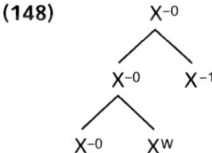

zhítoujiān 指头尖 finger-AFF-point 'fingertip', *zhítoudù* 指头肚 finger-AFF-stomach 'fingertip', *suōzixiè* 梭子蟹 shuttle-AFF-crab 'a kind of crab', *yǎnghuàwù* 氧化物 oxygen-AFF-material 'oxide', *guǒzilí* 果子狸 fruit-AFF-fox 'masked civet'

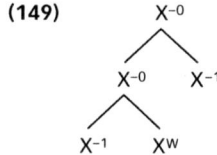

shìzijiāo 柿子椒 persimmon-AFF-pepper 'sweet bell pepper', *cíhuàlì* 磁化力 magnet-AFF-strength 'magnetizing force', *lǜhuàwù* 氯化物 chlorine-AFF-material 'chlorides', *mùhuàshí* 木化石 wood-AFF-stone 'woodstone'

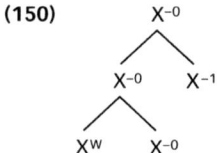

wúdìngxíng 无定形 AFF-fixed-form 'amorphous', *fēimàipǐn* 非卖品 AFF-sell-product 'items not for sale', *wúshénlùn* 无神论 AFF-god-theory 'atheism'

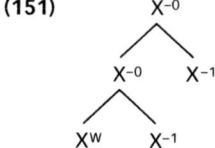

wújītǐ 无机体 AFF-organic-body 'inorganic matter', *wúzhǔwù* 无主物 AFF-master-material 'ownerless property', *wèihūnfū* 未婚夫 AFF-marry-man 'fiance', *wèizhīshù* 未知数 AFF-know-number 'unknown number'

(152)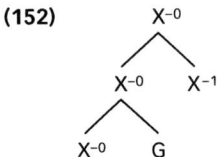

kāiguòdāo 开过刀 open-AFF-knife 'to have operated', *xǐlezǎo* 洗了澡 wash-AFF-bath 'to have washed', *jiēguòhūn* 结过婚 unite-AFF-marry 'to have gotten married', *jìbuzhù* 记不住 recall-AFF-firm 'unable to remember'

(153)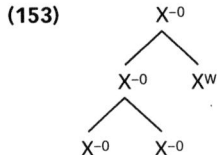

diànqìhuà 电气化 electric-force-AFF 'electrify', *tǔgǒuzi* 土狗子 dirt-dog-AFF 'mole cricket'

(154)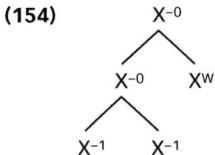

tuòhuāngzhě 拓荒者 open-wasteland-AFF 'pioneer', *zàokuángzhě* 躁狂者 impetuous-crazy-AFF 'maniac', *wēixínghuà* 微型化 small-form-AFF 'microminiaturize', *zìyuànzhě* 自愿者 self-willing-AFF 'volunteer', *yìtǐhuà* 一体化 one-body-AFF 'unify'

(155)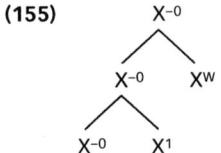

kāituòzhě 开拓者 open-open-AFF 'developer',[20] *wúshénlùnzhě* 无神论者 without-god-theory-AFF 'atheist'

(156)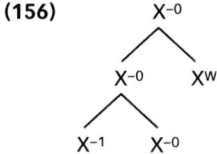

jūnshìhuà 军事化 military-affair-AFF 'to militarize', *zìdònghuà* 自动化 self-move-AFF 'to automate', *jiàochēhuà* 轿车化 sedan-car-AFF 'to sedanize',[21] *láodònghuà* 劳动化 work-move-AFF 'to integrate oneself with the working people', *láodòngzhě* 劳动者 work-move-AFF 'worker'

(157)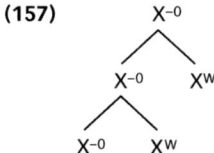

shuōtour 说头儿 speak-AFF-AFF 'something to talk about'

(158)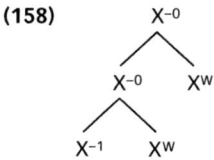

ǒuránxìng 偶然性 chance-AFF-AFF 'probability', *tíngzihuà* 亭子化 pavilion-AFF-AFF 'to pavilionize'[22]

(159)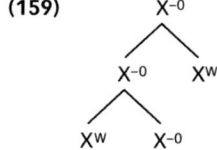

---

[20] Zhang and Sang 1986: 347.
[21] Baxter and Sagart 1997: 41.
[22] Baxter and Sagart 1997: 41.

wèidùzhě 未渡者 AFF-cross-AFF 'one who has not yet crossed', *kěnéngxìng* 可能性 AFF-able-AFF 'possibility'

(160)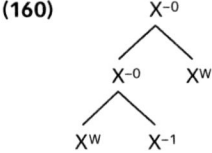

wúhéhuà 无核化 AFF-nuclear-AFF 'denuclearize', *wúchǎnzhě* 无产者 AFF-property-AFF 'proletarian', *kěsùxìng* 可塑性 AFF-plastic-AFF 'plasticity'

(161)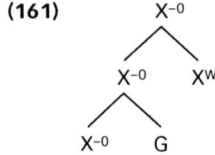

not observed

(162)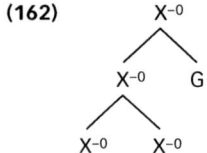

jièyòngle 借用了 borrow-use-AFF 'borrowed', *gōngrénmen* 工人们 work-person-AFF 'workers'

(163)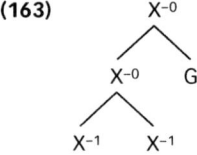

jiějuéle 解决了 undo-resolve-AFF 'solved', *fùmǔmen* 父母们 father-mother-AFF 'parents',[23] *péngyǒumen* 朋友们 friend-friend-AFF 'friends'

[23] Zhang and Sang 1986: 347.

(164)

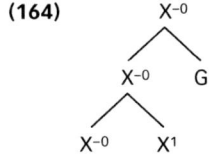

bāngzhùle 帮助了 help-help-AFF 'helped', *liúmángmen* 流氓们 flow-scoundrel-AFF 'ruffians'[24]

(165)

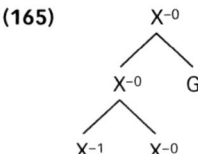

xiǎngshòule 享受了 enjoy-accept-AFF 'enjoyed'

(166)

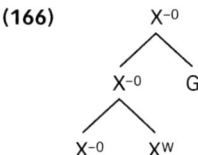

jiànshèzhěmen 建设者们 build-design-AFF-AFF 'builders'[25]

(167)

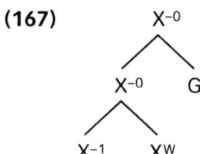

guīhuàle 归化了 return-AFF-AFF 'to have been naturalized', *háizimen* 孩子们 child-AFF-AFF 'children'

(168)

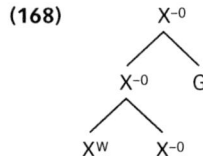

[24] Zhang and Sang 1986: 416.
[25] Zhang and Sang 1986: 347.

192   THE MORPHOLOGY OF CHINESE

fùhuóle 复活了 AFF-live-AFF 'to have come to life again'

(169)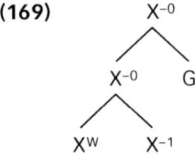

fùshěnle 复审了 AFF-investigate-AFF 'to have reinvestigated'

(170)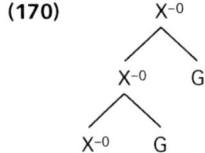

chīguòle 吃过了 eat-AFF-AFF 'to have eaten'

5.4.5.2.3   **Some examples of multiple embedding**
Although most of the examples above are restricted to only one degree of embedding and embedding from only one of two possible nodes, the system is generative and productive and so in principle would also allow multiple embeddings at a single level of recursion, as well as embeddings at even deeper levels (as long as the branching expansion node is X^{-0}). An exhaustive listing of the actual occurrences of such predicted structures would of course yield an enormous amount of data, and would have even more gaps than seen in the examples with one degree of embedding presented in (108)–(170). Instances of multiple and deeper embeddings are nonetheless predicted to be possible in principle. Some examples follow.

(171)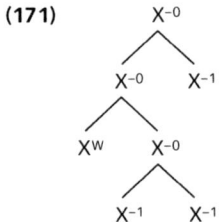

wúfǎngzhīwù 无纺织物 AFF-spin-weave-material 'adhesive-bonded fabric'

(172)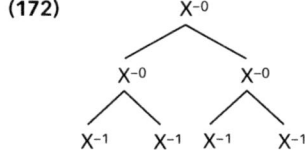

zīběnzhǔyì 资本主义 money-base-advocate-intention 'capitalism'

(173)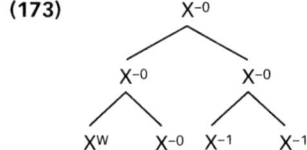

wútǔzāipéi 无土栽培 AFF-earth-grow-nourish 'hydroponic'

(174)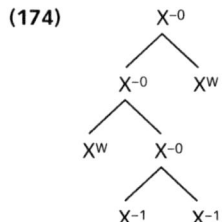

wúguójízhě 无国籍者 AFF-country-nationality-AFF 'stateless person', *fēijūnshìhuà* 非军事化 AFF-military-affair-AFF 'demilitarize'

(175)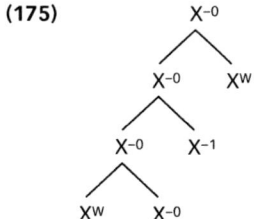

wúshénlùnzhě 无神论者 AFF-god-theory-AFF 'atheist'

5.5 The concept of 'head' applied to Chinese words

Sadock supports the idea that morphological structures have heads, with 'the head being the daughter whose featural composition is related to that of the mother node' (Sadock 1991: 27). Haspelmath suggests that the diachronic origins of word headedness derive from the lexicalization of headed syntactic structures (Haspelmath 1992). Of course, the question of whether words have heads in Chinese (or any other language) depends upon what we mean by 'head'. When it comes to words, scholars are quite equivocal, sometimes speaking of heads in structural terms, sometimes in semantic terms. Let us consider how this concept applies specifically to words in Chinese.

5.5.1 'Canonical head' vs. 'virtual head'

In Chinese (and possibly all languages; see, e.g., Di Sciullo and Williams 1987), the head of a word may be defined canonically, by its position within the word. For Chinese, the canonical head is defined as a function of the form class of the word, following the Headedness Principle: verbs have their canonical head on the left, and nouns have their canonical head on the right. The notion of the canonical head is posited to be knowledge that is intrinsic to a native speaker's knowledge of words, and is specific to the lexical component. So, for example, the head in syntax is identified by feature matching and is not identified canonically by position.

The intuition behind the notion of 'canonical head' is that knowledge about the form class identity of a word's internal constituents is, in the unmarked case, 'driven' by the gestalt word's form class identity. This means that given a speaker's knowledge of the form class of a word, there will exist a default value, or 'hypothesis', in the speaker's grammar regarding the nature of the word's internal constituents, specifically regarding the identity of the canonical head. Words that do not conform to the hypothesis will be treated exceptionally in the word-formation grammar (as seen in 6.1.3).

A word's 'virtual' head is a word constituent whose form class identity matches that of the gestalt word,[26] a notion that is closer to the

---

[26] Although technically (as defined here) a canonical head is redundantly a virtual head, unless otherwise noted we will use the term virtual head loosely to refer to a word constituent whose form class identity matches that of the gestalt word and does not appear in canonical head position.

traditional definition of head as understood from syntax. The intuition behind the notion 'virtual' head is that the word has an internal constituent that just happens to match the form class of the gestalt word, but beyond that coincidental fact has very little implication for the structure of the word.

For our purposes, therefore, an *endocentric* word is a word that has a canonical head, and an *exocentric* word is a word that has a virtual but not canonical head. A *headless* word in this framework is a word that has neither a virtual nor a canonical head.

5.5.2 'Semantic head' vs. 'structural head'

A semantic head is that part of the word which is a more general instance of what the entire word means, often defined in terms of the 'IS A' relation. So in the word *qìchē* 汽车 gas-vehicle 'automobile', a *qìchē* is a kind of *chē*, that is to say, an automobile IS A kind of vehicle, therefore *chē* is the semantic head of the word. A structural head is a head defined by reference to grammatical rather than semantic values. So, for example, a head defined by a grammatical form class or feature specification – as with the canonical head discussed in the previous sections – is a structural rather than semantic head.

The semantic and structural heads often match (as in the example above, where *chē* is both the semantic and the structural head of the word), but there are cases in which the structural and semantic heads are different. One such example is the word *kǒuàn* 口岸 mouth-coast 'harbour', in which a structural (canonical) head is on the right, but the semantic head is on the left (since a 'harbour' is more generally understood as a kind of 'mouth' than a kind of 'coast'). Another example is the word *yúncǎi* 云彩 cloud-colour which means 'cloud' even though the 'cloud' part is on the left. Another example, this time with a verb, is *tīnghòu* 听候 listen-wait 'to wait for'. The verb *tīnghòu* is more accurately characterized as a kind of 'waiting' and not a kind of 'listening', therefore, the semantic head is on the right, while the structural (canonical) head, because it is a verb, is on the left.[27] Discussion of the difference between a semantic head and a structural

---

[27] This framework predicts the existence of words that have semantic heads but no structural heads (i.e., neither a canonical nor a virtual head). I have not yet found examples of this.

head may be found in Zwicky 1985 and, especially with respect to Chinese, in Pan, Yip and Han (1993: 289).

5.5.3 Headless words

'Headless' words are words in which the form class category of the gestalt word fails to match that of at least one of its constituents (or, in my terminology, they are words that lack both a canonical and a virtual head; see 5.5.1). If the criterion for headhood is a match between the inner and outer form class category, it is predicted that a word whose form class category does not match one of its constituents either has no properties (at least none derivable through a head) or gets its properties through some type of default algorithm.

One possible resolution of this apparent problem is to posit that the more 'lexicalized' a word is (see 6.1.2), the less relevant the notion of 'headedness' is, and therefore the less the word is considered to be headed. In syntax, exocentric constructions are rather rare, but they are fairly common in the case of words. This implies that 'head' is not as all-encompassing a construct for words as for syntactic structures, since in syntax the dominating category invariably gets its grammatical identity from one of its components, unlike the case for words. The phenomenon of lexicalization and its relationship to Chinese wordhood is discussed in chapter 6.

5.6 The proposed analysis applied to English

The system proposed for Chinese in 5.4, as it turns out, also accounts for English word-formation data in a surprisingly straightforward and complete fashion. As is the case in Chinese, there are four morphological primitives: X^{-0}, X^{-1}, X^W and G. X^{-0} is a full word, and anything below the level of X^{-0} is bound. X^{-1} is a bound content (non-function) morpheme (bound root). X^W is a (non-inflectional) affix that is capable of being a head (as seen by its 'X' value) but does not participate in the bar level system (as seen by use of the constant 'W' rather than an integer as a superscript; Selkirk 1982: 124). In English, X^W includes both Class I and II derivational morphemes (they may be distinguished by the fact that Class I subcategorizes for X^{-0} and Class II subcategorizes for X^{-1}). G is an inflectional affix – a bound function morpheme that contains syntactic diacritical features.

X-BAR ANALYSIS OF CHINESE WORDS

These primitives, furthermore, are also combined using the rules that we used for Mandarin, repeated here as (176), which means that the set of specific rules generating possible English word structures are also the same as those used to generate Mandarin words, repeated in modified form as (177).

(176) Rule 1 $X^{-0} \rightarrow X^{-0,-1,\{W\}}, X^{-0,-1,\{W\}}$
      Rule 2 $X^{-0} \rightarrow X^{-0}, G$.

(177) $X^{-0} \rightarrow X^{-0}, X^{-0}$ (two words)
       $X^{-0} \rightarrow X^{-1}, X^{-1}$ (two bound roots)
       $X^{-0} \rightarrow X^{-0}, X^{-1}$ (word + bound root)
       $X^{-0} \rightarrow X^{-1}, X^0$ (bound root + word)
       $X^{-0} \rightarrow X^{-0}, X^W$ (word + II derivational affix)
       $X^{-0} \rightarrow X^{-1}, X^W$ (bound root + I derivational affix)
       $X^{-0} \rightarrow X^W, X^{-0}$ (II derivational affix + word)
       $X^{-0} \rightarrow X^W, X^{-1}$ (I derivational affix + bound root)
       $X^{-0} \rightarrow X^{-0}, G$ (word + inflectional affix)

Also as with Mandarin, the curly brackets around the W superscript in (176) are intended to represent the fact that only one X^W element may be selected, or in other words, that X^W may only attach to a root word or a bound root, and may not attach to another X^W. Even though this stipulation appears to apply to both English and Chinese, I am unsure of its status as a proposed universal rule (see n. 16).

Note in (177) that the traditional labels of 'Class I and Class II derivational affix' are given to word-forming affixes that attach to words and bound roots respectively. This is similar to Selkirk's proposal in that the distinction between these two traditional categories is not an inherent property of the affixes themselves, but rather is based upon the type of element to which they affix, or, in other words, their subcategorization specification. As noted previously, these rules conform to Selkirk's posited rule schemata (63) from which all languages are posited to draw a subset of possible word-formation rules. These rules will yield the structures in (178)–(249) below, restricted here to two levels of X^{-0} expansion.

The primitives of the system are words (X^{-0}), bound roots (X^{-1}), word-forming affixes (X^W) and grammatical affixes (G). A word, of course, may be any free word in English. Since the set of bound roots is much more restricted (and undoubtedly controversial) in English than in Mandarin, a selection of English bound roots is given in table 27. The criteria for bound roots is the same as that for Mandarin (see discussion in 3.4.3 and 3.4.3.1): they are 'bound' and 'content' (versus 'function').

Table 27 English bound roots (X⁻¹; partial list)

left-adjoining	right-adjoining
anti-	-aholic
auto-	-ese
bi-	-fer
circum-	-gram
counter-	-ism
di-	-itis
extra-	-morph
intra-	-mural
ling-	-osis
magni-	-pathy
meta-	-pede
mono-	-pedic
multi-	-phile
neuro-	-philiac
ortho-	-proof
para-	-vene
pedo-	-vert
photo-	
poly-	
post-	
pre-	
pro-	
semi-	
thermo-	
tri-	
ultra-	

Table 28 English word-forming affixes (X^W; partial list)

prefixes	suffixes
a-	-able
an-	-ar
de-	-ary
dis-	-ate
in-	-ed
non-	-ee
re-	-er
un-	-ful
ex-	-ify
	-ine
	-ish
	-ize
	-less
	-like
	-ment
	-oid
	-or
	-ous
	-tude
	-y

A selection of English word-forming affixes (X^W) is seen in table 28. The criteria for word-forming affixes is also the same as it is for Mandarin (see discussion in 3.4.3 and 3.4.3.1): they are 'bound' and 'function' (versus 'content'). Grammatical affixes in English are surprisingly few (as is the case in Mandarin), and include the plural marker -*s*, the third person singular marker -*s* and the past tense morpheme -*ed*. Grammatical affixes are distinguished from word-forming affixes using the same criteria as for Mandarin (see 3.4.3.1): grammatical affixes (and not word-forming affixes) are completely general, have a constant, predictable meaning across contexts, must attach to free words, and never change the form class of the words to which they attach.

The structures of English words formed using the rules in (177) are seen in (178)–(249) below. The judgments are mostly mine, with references cited otherwise. The single-branching structures are presented first in (178)–(186), followed by structures in which further branching occurs from the right (187)–(213) and the left (214)–(249). Note that of all the structures in (178)–(249) generated by the rules in (177), apparently only one type of structure – that of a grammatical affix (G) being embedded to the left of a non-word (X^{-1}, X^W or G) – predicts the existence of forms that some may find only marginally acceptable (e.g., (231) and (249)).[28] The fact that there are fewer gaps in the English word-formation data below than we found in the Mandarin data in (99)–(175) I believe may be attributed to the fact that I am a native speaker of English and not of Mandarin, and so lack the intuition necessary to create novel Chinese forms corresponding to many of the English forms below that are novel but that my intuition tells me are acceptable.

5.6.1 Single branching

(178)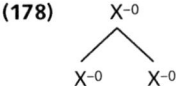

rugrat, keyboard, gutterball

(179)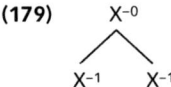

intervene, converse, complete, convene, neurosis, psychosis, orthopedic, corpocracy, chocaholic, interject, biology, microcosm, monologue, polygon, pseudonym, retrogress

[28] Selkirk faces the related problem of how not to generate forms such as *aprons-s, since there is nothing in the system to keep the plural suffix -s from applying more than once (1982: 56–7). She proposes to solve it by assigning the suffix a subcategorization for a sister element that is unspecified for the inflectional feature in question, and then require that lexical insertion and percolation apply cyclically.

(180)   X⁻⁰
        ╱ ╲
      X⁻⁰   X⁻¹

candygram, shatterproof, waterproof, Spoonerism, workaholic, videocam

(181)   X⁻⁰
        ╱ ╲
      X⁻¹   X⁻⁰

cranberry, multipack, biodata, micromanage, interbreed, bioethics, microchip, monorail, polysyllable, pseudoscience, retrofit, subacute, triangle, cardioscan

(182)   X⁻⁰
        ╱ ╲
      X⁻⁰   Xᵂ

ailment, spheroid, vulturish, pulpy, payment, argument, employer, employee, actor, sailor, drinkable, classify, testify[29]

(183)   X⁻⁰
        ╱ ╲
      X⁻¹   Xᵂ

rhomboid, toxic, squeamish, skittish, hapless, happy, ornament, excrement, hydrate, donor, donee,[30] criminate

(184)   X⁻⁰
        ╱ ╲
      Xᵂ   X⁻⁰

untie, relive, enjoy, uncola

---

[29] This is a verb created from the verb 'test' by my ten-year-old son Eric at the dinner table, when he said 'I'm going to testify this cake', clearly intending to mean that he wanted to 'test' the cake after he had helped bake it.

[30] Barker 1998: 699.

(185)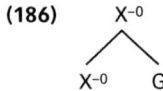

encrypt, decrypt, detox, attach, detach, decant, exhume

(186)

strings, climbed, ftp-ing[31]

5.6.2 Right branching

(187)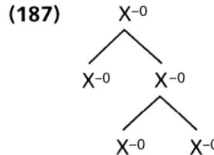

department chairperson

(188)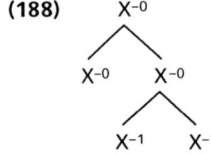

blood antigen, heart sonogram

(189)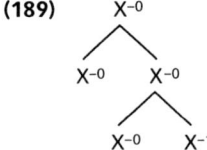

heart echogram, collision shatterproof[32]

---

[31] Taken from a conversation on the internet (11/16/97): 'Back to ftp-ing and installing software!'

[32] Selkirk 1982: 48.

(190)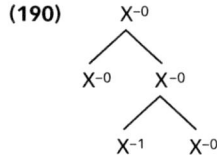

serum antibody

(191)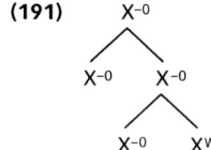

boat arrival, pasta eater, head-bonkee[33]

(192)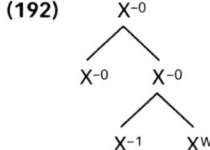

vitamin fortify, blood-squeamish, door ornament, heart surgery

(193)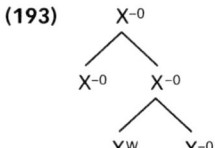

exam retest

(194)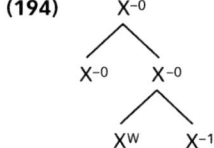

computer encrypt

[33] Barker 1998: 699.

(195)

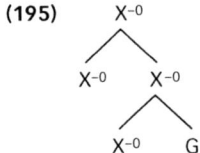

door hinges, house eaves, computer wires

(196)

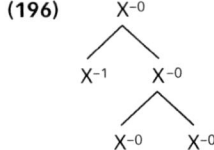

pro-reform-school, anti-leash-law, anti-sunburn

(197)

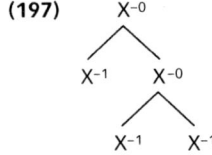

semi-introvert, pseudo-intramural

(198)

pseudo-Japanese

(199)

pseudo-antiChrist

X-BAR ANALYSIS OF CHINESE WORDS   205

(200)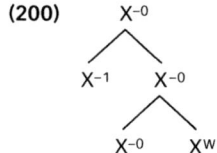

semitrailer, telemarketer, ultra-sheepish

(201)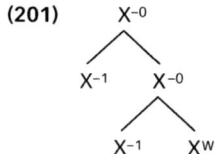

semirhomboid, semireticular, phototropic, ultra-skittish, camcorder

(202)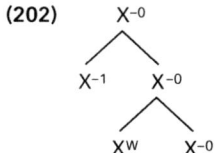

pro-retest, anti-exhusband, polyunsaturated, semiunkempt

(203)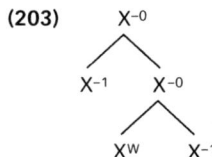

pro-detox, auto-extract, semi-exhume

(204)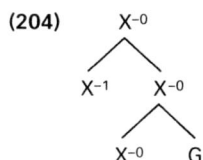

cross-listed, anti-smokers, pro-voters

(205)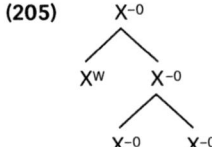

non-highschool, reoverlearn, reaircondition

(206)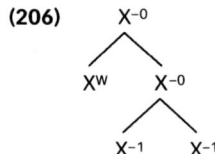

retelegraph

(207)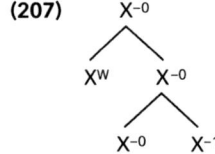

non-waterproof, re-rustproof

(208)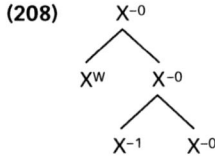

remicromanage

(209)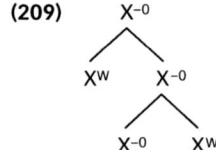

non-arrival, declassify

(210)

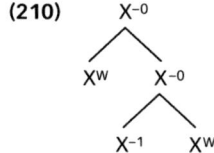

non-toxic, dehydrate, defenestrate, decapitate

(211)

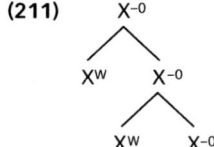

redebrief

(212)

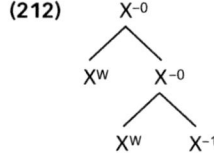

unencrypt, redecant, unretract

(213)

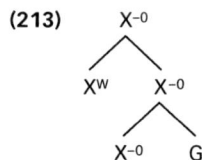

reclimbed

5.6.3 Left branching

(214)

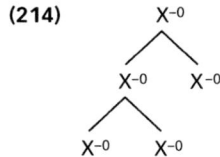

keyboard cover, blood-type analysis

(215)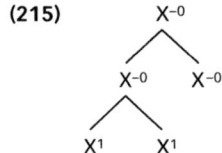

orthopedic ward

(216)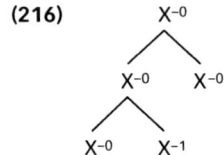

candygram receipt

(217)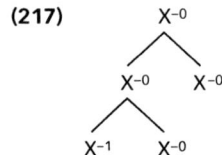

cranberry sauce, antilock brakes

(218)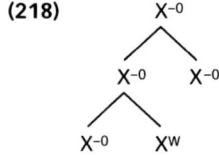

manly physique, teacher lounge

(219)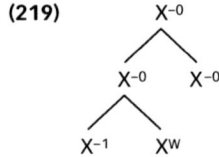

rhomboid body

X-BAR ANALYSIS OF CHINESE WORDS 209

(220)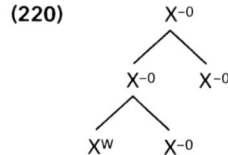

aplastic anemia

(221)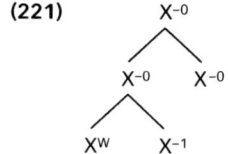

detox centre

(222)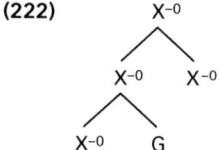

parks commissioner,[34] weeks-long

(223)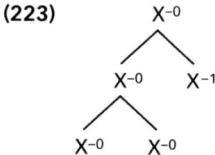

keyboard-itis, rugrat-proof, sunburn-proof, earthquake-proof

(224)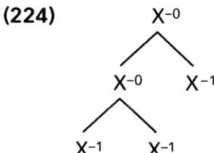

telegram-itis, technocrat-ese, prenup-ese, pre-nup-itis

[34] Selkirk 1982: 52.

(225)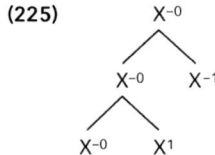

bureaucrat-ese

(226)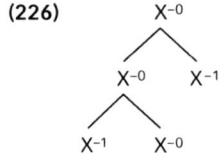

anti-Clinton-ism, televisionitis

(227)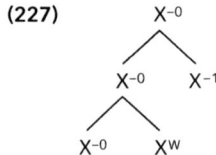

toddler-proof, computerese, tabloidaholic

(228)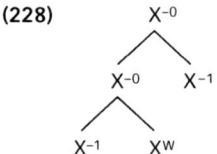

toxicology, excrementitis

(229)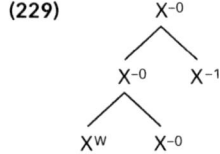

retestism, reuseproof

(230)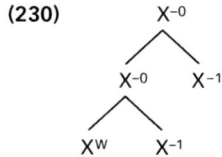

encrypt-proof, decrypt-proof, detox-itis, exhume-proof

(231)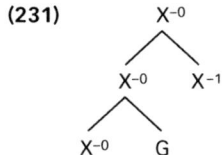

Bullsaholic, twinsproof

(232)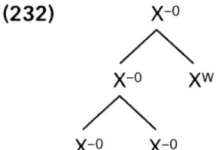

sunshiny, high-schoolish, slam-dunker, jetsetter, baby-boomer, double-decker

(233)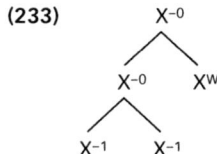

completely, postopify, prenupify

(234)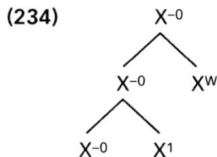

workaholic-like

(235)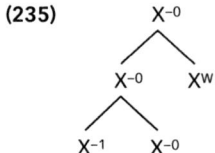

micromanager, micromanagement, anti-American, microencapsulate

(236)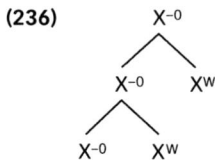

managerlike, teacherless

(237)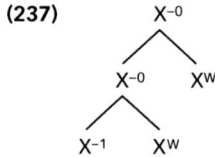

rhomboidlike, ornamentlike, excrementlike, techie-ish

(238)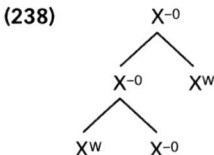

resurfacer, defibrillator, enjoyment, repayment, derailment, deicer, encapsulate, retrainee

(239)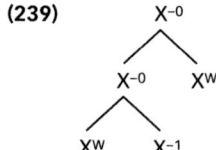

encryption, attachment, exhumable

(240)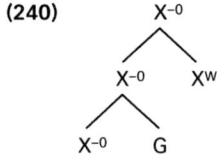

roastedlike, reportedly[35]

(241)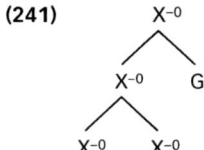

blackbirds

(242)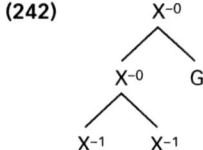

intervened, chocaholics

(243)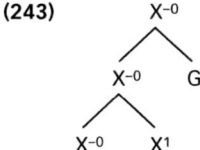

candygrams, Spoonerisms, workaholics

(244)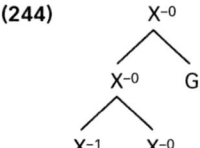

micromanaged, multipacks

[35] Thanks to Jerry Morgan for suggesting examples of this type.

214   THE MORPHOLOGY OF CHINESE

(245)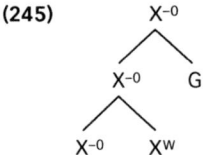

ailments, payments, panties

(246)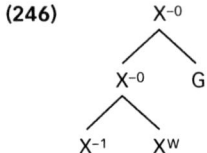

hydrates, ornaments, impediments

(247)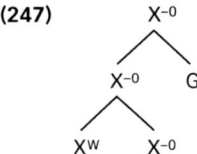

debugs, disarmed, de-ices, unbuttoned

(248)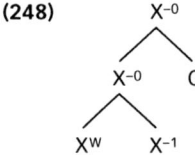

encrypted, decants

(249)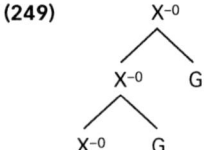

pantsed[36]

---

[36] 'The bull *pantsed* him' (*Life* magazine, Dec. 1997, p. 20; from a story about a bull ripping the pants off a bullfighter).

Having presented a theory of word formation using X-bar formalism with application to Chinese (and English), we now move on to consider some of the relationships between inner and outer constituent identity that are entailed by that theory. Specifically, we investigate why the 'head' doesn't have the same status in word formation as it does in syntax, and more to the point, why words in Chinese exhibit variability in their conformity to the Headedness Principle. We will find that the relation between the outer identity of the word and that of its inner constituents – including the notion of 'head' – breaks down as a word becomes more strongly lexicalized and more deeply ensconced in the lexical module.

6 | Lexicalization and Chinese words

Lexicalization is an important concept in Chinese, not only because it is an especially productive source of new words in the language, but also because it explains both the variable nature of the relationship between a word and its components and the general availability of word-internal information to the grammar at large. In the sections that follow, we will discuss lexicalization as a source of new words and as a way of explaining the nature of the component–word relationship.

Although the basic meaning of 'lexicalization' refers to something 'becoming a word', the term has been used by linguists to mean different things. Talmy (1985), for example, uses the term to focus on differences in concepts that happen to find instantiation at the word level in different languages. Another usage refers to abstract feature complexes leaving the realm of deep structure and taking on a concrete surface form (see, e.g., Sadock 1991: 36). Yet another common use of the term refers to the extent to which a complex linguistic form has taken on a non-compositional, idiomatic meaning. Harris and Campbell (1995) do not directly discuss lexicalization, but in their framework it would be considered a form of reanalysis in which the component that has been 'recruited' to become part of a word undergoes a change in *cohesion*, with the resulting formed word undergoing shifts in its constituency, hierarchical structure, category labeling and grammatical relations.

I will use the term 'lexicalization' to refer to cases in which 'material develops into or is recruited to form lexical items' (Hopper and Traugott 1993: 224 n. 5). This can be the recruiting of a component C to become part of an already existent word, in which case we say that the component C has been 'lexicalized' (e.g., *-re* being lexicalized as part of the word *we're*), or it can refer to multiple components C^N joining together to become a single word – as in the case of the lexicalization of V–O combinations discussed in 4.3.4 – in which case we say that the combination C^N has been 'lexicalized'.

I will also use the term to refer to how deeply ensconced in the lexicon a particular item is. According to this concept, a word may be considered strongly or weakly lexicalized, depending upon the extent to which the word components retain their individual identity. It is to this concept that we turn first.

6.1 Lexicalization and the relation between word and constituent

Lexicalization may be seen as possessing a gradient property: a word is 'weakly lexicalized' if its components remain semantically and grammatically transparent and available to the grammar at large, and 'strongly lexicalized' if the components become semantically and grammatically unavailable or opaque. Thus, the closeness of the relationship between a word and its constituents – including, I will argue, the applicability of the Headedness Principle – varies according to its degree of lexicalization: in general, the more strongly lexicalized a word is, the weaker the connection is between the properties of the gestalt word and the properties of its constituents.

6.1.1 Semantic and grammatical reduction in lexicalization

The loss of word component morpheme characteristics as a word increases its degree of lexicalization – which we may call *word component reduction* – involves both the loss of word component meaning ('bleaching'; Hopper and Traugott 1993: 87ff.) and the loss of word component grammatical information.

Remarking on the latter, purely grammatical, aspect of word component reduction, Anderson (1992: 194) says 'the longer a word exists in a language as a lexical item, the more various parts of its structure may become idiosyncratic, so that eventually this structure can become quite opaque from a synchronic point of view . . . In these cases, the amount of a word's structure that can be parsed . . . declines as a function of its lexicalization.' In this way, Anderson sees the 'interpretation' (i.e., semantics) and the 'compositional foundation' (i.e., grammatical structure) of words as independent, separable phenomena (Anderson 1985a: 42–3) that we may consider differentially susceptible to reduction due to degree of lexicalization.

Discussing the semantic aspect of word component reduction, Li and Thompson note in the case of Chinese that when a word is first formed, speakers are aware of both its literal and idiomatic senses, and that it becomes more idiomatic over time. Referring to the connection between the meaning of the word and the meanings of its components, Li and Thompson say: 'As time moves on, this semantic connection begins to recede from the realm of the knowledge of the native speakers until, finally, it is totally lost' (1981: 46–8). Li and Thompson also discuss degrees of semantic relatedness between the meanings of words and the meanings of their components, ranging from (a) no relation to (b) metaphorical relation to (c) direct relation, remarking that while discrete categories such as these are useful, 'in reality . . . the degree of relatedness between the meaning of a compound and the meaning of its parts forms a continuum' (1981: 47).

Note, however, that the reductions of word component meaning and of word component grammatical information do not necessarily occur in parallel: the meaning and grammatical information within word components are independent entities and their reduction proceeds at different rates as lexicalization increases, with meaning reduction often preceding loss of grammatical information.

Liberman and Sproat (1992: 150–1), for example, posit three 'stages' in the lexicalization of phrases, in which the meaning and grammatical structure undergo reduction independently, with semantic reduction occurring first. In their first stage, a phrase simply acquires a conventionalized meaning. It retains its internal structure, remains dominated by a phrasal category (N^1) and is 'listed in a phrasal lexicon of some sort' (1992: 150). In the second stage, a phrase has a conventionalized meaning and retains its internal structure but takes on the grammatical identity of a lexical category (N^0). In the third stage, the phrase has conventionalized meaning and lexical category status, but also loses its internal grammatical structure.

Givón (1992: 122–3) makes the same type of comparison between semantic and structural reduction in discussing grammaticalization (more on the relation between lexicalization and grammaticalization in 6.3), stating that the structural reduction tends to lag behind semantic reduction in grammaticalization. Nunberg, Sag and Wasow (1994) make a similar point in the case of phrasal idioms, positing the occurrence of semantic reduction in the absence of grammatical reduction. They argue that the meaning of phrasal idioms derives via the operation of extant, unreduced, grammatical rules upon phrasal components whose individual meanings have become conventionalized.

6.1.2 Categories of lexicalization

It seems, therefore, that we can posit different 'degrees' of lexicalization – sort of the 'depth' to which a form is ensconced in the lexical module – depending upon how much semantic and grammatical reduction has occurred within a word (cf Craig 1991: 467, 482). Based on these factors, I have set up the following five categories[1] corresponding to a gradient measure or 'degree' of a word's lexicalization.[2] The specific criteria used to determine degree of lexicalization are: (a) whether the word components retain their full original meaning, reflect a figurative, metaphorical sense, or lose their original meaning entirely; and (b) whether the grammatical information within word components remains available to the grammar as a whole.

Intuitively, the notion 'degree of lexicalization' is a recognition that a word's identity evolves, such that the identity of a word's individual components tends over time to be reduced or lost, due to their continued use as synthetic gestalt – rather than analytically decomposable – entities. The assignment of a degree of lexicalization to a word is an attempt to estimate the extent to which this loss of component identity has occurred in a given word form.

6.1.2.1 Conventional lexicalization

The first category is 'conventional' lexicalization, which constitutes the least lexicalized words. In many cases these are recent lexicalizations, and they at any rate completely retain the grammatical and semantic identity of their components. In conventional lexicalization, the meaning of the individual word components is retained and non-metaphorical, but nonetheless *conventionalized* with the possibility of extended (albeit generally non-metaphorical) associations. Some examples from Chinese are *chīfàn* 吃饭 eat-rice 'to eat a meal', *mùlì* 目力 eye-strength 'eyesight', *gāngbǐ* 钢笔 steel-pen 'fountain pen', *nǔlì* 努力 exert-strength 'try hard', *páchóng* 爬虫 crawl-insect 'reptile', *yìngdié* 硬碟 hard-saucer '(computer) hard drive', *jièyì* 介意 interpose-intention 'to mind, take offense', *huángdòu* 黄豆 yellow-bean 'soybean'. In these words, the grammatical relationships among components remain completely unreduced, and in some cases syntactic

---

[1] Or 'stages', if there is evidence of a diachronic process.
[2] This corresponds somewhat to the 'cline of lexicality' referred to in Hopper and Traugott 1993: 7.

rules may even continue to apply to reanalysed portions of the word-internal domain.

6.1.2.2 Metaphorical lexicalization

Metaphorical lexicalization refers to words whose components lose their original meaning and take on a related, figurative or metaphorical, interpretation, while the grammatical relationships within the word continue to obtain. It is possible to distinguish two types of metaphorical lexicalization: that which occurs at the component level (component metaphorical lexicalization) and that which occurs at the level of the gestalt word (word metaphorical lexicalization).

In component metaphorical lexicalization, one or both of the individual word components take on a metaphorical meaning (with the grammatical relationship among the parts continuing to obtain), while the overall meaning of the word continues to be a compositional sum of the meanings of its metaphorical parts.[3] Some examples are *tàshí* 踏实 step-reality 'to be realistic' (no 'stepping' takes place), *shísǔn* 石笋 stone-bamboo 'stalagmite' (not really bamboo), *chóngyá* 虫牙 insect-tooth 'cavity' (not really caused by an insect), *ěxin* 恶心 sicken-heart 'feel nauseous' (not really the heart that feels sick) and *chìdào* 赤道 red-band 'equator' (not really red).

In word metaphorical lexicalization the meaning at the level of the word is figurative or metaphorical while the individual morphemes retain their basic (non-metaphorical) meaning. In this case, figuration takes place not so much at the component level (as is the case with component metaphorical lexicalization described above) as at the level of the gestalt word. For example, in the word *diànyǐng* 电影 electric-shadow 'movie', the grammatical structure is retained (it is a noun composed of a noun modifying another head noun), and furthermore its meaning derives compositionally from the individual morpheme elements *diàn* 电 and *yǐng* 影 which retain their individual meanings of 'electric' and 'shadow' respectively, i.e., 'electric shadows'. However, at the word level the composition 'electric shadows' is metaphorically interpreted as 'movie'. Some other examples of 'word metaphorical' lexicalized words are *tiánfáng* 填房 fill-house 'second wife', *ruǎnmù* 软木 soft-wood 'cork', *pàoyǐng* 泡影 bubble-shadow 'visionary

---

[3] This is similar to Nunberg, Sag and Wasow's notion of 'idiomatically combining' (1994: 496), meaning that normal grammatical relations are used to combine elements that themselves have come to have a figurative meaning.

hope', *bóshì* 博士 abundant-scholar 'Ph.D. degree', *pàotǒngzi* 炮筒子 gun-barrel-AFF '(person with a) big mouth', *chīcù* 吃醋 eat-vinegar 'be jealous', *huǒchē* 火车 fire-car 'train' and *jīguāng* 激光 excited-light 'laser'.

6.1.2.3 Asemantic lexicalization

Category 3 is termed 'asemantic' lexicalization, because the meanings of individual morphemes may perhaps be recognizable in diachronic terms, but synchronically they no longer bear even a metaphorical semantic relationship to the meaning of the word. The word component meanings are thus lost, but the grammatical relationship between word components nonetheless continues to obtain. Some examples are *qiānzhang* 千张 thousand-sheet 'a kind of dried bean curd', *wènshì* 问世 ask-world '(said of a new book) to be published' and *chuānchā* 穿插 put:through-insert 'to alternate'. The grammatical form of the components or the grammatical relationship between word components is said to remain because there is some sense in which the grammatical form of the components or the grammatical relationships (e.g., modification, coordination) are perceived as present by the native speaker. For example, in *qiānzhang* there is a sense in which *qiān* does indeed modify *zhang*, and in *chuānchā* the speaker perceives the double verb identity of the components.

6.1.2.4 Agrammatical lexicalization

In agrammatical lexicalization, there is a semantic contribution of the components to the word (either full or metaphorical), but the grammatical relations are absent. In this degree of lexicalization, there are clear semantic relations perceived, but the grammatical relationship is non-standard, that is, it runs counter to native speaker intuition as to what the grammatical structure of words should be.

Examples of this are the words *gōutōng* 沟通 ditch-connect 'communicate', *bìguà* 壁挂 wall-hang 'wall hanging', *xuéjiū* 学究 study-research 'pedant' and *zhǔbǐ* 主笔 primary-pen 'editor-in-chief' in which there is a clear semantic relationship between the word components and the meaning of the gestalt word, but there is no clear non-ad hoc grammatical relationship between the word constituents.

Placed into this lexicalization category are the 'exocentric' words discussed in 5.5.1 because they do not conform to a grammatical convention, i.e., the Headedness Principle. This means these words are understandable even through they run counter to the word-formation intuitions of the native speaker. Words such as *liǎnhóng* 脸红 face-red 'embarrassed' and *mànpǎo* 慢跑 slow-run 'jog' are considered examples of agrammatical lexicalization because they retain their semantics, but their word-internal grammatical structure is inaccessible to the grammar (see 6.1.3) by virtue of their being exocentric (5.5.1).

6.1.2.5 Complete lexicalization

The final, 'most lexicalized' type of lexicalization may be termed 'complete' lexicalization, in which both the internal structure of the word and the original meanings of the components are completely opaque. Some examples are *huāshēng* 花生 flower-born 'peanut', *wùsè* 物色 thing-colour 'to search for', *yāgēn* 压根 pressure-root 'completely, totally', *zuǒyòu* 左右 left-right 'to influence', *shāomài* 烧卖 burn-sell 'a type of snack'. Phonetic loan examples such as *shāfā* 沙发 sand-emit 'sofa' and *jítā* 吉他 lucky-him 'guitar' fit naturally into this category.

These lexicalization categories are illustrated in table 29. Note that the categories are heuristically useful constructs used to demonstrate variation in the opacity of meaning and grammatical structure, but in reality the degree of meaning and grammatical transparency factors probably vary on a continuum, rather than being discrete 'plus or minus' entities; as noted by Li and Thompson (1981: 47).

Table 29 Categories of lexicalization

category	lexicalization type	word component meaning	grammatical identity of relations	examples
1	conventional	full	present	*páchóng* 爬虫 crawl-insect 'reptile'
2	metaphorical	metaphorical	present	*diànyǐng* 电影 electric-shadow 'movie'
3	asemantic	opaque	present	*wènshì* 问世 ask-world 'to be published'
4	agrammatical	full or metaphorical	absent	*xuéjiū* 学究 study-research 'pedant'
5	complete	opaque	absent	*yāgēn* 压根 pressure-root 'completely'

It is important also to note that these lexicalization categories are valid only in as much as the meaning and grammatical opacity characteristics constitute properties of those words that are present in the grammar of any given native speaker. So, for a speaker who has absolutely no knowledge or intuition of the internal semantics or structure of a word such as *jièshào* 介绍 interpose-continue 'to introduce', that word can be considered 'completely lexicalized'. For that speaker, *jièshào* would be considered a member of category 5 'complete lexicalization' instead of being a member of category 2 'metaphorical lexicalization'.

6.1.2.6 Validity of 'degree of lexicalization'

It might seem overly abstract or even circular to say a word is lexicalized to a greater or lesser degree, since, as I have defined it, 'how lexicalized' a word is is a completely predictable function of its semantic and grammatical transparency. The apparent circularity arises because how lexicalized a word is depends solely on its semantic and grammatical transparency, but its transparency is said to be a function of how lexicalized it is. Thus, how lexicalized a word is might be viewed as a derivative notion – simply a convenient label that actually refers to the independently existing degree of word-internal transparency, rather than existing as an independent construct that can stand on its own.

The reason why 'degree of lexicalization' is not merely an abstract entity constructed as a corollary function of word transparency is that these properties of transparency would not be present had the form not 'crossed over' and become a bona fide X^0 member of the lexicon. In other words, since I have argued for the existence of the lexical or morphological component as an independent linguistic module (see 4.3.4.3), my contention is that the transparency correlated with degrees of lexicalization is solely a property of forms that have 'become members' of the lexical module.

6.1.2.7 Categories of lexicalization and lexical strata

Since I shall make reference to the lexical morphological strata proposed in Packard (1997c), I should comment on the relationship between those strata and the categories of lexicalization discussed in 6.1.2. 'Categories of lexicalization' refers to degree of lexicalization as predicted by words' opacity of meaning and grammatical structure, while the lexical strata in Packard (1997c) refer to levels at which morphological

Table 30 Lexicalization categories and lexical strata

lexical stratum (Packard 1997c)	depth of lexical stratum	corresponding lexicalization category (see 6.1.2)	lexicalization type	degree of lexicalization	word component meaning	grammatical identity or relations
1	deep	5	complete	complete	opaque	absent
		4	agrammatical	high	non-opaque	absent
2	moderate	4	agrammatical	high	non-opaque	absent/reduced
		3	asemantic	moderate	opaque	present
3	moderate	3	asemantic	moderate	opaque	present
		2	metaphorical	low	metaphorical	present
4	shallow	2	metaphorical	low	metaphorical	present
		1	conventional	low	full	present

and phonological rules are posited to apply. While a one-to-one correspondence between the categories and the strata is unlikely (although that would be the ideal), clearly the properties are highly correlated. Suffice it to say that, in general, the words that are formed at the deepest lexical stratum will correspond to those that are the most highly lexicalized, and vice versa. A rough depiction of this relationship is presented in table 30.

It is most useful to view both the categories and the strata, as well as their posited relationship as depicted in table 30, as a working hypothesis rather than a rigorous computational formalism meant to mechanistically assign forms and processes to specific strata or categories. I have presented the data in this way to serve as a heuristic device: that is, I wish to make the point that there does exist a general relationship – a correlation – between a word's status as a member of the lexicon and its opacity, including the degree to which its internal semantics and structure are recognized by the grammar as a whole. Clearly, there are likely to be many failures of correspondence between the strata and the categories as presented in table 30. These failures of correspondence could be avoided simply by positing a general correlation, and leaving it at that. But I believe that offering a correspondence hypothesis as in table 30 will allow us to see where failures of correspondence occur, positing which forms and processes are more unexpected and therefore more systemically 'costly' in terms of the theory presented here.[4]

6.1.3 Explaining exceptions to the Headedness Principle

Now that a characterization of the different degrees of lexicalization has been presented, I would like to offer an explanation for how this characterization accounts for exceptions to the Headedness Principle. Note that there is indeed a non-trivial number of exceptions to the Headedness Principle to be accounted for in Mandarin. The statistics

---

[4] I should also point out that the general theory of lexical strata posited in the theory of Lexical Phonology and Morphology (e.g., Kiparsky 1982, Mohanan 1986), would imply that words with grammatical affixes such as G are formed at very shallow strata, and those formed with word-forming affixes like X^w are formed at strata less shallow than G but more shallow than, e.g., bound root words. The precise nature of the relationship between the all phenomena related to 'depth' of lexical strata must await a more complete theory of the lexicon.

from Huang (1997) listed earlier (table 18 in 4.4) indicate that 10.1 per cent of nouns and 15 per cent of verbs do not adhere to the Headedness Principle. This was also seen in the various exceptions to the Headedness Principle noted in 3.2.

Earlier I proposed that the more lexicalized a word is, the less it is subject to the Headedness Principle. I would like to make that general proposal more specific now by suggesting that bisyllabic Chinese words that do not conform to the Headedness Principle belong to one of the two 'most lexicalized' categories proposed in 6.1.2 – either agrammatical or complete lexicalization – since, by definition, grammatical relations and identities are absent in components of words with those lexicalization types. Since the Headedness Principle refers to a grammatical relationship that obtains between words and their constituents, we would expect such a relationship to be weakened or suspended in words whose inner–outer relation has become opaque due to lexicalization.

Now, what exactly are the grammatical consequences for words that do not conform to the Headedness Principle? The Headedness Principle is posited to be a language-specific constraint in Chinese (see section 5.4.3.1) that militates against the occurrence of words without a canonical head (see 5.5.1). When these words do occur, they are predicted to behave exceptionally in the grammar.

What does it mean to behave exceptionally in the grammar? Intuitively speaking, if a word does not conform to the Headedness Principle, it means that native speakers do not possess the knowledge of the grammatical structure of the word that the Headedness Principle entails, namely, that nouns have nouns on the right and verbs have verbs on the left. This means that the non-conforming word is predicted not to be subject to the grammatical processes that normally operate on words, especially head operations – i.e., those grammatical processes that critically involve identification of the word's head. So to say that such words are predicted to behave exceptionally in the grammar means that they will tend not to be subject to those grammatical processes that involve (word) head operations.

To give an example, let us take what is probably the largest and most obvious class of exceptions to the Headedness Principle: verbs that have non-verbs on the left ([–V X]v), like *bùxíng* 步行 step-travel 'to go on foot', *qiāngbì* 枪毙 gun-kill 'to shoot dead', *mànpǎo* 慢跑 slow-run 'to jog', *lǎngdú* 朗读 bright-read 'to read aloud', *dúshā* 毒杀

poison-kill 'to kill with poison', *yǎnhóng* 眼红 eye-red 'to be envious of',[5] *cǎipái* 彩排 colour-perform 'to dress rehearse', etc. Since these words do not conform to the Headedness Principle because they do not have verbs on the left, we would predict that certain grammatical operations that normally apply to the heads of verb words will not be allowed to apply – i.e., will be ungrammatical – if applied to these words. One of the best-known grammatical operations that demonstrates morphological operation on a verb word head is the 'A-not-A' question operation which duplicates the first part of a verb and inserts the negation word *bu* 不 'no, not' to make a disjunctive-type question.[6]

(250) xǐhuān → xǐ-bu-xǐhuān?
喜欢 → 喜不喜欢
like-happy → like-not-like-happy
'to like' → 'like or not?'

A standard example is *xǐhuān* → *xǐ-bu-xǐhuān*, as seen in (250). This operation applies to verbs except when the left-hand constituent is transparently not a verb as construed by the speaker. Notice that the 'A-not-A' operation is generally not allowed to apply to verbs that run afoul of the Headedness Principle, as demonstrated by (251)–(257).

(251) bùxíng → *bù-bu-bùxíng?
步行 → *步不步行
step-travel → step-not-step-travel
'to go on foot' → 'go on foot or not?'

(252) qiāngbì → *qiāng-bu-qiāngbì?
枪毙 → *枪不枪毙
gun-kill → gun-not-gun-kill
'to shoot dead' → 'shoot dead or not?'

(253) mànpǎo → *màn-bu-mànpǎo?
慢跑 → *慢不慢跑
slow-run → slow-not-slow-run
'to jog' → 'jog or not?'

---

[5] Zhang and Lu (1986) give an example of *yǎnhóng* used as a transitive verb followed directly by an object: 他知道有许多人眼红他，嫉妒他 'He knew a lot of people envied him, were jealous of him' (Zhang and Lu 1986: 262).

[6] This is argued by Huang (1982) to be a word-internal inflectional, rather than syntactic, operation.

(254) lǎngdú → *lǎng-bu-lǎngdú?
朗读 → *朗不朗读
bright-read → bright-not-bright-read
'to read aloud' → 'read aloud or not?'

(255) dúshā → *dú-bu-dúshā?
毒杀 → *毒不毒杀
poison-kill → poison-not-poison-kill
'to kill with poison' → 'kill with poison or not?'

(256) yǎnhóng → *yǎn-bu-yǎnhóng?
眼红 → *眼不眼红
eye-red → eye-not-eye-red
'to envy' → 'envy or not?'

(257) cǎipái →*cǎi-bu-cǎipái?
彩排 → *彩不彩排
colour-perform → colour-not-colour-perform
'to dress rehearse' → 'dress rehearse or not?'

One might argue that the unacceptability of the forms in (251)–(257) is due to pragmatic and other factors, and not due to a grammatical constraint per se (see, e.g., Sproat and Shih 1993). But this cannot be the sole explanation, as shown by the contrast in acceptability of (258) as compared with (259).

(258) Tā měitiān pǎobù bu pǎobù? → Tā měitiān pǎo-bu-pǎobù?
他每天跑步不跑步? → 他每天跑不跑步?
he every-day run-step not run-step → he every-day run-not-run-step
'Does he jog every day?' → 'Does he jog every day?'

(259) Tā měitiān mànpǎo bu mànpǎo? → *Tā měitiān màn-bu-mànpǎo?
他每天慢跑不慢跑? → 他每天慢不慢跑?
he every-day slow-run not slow-run → he every-day slow-not-slow-run
'Does he jog every day?' → 'Does he jog every day?'

The fact that *pǎo-bu-pǎobù* in (258) is acceptable but the pragmatically and semantically identical **màn-bu-mànpǎo* in (259) is not, demonstrates that it is the constraint against reduplication of the head in (259) rather than pragmatic and other factors that results in its unacceptability.

One could also argue that forms such as those in (251)–(257) are in fact acceptable in certain narrow or forced contexts (see, e.g., Chi 1985: 106; Sproat and Shih 1993). This must be true for some speakers, and in fact, Chi lists *qiāng-bu-qiāngbì?* in (252) as acceptable (1985: 106). This would appear to constitute counterevidence to the claim that words that do not conform to the Headedness Principle behave exceptionally in the grammar.

However, rather than constituting counterexamples, these forms are evidence that, for these speakers in these contexts, verbs such as *qiāngbì conform* to the Headedness Principle, because in producing such forms, these speakers are actually performing a form of reanalysis, construing the left-hand constituents of these words as verbs. The prima facie evidence for this is the fact that such speakers reduplicate the first syllable to form a question, which suggests that they are treating the first syllable as a verb. Other investigators have counterargued that the first syllable in such verbs is allowed to reduplicate regardless of its form class, as with – in the most extreme case – two-syllable English verbs inserted into Chinese sentences during code switching, such as *sup-bu-supply* 'supply or not?' (Sproat and Shih 1993), *re-bu-realize* 'realize or not?' and *ha-bu-happy* 'happy or not?' (Chi 1985: 106). It cannot be the case, the argument runs, that speakers who create these forms construe meaningless submorphemic syllables borrowed from another language as verbs.

However, Chi also gives *qiāng-le-bì* gun-ASP-kill 'shot to death' (1985: 106) and Huang gives *yōu-le tā yi mò hu*-LE he one-*mour* 'teased him once' (1984: 65; see (52)) as examples demonstrating that the non-verb first syllables of these two-syllable verbs allow suffixation of the verbal aspect marker -*le*. Since the aspect marker -*le never* suffixes to anything other than a verb,[7] this is clear evidence that these elements – whatever their original form class identity (or lack thereof!) – must have been reanalysed as verbs by virtue of their being the left-hand members of gestalt verb words, and that native speakers who produce these forms construe them as such. Chi makes this claim explicitly: 'when a disyllabic or polysyllabic word is used as a verb ... the first syllable is always favored as the main verb. This is true even when such a polysyllabic verb is a compound whose first constituent is a noun' (1985: 105). Therefore, the existence of

---

[7] We are, of course, speaking here of the 'verbal' -*le* with scope only over the verb and not the 'sentence' *le* which has scope over a larger phrasal or sentential unit.

forms such as *sup-bu-supply* and *ha-bu-happy* notwithstanding,[8] forms such as *qiāng-le-bì* and *yōu-le tā yi mò* show conclusively that for speakers who form 'V₁-not-V₁V₂' questions on canonically headless verbs (and by no means is it the case that all can do so), the left-hand element is construed as a verb, in de facto conformity with the Headedness Principle.

The hypothesis that words which are exceptions to the Headedness Principle behave differently in the grammar is much more difficult to demonstrate using nouns, since there are virtually no lexical grammatical operations that are performed on complex Chinese noun words in general, much less on the noun's right-hand head in particular.

However, notice that – even without the benefit of direct evidence such as that from verbs just presented – the notion that 'canonically headless' forms behave exceptionally follows as a matter of simple logic. That is (taking the case of nouns as an example), logic tells us that if noun words were subject to an operation in the grammar that crucially depended on the identification of the right-hand member as a noun, that operation would not be possible for native speakers who do not construe the right-hand member as a noun. The only way this could fail to be true is if the operation in question does not actually depend on the identification of the right-hand member as a noun.

6.1.3.1 Systematic exceptions

Let us now consider various other systematic exceptions to the Headedness Principle. By 'systematic exceptions' I mean words in Mandarin whose formation pays little or no heed to keeping verbs and nouns on the left and right respectively.

6.1.3.1.1 Phonetic loans

Phonetic loan words generally do not follow the Headedness Principle because the syllables representing the borrowed word are meaningless, used for their phonetic content alone. For example, the phonetic loan word *shāfā* 沙发 sand-emit 'sofa' does not have a noun on the right even though it's a noun, and *bēigé* 杯葛 cup-*dolichos* 'boycott',[9] although a verb, does not have a verb on the left. If the syllables *shā* 沙 'sand'

---

[8] Examples of the '*sup-bu-supply*' sort may well be a case of question marking by phonological reduplication, albeit reduplication of a head that is construed as verbal in nature (cf, Huang 1982).

[9] Thanks to Bob Good and Picus Sizhi Ding for this example.

and *fā* 发 'emit' used to represent the borrowed word *shāfā* carry the meanings of 'sand' and 'emit', it is only by happenstance association with the orthographic symbols used to represent the sounds. Since the meanings usually represented by 沙 and 发 are not in any sense related to the meaning of the gestalt word *shāfā*, it makes little sense to say, for example, that the Headedness Principle applies to *shāfā*, or that the 'noun' form class identity of the word *shāfā* determines that of the right-hand word constituent *fā* (as was argued to be the general case in 3.3).[10] Therefore, phonetic loans must be considered to belong to category 5 of lexicalization ('completely lexicalized') as soon as they enter the lexicon (see 6.1.2.5), simply because the relation between the word and its constituents is one of complete opacity.

There are two other points we may note here. The first is that some phonetic loans will conform to the Headedness Principle simply by coincidence: the noun *yāpiàn* 鸦片 crow-slice 'opium' and the verb *kǎobèi* 拷贝 hit-shell 'to copy' vacuously conform to the Headedness Principle because *yāpiàn* has a noun on the right and *kǎobèi* has a verb on the left. This is sheer coincidence, and has little to do with the native speaker knowledge that the Headedness Principle is posited to reflect.

The second point to note is that some phonetic loans – namely, phonetic calques, those borrowings that take the meaning as well as the sound of the source word into account – do indeed conform to the Headedness Principle. The phonetic calque noun *píjiǔ* 啤酒 beer-alcoholic:beverage 'beer' is just such a case, since the word was formed with the noun *jiǔ* 'alcoholic:beverage' on the right by design.

6.1.3.1.2 Neologisms

Most neologisms are probably created in conformity with the Headedness Principle. So, as seen in (260), *cǎisè diànshìjī* 'colour television' does indeed conform to the Headedness Principle when it is abbreviated as *cǎidiàn*, with the noun *diàn* 'electricity' acting as the right-hand member of the new word (ostensibly taking on the semantic and grammatical identity of a bound noun whose meaning is 'television'; see 6.4.3).

---

[10] Of course, if the syllable in question (*fā* 发) begins to be used itself as a word or word component representing the larger word ('sofa'), then we may indeed posit such a deterministic relationship.

(260) căisè   diànshìjī   → căidiàn
       彩色   电视机   → 彩电
       colour-colour   electricity-view-machine   → colour-electricity
       'colour'   'television'
                'colour television'   → 'colour television'

In (261), the verb *chuànglì*, created from the phrase *chuàngzào lìrùn* 'create profit',[11] retains the verb *chuàng* 'create' in canonical verb head position on the left.

(261) chuàngzào   lìrùn   → chuànglì
       创造   利润   → 创利
       create-make   profit-profit   → create-profit
       'create'   'profit'
                'make profit'   → 'make profit'

However, some newly coined words do not appear to follow the Headedness Principle. For example, in (262) *gōngtuō* 公托 public-entrust 'public daycare centre' (derived from *gōngbàn tuōérsuǒ*) is a noun that has a verb on the right ('entrust') following its formation by abbreviation.

(262) gōngbàn   tuōérsuǒ   → gōngtuō
       公办   托儿所   → 公托
       public-manage   entrust-child-place   → public-entrust
       'public run'   'daycare centre'
            'public daycare centre'   → 'public daycare centre'

As in the case of phonetic loans, the Headedness Principle may appear not to apply here, and as a result these new words would be posited to belong to lexicalization category 4 ('agrammatical lexicalization') at the time they enter the lexicon, i.e., when they are coined.

But this lack of conformity with the Headedness Principle is more apparent than real. By this I mean that when such a word is formed that places, e.g., a *verb* in canonical *noun* head position, the verb often will be reanalysed as a noun by virtue of its occurrence in that position in the new word. So when *gōngbàn tuōérsuǒ* 'public daycare centre' (with the structure [[N V]v [V N N]n]n) is lexicalized as *gōngtuō* (with the structure [N V]n), the erstwhile verb *tuō* actually comes to

---

[11] Yu 1993: 79.

be reanalysed as a noun meaning 'daycare centre'. This is further demonstrated by the existence of the V–O word *rùtuō* 入托 enter-entrust > enter-daycare:centre > 'to enter a public daycare centre', in which *tuō* clearly is being used as a (bound root) noun meaning 'daycare centre'.

It should be clear that neologisms that do not conform to the Headedness Principle will belong to lexicalization category 4 ('agrammatical lexicalization') when they are formed (see 6.1.2.4), because the grammatical, but not necessarily the semantic, relation between the word and its constituents is opaque. Either that, or in the grammar of a native speaker – in the case of *gōngtuō* for example – the (normally) verbal element *tuō* actually comes to be construed as a noun because of its use in canonical noun position.

6.1.3.1.3 Left-modified verbs

This rather large class of exceptions to the Headedness Principle was discussed in 6.1.2.7 in our analysis of words like *qiāngbì* 枪毙 gun-kill 'to shoot dead' and *mànpǎo* 慢跑 slow-run 'to jog' (see (251)–(257)).

These exceptions of the form [–V X]v – that is, a gestalt verb with non-verb modifier on the left – are allowed because the salient modifier–modified property of Chinese grammar permits complex verbs to be composed using a verb on the right modified by an element to its left. This, of course, is a perfectly acceptable word form in Chinese. So these [–V X]v forms can be 'explained' in one of two ways: (a) by saying that there is really no such thing as the Headedness Principle, or (b) by saying that there is a Headedness Principle, to which the [–V X]v forms are exceptions, and this exceptionality causes them to be treated differently in the grammar of Chinese word formation.

Choice (b) is of course the option that I have proposed, with one specific contention being that any word of the form [–V X]v will not be allowed to form a question by duplicating the left-hand non-verb ([–V]) element. My argument is that the verbal element on the right is a 'virtual' rather than 'real' word head – virtual because it is a verb that occurs within a verb, albeit on the right (see 5.5.1), and therefore does not possess the predicted properties of a bona fide verb word head. Even though these [–V X]v examples are argued to be exceptional in Mandarin, and are predicted to behave exceptionally in the grammar, they are in fact permitted to exist by universal rule (see section 5.3.5,

p. 171). Therefore the existence of [–V X]v in violation of the Headedness Principle is a violation of a language-specific rather than universal constraint, and so its 'violation' incurs much less of a 'cost' than would the violation of a universal constraint.

These [–V X]v words are instances of category 4, 'agrammatical lexicalization', because although the grammatical relations are not present (in terms of the Headedness Principle[12]), the semantic information is retained. This is evident from the fact that the meanings of these words (e.g., *mànpǎo* 慢跑 slow-run 'to jog') would be expected to be fully transparent to a learner of Chinese hearing them for the first time.

6.1.3.1.4 Zero-derived complex nouns

Another large class of exceptions to the Headedness Principle are zero-derived nouns that are the concatenation of two verbs (i.e., [V V]N), such as *mǎimài* 买卖 buy-sell 'business', *páiguàn* 排灌 drain-irrigate 'drainage and irrigation', *chīhē* 吃喝 eat-drink 'eating and drinking' and *dòngzuò* 动作 move-do 'activity'. The word-formation process in this case is considered to be zero derivation because the gestalt noun is derived from constituent verbs without the use of an overt grammatical marking process.

Although [V V]N zero-derived nouns are permitted to exist by rule (see table 23), they are predicted to behave exceptionally in the grammar because they violate the Headedness Principle. As is the case with all canonically headless nouns, it is very difficult to demonstrate how they would be treated exceptionally by the grammar since virtually no grammatical operations are performed on noun word heads in Mandarin. As I argued in 6.1.2.7, however, their exceptionality is predicted (tautologously) by hypothesis: any grammatical operations that would depend on the right-hand member being construed as a noun would not be possible if the native speaker did not construe the right-hand member as a noun.

---

[12] This may appear to involve specious reasoning, since its lack of grammatical transparency is defined in terms of the Headedness Principle, and not by what might seem to be the more intuitive 'actual' transparency of the [Mod V]v grammatical structure. The reasoning is sound, however, on the assumption that its failure to conform to the Headedness Principle enables us to predict something about its grammatical behaviour in the grammar as a whole that we could not otherwise predict, in this case its inability to undergo the 'V₁-not-V₁V₂' question operation.

6.1.3.1.5 Induced constituent reanalysis

This refers to words that appear to violate the Headedness Principle because they have constituents that are not identified as verbs and nouns (for left-hand and right-hand constituents respectively), e.g., in dictionary listings, even though they clearly are used as verbs and nouns due to reanalysis that is induced by the gestalt word.

We have seen several instances of this so far, as noted in 3.2. For example, the word *diāo* 雕 'to carve' is listed solely as a verb in major dictionaries,[13] but it clearly functions as a noun when it occupies the right-hand side of such gestalt nouns in words like *shídiāo* 石雕 stone-carve 'stone carving', *bèidiāo* 贝雕 shell-carve 'shell carving', *fúdiāo* 浮雕 float-carve 'relief sculpture', *qīdiāo* 漆雕 paint-carve 'carved lacquerware' and *yádiāo* 牙雕 tooth-(> ivory)-carve 'ivory carving'. Thus, despite its failure to be listed as a noun in dictionaries, it would appear that *diāo* has in fact begun to take on the functional identity of a noun ('carving') in the synchronic grammar of Mandarin word formation.

Induced constituent reanalysis represents a kind of gestalt word 'dominance', since *diāo* is a lexical verb that receives a noun form class interpretation by virtue of its being the right-hand member of a gestalt noun. In other words, the 'verb' form class of *diāo* is in a sense 'overridden' by the form class of the gestalt nouns *shídiāo*, *bèidiāo*, etc. Given this – apparently productive – use of *diāo* as a noun in this way, it should probably be listed in dictionaries as a noun (albeit perhaps only when used as a bound morpheme, at this point in its linguistic history). The fact that it is not now so listed is understandable, as it may be unreasonable to expect lexicographers to remain completely up to date regarding the changing morpheme usage, especially when those morphemes are bound.

Some other examples of induced constituent reanalysis, some of which appeared in 3.2, are:

- *lǐ* 理 listed in dictionaries as a verb meaning 'run, manage' but used as a noun meaning 'one in charge; manager' in such words as *jīnglǐ* 经理 manage-manage 'manager' and *zǒnglǐ* 总理 chief-manage 'premier'

---

[13] *Xiàndài Hànyǔ Cídiǎn*, 1988; *Xīnhuá Zìdiǎn*, 1988; *Hànyīng Cídiǎn* (Wu) 1982; *Yuǎn Dōng Hànyīng Dà Cídiǎn* (Liang) 1992.

- *-zhù-* 助 listed in dictionaries as a verb meaning 'help' but used as a noun meaning 'help, helper' in such words as *tánzhù* 谈助 chat-help 'topic of conversation', *bìzhù* 臂助 arm-help 'helper' and *nèizhù* 内助 inside-help 'wife'
- *tuō* 托 listed in dictionaries as a verb meaning 'entrust' but used as a noun meaning 'daycare centre' in such words as *gōngtuō* 公托 public-entrust 'public daycare centre', *rùtuō* 入托 enter-entrust 'to enter a public daycare centre' (as seen in (262)) and *sītuō* 私托 private-entrust 'private daycare centre'

It should be clear that examples of induced constituent reanalysis such as these are only apparent exceptions to the Headedness Principle, because the constituents in question undergo reanalysis; and do so precisely because of the influence of the Headedness Principle.

6.1.3.2 Other exceptions

This brings us to the words that do not conform for other reasons: they are not recent phonetic loans or neologisms, zero-derived complex nominalized forms such as *mǎimài*, instances of constituent reanalysis forced by the gestalt word like *gōngtuō* 公托, and not left-modified verbs like *qiāngbì* 枪毙 gun-kill 'to shoot dead'. A selection of these may be seen in table 31. Some are instances of category 4 'agrammatical

Table 31 Other exceptions to the Headedness Principle

word	form class	constituent form classes
bìguà 壁挂 wall-hang 'wall hanging'	noun	noun–verb
gōutōng 沟通 ditch-connect 'communicate'	verb	noun–verb
gòuzào 构造 compose-create 'structure'	noun	verb–verb
guōtiē pot-stick 锅贴 'fried dumpling'	noun	noun–verb
wùsè 物色 thing-colour 'to search for'	verb	noun–noun
zuǒyòu 左右 left-right 'to influence'	verb	noun–noun

lexicalization' (like *bìguà* 壁挂 wall-hang 'wall hanging') and some of category 5 'complete lexicalization' (like *wùsè* 物色 thing-colour 'to search for'). In both types of lexicalization, the semantic and grammatical opacity of the word constituents has increased over time, as the word constituents slowly become more and more lexicalized.

The main point of 6.1 has been that lexicalization may be considered a graded or variable phenomenon based on semantic and grammatical opacity, and that in all but the final two stages of lexicalization ('asemantic' and 'complete' lexicalization), speakers possess at least an implicit knowledge of the grammatical relationships that obtain between a word and its components. These two final, most strongly lexicalized stages in the lexicalization of a word are precisely the level at which the Headedness Principle and the X-bar principles in 5.4 are posited to cease being relevant.

6.2 Lexicalization and the availability of word-internal information

In 6.1 we discussed how the degree of word lexicalization determines the extent to which the word is subject to the Headedness Principle. A corollary to that finding is the fact that the degree of a word's lexicalization also determines how available word-internal information is to the grammar in a more general sense: that is, the more strongly lexicalized a word is, the less information from the individual word components is available to the operation of the grammar as a whole. In more specific terms, the more highly lexicalized a word is: (a) the more its components are susceptible to phonological reduction; (b) the less its components are subject to phonological rule application; (c) the less its components are subject to morphological rule application; (d) the less the syntactic information contained in individual components is available to the grammar and (e) the less other semantic information contained in word components is accessible by the grammar.

The intuition behind these generalizations regarding the availability of word-internal linguistic information is that when lexicalization occurs, word-internal information – be it phonological, morphological, syntactic or semantic – is rendered less salient to the grammar as a whole because of the opacity of the word-internal environment. In the case of phonological reduction, the individual phonological features begin to lose their saliency and therefore undergo a loss of phonological distinction. In the case of failure of phonological rules to apply, the opacity of the word-internal environment results in phonological rules failing to 'read' the word-internal phonological information as a suitable context for the application of the rules. The same reasoning applies in the case of morphological rules, where word-internal morphological information fails to trigger a morphological rule due to the opacity of that information. The same is true for word-internal syntactic information – such as the theta role information on individual members of complex verbs (see 6.2.3) – which becomes unavailable due to the opacity of the word-internal environment. This loss of information is also true for the compositional semantics of complex words in an almost trivial or redundant sense, since, as I have already explicitly argued, lexicalization directly entails the reduction of word-internal semantic information.[14]

Specific examples of the above processes are presented in the following sections.

6.2.1 Phonological information

Lexicalization is often accompanied by phonological change, which most often takes the form of phonological attrition or reduction in prominence. Hopper and Traugott make this generalization with respect to morphologized elements (1993: 145–6), but it applies to lexicalized elements as well. One type of phonological reduction commonly noted is loss of stress, tone or accent, which is precisely what occurs in the case of Mandarin Chinese. A change from full tone to neutral tone is what would be expected in cases of Mandarin lexicalization, especially if neutral tone is viewed as an accentual or stress phenomenon (as is argued, for example, in Packard 1997c).

The phonological reduction of lexicalized elements in Chinese is implied by Chao in his discussion of V–O compounds (1968: 415, 417), in which he designates neutral tone on the object as a diagnostic for determining whether a V–O form has been lexicalized as a word. The problem with this, as noted by Chi (1985: 74; see also 4.3.4.2), is that the presence of neutral tone is neither necessary nor sufficient to identify lexicalized V–O elements. We are correct to suspect, however, that a

---

[14] See also Lipka (1990: 95, as cited in Traugott forthcoming), who describes compounding as involving loss of semantic compositionality.

strong correlation nonetheless exists between the presence of neutral tone and of lexicalization. This being the case, we may hypothesize a correlation in Mandarin between the appearance of neutral tone and another characteristic associated with words that are considered strongly lexicalized, namely, opacity of gestalt word meaning and grammar.

In order to test this hypothesis, I selected a random dictionary sample of neutral-toned words, to see if the words with neutral tone are more 'opaque' in terms of meaning and grammar than words without neutral tone. My method was to begin near the front of *A Chinese–English Dictionary* (Wu 1988) and randomly flip forward several pages at a time, selecting all the neutral-toned words on the two adjoining pages where I stopped to take the sample. The word directly beneath the neutral-toned word was chosen as the counterpart example of a non-neutral-toned word to be used as a 'control' item. For each neutral-toned word and its full-toned control, I noted whether both the meaning of the word and its 'grammar' (i.e., the form classes of the elements and the nature of their relationship) were opaque or transparent. The specific hypothesis was that more neutral-toned than full-toned words would have opaque meaning and grammar.

Some notes on the methodology of this procedure: (a) words of three of more syllables were not included; (b) forms which are suspected of being V–O phrases were not included, since they would be expected to have conventionalized meaning if they were dictionary-listed phrases; (c) where there exists no entry with the same head word directly following the neutral tone word, I selected the word directly preceding; where there exists no entry with the same head word following or preceding the neutral tone word, I selected the first word in the following head word entry; (d) in deciding opaque versus transparent, I took a conservative approach and (i) weighted the decision in favour of transparency for debatable cases, and (ii) granted transparency to the word if one morpheme had a transparent meaning.

This procedure yielded twenty neutral-toned words and twenty non-neutral-toned word counterparts, which usually shared the same first morpheme. Note that in some cases this 'same' morpheme is glossed as having different meanings in the two words. This is due to the fact that most morphemes are intrinsically polysemous, with the different meanings normally listed under the single entry for that morpheme. The dictionary entry data and opacity judgments are given in table 32.

Table 32 Meaning transparency in neutral-toned words

Neutral or Full tone	word	meaning	Opaque or Transparent meaning?	Opaque or Transparent grammar?
N	cuōhe 撮合 gather-join	'make a match'	T	T
F	cuōnòng 撮弄 gather-tease	'make fun of'	T	T
N	cuòchu 错处 wrong-place	'fault'	T	T
F	cuòguài 错怪 wrong-blame	'blame wrongly'	T	T
N	jūni 拘泥 constrain-mud	'be a stickler for'	O	O
F	jūpiào 拘票 constrain-ticket	'arrest warrant'	T	T
N	juéhu 绝户 finish-household	'without offspring'	T	T
F	juéjī 绝迹 finish-trace	'vanish'	T	T
N	láiwang 来往 come-go:toward	'dealings' (cf láiwǎng 'come and go')	O	T
F	láiwén 来文 come-writing	'document received'	T	T

LEXICALIZATION AND CHINESE WORDS

Table 32 *(cont'd)*

Neutral or Full tone	word	meaning	Opaque or Transparent meaning?	Opaque or Transparent grammar?
N	lìba 力巴 strength-close	'clumsy'	O	O
F	lìbì 力臂 strength-arm	'arm of force (physics)'	T	T
N	língsan 零散 part-scatter	'scattered'	T	T
F	língshí 零时 zero-hour	'zero hour'	T	T
N	luànteng 乱腾 disorder-soar	'disorder'	T	T
F	luànzhēn 乱真 confuse-real	'look genuine'	T	T
N	máli 麻俐 numb-sharp	'deft'	T	T
F	mámù 麻木 numb-numb	'numb'	T	T
N	mǎhu 马虎 horse-tiger	'careless'	O	O
F	mǎjiǎo 马脚 horse-foot	'something that gives someone away'	O	O

Table 32 (cont'd)

Neutral or Full tone	word	meaning	Opaque or Transparent meaning?	Opaque or Transparent grammar?
N	mùxi 木犀 wood-rhinoceros	'scrambled egg'	O	O
F	mùxiān 木锨 wood-spade	'wooden winnowing spade'	T	T
N	rènshi 认识 identify-know	'know, recognize'	T	T
F	rènshū 认输 admit-lose	'admit defeat'	T	T
N	rènwu 任务 assume-serve	'assignment, job'	T	T
F	rènxìng 任性 allow-'-ness'	'wilful'	O	T
N	róucuo 揉搓 rub-rub	'rub'	T	T
F	róuhé 糅合 mix-combine	'mix'	T	T
N	ròushi 肉食 meat-food	'meat' (cf ròushí 'carnivorous')	T	T
F	ròusī 肉丝 meat-thread	'shredded meat'	T	T
N	tèwu 特务 special-task	'secret agent' (cf tèwù 'special task')	O	T

LEXICALIZATION AND CHINESE WORDS

Table 32 (cont'd)

Neutral or Full tone	word	meaning	Opaque or Transparent meaning?	Opaque or Transparent grammar?
F	tèxiào 特效 special-effect	'specially good effect'	T	T
N	tōngrong 通融 open-blend	'make an exception to the rules'	O	T
F	tōngshāng 通商 open-commerce	'have trade relations'	T	T
N	wěiqu 委屈 indirect-injustice	'feel wronged'	T	T
F	wěirèn 委任 appoint-job	'appoint'	T	T
N	xīhan 稀罕 rare-scarce	'rare'	T	T
F	xīkè 稀客 rare-guest	'rare visitor'	T	T
N	xīla 锡鑞 tin-wax	'solder'	T	T
F	xīshí 锡石 tin-stone	'tinstone'	T	T
		neutral-toned	T = 13 O = 7	T = 16 O = 4
		full-toned	T = 18 O = 2	T = 19 O = 1

As seen in the last two rows of table 32, it is clear that, in the case of meaning, the percentage of neutral-toned words that are semantically opaque is higher than the percentage of full-toned words (7 of 20 = 35% vs. 2 of 20 = 10%, respectively) at a level that reaches statistical significance (population proportion significance test, 35% vs. 10%: Z = 1.89, one-tailed p < .03). For grammar, the percentage of opaque neutral-toned words is also higher than that of full-toned words (4 of 20 = 20% vs. 1 of 20 = 5%), though the difference approaches, but does not reach, statistical significance (population proportion significance test, 20% vs. 5%: Z = 1.43, one-tailed p = .076). Collapsing the two categories of semantic and grammatical opacity, neutral-toned words had a 27.5% (11 of 40) incidence of opacity as compared with 7.5% (3 of 40) of the full-toned words, a difference which is highly significant (population proportion significance test, 27.5% vs. 7.5%: Z = 2.35, one-tailed p < .01). These results demonstrate that the words with a neutral tone were more semantically and grammatically opaque – characteristics that go hand and hand with a greater degree of lexicalization.

Another example of phonological opacity in highly lexicalized words is the non-application of the third tone sandhi rule in certain highly lexicalized environments. There is a class of complex noun words (such as *ěrduo* 耳朵 ear-cluster 'ear' and *lǐji* 里脊 inside-spine 'tenderloin') that, although composed of two morphemes with third tones, do not undergo the expected obligatory tone sandhi rule (whereby the first of two consecutive third tones changes to a second tone: 3–3 ⇒ 2–3). These words do not undergo the rule because this class of words has been lexicalized to the point where the right-hand morpheme is 'phonologically opaque', i.e., not analysed by the native speaker as a third-toned word, and so does not trigger the 3–3 ⇒ 2–3 sandhi operation (Packard 1997c). Thus, we have an example from Mandarin of phonological information (viz., the fact that one of the morphemes is third-toned) being 'unavailable' for phonological rule application in a highly lexicalized environment.

A final example of phonological opacity in highly lexicalized words is the failure of a sandhi-changed 3–3 ⇒ 2–3 'second' tone to revert back to its original 'third' tone following the removal of the sandhi-triggering context, e.g., when the lexicalized word containing the tone change is shortened. As an example, the word 'ballet' entered the Mandarin lexicon as a phonetic loan, with the underlying phonological form of *bālěiwǔ* (芭蕾舞 banana-bud-dance). The 3–3 ⇒ 2–3 tone sandhi rule changes the surface tone pattern to *bāléiwǔ*, with the third tone of *lěi* changing to a second tone *léi*. However, in using the common shortened form which drops the last syllable of the word (*wǔ*), most speakers pronounce the syllable *lei* as *léi* in second tone, yielding the form *bāléi*. The anomaly here is that in producing the shortened form, speakers should 'undo' the tone sandhi rule, pronouncing the shortened word for 'ballet' as *bālěi*, since *lěi* has a (underlying) third tone, and the syllable *wǔ* that triggered the sandhi in the full-form word has been removed. This, however, does not occur, because the word *bāléiwǔ*, as a phonetic loan, is the most highly lexicalized type of word (category 5 'complete lexicalization'; see 6.1.2.5) and therefore the underlying phonological identity of *léi* as *lěi* cannot be 'seen' by the grammar (i.e., the native speaker) following the removal of the triggering context, due to its opacity as a highly lexicalized phonetic loan.

This is in contrast with, for example, the word *láobǎo* 劳保 work-protect 'labour insurance', abbreviated from the term *láodòng bǎoxiǎn* 劳动保险 work-move-protect-risk 'labour insurance'. The 3-3 ⇒ 2-3 tone sandhi rule occurs in the long form of this word, resulting in the change from *láodòng bǎoxiǎn* to *láodòng báoxiǎn* (*bǎo* ⇒ *báo*). But notice the sandhi rule is 'undone' when the word is abbreviated, yielding *láobǎo* rather than *láobáo, since the word *bǎoxiǎn* (⇒ *báoxiǎn*) which contains the changed syllable *báo* is not as highly lexicalized as, e.g., the phonetic loan *bāléiwǔ*, and therefore the underlying phonological identity of *bǎo* has not become opaque. Thus, when the triggering context for sandhi (*xiǎn*) is removed following abbreviation, the syllable *báo* reverts back to its original tone *bǎo*, since its underlying phonological identity remains transparent to the grammar (i.e., native speaker).

6.2.2 Morphological information

The more highly lexicalized a word is, the less its components are subject to morphological rule processes. Anderson (speaking of inflection) says:

> when an inflected form develops such a specialized sense, not predictable from the semantics of its base form taken together with the category in which it appears, the result is that this surface form is separately lexicalized... As a consequence, changes in regular morphology have no effect on the new item, insofar as the Word Formation Rules in question are no longer involved in its formation. (1992: 371)

In Chinese, one of the most common morphological processes – affixation of the -*zi* 子 -*tou* 头 and -*r* 儿 'nominalizing' suffixes – cannot occur internal to a lexicalized environment. In other words, -*zi*, -*tou* and -*r* can never attach to one of the two morphemes of a two-morpheme noun word once the word has been formed. Rather, such affixation must operate on the gestalt word.

The occurrence of -*zi*, -*tou* and -*r* affixed nouns as constituents within complex nominals is generally disfavoured in Mandarin in any case. Using *cuò* 错 'incorrect, mistake' as an example, the noun *cuòr* 错儿 mistake-SUF 'mistake' may be derived from *cuò* by -*er* suffixation. But while the words *cuòwù* 错误 mistake-mistake 'mistake' and *chācuò* 差错 mistake-mistake 'mistake' are allowed, the words **cuòrwù* 错儿误 or **chācuòr* 差错儿 are not. In columns 3 and 6 of table 33, we see that what is true in the case of *cuòr* is true in Mandarin in general: complex nouns that have -*zi*, -*tou* and -*r* affixed nominals as constituents are generally bad.[15]

The fact that the constraint against affixed nominals within noun words is a strong tendency rather than an absolute prohibition is shown by the acceptability of such words as *bàngzimǐ* 棒子米 club-AFF-rice 'corn', *gērmen* 哥儿们 brother-AFF-PL 'brothers', *shítoulù* 石头路 stone-AFF-road 'gravel road', *tǔbāozi* 土包子 dirt-bag-AFF 'country bumpkin', *bīnggùnr* 冰棍儿 ice-stick-AFF 'popsicle' and *shǒuzhǐtou* 手指头 hand-finger-AFF 'finger'.

But although -*zi*, -*tou* and -*r* affixed words occurring as constituents within complex nouns are allowed, such affixation occurring on word-internal constituents *subsequent to* the formation of the complex noun is an absolute prohibition: in no case does the affixing of -*zi*, -*tou* and -*r* occur on one of the two morphemes 'after' they have combined to form a word. This means that for all complex noun words that have the forms [[N₁ AFF]N₂]ₙ or [N₁[N₂ AFF]]ₙ, the respective words [N₁ AFF]ₙ and [N₂ AFF]ₙ must independently exist a priori in order for such internally affixed complex noun words to be acceptable.

This is borne out by the data, since all nouns that have the -*zi*, -*tou* or -*r* affix on their left-hand member, like *bàngzimǐ*, *gērmen* and *shítoulù* (with the respective structures [[bangzi]mi], [[ger]men] and [[shitou]lu]),

---

[15] If in fact some of the complex words containing -*zi*, -*tou* and -*r* affixed nominals in table 33 are acceptable, it is either because the affixation occurs on the word boundary rather than word-internally, or because the affixed nominal independently exists as a word. See discussion accompanying table 33.

Table 33 Internally affixed words

nominal affixed word	word using the first morpheme of nominal affixed word	unacceptable internally affixed word	nominal affixed word	word using the first morpheme of nominal affixed word	unacceptable internally affixed word
cír 词儿 word-SUF 'word'	cídiǎn 词典 word-canon 'dictionary'	*círdiǎn 词儿典	lìzi 例子 example-SUF 'example'	lìjù 例句 example-sentence 'example sentence'	*lìzijù 例子句
	gēcí 歌词 song-word 'lyrics'	*gēcír 歌词儿		shìlì 事例 matter-example 'instance'	*shìlìzi 事例子
diǎnr 点儿 dot-SUF 'bit'	diǎnxīn 点心 dot-heart 'pastry'	*diǎnrxīn 点儿心	màozi 帽子 hat-SUF 'hat'	màoshé 帽舌 hat-tongue 'visor'	*màozishé 帽子舌
	bāndiǎn 斑点 spot-dot 'spot'	*bāndiǎnr 斑点儿		cǎomào 草帽 straw-hat 'straw hat'	*cǎomàozi 草帽子
diàotou 调头 tone-SUF 'tone'	diàozhí 调值 tone-value 'pitch'	*diàotouzhí 调头值	miáotou 苗头 seedling-SUF 'symptom'	miáochuáng 苗床 seedling-bed 'seed bed'	*miáotouchuáng 苗头床
	shēngdiào 声调 sound-tone 'pitch'	*shēngdiàotou 声调头		yúmiáo 鱼苗 fish-seedling 'fry'	*yúmiáotou 鱼苗头
diàozi 调子 tone-SUF 'tone'		*diàozizhí 调子值	mùtou 木头 wood-SUF 'wood'	mùliào 木料 wood-material 'lumber'	*mùtouliào 木头料
		*shēngdiàozi 声调子		zhěnmù 枕木 pillow-wood 'railroad tie'	*zhěnmùtou 枕木头
dīngzi 钉子 nail-SUF 'nail'	dīngxié 钉鞋 nail-shoe 'spiked shoes'	*dīngzixié 钉子鞋			
	luódīng 螺钉 snail-nail 'screw'	*luódīngzi 螺钉子			

Table 33 (cont'd)

nominal affixed word	word using the first morpheme of nominal affixed word	unacceptable internally affixed word	nominal affixed word	word using the first morpheme of nominal affixed word	unacceptable internally affixed word
gēr 歌儿 song-SUF 'song'	gēqǔ 歌曲 song-song 'song'	*gērqǔ 歌儿曲	páizi 牌子 sign-SUF 'sign'	páizhào 牌照 sign-licence 'licence plate'	*páizizhào 牌子照
	zhàngē 战歌 war-song 'fighting song'	*zhàngēr 战歌儿		ménpái 门牌 door-sign 'door sign'	*ménpáizi 门牌子
gēr 哥儿 brother-SUF 'brother'	gēge 哥哥 brother-brother 'older brother'	*gērge 哥儿哥	rénr 人儿 person-SUF 'person'	réngōng 人工 person-work 'manpower'	*rénrgōng 人儿工
		*gēger 哥哥儿		gōngrén 工人 work-person 'worker'	*gōngrénr 工人儿
huǒr 火儿 fire-SUF 'fire'	huǒchē 火车 five-vehicle 'train'	*huǒrchē 火儿车	shétou 舌头 tongue-SUF 'tongue'	shéyán 舌炎 tongue-inflammation 'glossitis'	*shétouyán 舌头炎
	dēnghuǒ 灯火 lamp-fire 'lights'	*dēnghuǒr 灯火儿		huǒshé 火舌 fire-tongue 'flame'	*huǒshétou 火舌头
làngtou 浪头 wave-SUF 'wave, trend'	làngcháo 浪潮 wave-wave 'tide'	*làngtoucháo 浪头潮	wèir 味儿 odour-SUF 'odour'	wèidào 味道 odour-course 'smell'	*wèirdào 味儿道
	bōlàng 波浪 wave-wave 'wave'	*bōlàngtou 波浪头		qìwèi 气味 air-odour 'smell'	*qìwèir 气味儿
			xiézi 鞋子 shoe-SUF 'shoes'	xiéshé 鞋舌 shoe-tongue 'shoe tongue'	*xiézishé 鞋子舌
				bùxié 布鞋 cloth-shoe 'cloth shoes'	*bùxiézi 布鞋子

or on their right, like *tǔbāozi*, *bīnggùnr* and *shǒuzhítou* (with the respective structures [*tu*[*baozi*]], [*bing*[*gunr*]] and [*shou*[*zhitou*]]), are only acceptable because the words *bàngzi* club-AFF 'club', *gēr* brother-AFF 'brother', *shítou* stone-AFF 'stone', *baōzi* bag-AFF 'steamed stuffed bun', *gùnr* stick-AFF 'stick' and *zhítou* finger-AFF 'finger' already independently exist as lexical items.[16] If the affixation appears on the word-internal constituent, the affixed form must already exist. I know of no exceptions to this generalization.

Note that this prohibition against word-internal affixation does not rule out words of the form [[N₁ N₂]AFF], since 'external' affixation (i.e., affixation to the word itself) is not disallowed. So we do in fact find examples such as *èrhūn*r 二婚儿 two-marriage-AFF 'remarried woman', *shuōtou*r 说头儿 speak-AFF-AFF 'something to talk about', *niànxīn*r 念心儿 recall-heart-AFF 'memento' and *xīnlù*r 心路儿 heart-road-AFF 'scheme' (with the respective structures [[*erhun*]*r*], [[*shuotou*]*r*], [[*nianxin*]*r*] and [[*xinlu*]*r*]), which are acceptable because they are instances of affixation 'external' to the gestalt word.

Other examples of more highly lexicalized words being less subject to morphological rules can be seen in Packard 1997c, where it is argued that the most productive morphological processes that occur in the lexicon (reduplication of complex adjectives and verbs, non-complex verb reduplication, and 'V₁-not-V₁–V₂' question inflection) occur at the 'least lexicalized' strata of the lexicon, namely strata 3 and 4 (Packard 1997c). In that theory, the only morphological reduplication processes occuring at the 'most lexicalized' stratum (stratum 1) are kinship/hypercoristic reduplication (e.g., *jiě* 姐 sister ⇒ *jiějie* 姐姐 sister-sister 'sister', *nǎi* 奶 grandmother ⇒ *nǎinai* 奶奶 grandmother-grandmother 'grandmother', *bǎo* 宝 precious ⇒ *bǎobao* 宝宝 precious-precious 'precious one' and *gǒu* 狗 'dog' ⇒ *gǒugou* 狗狗 dog-dog 'doggy') and adverbial reduplication (e.g., *hǎo* 好 'good' ⇒ *hǎohāorde* 好好儿地 good-good-AFF-AFF '(to do something) well'). While these highly lexicalized forms do undergo the morphological process of reduplication, crucially, the reduplicated forms are opaque to phonological rules in the sense discussed in 6.2.1, since they are not subject to the phonological 3–3 ⇒ 2–3 tone sandhi operation. This being the

---

[16] Also acceptable are words such as *mùtourénr* 木头人儿 wood-AFF-person-AFF 'blockhead', which have *-tou* and *-r* affixes on *both* the right-hand and left-hand members. This form is acceptable because both *mùtou* 'wood' and *rénr* 'person' exist independently as words.

case, the morphemes *jiě, năi, băo* and *gŏu* in the examples above all retain their original third tone in the reduplicated form (Packard 1997c: 315–16).

6.2.3 Syntactic information: theta roles in complex verbs

As stated by Traugott (forthcoming: 6), 'L[exicalization] results in morphosyntactic opacity'. That principle – i.e., that the more lexicalized a word is, the less information is available from the components of that word – is instantiated in Mandarin complex verb words[17] as the unavailability of thematic role or argument structure information from the verb's right-hand or 'non-head' component. Intuitively speaking, the more lexicalized the verb is, the less the argument structure information of the verb components is contributed to the gestalt verb. This can be seen in two types of complex verbs: V_1–V_2 resultative verbs (see 4.3.3) and V–O verbs (see 4.3.4). In the case of resultative verbs, the more lexicalized the gestalt verb is, the less the argument structure of the V_2 non-head becomes part of the argument structure of the gestalt verb. In the case of V–O verbs, the more lexicalized the gestalt verb is, the less the information from the non-head 'object' is available to satisfy the argument structure of the gestalt verb. Let us look at resultatives first.

6.2.3.1 Availability of resultative V_2 argument structure

It was stated in 4.3.3.1 that the argument structures of V_1–V_2 resultative verbs are usually a straightforward composite of the argument structures of the V_1 and V_2 components. I will now illustrate this with examples from the three classes of resultatives discussed in 4.3.3.1 (stative resultatives, directional resultatives and attainment resultatives), and then demonstrate how lexicalization causes this argument structure information to become unavailable.

Every verb has an argument structure, which is a specification of the types of arguments (subject, object, indirect object, etc.) it optionally or obligatorily takes, normally specified in terms of thematic roles

---

[17] In the case of complex noun words, this principle might predict that, e.g., anaphoric coreference relations between components of such words and sentence arguments would be more possible the less lexicalized the complex noun is. This prediction does not hold, however, because anaphoric coreference between sentence- and word-internal constituents is impossible for any word, independent of its degree of lexicalization, due to the Lexical Integrity Hypothesis.

Table 34 Thematic roles

thematic role	symbol	description
Agent	A	initiator of action
Theme	T	entity undergoing action or to which state is ascribed
Stative	S	entity to which state is ascribed
Location	L	final endpoint of action
Goal	G	recipient of Theme

or *theta roles*. I will use the theta roles Agent, Theme, Stative, Location and Goal corresponding to the labels seen in table 34 (modified from Ross 1990), where Agent is the primary 'actor', traditionally associated with subject, Theme refers to the entity that is the receiver of the action, Stative refers to that entity whose description is specified by the stative verb, Location is the final endpoint of the action and Goal is the recipient of Theme, or the 'indirect object' in traditional terms. Goal and Location are traditionally considered the 'object of the preposition' in English. Although I have chosen these thematic roles A, T, S, L and G for demonstration purposes, the specific names and exact properties of the theta roles are not crucial to the argument.

To demonstrate, the verb *gěi* 给 'give' takes an Agent (subject), a Theme (direct object) and a Goal (indirect object), so the argument structure is listed in its *thematic grid* as [$A_i\ G_j\ T_k$] in (263), with the subscript indexes (i, j, k) indicating the specific referents in the sentence that fill those respective roles.

(263) wǒ$_i$ gěi   tā$_j$ shū$_k$ le
       我   给   他   书   了
       I   give   him   book   ASP
       'I gave him the book'

       gěi   'give'   [$A_i\ G_j\ T_k$]

If there is a single referent in the sentence that fills two thematic roles (for example, the same person being the Agent of one sentence verb and the Theme of another), this is indicated by coindexing the two theta roles with the same subscript index. This is illustrated in (264), where the person who is walking and the person who is tired are the same person, so the Agent of *zǒu* and the Stative quality of *lèi* are ascribed to the same referent (*tā*), and therefore the theta grids of both *zǒu* and *lèi* are coindexed with 'i'.

(264) tā$_i$ zǒu lèi le
他 走 累 了
he walk tired ASP
'He got tired from walking'

zǒu 'walk' [A$_i$]
lèi 'tired' [S$_i$]

Turning first to examples of stative resultatives, notice that whether V$_1$ is intransitive ((265), (269)), or transitive ((266), (267), (268)), and regardless of whether V$_1$ shares an argument with the V$_2$ ((267), (268)) or not (269), the argument structures of V$_1$ and V$_2$ always combine perfectly to yield the argument structure on the gestalt verb, under the reasonable assumption that when the arguments on V$_1$ and V$_2$ are coreferential, they are 'collapsed' on the gestalt verb, a process termed 'theta identification' by Li (1990).

(265) mèimèi$_i$ zhǎngdà le
妹妹 长大 了
sister grow-big ASP
'Little sister has grown up'

zhǎng 'grow' [A$_i$]
dà 'big' [S$_i$]
zhǎngdà 'get big from growing' [A$_i$ S$_i$]

(266) dìdi$_i$ chuānlànle yīfu$_j$
弟弟 穿烂了 衣服
brother wear-worn:out-ASP clothes
'Little brother wore out the clothes'

chuān 'wear' [A$_i$ T$_j$]
làn 'worn out' [S$_j$]
chuānlàn 'wear out (from wearing)' [A$_i$ S$_j$ T$_j$]

(267) tā$_i$ hēzuìle jiǔ$_j$
他 喝醉了 酒
he drink-drunk-ASP wine
'He got drunk by drinking wine'

hē 'drink' [A$_i$ T$_j$]
zuì 'drunk' [S$_i$]
hēzuì 'get drunk (from drinking)' [A$_i$ S$_i$ T$_j$]

(268) kèrén_i   chībǎole   fàn_j
      客人   吃饱了   饭
      guest   eat-full-ASP   rice
      'The guests are full from eating rice'

      chī   'eat'   [A_i T_j]
      bǎo   'full'   [S_i]
      chībǎo   'eat one's fill'   [A_i S_i T_j]

(269) háizi_i   kūhóngle   yǎnjīng_j
      孩子   哭红了   眼睛
      child   cry-red-ASP   eyes
      'The child has cried his eyes red'

      kū   'cry'   [A_i]
      hóng   'red'   [S_j]
      kūhóng   'turn red from crying' [A_i S_j T_j]

Notice also that although there are clear cases of theta role identification (and there is also the apparent 'creation' of a theta role ([T_j]) for *kūhóng* in (269)), there are no cases of theta role 'loss', i.e., cases where the theta role on any V₁ or V₂ fails to be realized on the gestalt verb.[18]

Looking now at examples of directional resultatives, notice again that whether V₁ is intransitive (270) or transitive (271), the theta roles of V₁ and V₂ nonetheless all show up to yield the argument structure on the gestalt verb.

(270) xuéshēng_i   zǒujìnle   túshūguǎn_j
      学生   走进了   图书馆
      student   walk-enter-ASP   library
      'The student walked into the library'

      zǒu   'walk'   [A_i]
      jìn   'enter'   [A_i L_j]
      zǒujìn   'enter by walking' [A_i L_j]

(271) lǎoshī_i   bǎ   shū_j   náhuí   túshūguǎn_k   le
      老师   把   书   拿回   图书馆   了
      teacher   BA   book   take-return   library   ASP
      'The teacher took the book back to the library'

      ná   'take'   [A_i T_j]
      huí   'return'   [A_i L_k]
      náhuí   'take back'   [A_i T_j L_k]

---

[18] Except, as I shall demonstrate below, in the case of lexicalized words.

Although theta role identification when there is coreference is the norm, there are once again no cases of theta role 'loss', in which a theta role on any V₁ or V₂ fails to be realized on the gestalt verb. That is, as in the case of stative resultatives, the argument structures of V₁ and V₂ combine perfectly to yield the argument structure on the gestalt verb, with no cases in which a referent of V₂ is not realized on the gestalt verb.

Taking a look now at attainment resultatives, as with the stative and the directional resultatives, irrespective of which actual theta roles are employed and regardless of which roles and referents are shared by V₁ and V₂, in (272)–(277) the argument structures of the V₁V₂ verbs are derived completely by combining the individual argument structures of V₁ and V₂, with allowance for theta role identification.

(272) wǒmen$_i$ zǒudào   túshūguǎn$_j$ le
       我们   走到   图书馆   了
       we   walk-arrive   library   ASP
       'We walked to the library'

       zǒu   'walk, go'   [A$_i$]
       dào   'arrive'   [A$_i$ L$_j$]
       zǒudào   'walk to'   [A$_i$ L$_j$]

(273) zéi$_i$ názǒule   píbāo$_j$
       贼   拿走了   皮包
       thief   take-go-ASP   handbag
       'The thief took the handbag'

       ná   'take'   [A$_i$ T$_j$]
       zǒu   'walk, go'   [A$_i$]
       názǒu   'take away'   [A$_i$ T$_j$]

(274) xiǎogǒu$_i$ èsǐ   le
       小狗   饿死   了
       small-dog   hungry-die   ASP
       'The puppy starved to death'

       è   'hungry'   [S$_i$]
       sǐ   'die'   [T$_i$]
       èsǐ   'starve to death' [S$_i$ T$_i$]

(275) Zhèzhǒng   yàopǐn$_i$ néng   shāsǐ   xìjūn$_j$
       这种   药品   能   杀死   细菌
       this-kind   medicine   can   kill-die   bacteria
       'This kind of medicine can kill bacteria'

LEXICALIZATION AND CHINESE WORDS

        shā   'kill'   [$A_i\ T_j$]
        sǐ   'die'   [T_j]
        shāsǐ   'kill'   [$A_i\ T_j$]

(276) wǒ$_i$ kànjiàn   tā$_j$ le
       我   看见   她   了
       I   look-perceive   her   ASP
      'I saw her'

        kàn   'look'   [$A_i\ T_j$]
        jiàn   'perceive'   [$A_i\ T_j$]
        kànjiàn 'see'   [$A_i\ T_j$]

(277) wǒmen$_i$ tīngdǒng   Hànyǔ$_j$
       我们   听懂   汉语
       we   hear-understand Chinese
      'We understand (spoken) Chinese'

        tīng   'hear'   [$A_i\ T_j$]
        dǒng   'understand'   [$A_i\ T_j$]
        tīngdǒng 'understand (via hearing)' [$A_i\ T_j$]

Examples (263)–(277) are highly representative of the class of V_1–V_2 resultative verbs, and demonstrate that, in general, resultative verbs – whether they are stative, directional or attainment – freely allow the percolation of argument structure information from both V_1 and V_2, and thus are remarkably compositional in terms of the argument structures of their components.

Now, there is a group of V_2 components that behave in all other respects like resultative endings, but are exceptions to this general property of compositionality, since they do not contribute full theta role information to the resultative verbs they form. These are the V_2 endings that serve to modify the action of V_1 instead of describing its result. Chao (1968: 446) and Li and Thompson (1981: 65) call resultatives with these endings 'phase' resultatives, and Chang describes these endings as 'degenerate' (Chang 1997: 81, 98 n. 4).

Some examples of these are the V_2 endings in the following words: *kàndào* 看到 look-arrive 'see', *dǎwán* 打完 hit-finish 'to finish hitting', *bànchéng* 办成 do-complete 'to finish doing', *zhuājǐn* 抓紧 grab-tight 'to grasp tightly', *jìzhù* 记住 remember-fixed 'to remember well', *zuòxià* 坐下 sit-descend 'to (have room to) seat', *zhàoshang* 照上 photograph-ascend 'to (fit into the) photograph', *shuìzháo* 睡著 sleep-touch 'to fall asleep' and *xǐdé* 洗得 wash-attain 'to be able to be washed'.

Readers familiar with these words will notice that in all cases, the V₂ component is more properly seen as modifying the nature of V₁ predication rather than necessarily describing the result of V₁ on one of the verb arguments. The reason for this is that these 'degenerate' resultatives – unlike regular resultatives – percolate theta role information from V₁ – but not V₂ – to the gestalt verb. The reason V₂ theta role information does not percolate – following our discussion in 6.2 – is that these resultatives are more highly lexicalized than regular resultatives.

The non-percolation of theta roles in these V₂ endings is best demonstrated by contrasting their usage as lexicalized 'degenerate' endings with their usage as full, non-lexicalized, 'non-degenerate' resultative endings. Compare, for example, the resultative verbs *zǒudào* and *kàndào* in (278a–c).

(278) a. wǒmenᵢ   zǒudào   túshūguǎnⱼ   le
         我们   走到   图书馆   了
         we   walk-arrive   library   ASP
         'We walked to the library'

   b. wǒmenᵢ   kàndào   túshūguǎnⱼ   le
         我们   看到   图书馆   了
         we   look-arrive   library   ASP
         'We saw the library'

   c. zǒu   'walk, go'   [Aᵢ]
      kàn   'look'   [Aᵢ Tⱼ]
      dào   'arrive'   [Aᵢ Lⱼ]
      zǒudào   'walk to'   [Aᵢ Lⱼ]
      kàndào   'see'   [Aᵢ Tⱼ]

In (278c), from the theta grids we see that the argument structure on *zǒudào* is a perfect concatenation of the argument structures on *zǒu* and on *dào* (as we saw in (272)). The argument structure on *kàndào*, however, is not a composite of the argument structures of *kàn* and *dào*: the [Lⱼ] Location theta role that is ascribed to *dào* has been 'lost' in the gestalt resultative verb *kàndào*. Intuitively, what has happened is that while it is the Location 'library' that has been 'arrived at' by the Agent in *zǒudào*, the library is no longer 'arrived at' by the Agent in *kàndào*: the 'arrival' meaning that is usually discharged onto the Location argument of *dào* has now come to modify the verb *kàn*, so that the 'arrival' meaning has been 'transferred' to and associated with the verbal action of *kàn*. This means that, in a sense, it is something about the action of 'looking' itself – rather than a syntactic argument of 'look' – that has arrived at the library in the word *kàndào*.

To demonstrate the point in a slightly different way, compare the resultative verbs *zājǐn* 扎紧 tie-tight 'to tie tightly' in (279a) and (279c), and *zhuājǐn* 抓紧 grab-tight 'to grasp tightly, to seize' (279b) and (279d).[19]

(279) a. lǎorén$_i$ zājǐnle   kǒudài$_j$
老人   扎紧了   口袋
old man   tie-tight-ASP   bag
'The old man tightened the bag'

b. wǒmen$_i$ zhuājǐnle   shíjī$_j$
我们   抓紧了   时机
we   grab-tight-ASP   opportunity
'We seize the opportunity'

c. zā   'tie'   [A$_i$ T$_j$]
jǐn   'tight'   [S$_j$]
zājǐn   'tighten'   [A$_i$ S$_j$ T$_j$]

d. zhuā   'grab'   [A$_i$ T$_j$]
jǐn   'tight'   [S$_j$]
zhuājǐn   'grab tightly'   [A$_i$ T$_j$]

The stative verb ending *jǐn* 'tight' is exactly the same lexical item with identical argument structures in both words *zājǐn* and *zhuājǐn*, but the verb *zājǐn* is a 'regular' resultative, while the word *zhuājǐn* has become much more highly lexicalized in Mandarin, thereby changing its status to that of 'degenerate' resultative. The argument structure of the regular resultative *zājǐn* is a perfect sum of the argument structures on *zā* and on *jǐn* (with the usual theta identification due to coreference), as seen in the theta grid in (279c). The more highly lexicalized verb *zhuājǐn*, on the other hand, has 'lost' the [S$_j$] theta role that is inherently part of the stative verb *jǐn*. Once again, in contrast to the formal description just offered, a more intuitive, verbal description is that lexicalization has caused the 'tight' meaning of *jǐn* to be 'transferred'

---

[19] The '$_j$' subscript index that occurs on *jǐn* when it occurs in isolation in (279d) is not meant to indicate that *shíjī* is the referent associated with it, but rather may be considered an arbitrary label intended to indicate that the stative verb *jǐn* should indeed take an argument.

to V_1 rather than remaining a 'result' of V_1: the verb *zhuājǐn* as a 'degenerate' resultative no longer has a sentence argument to which the 'tightness' of *jǐn* can be ascribed – it is certainly not ascribed to the the direct object *shíjī* 'opportunity'.

What I have just demonstrated for *kàndào* and *zhuājǐn* is generally true for all the 'degenerate' resultatives listed above: the theta roles of these V_2 resultative endings do not percolate, with the information that would normally discharge onto the now-defunct theta role discharging instead semantically onto V_1. The reason V_2 theta role information does not percolate in these 'degenerate' resultatives is that they are more highly lexicalized than regular resultatives, and have as a result 'lost access' to the grammatical information in V_2.

6.2.3.2 Availability of 'object' theta roles to [V–O]$_V$ verbs

As noted in 4.3.4, V–O phrases become words by virtue of their lexicalization. This fact conforms with the principle 'the more lexicalized a word is, the less information is available from the components of that word' because the more lexicalized the gestalt V_x–O_y verb,[20] the more able it is to take an external object. This is to say that the more lexicalized the V_x–O_y verb, the less available the thematic information from its non-head O_y is to satisfy the 'object' (i.e., Theme) theta role requirement of V_x.

Recall from 4.3.4.3.2 that three lexicalization criteria were presented for V–O forms: first, when the V–O form may take an object (by Huang's PSC; Huang 1984: 54); second, when one of the constituents is a bound morpheme; and third, when the meaning of the V–O form is specialized. This means that V_x–O_y forms may be considered lexicalized verbs even if they do not take external objects. For example, the lexicalized V_x–O_y verbs *zhàoxiàng* 'to photograph', *tōngfēng* 'to ventilate', *bìyè* 'to graduate' and *jiāoshū* 'to teach' may not take objects (i.e., are intransitive), as seen in (280)–(283).

(280)   *zhàoxiàng   Zhāngsān
        照相   张三
        photograph-likeness Zhangsan
        'photograph'
        'to photograph Zhangsan'

---

[20] I will use the notation V_x and O_y to refer unambiguously to the verb and object components respectively of the gestalt [V_x O_y]$_V$ form.

(281) *tōngfēng wūzi
 通风 屋子
 pass-wind room
 'ventilate'
 'to ventilate the room'

(282) *bìyè dàxué
 毕业 大学
 end-career college
 'graduate'
 'to graduate college'

(283) *jiāoshū lìshǐ
 教书 历史
 teach-book history
 'teach' history
 'to teach history'

For these words, the [T] theta role information in O_y is available to V_x because it 'percolates' to the gestalt verb, thus allowing the argument structure of V_x to be satisfied internally by O_y. Since the argument structure of V_x is satisfied by O_y, satisfaction by an external object is disallowed by the constraint of the PSC, ruling out (280)–(283).

When V_x–O_y verbs are more fully lexicalized, they are able to take external objects. This is seen in the examples *dòngyuán* 'mobilize, arouse', *fùzé* 'be responsible for, be in charge of' and *tóuzī* 'invest' in (284)–(286).

(284) dòngyuán tāmen zǒu
 动员 他们 走
 move-person them go
 'to arouse'
 'to arouse them into going'

(285) fùzé bǎowèi gōngzuò
 负责 保卫 工作
 bear-responsibility security work
 'be in charge of'
 'to be in charge of security affairs'

(286) tóuzī wǔwàn yuán
 投资 五万 元
 throw-money 50,000 dollar
 invest
 'to invest 50,000 dollars'

These highly lexicalized V_x–O_y verbs are able to take an external object because when they are more fully lexicalized, the [T] theta role properties of O_y do not percolate and therefore are not available or 'visible' to V_x. This allows for the satisfaction of the V_x argument structure by means of an external object without violating the PSC.

6.2.3.3 A note on non-head opacity

It is worth pointing out that in 6.2.3.1 and 6.2.3.2 lexicalization affects the availability of information within V_1–V_2 resultative verbs and V–O verbs in much the same way. In both cases, lexicalization results in the inaccessibility of theta role information from the right-hand member or non-head of the verb. Furthermore, in both cases, information from the non-head semantically shifts onto the verb head as the grammatical information from the non-head becomes unavailable to the gestalt verb. So in both cases it is non-head information that is 'cut off' when lexicalization occurs.

We might ask: why is it in both cases information from the *non-head* that is first to become unavailable with the onset of lexicalization? The natural explanation is that the head of a word is the 'main conduit' of information 'upwards' to the gestalt word, while the non-head is a secondary route. Thus, the less important non-head conduit is the first to be cut off when lexicalization occurs.

6.2.4 Semantic information

As discussed in 6.1.1, the word component reduction that accompanies lexicalization usually results in the loss or weakening of word component meaning. The more highly lexicalized a word is, the less the semantic information contained in word components remains a visible part of the gestalt word. This is implicit in the discussion of lexicalization in 6.1.1 and 6.1.2, and the lexicalization categories given in table 29 and table 30. When a word is highly lexicalized, native speakers tend not to perform even casual analysis of the original meanings of word components, unless they are asked to reflect upon the word or give an opinion regarding why it means what it does. A good example of this from English is the word 'awful' which historically has a literal meaning of 'full of awe' or 'awe inspiring', but now more often means 'terrible' or 'very', especially in colloquial speech.

Table 35 Semantic opacity and metaphor in lexicalized words

left-hand side metaphorical	left-hand side opaque	right-hand side metaphorical	right-hand side opaque	both sides metaphorical	both sides opaque
chóngyá 虫牙 insect-tooth 'tooth cavity'	cǎipái 彩排 colour-perform 'dress rehearse'	bìhǔ 壁虎 wall-tiger 'gecko'	chángchuān 常川 often-river 'frequently'	chēmǎ 车马 car-horse 'travel'	chuānchā 穿插 put:through-insert 'to alternate'
féizào 肥皂 fat-soap 'soap'	chējiān 车间 car-room 'workshop'	chuānghù 窗户 window-door 'window'	chēpí 车皮 car-skin 'railway wagon'	diànchí 电池 electricity-pool 'battery'	dōngxi 东西 east-west 'thing'
máojīn 毛巾 hair-cloth 'towel'	chénxiāo 尘嚣 dirt-clamour 'clamour'	diànnǎo 电脑 electricity-brain 'computer'	chěpí 扯皮 wrangle-skin 'argue'	fēngshuǐ 风水 wind-water 'geomancy'	fēngliú 风流 wind-flow 'amorous'
shuǐpíng 水平 water-level 'level'	mǎtǒng 马桶 horse-bucket 'toilet'	diànyǐng 电影 electricity-shadow 'movie'	guójiā 国家 country-home 'country'	qíngyóu 情由 affair-reason 'the hows and whys'	shāomài 烧卖 bake-sell 'type of snack'
yínháng 银行 silver-shop 'bank'	qìchē 汽车 vapour-car 'automobile'	ěrduo 耳朵 ear-bunch 'ear'	qūbǐ 曲笔 crooked-pen 'distortion of the facts'	qūzhí 曲直 crooked-straight 'right and wrong'	wènshì 问世 ask-world 'to be published'
yùmǐ 玉米 jade-rice 'corn'	tiānqiáo 天桥 sky-bridge 'footbridge'	yúncǎi 云彩 cloud-colour 'clouds'	xīnshuǐ 薪水 salary-water 'salary'	zhǎoyá 爪牙 claw-tooth 'lackeys'	yāgēn 压根 pressure-root 'completely'

Native speakers are not normally aware of the literal meaning unless they stop and think about it.

In table 35, I give some examples of Chinese words that are moderately and highly lexicalized, as seen from the fact that certain of the word components are either metaphorical, thereby transmitting only limited meaning from that component to the gestalt word, or opaque, thereby transmitting virtually no meaning to the word. By hypothesis, the words that have metaphorical components are less highly lexicalized than words that have opaque components.

6.3 Lexicalization and grammaticalization

The lexicalization of morphemes often involves their *grammaticalization*. Grammaticalization (also known as 'grammaticization') refers to 'the process whereby lexical items and constructions come in certain linguistic contexts to serve grammatical functions, and, once grammaticalized, continue to develop new grammatical functions' (Hopper and Traugott 1993: xv).[21]

The 'degenerate' resultative V₂ endings such as -*dào* 到 'attain' discussed in 6.2.3.1 (see (278)) are a good example of grammaticalization in modern Mandarin. Recall that in gestalt V₁–V₂ words containing these endings, the theta role and semantic information that had been ascribed to the 'erstwhile-V₂-words-turned-degenerate-endings' became part of the head verb V₁ rather than remaining part of the erstwhile V₂ words. As a result, these forms have evolved into endings that reflect aspectual properties of the V₁ verb (viz., perfectivity; referring to the completion of verb action) rather than reflecting the full meaning and argument structure of the erstwhile V₂ words. Thus, 'degenerate' endings like *dào* have lost some of their 'content' and evolved toward indicating grammatical 'function'. Other instances of grammaticalization in Chinese are verb suffixes such as -*le* 了, -*guo* 过, -*zhe* 著 and -*de* 得 and the free direct object marker *bǎ* 把, all of which have their origins in content words (for fuller treatment of grammaticalization in Chinese, see Li and Shi 1997 for a discussion of -*le*, -*zhe*, -*guo* and -*de*; Sun 1996 for a discussion of -*de*, -*le* and *bǎ*; and Peyraube forthcoming for a detailed theoretical discussion of grammaticalization in general terms, and of how the concept applies to Chinese in particular).

Polysemy (see discussion in 4.3.3.3) often occurs in grammaticalization when the content form of origin continues to coexist contemporaneously with its grammaticalized function form counterpart (also conceptualized as a form of 'layering'; see Heine, Claudi and Hünnemeyer 1991a: 5; Traugott forthcoming: 10; Peyraube forthcoming: 6). In such a situation, the degree of polysemy may depend upon

---

[21] Compounding such as is seen in Chinese (qua combining; see n. 25) has been described as a process analogous to grammaticalization. According to Haspelmath (1992: 71): 'Although the increasing use of a word as the second member of a compound with accompanying semantic generalization and phonological erosion is not exactly the paradigm case of grammaticization . . . it is clearly a completely analogous diachronic process.'

just how grammaticalized the derived function form has become (Craig 1991: 456). For a time, the original 'content' and incipient 'function' forms may be construed by the native speaker as polysemous variants of the 'same' word. Then at some point in the diachronic process the two forms may cease being construed as the same word, and be seen instead as different words – perhaps homonyms – that are historically or derivationally related (Heine, Claudi and Hünnemeyer 1991b: 180).

As examples of this phenomenon from English we have the derivational suffixes '-ful' and '-able' and their respective words of origin 'full' and 'able'. The members of these suffix–word pairs are now considered different morphemes, but at one time they doubtlessly were considered polysemous variants of the 'same word'. An example from historical Chinese is the 'completed action' verb suffix -*le* 了. This suffix derives historically from the full verb *liǎo* 了, meaning 'to finish', which had grammaticalized as a verb suffix by the time of the Tang dynasty (7th–10th centuries AD; Li and Shi 1997). According to Li and Shi, at some point in time both the full verb and verb suffix forms would have coexisted (1997: 90–1). Presumably at that time the two forms would have been considered polysemous variants of the 'same word'.

Examples from modern Mandarin of such polysemy include the free-form and V₂ uses of *dào* 到 discussed above, and also the full verb and verb suffix forms of *guò* 过, with the lexical verb *guò* meaning 'to pass, cross', and the verbal aspect suffix -*guò* indicating the prior occurrence of an event (e.g., *kànguò* 看过 see-ASP 'to have seen before'). The verbs *dào* and *guò* and their respective grammaticalized counterparts could be construed as polysemous variants of the 'same morpheme' because of their near-complete phonological identity (the verbal aspect variant often occuring in neutral rather than fulltoned form), their complete orthographic identity, and their close semantic and historical relationship.[22] Sun (1996: 170–4, 179–86) further discusses the role of polysemy in Chinese grammaticalization.

Regarding the nature of the relationship between lexicalization and grammaticalization, the data in Craig (1991) from Rama (an SOV language spoken in Nicaragua) show a clear positive correlation between

---

[22] Actually, even though the verbal aspect and full verb forms of *guò* seem closely related in contemporary Mandarin, the verb *guò* was already grammaticalized as an aspect marker by the time of the Yuan and Ming dynasties (13th–14th centuries AD; Li and Shi 1997: 91–2).

a relational preverb's 'degree of lexicalization' (Craig 1991: 467; see also 6.1.2) and the extent to which the preverb has undergone grammaticalization. The Rama relational preverb *ba-* is given as an example of 'advanced' lexicalization (cf 6.1) because it has been lexically incorporated by a relatively large number of verbs, and it is highly grammaticalized because there are no instances of *ba-* in the original postposition form from which it evolved (see table 1 in Craig 1991: 463, and accompanying discussion). The relational preverb *yu-*, on the other hand, is an example of 'incipient' lexicalization because it has been incorporated by relatively few verbs, and it is less grammaticalized than *ba-* because of its relatively large number of appearances in its original postpositional form (Craig 1991: 463).

An important point to keep in mind about the relationship between grammaticalization and lexicalization is that although they are highly correlated and do often cooccur, they are nonetheless demonstrably independent phenomena. The most obvious and important difference between the two is that 'L[exicalization] involves word-formation processes within the lexicon, and recruitment of form–meaning pairs into open class categories', while 'G[rammaticalization] involves processes that recruit form–meaning pairs out of the lexicon into specifier and operator (grammatical) status' (Traugott forthcoming: 12).[23] That is, a grammaticalized element by definition always becomes more 'grammatical', but does not always 'lexicalize' to become a word or part of a word, and lexicalized elements by definition become words or word parts, but do not necessarily become more 'grammatical'. So, for example, a free content word may grammaticalize to become a free function word with no lexicalization implied. By the same token, although lexicalized elements often lose or change their semantic content as they become part of a new word, that meaning loss or change does not necessarily entail a shift to a more 'grammatical' meaning. As an example of the latter (examples of the former are legion), the Mandarin content word *féi* 肥 'fat' no longer makes any significant semantic contribution to the meaning of the gestalt word *féizào* 肥皂 fat-soap 'soap' (seen in table 35). But *féi* did not become more 'functionlike' as it lost its meaning after becoming lexicalized as part of the gestalt word *féizào* – it simply ceased contributing its

---

[23] Although, as noted in the quote from Hopper and Traugott (1993: 2), grammaticalization often involves a form simply becoming more grammatical, and does not necessarily involve recruiting a form from the lexicon.

'content' meaning to the word. So while grammaticalization and lexicalization may often involve each other, they are logically and empirically independent.

In Chinese we can clearly see the two separate processes of grammaticalization and lexicalization independently at work. Given the framework presented here, morphemes that have been lexicalized as part of a larger word often have become or are in the process of becoming *either* bound roots (content forms) *or* affixes (function forms), and morphemes that are grammaticalized have become or are becoming *either* function words (free forms) *or* affixes (bound forms).

6.4 Lexicalization and the formation of new words

6.4.1 Historical factors

A long period of lexicalization in the history of the Chinese language began with the shift from monosyllabic to bisyllabic words that happened sporadically as early as the Zhou dynasty (1000–700 BC; Cheng 1981b: 44; Boltz 1994: 171), continuing on a small scale into the Qin period (before the third century BC), and undergoing relatively large scale development during and after the Han dynasty (206 BC–AD 220; Peyraube 1996: 197; Feng 1997). This shift toward the use of bisyllabic words occurred when free monosyllabic words combined into new bisyllabic words both through compounding (qua combination; see n. 25) and through abbreviation of longer phrases. The newly juxtaposed morphemes subsequently often lost their status as free words, undergoing semantic shift or reduction due to the general effects of lexicalization described in 6.1.

The general criteria for considering a form to be a lexicalized word rather than a phrase are (a) non-compositionality of meaning; (b) strength of the boundness relation between the erstwhile phrasal elements (i.e., the separability of those elements); (c) parallelism of structure with adjacent units; (d) whether it can stand as a single constituent (for example, whether a [V N]$_N$ form can serve as the object of a preposition) and (e) frequency of occurrence (Cheng 1981b, Zhou 1982).

The statement 'today's morphology is yesterday's syntax' (Givón 1971: 413) is quite applicable in Chinese, since many of today's Chinese word structures arose from lexicalizations of syntactic structure. Parallel compounds (such as [V V]v and [N N]N; see 3.1.1.2) were lexicalized as early as the pre-Qin period (before the third century BC), achieved maturity in the Han dynasty (206 BC–AD 220) and enjoyed wide usage by the time of the beginning of the fifth century AD. Of the modifier–head word types (such as [Mod N]N and [Mod V]v; see 3.1.1.2), the [Mod N]N type were being formed as early as the pre-Qin period, and all types had achieved maturity by the time of the Han dynasty except for [V N]N, which did not see significant usage until the Northern and Southern dynasties period (fifth century AD). Modifier–head constructions of the type [Mod V]v are seen only infrequently in the pre-Qin period, slowly achieving status as a bona fide word-formation pattern after the Wei-Jin period (fourth century AD). [V O]v constructions (see 3.1.1.4 and 4.3.4) are seen in the pre-Qin period, but mostly served as the names of official titles. That situation did not change much until the time of the Northern and Southern dynasties, when the pattern became productive (Zhou 1982: 82–4).

There has been some discussion as to whether this shift toward the use of bisyllabic words in the diachronic development of Chinese was the cause or the result of the simplification of the phonological system (if indeed a cause–effect relation is necessarily to be inferred) that happened at approximately the same time (see discussion in Packard 1997b: 6–7; also Feng 1997: 211–19). The 'functional' explanation (see, e.g., Cheng 1981b: 44) is that at the time of rapid societal growth that occurred from 1100 to 300 BC, the pressure to communicate new concepts was met by the creation of increasing numbers of two-syllable words by the populace to expand the size of the lexicon. This in turn caused the phonological system to simplify, since the myriad phonological distinctions that originally functioned to keep homophonous words apart were no longer needed.

The alternative, 'phonological', explanation is that simplification of the phonological system occurred as a natural linguistic process of phonetic attrition (eliminating 'super-heavy' syllable types; see Feng 1997). This phonetic simplification caused single-syllable words which had been phonologically distinct to become homophones, and compounds consequently were created in the language to keep the homophonous words distinct. To give a concrete example of this process, in American English dialects in which the contrast between the vowels [ɪ] (as in 'bit' or 'pin') and [ɛ] (as in 'bet' or 'pen') has become neutralized to [1] (in certain phonological environments), speakers use the compounds 'safety-pin' and 'straight-pin' versus 'writing-pin' and 'ink-pin' to distinguish 'pin' from 'pen' respectively.[24]

The 'non-functional' phonological explanation seems more likely, because it involves two processes that remain operative in the modern language: the continued simplification of the Chinese phonological system (see, e.g., Chen 1975, Barale 1982), and the continuation of 'compounding' as a way of forming new words (see discussion of Sawer 1995 in 6.4.2). But regardless of whether it was the first ('concept-driven') or the second ('phonology-driven') impetus that caused bisyllabic words to proliferate, the shift from monosyllabic to bisyllabic words would have occurred by the wholesale lexicalization of combined or abbreviated forms, making it clear that lexicalization has been a particularly rich source of new words in the historical evolution of Chinese.

6.4.2 The modern language

In modern Chinese, the coining of new words still overwhelmingly yields forms that are bisyllabic rather than monosyllabic: less than 1 per cent (from 0.13 per cent to 0.32 per cent) of new words were monosyllabic in a study done by Sawer (1995). Furthermore, such word creation rarely occurs anew, 'out of thin air' as it were, but rather derives from the combination of extant morphemes using existing word structure rules.

Sawer gives five different methods of creating new words in Chinese: combination[25] (the novel concatenation of morphemes, often on analogy with existing words), abbreviation (shortened forms of preexisting words or phrases), borrowing (words whose sound or meaning is imported from another language), shifting (existing words used with a new meaning) and 'creating numerical formulae' (the use of a number-plus-noun to refer to several instances of the same noun; e.g., *sānqū* 三区 three-area 'the three areas', *jìnqū* 禁区 forbidden-area

[24] My thanks to Mike Wright for this example.
[25] Sawer's term is 'compounding'. I prefer to use the term 'combination' instead because the morphemes that come together to form words in this process may either be free (in which case the resulting word is a true compound) or bound (in which case the resulting word is a bound root word; see 4.1). By using the term 'combination' I hope to avoid the implication that words formed using this process are all true compounds, when in fact most of the time in Chinese they are actually bound root words.

'forbidden areas', *mángqū* 盲区 blind-area 'blind areas', *nánqū* 难区 difficult-area 'difficult areas').

6.4.2.1 Abbreviation and combination ('compounding')

In his study, Sawer found that by far the majority of contemporary new words in Chinese arise through combination (70.2 per cent) and abbreviation (18.7 per cent), with borrowing, shifting and numerical formulae constituting 4.9, 3.3 and 2.9 per cent of the sample respectively. New words formed through combination and abbreviation are clearly instances of lexicalization, because in both cases morphemes are joined and anointed as new gestalt words.

A new word is considered an abbreviated form if (a) there is a clear preexisting word or phrase that contains all the constituents of the abbreviation, and (b) the abbreviation is considered to be derived directly from that longer word or phrase. It is considered a combined form if there is no obvious preexisting longer form, with consideration also given to whether the new word is formed on analogy with an existing word. Sometimes, however, it is difficult to make a clear distinction between the two. This is because almost every word formed by combination can be paraphrased with longer words or phrases, and may therefore 'masquerade' as an abbreviation.

Take, for example, the word *gōngtuō* 公托 public-entrust 'public daycare centre', seen in (262) and table 38. This word is taken to be a combined form rather than an abbreviation of, e.g., *gōngbàn tuōérsuǒ* (公办托儿所 public-manage-entrust-child-place), because it is seen as having been created on analogy with the term *sītuō* 私托 private-entrust 'private daycare centre' (Yu 1993: 132). To give another example, in Yu (1993: 34) *guǎnfēng* 管风 manage-style 'style of management' is considered an abbreviation (of *guǎnlǐ zuòfēng* 管理作风 manage-order do-style 'management style'), while *jiàofēng* 教风 teaching-style 'style of teaching' is considered a combination, because the latter is said to be formed on analogy with *xuéfēng* study-style 'style of studying'. Yu says that although *guǎnfēng* is also created on analogy with *xuéfēng*, the fact that it can be considered derived from *guǎnlǐ zuòfēng* carries the most weight in its classification as an abbreviation.

But what about an example such as *dǎtiě* 打铁 hit-iron 'to abolish the system of guaranteed jobs', which, although clearly derived from *dǎpò tiěfànwǎn* 打破铁饭碗 'smash the iron rice bowl', is nonetheless not considered to be an abbreviation (see 6.4.3 and table 38)? In Yu

(1993: 14–15), the decision of which category to assign it to boils down to whether *dǎpò tiěfànwǎn* is considered to be a 'preexisting phrase'. It is not clear why *dǎpò tiěfànwǎn* is not to be considered a preexisting term whose abbreviation gave rise to *dǎtiě*. Such is the nature of the arbitrariness sometimes encountered in categorizing new words as combinations versus abbreviations.

Now, even though a clear distinction cannot always be made between combination and abbreviation, in unambiguous cases the latter usually gives us more information about the original form class identity of the neologized constituents. In other words, abbreviation gives us more information regarding, for example, whether the derived usage represents a shift in the form class identity of the neologized constituents. The reason for this is that we are usually more certain in the case of (unambiguous) abbreviations what the form classes of the original elements are prior to abbreviation.

To illustrate, consider the combined neologism *xuémáng* 学盲 study-blind 'one who is unable to study without a teacher' (my translation; example taken from Sawer 1995: 217, citing Yu 1994: 827). First of all, *xuémáng* is a combined form rather than an abbreviation, because it is derived by combining the independent elements *xué* and *máng* on analogy with, e.g., *wénmáng* 文盲 writing-blind 'one who is illiterate', and it is clearly not the shortened version of an existing word or phrase. Now, the word *xué* 'study' can normally function as either a noun ('the study of') or a verb ('to study'), and so while we know how it is being used in the neologism *xuémáng* (i.e., as a noun) because we perceive the structure (it cannot be a verb because *máng* is used as a noun in this context and is not functioning as an object), strictly speaking we have little evidence as to whether the use of *xué* in the neologized form derives from its original verbal or nominal meaning. This may be contrasted with a neologized combined form such as *cúnxiū* 存休 save-rest 'to accumulate vacation time' (Chinese Academy of Social Sciences 1992: 89), in which the word *xiū* 'vacation time' is used as a noun, but we know it must represent derivation from a verb because *xiū* is unambiguously a verb in origin. So, in other words, we can't always tell the form class derivation of a component in a combined form unless that component has an unambiguous form class to begin with.

In contrast, abbreviations are necessarily derived from longer words or phrases whose members have relatively distinct form class identities. Consider, for example, the abbreviation *qīngbǎo* 青保 young-protect 'protection of juveniles' seen in table 36 (Sawer 1995: 207, citing Yu 1993: 82), abbreviated from *qīngshàonián bǎohù* 青少年保护 (*qīngshàonián* young-young-year 'juvenile'; *bǎohù* protect-protect 'protect' > 'protection of juveniles'). The word *bǎo*,[26] while ordinarily a verb, can also be used as a noun (e.g., *zuòbǎo* 作保 do-guarantee 'to act as guarantor'). In the abbreviated term *qīngbǎo*, *bǎo* is used as a noun, and the fact that it is derived from the verb *bǎohù* within the term *qīngshàonián bǎohù* tells us clearly that *bǎo* has shifted its form class in the abbreviated term, deriving from its original verbal, rather than nominal, meaning.[27] This demonstrates that, as a way of forming new words, abbreviation generally provides more evidence than combination about the form classes of the participating morphemes.

Some examples of abbreviation are presented in table 36 (from Chinese Academy of Social Sciences 1988, 1992, Yu 1993, Chiang 1995 and Chen 1998).

Chen (1998) distinguishes several subcategories of abbreviation (which she terms 'acronyms'), with assignment to subcategory based upon which components of the original word or phrase are retained in the shortened form. Chen observes that most abbreviations by far are bisyllabic (96 per cent of her sample), and that abbreviations are predominantly formed by taking the first morpheme of each word in the original form (constituting 61.5 per cent of all two-syllable abbreviations in her sample), but that this method is not used when it results in semantic problems, i.e., potential non-recoverability of the original form. This observation is corroborated by a psycholinguistic experiment involving abbreviation in Chinese performed by Chiang (1995), who found that when subjects are asked to abbreviate four-syllable forms (each consisting of two two-syllable words) into a single two-syllable word, they tend to select the first morpheme of each original word, unless that choice is overridden by semantic considerations. This observation is also confirmed in general by the entries in table 36.

[26] Actually, a bound root.
[27] Of course, one might argue that there are intermediate stages in the nominalization, since the *bǎohù* in the term *qīngshàonián bǎohù* may be considered a syntactic nominalization. The point is, however, that the form class of *bǎo* within the lexical item from which *qīngbǎo* is derived is clearly verbal.

Table 36 Modern Mandarin abbreviations

abbreviation	abbreviated from	
Běitú 北图 north-chart 'Beijing library'	Běijīng 北京 north-capital 'Beijing'	túshūguǎn 图书馆 chart-book-establishment 'library'
	'Beijing library'	
gōngchē 公车 public-vehicle 'bus'	gōnggòng 公共 public-common 'public' 'bus'	qìchē 汽车 vapour-vehicle 'car'
guǎnfēng 管风 manage-style 'style of management'	guǎnlǐ 管理 manage-order 'management' 'style of management'	zuòfēng 作风 do-style 'style'
guāngxiān 光纤 light-tiny 'fibre optics'	guāngxué 光学 light-study 'optics' 'fibre optics'	xiānwéi 纤维 tiny-fibre 'fibre'
huánfā 环发 surround-emit 'environment and development'	huánjìng 环境 surround-border 'environment'	yǔ fāzhǎn 与 发展 and emit-expand and 'develop'
	'environment and development'	
láobǎo 劳保 work-protect 'labour insurance'	láodòng 劳动 work-move 'labour' 'labour insurance'	bǎoxiǎn 保险 protect-risk 'insurance'
láogǎi 劳改 labour-change 'reform through work'	láodòng 劳动 work-move 'labour' 'reform through work'	gǎizào 改造 change-create 'reform'

Table 36 (cont'd)

abbreviation	abbreviated from			
lǜhán 律函 law-mail 'law correspondence school centre'	lǜshī 律师 law-master 'lawyer'	hánshòu 函授 mail-teach 'correspondence school'		zhōngxīn 中心 middle-heart 'centre'
	'law correspondence school centre'			
ménzé 门责 door-duty 'doorstep environment hygiene responsibility system'	ménqián 门前 door-front 'doorstep' zhì 制 system 'system'	huánjìng 环境 surround-border 'environment'	wèishēng 卫生 protect-life 'hygiene'	zérèn 责任 duty-job 'responsibility'
	'doorstep environment hygiene responsibility system'			
qīngbǎo 青保 young-protect 'protection of juveniles'	qīngshàonián 青少年 young-young-year 'juvenile' 'protection of juveniles'	bǎohù 保护 protect-protect 'protect'		
wàiláo 外劳 out-work 'foreign workers'	wàilái 外来 out-come 'foreign' 'foreign workers'	láowù 劳务 work-serve 'work'	rényuán 人员 person-person 'person'	

Combination (qua compounding; see n. 25) is a form of reanalysis in which a juxtaposed, novel concatenation of morphemes (with no obvious preexisting longer form from which it is abbreviated) becomes lexicalized as a single word (Hopper and Traugott 1993: 49). The juxtaposition can be one of happenstance collocation, with increased frequency of use leading to eventual lexicalization (for example, *yào* 要 'want' + *shì* 是 'be' > *yàoshi* 要是 'if'), or it can be the conscious juxtaposition by a language user in order to express a concept (for example, *dàng* 当 'pawn' + *mài* 卖 'sell' > *dàngmài* 当卖 'pawning and selling'; Chinese Academy of Social Sciences 1992: 107).

LEXICALIZATION AND CHINESE WORDS

Table 37 Function words formed through combination

word 1	word 2	lexicalized word	word 1	word 2	lexicalized word
bù 不 not	guò 过 pass	búguò 不过 'however'	rú 如 as	guǒ 果 result	rúguǒ 如果 'if'
dàn 但 but	shì 是 be	dànshi 但是 'however'	rán 然 like	hòu 后 after	ránhòu 然后 'afterward'
ér 而 and	qiě 且 and	érqiě 而且 'furthermore'	suī 虽 though	rán 然 like	suīrán 虽然 'although'
hòu 后 after	lái 来 come	hòulái 后来 'afterward'	suǒ 所 which	yǐ 以 as	suǒyǐ 所以 'therefore'
jiǎ 假 false	rú 如 as	jiǎrú 假如 'supposing'	yào 要 want	shì 是 be	yàoshi 要是 'if'
kě 可 may	shì 是 be	kěshi 可是 'however'	yīn 因 cause	wéi 为 as	yīnwei 因为 'because'

Combination may yield either function words or content words. Some complex function words formed through combination are listed in table 37.[28] Combination function words are formed through lexicalization and grammaticalization of forms that were once entirely independent elements. Although these words are lexicalized and for all practical purposes their constituents are functionally opaque, they are still semantically decomposable, and sometimes single-morpheme versions of these words are used, especially in written communication (e.g., *suīrán* 'although' > *suī*, *kěshi* 'however' > *kě* or *dànshi* 'however' > *dàn*).

Table 38 lists some combined, relatively 'new' content words in Modern Mandarin (some from Chinese Academy of Social Sciences 1992 and Yu 1993). Many of these were taken from modern newspapers, and used by writers who either saw or heard them used

---

[28] Most, if not all, of these bisyllabic function words had already become lexicalized as words prior to the modern era.

Table 38 Combined content words in modern Chinese

first morpheme	second morpheme	combined form
ài 爱 love	liáo 疗 cure	àiliáo 爱疗 'cure by love'
bāo 包 include	hù 户 protect	bāohù 包户 'all-inclusive protection'
cān 参 participate	gǎi 改 change	cāngǎi 参改 'participate in reform'
chāi 拆 take apart	xǐ 洗 wash	chāixǐ 拆洗 'take apart and wash'
dǎ 打 remove	tiě 铁 iron > guaranteed job	dǎtiě 打铁 'abolish guaranteed jobs'
dì 地 earth	tiě 铁 iron > railroad	dìtiě 地铁 'subway'
gōng 公 public	tuō 托 entrust > day care centre	gōngtuō 公托 'public day care centre'
guāng 光 light > optic	xiān 纤 tiny > fibre	guāngxiān 光纤 'fibre optic'
píng 评 evaluate	zhì 质 quality	píngzhì 评质 'evaluate quality'
qǐ 启 inspire	dǎo 导 lead	qǐdǎo 启导 'inspire and lead'
qīng 清 clear	kā 咖 coffee	qīngkā 清咖 'black coffee'
sāng 丧 funeral	kǎ 卡 card	sāngkǎ 丧卡 'funeral invitation'
shè 涉 involve	nóng 农 agriculture	shènóng 涉农 'involving agriculture'
shuǐ 水 water	chuáng 床 bed	shuǐchuáng 水床 'waterbed'
tuō 脱 remove	cán 残 disability	tuōcán 脱残 'cured of disability'
wēi 微 small	miàn 面 bread > van	wēimiàn 微面 'minivan'
xī 息 interest	yé 爷 grandfather	xīyé 息爷 'one who lives off interest'

Table 38 (cont'd)

first morpheme	second morpheme	combined form	first morpheme	second morpheme	combined form
guāng 光 light > photon	nǎo 脑 brain > computer	guāngnǎo 光脑 'photon computer'	yǎ 哑 mute	xīng 星 star	yǎxīng 哑星 'star whose voice is dubbed'
háng 行 profession	píng 评 appraise	hángpíng 行评 'profession appraisal'	yǎn 眼 eye	yuán 缘 fate	yǎnyuán 眼缘 'actor and audience fate'
jiē 接 take control	quán 权 power	jiēquán 接权 'take over power'	yóu 游 travel	pǐn 品 product	yóupǐn 游品 travel souvenir
kǎo 考 test	fēng 风 custom	kǎofēng 考风 'obsession with testing'	zhèng 正 proper	pìn 聘 hire	zhèngpìn 正聘 'formally hire'
kōng 空 atmosphere	tiáo 调 adjust	kōngtiáo 空调 'air conditioner'			

elsewhere, or coined the neologized forms themselves. Simply because they appear in contemporary newspapers and new word lists (e.g., Yu 1993) does not guarantee that they will be adopted by the language in perpetuity. Whether such coinings become 'permanent' depends on whether they are generally adopted by the media, entertainment and the populace at large, and subsequently appear as permanent dictionary entries.

6.4.3 The creation of new morphemes in Chinese

The most remarkable thing to notice about the formation of new words through abbreviation and combination in Chinese is how new morphemes may arise as a result of this process. The creation of new morphemes in this way is likely a major source of morphological productivity and development in the history of the Chinese language.

New morphemes[29] are created when a basic morpheme M with an original meaning M^1 comes to be used in a new word W^2 that has a meaning different from the original M^1 meaning. Under these conditions, M^1 acquires the new word's meaning ($> M^2$) by virtue of its association with and role in W^2. The morpheme M^2 is then considered a bona fide 'new' morpheme when it is used in another new word W^3, with M^2 being the only representative of the new meaning in that word.

To give a concrete example, *dǎtiě* 打铁 hit-iron is a new word meaning 'to abolish the system of guaranteed jobs' (Yu 1993: 14–15). This word is derived from *dǎpò tiěfànwǎn* 打破铁饭碗 'smash the iron rice bowl' (*dǎpò* hit-broken = 'smash'; *tiěfànwǎn* iron-rice-bowl = 'guaranteed job'). In this example, the morpheme *tiě* 'iron' (M^1) appears in the new word *tiěfànwǎn* 'guaranteed job' (W^2). Thus, *tiě* has acquired the new word's meaning of 'guaranteed job' ($> M^2$) by virtue of its association with *tiěfànwǎn* (W^2). Finally, we can consider *tiě* a new morpheme when it is used in the new word *dǎtiě* (W^3), because *tiě* is the only element representing the notion 'guaranteed job' in that word.

Another example also involving *tiě* is *dìtiě*, 地铁 earth-iron 'subway', an abbreviation of *dìxià tiědào* 地下铁道 earth-beneath 'underground', iron-road 'railroad' (Chinese Academy of Social Sciences 1988: 238). In this case, *tiě* has come to have the meaning of 'railroad', which it acquired from its use in the word *tiědào*.

Note that in both the *dǎtiě* and *dìtiě* examples, the morpheme *tiě* is bound (X^{-1}) when used with its new derived meanings 'guaranteed job' and 'railroad'. This is because even though *tiě* is a free word (X^0) when used in its original sense of 'iron', it cannot be used as a free word when it is used to mean 'guaranteed job' or 'railroad'.

Another example of new morpheme creation is seen in the word *guāngnǎo* 光脑 light-brain 'photon computer' (Yu 1993: 34; see also table 38), derived from *guāngzǐ* 光子 light-particle 'photon' and *diànnǎo*

---

[29] Strictly speaking, the distinction between spoken 'morpheme' and written 'character' does not affect the present analysis. For those who take the position that the written character rather than the morpheme should more properly be the point of departure here, instead of considering the derived form to be a 'new morpheme', it will be more useful to consider the derived form to be a 'new meaning entry under an existing character'.

电脑 electricity-brain 'computer'. Although the basic meaning of *nǎo* is 'brain', in the word *guāngnǎo* it specifically means 'computer'. Therefore, the original meaning of *nǎo* has shifted from 'brain' to 'computer' as expressed in the word *guāngnǎo*.

We see meaning shift in both morphemes of the word *guāngxiān* 光纤 light-tiny 'fibre optic' (Chinese Academy of Social Sciences 1992: 190), as seen in (287).

(287)   guāngxué   光学   light-study = 'the study of light' > 'optics'
             xiānwéi   纤维   tiny-connection = 'fibre'
        → guāngxué xiānwéi   光学纤维   optics-fibre = 'fibre optics'
        → guāngxiān   光纤   optic-fibre = 'fibre optic'

In this example, the morpheme *xiān* 纤, which has an original meaning of 'tiny, minute', has come to mean 'fibre' because of its occurrence in the common word *xiānwéi* 'fibre', and the word *guāng* (光; original meaning 'light') has come to mean 'optic' because of its use in the word *guāngxué* light-study > 'the study of light' > 'optics'. This example is interesting because the meaning of *xué* 'study' in *guāngxué* 光学 'optics' is completely lost in the intermediate term *guāngxué xiānwéi* ('fibre optics'), since it is a loan translation (calque) from English.

For an even more interesting example, consider the morpheme *miàn* 面 (traditional character: 麵) 'flour, dough, noodles', which has now come to mean 'van' in modern Mandarin, and is used to create new words such as *miàndī* 面的 'van taxi' and *wēimiàn* 微面 'minivan', as seen in (288) (Yu 1993: 72).

(288)   miàn   面   'flour, dough, noodles'
        → miànbāo   面包   dough-package = 'bread'
        → miànbāochē   面包车   bread-vehicle = 'vehicle-shaped-like-a-loaf-of-bread' = 'van'
        → miànbāo dīshì   面包的士   bread-taxi (*dīshì* is a phonetic loan for 'taxi') = 'van taxi'
        → miàndī   面的   van-taxi = 'van taxi' (derived from *miànbāo dīshì*)
        → wēimiàn   微面   small-van = 'minivan'

In this example not only does the semantic identity of *miàn* change as it diachronically participates in ever-increasing numbers of words, it also changes its status from a free morpheme (as in *miàn* 'flour, dough, noodles') to a bound morpheme (as in *miànbāo*[30] and *wēimiàn*), the same as we saw with *tiě* in the *dǎtiě* and *dìtiě* examples above. These examples clearly show the remarkable productivity of the morpheme creation process, and how a morpheme's identity – including both its meaning and its bound–free status – is likely to change over time.

The productive use of morphemes in this manner also causes them to undergo shifts in their grammatical form class identity. For example, the neologism *gōngtuō* 公托 public-entrust 'public day care centre' (Yu 1993: 32; see also example (262)) demonstrates the creation of a morpheme with a different grammatical form class as well as a new meaning. The word *gōngtuō* in example (262) is derived from *gōngbàn tuōérsuǒ* 公办托儿所 'public run day care centre' (*gōngbàn* public-run 'public run' *tuōérsuǒ* entrust-child-place 'day care centre'). This example shows the change in meaning, form class and distribution undergone by the morpheme *tuō*: it is originally a free morpheme (i.e., a root word X⁰) with the meaning 'entrust', with an original form class identity of 'verb'. Through its combination with *tuōérsuǒ* and subsequent appearance in the word *gōngtuō*, *tuō* has taken on the meaning of 'day care centre', and in so doing, changed its form class from verb to noun and its morphological status from that of root word to bound root. These changes are also clearly seen in the word *rùtuō* 入托 enter-(entrust>)-day:care:centre 'to enter a day care centre'.

The words *láobǎo* 劳保 work-protect 'labour insurance' and *láogǎi* 劳改 labour-change 'reform through work' both involve a morpheme changing its grammatical form class. The word *láobǎo* is abbreviated from *láodòngbǎoxiǎn* 劳动保险 (work-move 'labour', protect-risk 'insurance' = 'labour insurance'), and the word *láogǎi* is abbreviated from *láodònggǎizào* 劳动改造 (work-move 'labour', change-create 'reform' = 'reform through work'). Both *bǎo* and *gǎi* are originally verbs ('protect' and 'change' respectively), and in *láobǎo* and *láogǎi* they are transformed into nouns (because they are right-hand members of the nouns *láobǎo* and *láogǎi* respectively). Use of the verb *gǎi* as a noun is also demonstrated in the new word *cāngǎi* 参改 'participate in reform' (derived from *cānyù gǎigé* 参与改革: *cānyù* participate-participate 'participate'; *gǎigé* change-reform 'reform'; Yu 1993: 10).

An example of change in form class without meaning shift may be seen in the neologized noun *hángpíng* 行评 profession-appraise

---

[30] Thanks to Jim Dew for the observation on *miànbāo*.

'profession appraisal', derived from *hángyè píngbǐ* 行业评比 (*hángyè* profession-profession 'profession', *píngbǐ* appraise-compare 'appraise through comparison'; Yu 1993: 38–9). Originally, *háng* is a noun and *píng* is a verb, but the word *hángpíng* is a noun, which converts the right-hand morpheme (*píng*) from a verb to a noun, since the right-hand morpheme is the structural head of the complex noun word, and possesses a 'noun' form class identity (see 5.5.1 and 5.5.2). The lexical meaning, however, has not undergone a change since it retains the same basic meaning of 'appraise/appraisal'.

We may ask whether in fact 'new morphemes' are 'created' in the development of entities like *tiě* 铁 'iron' > *tiě* 'guaranteed job' or 'railroad'; or *miàn* 面 'flour, dough, noodles' > *miàn* 'van'.[31] In other words, does a simple change in grammatical form class, bound–free status or even a change in meaning justify considering a morpheme to be 'new', or should these simply be considered derived instances of the 'same' morpheme? This question once again critically involves the issue of polysemy (see discussion in 4.3.3.3 and 6.3): in particular, at what point in the evolution of a morpheme's meaning does the degree of semantic shift justify our calling it a 'new' morpheme? No doubt some will say that the examples I have presented above are not really 'new' morphemes at all, but are merely derived, polysemous variants of extant morphemes. My response is that the examples I have given may indeed not see further use or be recognized by authorities as new morphemes. But one need only look at any lexicon of the Chinese language to realize that morphemes commonly undergo the kind of meaning shift that I have demonstrated.

For example, *mù* 木 is listed in most dictionaries (e.g., *Xīnhuá Cídiǎn* 新华词典; *Modern Chinese Dictionary*, Chinese Academy of Social Sciences 1988: 807) as meaning (among other things) 'tree', 'wood' and 'numb'. At some point in the history of the Chinese language, the lexicographical authorities decided that *mù* as 'wood' was distinct enough from *mù* as 'tree', and subsequently that *mù* as 'numb' was distinct enough from *mù* as 'wood' – in both meaning and popular usage – that they warranted their own separate entries under the dictionary heading *mù* 木.

[31] Or, e.g. (following n. 29), whether 'guaranteed job' or 'railroad' might someday be listed together with 'iron', 'determined', 'indisputable', etc. under the entry for *tiě* 铁, and whether 'van' might someday be listed under the entry for *miàn* along with 'flour', 'noodles', 'dough', etc. in a dictionary.

To give another example, *yá* 牙 is listed as meaning both 'tooth' and 'ivory'. Not only did lexicographers at some point decide – as with *mù* 木 above – that 'ivory' was sufficiently distinct from 'tooth' to warrant its own entry under *yá*, it is also fairly certain that the 'ivory' meaning of *yá* arose as a result of the participation of *yá* in the word *xiàngyá* 象牙 elephant-tooth 'ivory', in just the same way that *miàn* 面 has acquired the meaning of 'van' by its appearance in the word *miànbāochē* 面包车 as seen in (288). Finally, it should also be clear that the bound root *yǐng* 影 'shadow' has acquired the meaning of 'movie' (Chinese Academy of Social Sciences 1988: 1387) by its appearance in the word *diànyǐng* 电影 electric(ity)-shadow 'movie', as independently confirmed by the existence of such words as *yǐngpíng* 影评 (shadow >) movie-appraise 'movie review'.

It is abundantly clear that the type of meaning shift that I have demonstrated is often caused by the shift in the role of an 'old' morpheme within a new word. So while it is correct to question whether the specific examples I have chosen to illustrate this process will actually end up being considered 'new' morphemes, the existence of the general process I have described that leads to the creation of new morphemes is surely beyond doubt.

6.4.3.1 Most new Chinese morphemes are bound roots

It is significant to note that, as seen from our discussion in the previous section, most new morphemes created in Chinese are bound roots (X^{-1}). For example, in both the *dǎtiě* and *dìtiě* examples shown in the previous section (and presented again in table 39), the morpheme *tiě* is bound (X^{-1}) when used with its new, derived meanings 'guaranteed job' and 'railroad', even though it is a free word (X^0) when it is used to mean 'iron'. This may also be seen for the rest of the examples in table 39, which show that the morphemes are free words when used with their original meanings, but bound roots when used with their new meanings.

This tendency to create bound roots in deriving new morphemes contributes to the continued proliferation of bound morphemes in the Chinese language. This is because in the creation of new complex words, bound roots will necessarily remain bound roots[32] (whether they are used with a new meaning or not), but (root) words are likely

---

[32] This is a truism because a bound root becoming free could only be demonstrated by its independent use as a single-syllable word.

Table 39 Creation of bound roots

morpheme	original meaning (X^{-0})	→	new meaning (X^{-1})	examples
diàn 电	electricity	→	television	cǎidiàn 彩电 colour-television 'colour television'
diāo 雕	carve	→	carving	shídiāo 石雕 stone-carving 'stone carving'
gǎi 改	to change	→	reform	cāngǎi 参改 participate-reform 'participate in reform'
guà 挂	hang	→	hanging	bìguà 壁挂 wall-hanging 'wall hanging'
guāng 光	light	→	photon	guāngnǎo 光脑 photon-computer 'photon-computer'
		→	optic	guāngxiān 光纤 optic-fibre 'fibre optic'
mí 迷	to be fascinated	→	fan	yǐngmí 影迷 movie-fan 'movie fan'
miàn 面	flour	→	bread	miànbāo 面包 bread-package 'bread'
		→	van	wēimiàn 微面 small-van 'minivan'
tiáo 调	to adjust	→	adjuster	kōngtiáo 空调 atmosphere-adjuster 'air conditioner'

Table 39 (cont'd)

morpheme	original meaning (X^{-0})	→	new meaning (X^{-1})	examples
tiě 铁	iron	→	guaranteed job	dǎtiě 打铁 smash-job 'abolish guaranteed jobs'
		→	railroad	dìtiě 地铁 earth-railroad 'subway'
tuō 托	entrust	→	day care centre	gōngtuō 公托 public-care:centre 'public day care centre'
xiān 纤	tiny	→	fibre	xiānwéi 纤维 fibre-connect 'fibre'

to change into bound roots ($X^{-0} \to X^{-1}$) as well. Also, there appear to be no tendencies in the opposite direction: that is, bound roots tend not to become free (which would be demonstrated by the creation of new single-syllable words from bound roots). In Chinese, therefore, linguistic forces seem to 'conspire' to create bound roots.

The reason for this is, in part, simple probability: since by far the majority of Chinese morphemes are already bound roots, it is a simple statistical fact that the morphemes used to make new words have a greater likelihood of being bound. Since there is apparently no constraint *against* the use of bound forms in the creation of words, unless other factors intervene, there will be a propensity for new words to be created from bound roots.

But there is another reason for this tendency as well, having to do with the phenomenon of homophony in Chinese. The relatively small inventory of syllables in Mandarin Chinese (around 1,200; compared with estimates of between 6,000 and 7,000 in English) means that a single-syllable word stands a good chance of being homophonous with other single-syllable words, resulting in potential ambiguity.

When a 'new' morpheme is created by an 'old' morpheme participating in a new word (as demonstrated in 6.4.3), because of homophony the new morpheme might not serve as a clear representative of the new meaning if that new morpheme were to occur as a free, one-syllable form. To give an example, that would be like using the the single syllable *diàn* in a sentence, expecting to communicate the meaning 'television' based on the existence of *cǎidiàn* 彩电 'colour television' (the first entry in table 39). A quick glance at the dictionary reveals that not only would the 'television' meaning have to compete with the original meaning of 'electricity', it would in theory also have to compete with all the other homophonic nouns pronounced *diàn* as well: 'shop' (店), 'pad' (垫), 'palace' (殿), etc. Furthermore, the degree of potential homophony is continually on the increase due to the ongoing reduction in the phonological complexity of the Chinese syllable (e.g., the loss of final nasal endings as outlined, for example, in Chen 1975 and Barale 1982).

From the above we can see that both new and old morphemes in Chinese are moving in the direction of being *bound*, and they are particularly moving in the direction of becoming *bound roots*. Critically, Chinese morphemes are generally *not* becoming more *grammatical* as rapidly as they are becoming more bound. The evidence is that there is no similar prolific creation of grammatical morphemes – either word-forming affixes or grammatical affixes – in present-day Mandarin akin to the proliferation of bound roots. Although there are quite a few relatively new affixes in Mandarin (see table 26), clearly they are not being created as quickly as bound roots. Given the traditional view of 'content' morphemes as 'open-class' items and 'function' morphemes as 'closed-class' items, the creation of content forms outpacing function forms might be expected.

When viewed in total, these facts about compounding and the tendency of morphemes to move toward bound status give us a picture of how words are formed in contemporary Chinese, and also provide us with a hypothesis regarding the creation of words and evolution of morphemes in the history of the Chinese language. The historical shift from monosyllabic to bisyllabic words in Chinese most likely began with free, largely single-syllable words combining through compounding, abbreviation and lexicalization of syntactic structures, with the free words subsequently becoming bound following the increasing lexicalization of the bisyllabic words in which they appeared as constituents.

7 | Chinese words and the lexicon

Issues involving the relationship between Chinese words and the lexicon are addressed in this chapter. Some of the questions we will consider are: What is 'the lexicon'? What is and what is not 'listed' there in Chinese? Are words 'stored' in and 'accessed' from the lexicon as gestalt wholes or by their component morphemes? What role does character orthography play in accessing the Chinese lexicon?

A first common source of confusion in thinking about Chinese words and the lexicon is that Chinese words are for the most part composed out of *open*-class items that are *bound*. This starkly contrasts with other languages in which bound morphemes are usually closed class, functional elements (i.e., affixes of some sort). Therefore, the discussion of composed and decomposed lexical storage in those languages (e.g., English) tends to centre on whether word roots and their affixes are stored in precompiled or decomposed fashion. This makes the question of composed or decomposed storage in the case of Chinese somewhat different, but very interesting and important.

A second common source of confusion is the relationship between the Chinese natural speech lexicon and the processing of Chinese character orthography. This is confusing because the Chinese character orthographic system in a very real sense *drives* the concept of lexical processing for many investigators who have worked on Chinese language processing. Below we will consider these two issues separately, and try to determine what role Chinese characters play in Chinese natural language processing.

7.1 What is 'the lexicon'?

It is a strong intuition of speakers of any language that pieces of the language are strung together to make meaningful utterances such as sentences. The sentences are built up using rules of grammar, and the rules of grammar manipulate individuated entities. These individuated entities are strung together using rules of grammar to form intelligible output, which is parsed by the hearer using those same rules of grammar. What are those things that the rules of grammar manipulate? They are grammatical form class categories, like nouns and verbs etc.: these are the constituents that grammatical rules string together and manipulate as 'variables', sort of like chess pieces or poker chips rather than meaning-containing elements (see, e.g., Pinker 1997: 106).

The elements that are manipulated by sentence syntax – the syntactic constituents – may be nouns and verbs etc., but we don't store away in memory those larger noun and verb categorial elements. The things that are filed away for repeated use by the speaker on demand are further broken down into the smallest, most fully reduced occupants of one of those syntactic constituent slots. This is the definition of 'word' – i.e., syntactic word – given in 2.3 that we have used throughout this study.

Now, having posited the existence of these discrete entities called 'words' that are selected for insertion in sentence syntactic slots, we may assume that the speaker has access to or 'knows' a set of such items. That set, linguists, psychologists and psycholinguists presume, constitutes the lexicon. So the lexicon is a set of form–meaning pairs that are used in the production of utterances, and in the comprehension of utterances they are the elements that are identified in the speech stream as the carriers of meaning.

7.2 The lexicon and lexical access

There are many issues involved in lexical access. For example, is lexical access triggered by meaning, or sound? Also, are there multiple lexicons, e.g., one for production and one for comprehension? And what is the actual lexical unit that is accessed: the morpheme, the word or maybe even the written character?

The answer to the question of what initiates lexical access depends on whether the language activity is one of comprehension or of production. Most models assume that meaning – the speaker's intent to communicate a message with a certain semantic content – initiates lexical access in the case of speech production, and that the phonological form of an item in the perceived speech stream ('sharpened' by semantic and other contextual factors) initiates lexical access in the case of speech comprehension. These will be further discussed with specific reference to Chinese in 7.3.1 and 7.3.2.

Regarding the number of lexicons, the most reasonable assumption (and the one adopted by most investigators) is that the lexicon accessed in production and the one accessed in comprehension *is the 'same' lexicon*, i.e., a representation of sound–meaning pairs that are shared by the production and comprehension systems. For it to be otherwise we would have to assume the existence of two separate lexicons: a lexicon used for production output and one used for comprehension input. If that were the case, then when, for example, a speaker heard a new word, it would enter the 'comprehension' lexicon and be redundantly entered into the 'production' lexicon ready for output use, and when the speaker formed a new word it would become part of the speaker's 'production' lexicon but presumably also redundantly take up residence in the 'comprehension' lexicon. This seems implausible a priori, so we will consider the lexicon to be a single common representation serving both production and comprehension. This assumption involves the concept of the *modality-neutral* lexicon (Butterworth 1983: 260–1): the idea that lexical representations are in principle neutral with respect to modalities serving comprehension and those serving production.[1]

Finally the issue of what constitutes the actual unit of lexical access is essentially the question of what is 'listed' in the lexicon in precompiled form, ready to be accessed and brought on line as a single gestalt processing unit. Without wishing to prejudge the issue with respect to Chinese at this point, usually it is theories of visual access of orthographic word representations that allow the possibility of morpheme-based versus word-based lexical access. This and other issues will be discussed in the sections that follow.

7.3 Lexical access in Chinese

Issues surrounding lexical access have been unusually prone to misconception in the case of Chinese, for two reasons. The first is that

[1] Such a modality-neutral lexicon is ostensibly as independent of natural speech production and comprehension as it is of visual perception of orthography. However, the abstract lexical representation is weighted quite heavily in favour of natural speech and away from orthography, rather than being strictly 'neutral' with respect to modality. This is because although orthographic word meaning is logically and empirically dissociable from its phonetic form, the visual apprehension of word meaning is still heavily dependent upon the form–meaning connection that exists in natural speech (see discussion in 7.5).

psycholinguistic research on the Chinese lexicon has tended to focus on the visual processing of character orthography rather than natural speech, and it is only within this subfield of visual processing that morpheme access has been generally considered a viable possibility. The second reason is that Chinese orthographic units (characters) happen to be virtually isomorphic with morphemes (i.e., a character is almost always a morpheme and vice versa). These two facts have caused an unusually strong bias in favour of considering the morpheme to be the unit of lexical access in Chinese. We will evaluate the likelihood of morphemic lexical access in the sections that follow, in the context of specific Chinese speech comprehension and production models.

7.3.1 Chinese speech comprehension and the lexicon

The process of on-line speech comprehension involves perceiving and discriminating language sounds, parsing them into 'sound bundles' that match entries in a lexicon of sound–meaning combinations ('lexical retrieval'), and then decoding the meanings of those entries as combined by the speaker using rules of syntax. We are largely going to ignore the perception, discrimination and syntactic analysis stages, and focus on how the lexical retrieval process works, i.e., how the 'sound bundle' sequences match those of the lexical entries, resulting in sound–meaning combinations being accessed from the lexicon.

To investigate this question we will use Marslen-Wilson's *cohort* model of speech comprehension lexical retrieval (Marslen-Wilson 1989b). The cohort model assumes that certain 'lexical units' are activated and accessed by a process of successive approximation, in which more of the target lexical unit is 'ruled in' and its competitors 'ruled out' as increasingly more of the auditory sensory input is processed. We use this model because it is easily used to illustrate the general case of Chinese, because it is modality-neutral (see Butterworth 1983: 260, 289 for discussion), and because it allows in principle any arbitrarily sized meaningful unit to be posited as the unit of lexical access, allowing us for the moment to remain pretheoretically agnostic on the issue of morphemes or words as units of lexical access. I will therefore use the term 'Lexical Unit' in just such a pretheoretical sense in my description of the model below.

The cohort lexical retrieval model is proposed to work as follows (Marslen-Wilson 1989b: 7). The Lexical Unit selection process begins with the multiple access of candidates – the 'cohort' – as the first one or two phonetic segments of the Lexical Unit are heard as sensory input. All the Lexical Units in the hearer's mental lexicon that share the onset segment sequence are assumed to be activated as candidate units, representing the primary decision space within which the subsequent Lexical Unit selection process occurs. As more of the auditory sensory pattern is input, that pattern diverges from the patterns of successively more members of the cohort in the initial decision space, reducing the size of the cohort. At the same time, content-based contextual evaluation takes place, further reducing the size of the cohort according to the syntactic, semantic and discourse context requirements of the target Lexical Unit. This process continues until there is a single unique (in the ideal case) Lexical Unit candidate left that matches both the sensory input and contextual information.

The instant in time at which the target Lexical Unit is correctly identified from among its cohort competitors is called the *recognition point*. Shadowing, monitoring and gating experiments (Marslen-Wilson 1989b: 5) reveal that at the recognition point, neither the contextual information nor the auditory sensory pattern of the input form is by itself sufficient to identify the target Lexical Unit uniquely. This indicates that the Lexical Unit is identified by a convergence of contextual and phonetic information.

In the case of Chinese speech comprehension, the question of interest is the identity of the Lexical Unit: is it the morpheme or is it the word? If it is the word, then the pool of candidates that constitutes the cohort consists of words, and it is words that are eliminated and finally selected. On the other hand if it is the morpheme that is accessed as the Lexical Unit, then it is individual morphemes that are accessed, eliminated and finally selected. Let us now consider what each of these possibilities would mean for on-line comprehension of Chinese speech.

First let us consider what would happen under the assumption that the *word* is accessed as the Lexical Unit, using *huǒchē* 火车 fire-vehicle 'train' as an example. According to the cohort model, at a certain point following the onset of *huǒchē*, the phonetic form, along with contextual syntactic, semantic and pragmatic information, converge to retrieve the identity of the word *huǒchē* 'train' from the mental lexicon.

It may not be reasonable to think that the recognition point for *huǒchē* could be located, for example, at [hu . . .], since at this point in the acoustic sensory input stream[2] there would be over one thousand – by my estimate, 1,207 – phonetic word candidates: i.e., all single-syllable words consisting of the syllables *hu, hua, huai, huan, huang, hui, hun* and *huo*, as well as any multisyllabic words that begin with any of those syllables[3] (see Packard 1999 for detailed discussion). But note that even though the list of 1,207 phonetic candidates is large, the cohort would have been considerably reduced in size by the following requirements of the context: (a) the fact that the target Lexical Unit is a noun (syntactic context); (b) the meaning of the target Lexical Unit involves something that could 'move along a track' or 'be ridden' or 'be used to transport goods' (semantic context) and (c) the interlocutors were presumably discussing something having to do with travel or transportation, etc. (pragmatic context). Thus, the convergence of information from the acoustic sensory input stream and context would have reduced the cohort size to considerably fewer than the 1,207 entailed by the phonetic stream [hu . . .] alone.

Now if we assume recognition point occurs at the next phonetic segment, i.e., [huǒ . . .], there would be 116 phonetic candidates, namely, all words that begin with [huǒ . . .]. And once again, the cohort would have been reduced in size by the same syntactic, semantic and pragmatic contextual requirements listed above. Of the 116, about 45 of the candidates are nouns, and perhaps only one of these 45 fits the pragmatic context of 'travel or transportation' – i.e., *huǒjiàn* 'rocket' – but its semantic context is inappropriate. If we add yet another segment to the sensory input stream, the phonetic string [huǒç . . .] would have only four phonetic candidates: *huǒchái* 火柴 'match', *huǒcháng* 火场 'fire scene', *huǒchē* 火车 'train' and *huǒchéngyán* 火成岩 'igneous rock'. Thus, we might reasonably presume that identification of *huǒchē* – its recognition point – would occur at [huǒ . . .], or at some point 'between' [huǒ . . .] and [huǒç . . .].

Now let us consider what would happen if it were the *morpheme* that is accessed as the Lexical Unit. Once again using the example *huǒchē*, we assume that the Lexical Unit accessed is the morpheme

---

[2] Assuming that tone would not yet be perceptible at that point.
[3] My method was to use the *Hànyǔ Pīnyīn Cíhuì* (Lexicon Group, Committee on Script Reform, 1964), which uses a single alphabetic pinyin sort, to estimate the number of two-syllable entries between [hu] and [huzhu].

huǒ 火 'fire'. According to the model, given the acoustic sensory input [hu . . .], the selected group of phonetic morpheme candidates would be much smaller than the estimated 1207 for the word as the Lexical Unit (given the same amount of sensory input), because the number of potential *morphemes* that start with [hu . . .] is only, by my estimate, approximately 170 compared to the approximately 1207 *words* that are estimated to start with [hu . . .].[4] Recognition, therefore, might be presumed to occur much more quickly in the case of morpheme access.

But now notice the effect of the context requirements as outlined above. Will the number of phonetic candidates for the morpheme huǒ 火 'fire' as the Lexical Unit be reduced by context? Recall that the context is asking for a noun that can be 'ridden', 'used to transport' etc., in a situation involving travel. How do these contexts help to select the morpheme huǒ 火 'fire'?

The answer is that they do not, since the morpheme huǒ 火 'fire' has only a very general relation, if any, to that specific context. For the context to be able to assist in selecting the morpheme huǒ 火 'fire' as a processing constituent would only make sense if we assume a combinatorial grammar for (modern) Chinese that operates on morphemes as the primary units, rather than on the syntactic categories of noun, verb, etc. To date, no such grammar has been proposed that I am aware of.

But let us for the sake of argument assume that the amount of acoustic sensory input increases to [huǒ . . .]. At that point, we could argue that – no matter what the context – the morpheme huǒ 火 'fire' is easily distinguished from its two competitors: huǒ 伙 'group' and huǒ 钬 'holmium'.[5] And if we assume perception of that longer acoustic sensory input string [huǒ . . .], the identification of the morpheme huǒ 火 as the Lexical Unit may indeed occur much more rapidly than for the word huǒchē, because (a) huǒ 火 is phonetically shorter than huǒchē and (b) the number of formal competitors is much smaller for huǒ 火 (only 2) than for huǒchē (around 170).

---

[4] The estimate compiled from Wu (1988) of 170 is conservatively large, i.e., I counted *all*, and not just likely (e.g., non-archaic) characters from (hū 乎) to (huò 蠖).

[5] The issue of polysemy could be relevant here: are the huǒ 火 that means 'fire' and the huǒ 火 that means 'red' considered 'different morphemes' for the purposes of lexical access, even though they are listed in dictionaries as the 'same character/morpheme'? See discussion of polysemy in 4.3.3.3 and 6.3.

But now, given the lexical retrieval of the morpheme *huǒ* 火, what happens next? If we are true to our model of using the morpheme as the access unit, then the very same morpheme identification process must now be performed for the second morpheme, *chē* 车, followed by some kind of combination whereby the *huǒ* and the *chē* get put together to form the word *huǒchē*. Assuming such a model, the increased speed in identifying the morpheme *huǒ* 火 over the word *huǒchē*, assuming the acoustic sensory input [huǒ . . .], would be more than offset by the need to search for the second morpheme *chē* 车 and then combine the two to form *huǒchē*.

But let us remain conservative and say that the same morpheme search process need not occur for the second syllable, and that instead what takes place after the identification of *huǒ* 火 is some sort of lexical search performed by initial morpheme, with, e.g., *huǒ* 火 serving as the initial morpheme 'index' to lexical entries (as, e.g., in a Chinese language dictionary). The problem with this approach is that such a search process must assume the existence of *huǒchē* as a compiled lexical entry, i.e., as a *word*: why would a *word* identification algorithm bother to identify a *morpheme* as a preliminary step in identifying the *word*? Identification via the word gives you the whole item 'for free', simply because it is that gestalt item, and not its subcomponents, that is stored and accessed. Since the identification of morphemes is, as we saw above, a time consuming procedure that benefits little from contextual syntactic, semantic and pragmatic information, it would be quite inefficient for morpheme identification to occur as a way of accessing a precompiled word.

I have argued that parsing the input string into morphemes rather than words for lexical access in speech comprehension would require an improbable lexical processing mechanism. I have used the 'cohort' model of speech perception to make my point, but it could have been demonstrated equally well regardless of the speech comprehension model employed (though perhaps in slightly different fashion), unless the model were specifically designed to posit morphemes as the primary units of lexical access, and were to assume (as demonstrated with the example *huǒchē* 'train' above) *a sentence grammar of modern Chinese that consists of rules that combine morphemes, and takes morphemes rather than words as its 'primitives' or basic combinatory units*. While there are models that posit morphemes as lexical access units (athough most are based upon visual word recognition),[6] I am not aware of the existence of any grammatical models of modern Chinese that posit morphemes as the primary combinatorial units (for a possible exception, see Xu 1997).

7.3.2 Chinese speech production and the lexicon

Models of speech production must account for the utterance of strings of appropriately formed words, selected from a set of thousands, that are then strung together in the proper order. As in our discussion of speech comprehension above, what we will be concerned with is the selection of lexical units for output from the thousands available, and although I will briefly mention how sentence structure is implemented in each model, we will be relatively unconcerned with that aspect of sentence production. Also, as in our discussion of speech comprehension, I will deal with the lexical access unit in a pretheoretical sense, to consider the question of whether it is the word or the morpheme that is the unit of lexical access, i.e., the Lexical Unit.

---

[6] Some experimental results have been interpreted as suggesting that the morphemes could serve as units of lexical access. Murrell and Morton (1974) found that facilitation occurred in recognition of words when they were identical to or contained the same morpheme as words memorized from a pretest list (e.g., list word = 'car', test word = 'cars'), but not when the test word had a component that was visually and acoustically similar but otherwise unrelated to the list word (e.g., list word = 'car', test word = 'card'). These results suggested to the authors that root and suffix morphemes might be recognized independently, which would be consistent with the linguistic analysis of words into morphemes. In another study, Snodgrass and Jarvella (1972) found that subjects making a lexical decision task on actual, possible and impossible words, as well as prefixed and suffixed versions of each, were slowest with possible stems, fastest with real stems and intermediate with impossible stems, with affixation increasing reaction time for real and impossible words, but not for possible words. The authors interpret these results as possibly supporting the existence of a derived lexicon. The results from these two studies may indeed show that lexical access is compositionally facilitated by individual morphemes (Murrell and Morton), or that the lexicon is derived (Snodgrass and Jarvella), but this is clearly not the same as saying that the morpheme versus the word is the primary unit of lexical access. Also, in both studies the use of orthography as testing stimuli is a possible confusion in the discussion of lexical access in the comprehension or production of *speech*. Butterworth also discusses models positing morphemes rather than words as possible candidate units for lexical representations, and concludes that such models are not well supported (1983: 279–80, 289).

Most models of Lexical Unit retrieval in speech production propose that meaning is the trigger for initial lexical selection, and that a separate process is required to retrieve phonological form. Thus most approaches posit a 'two-stage' model, in which access to a Lexical Unit's form and access to its meaning occur separately, with the initial selection occurring by meaning. The initial meaning stage starts with a non-linguistic conceptual or 'message' level, which results from the speaker's intent to communicate information. What follows the message level differs according to investigator. I will demonstrate with two of the best-known theories, those of Garrett (1988) and Levelt (1989, 1992).

In Garrett's model, the message gives rise both to (a) the selection of abstract lexical items that contain semantic and grammatical specification but not phonological form, and to (b) the construction of abstract functional phrasal structures. On this view, lexical retrieval is relatively independent of phrasal construction. In Levelt's model the message causes activation of the *lemma* – a lexical entry that contains semantic and grammatical (e.g., form class category, subcategorization, argument structure, etc.) information, but is unspecified for phonological form. The lemmas in turn trigger the construction of phrases using information from their grammatical content.

One area where the two models differ (and this is relevant but not crucially important for us) is that the Levelt model implies that sentence structure is 'projected' via grammatical information contained in the lemma, whereas the Garrett model implies that although abstract lexical items contain grammatical information, sentence structure is nonetheless built using relatively independent principles. The important thing for us to note is that in both models, the 'message' causes retrieval of abstract Lexical Units that contain semantic and grammatical information.

So the question once again – as in the case of speech comprehension – is: what is the identity of the Lexical Unit, the morpheme or the word? If we assume the morpheme as the Lexical Unit, that means that following the message stage, the abstract bundle of semantic and grammatical information that is accessed is the morpheme, and that the grammatical information contained in the morpheme would have to be *morpheme combination* rather than *word combination* information. Whereas, of course, if we assume the word as the Lexical Unit, then that unit would contain grammatical information about the order of words (as minimal occupants of syntactic phrasal slots) as combinatory units.

If we assume morphemes as Lexical Units, in the Garrett model the sentence frames that are formed post-message must be frames that would accept morphemes rather than words as units. In the Levelt model, the grammatical information contained in lemmas would have to be information about the combination of morphemes with other morphemes. So regardless which model we use, if we assume the morpheme as the Lexical Unit, implicit in the assumption would be – just as we saw in our discussion of speech comprehension in 7.3.1 – *the requirement that the sentence grammar of modern Chinese be a grammar that consists of rules that combine morphemes, and takes morphemes rather than words as its 'primitives' or basic combinatory units.*

It is not hard to imagine how such a grammar would have to work in principle. It would have to assume that units larger than morphemes are not selected as gestalt combinatorial units, and that such larger units (words, phrases) are built up by a combinatorial syntax using morphemes as primitives. For comprehension and production models, it would assume that both the selection from the mental lexicon and the composition into larger units occur on a morpheme-by-morpheme basis.

But being easy to imagine how such a system might operate in theory does not translate in this case into providing an accurate picture of how it actually works. Such a morpheme-based system is implausible – intuitively, because it is hard to envision the on-line production and comprehension of Chinese (or any) speech actually occurring on a morpheme-by-morpheme basis; and theoretically, because it gives up the efficiency that the system gains for free by having the precompiled word serve as the basic access unit.

7.3.3 Experimental evidence demonstrating whole-word processing

There is strong experimental evidence demonstrating that Chinese words are represented in the mental lexicon as gestalt units, supporting the arguments above presented in favour of whole-word rather than morpheme-by-morpheme processing.

In natural speech experiments employing lexical decision tasks, Zhou and Marslen-Wilson (1994) found that when word, morpheme and syllable frequency were varied, only word frequency had an effect on the lexical decision response times to real words, suggesting that Chinese words are represented as wholes in the mental lexicon and that lexical access occurs via those whole-word units.

In a series of twelve natural speech experiments using auditory–auditory primed lexical decision tasks, Zhou and Marslen-Wilson (1995) found that the results of all their experiments were consistent with lexical representation and access occurring at the whole-word level, while other of their results (especially their experiments 2a–2d) were inconsistent with representation and access occurring at the level of the morpheme. These results led the authors to conclude for Chinese that 'lexical representation . . . is word-based' and that 'In lexical access, the speech input ultimately projects onto a level of word representation' (p. 595).

In experiments involving semantically primed lexical decision tasks using Chinese character orthography, Liu and Peng (1997) found that gestalt word meanings are accessed before the meanings of the individual morphemes that make up the word. The task was to present a priming word followed by a target word, to see if the characteristics of the priming word caused the reaction to the target word to occur more quickly. The logic of the experiment is that if the meaning of either the priming word itself or a morpheme within a priming word is accessed within the time that the priming word is presented, then the recognition of a following target word related to that meaning should be facilitated. The experimenters found that at the shortest prime duration, whole-word primes, but not their components, prime target words, while at longer prime durations both whole-word primes and their components prime target words. These results indicate that in visual word recognition, gestalt word meaning is processed faster than and prior to the meaning of the word component morphemes.

Taft and Zhu (1997) also carried out experiments using Chinese character orthographic stimuli to determine whether two-character words are represented as whole words or via their component morphemes. The experimenters used a primed naming task in which a mask occurs just before the presentation of the prime to reduce low-level episodic trace effects. Subjects had to name the first character of a target word that had been preceded by a prime consisting of either the first or second character of that target word. The rationale behind this experiment is that although the first character of the word might be expected to prime itself, if the second character were found to prime the naming of the first character, then we could assume that the connection between the two must occur at the whole-word level, since only via a whole-word representation that includes both characters would the second character be expected to prime the first. Remarkably, the experimenters found that the second character of the word primed the naming of the first character of the word even more than the first character primed itself, a result that held for both monomorphemic and bimorphemic two-character words. The authors concluded that 'there are whole word representations in lexical memory despite the fact that they are highly redundant'.

The results of Zhou and Marslen-Wilson clearly show that in Chinese natural speech, complex words are psycholinguistically processed as gestalt units. Furthermore, even though the experiments of Liu and Peng (1997) and Taft and Zhu (1997) were conducted using Chinese character rather than natural speech stimuli, their results still lend strong support to the notion that gestalt word retrieval is more likely than morpheme-by-morpheme retrieval (as was argued in 7.3.1 and 7.3.2), for the following reason: if morpheme-by-morpheme lexical processing were primary in Chinese, we would expect it to show up in experiments involving Chinese characters to an even greater extent than in spoken language experiments, due to the fact that the morphemic units are uniquely individuated and unambiguous in visual presentation – more so than in spoken presentation. Morphemic primacy should therefore be easier to demonstrate using visual presentation in Chinese if it were in fact present.

7.4 The Chinese lexicon: what is 'listed'?

Most investigators would probably agree that Chinese word component morphemes – root words, bound roots, word-forming affixes and grammatical affixes – are listed in the lexicon. Now if, as I argued in 7.3.1 and 7.3.2, the basic, precompiled combinatory unit is the word, then why does the issue of what is listed in the lexicon and accessed as a precompiled form in Chinese arise? Isn't it simply the case that all words are listed in the lexicon (together with the individual word component morphemes that compose them) and are accessed and retrieved as needed for the comprehension and production of Chinese sentences?

This has become an issue partly because of the positions taken by other investigators on the question of lexical listing in Chinese (e.g., Hoosain, Dai, Zhang and Peng, and Sproat and Shih; see below), and also in consideration of the productive word-forming properties of other languages, e.g., agglutinating inflectional languages like Turkish. In these languages (see, e.g., Hankamer 1989), the number of productively formed potential complex words is so huge that it is difficult to imagine that they are not created on-line by rule.

The view that every (morphologically complex) word the speaker knows is explicitly listed in the lexicon (with or without a representation of its morphological structure) is called the Full Listing Hypothesis (FLH; Butterworth 1983), and assumes whole-word listing for known words, and suggests 'fall-back procedures' involving rules or analogy for the creation and comprehension of new words (1983: 290). At the other extreme are models which would posit that what are listed in the lexicon are morphemes, and that all complex-word formation is accomplished by rule (e.g., Taft and Forster 1975). Most models of the latter are restricted to orthographic word recognition.[7] Intermediate models propose full listing for some words and on-line productive generation by rule for some others, e.g., the Augmented Addressed Morphology (AAM) proposal of Caramazza, Laudana and Romani (1988), which assumes whole-word listing for known words, and morpheme listing for novel ones. For Chinese, the question of lexical listing versus on-line generation of complex words is discussed in the works of Hoosain (1992), Dai (1992), Zhang and Peng (1992) and Sproat and Shih (1996).

Hoosain (1992: 126–8) argues that the FLH is unlikely for Chinese, given his view of the 'fluid' notion of 'word' in Chinese, and cites the inability of Chinese speakers to assign word boundaries reliably. Hoosain further states that it is likely that a larger proportion of Chinese multimorphemic words, in contrast to English, are not listed in the

---

[7] Butterworth says that Morton's early 'logogen' model is morpheme-based, but that in later work the logogen actually corresponds to word-level elements. Butterworth expresses doubt as to whether later logogen models maintain the early morphemic character of logogens (1983: 270).

lexicon but rather 'have meanings that are arrived at in the course of language use', and that the Chinese lexicon contains a large number of individual morphemes and a 'lexical tool-kit' which allows the creation and understanding of multimorphemic words (Hoosain 1992: 126). Hoosain's position on lexical listing therefore appears to be that the Chinese lexicon does not, in general, list complex words. Hoosain does note, however, that with frequency of use, complex words may come to exist as lexical entries, with perhaps parallel activation for both the gestalt word and the component morphemes. He further argues that even if the Chinese lexicon does store all multimorphemic words, the individual components play a greater role than in English (Hoosain 1992: 126–8).

Dai's position is that the vast majority of complex words (namely, my bound root words – those composed of bound roots; see 3.4.3 and 4.1) are listed in the lexicon rather than generated by rule (Dai 1992: 63). Furthermore, Dai says that words in Chinese are formed using productive rules when the word components are, in essence, either free words themselves or affixes (Dai 1992: 59–63).

Zhang and Peng (1992) propose that Chinese words are stored in the lexicon in decomposed fashion, and that they are accessed via the 'character'. There are two important points to keep in mind regarding this proposal. The first is that it is by no means clear that the authors intend for 'character access' to be understood as being functionally equivalent to 'morpheme access', equivalent to that which occurs for example, in natural speech processing. The second point, closely related to the first, is that the Zhang and Peng proposal is based on experimental results on the visual recognition of words presented in Chinese character orthography, and addresses specifically what they term the 'orthographic lexicon'. It is therefore clear that their proposal is modality-specific, involving lexical access to a visual 'orthographic lexicon' with the (character) orthography serving at best as a medium via which the natural speech lexicon is accessed. It may indeed be possible to use results on visual 'orthographic lexicon' access such as those of Zhang and Peng as evidence for models of a Chinese natural speech lexicon. We know that the visual processing of characters in reading must be related somehow to the Chinese spoken language lexicon, otherwise we would be hard-pressed to explain how reading in Chinese occurs. To date there are relatively few explicit theories proposing what the nature of that relationship might be, despite the volumes that have been written on the visual information processing of Chinese orthography. The most comprehensive and explicit theory is that of Taft, as outlined in Taft and Zhu (1997). We will discuss this further in 7.5, along with the idea that lexical access in speech and in reading are, in principle, independent processes.

Sproat and Shih (1996) propose that morphemes[8] as well as many morphologically complex words (e.g., those with idiosyncratic meanings) are listed, and that the rules used to form complex words from these morphemes in Chinese constitute a generally productive system, with, e.g., bound roots available for productive word formation.[9]

7.4.1 What is 'listed'?: a proposal

My proposal is that every complex word known by the speaker is listed in precompiled form in the Chinese lexicon, except for those that contain the morphological element G (grammatical affixes). This follows naturally from the proposal in 7.3.1 and 7.3.2 that the word constitutes the basic unit of Chinese lexical access, and that in Chinese speech production and comprehension, grammatical affixes are added and parsed respectively by rule. The model I propose thus differs from the FLH (Butterworth, 1983) and the AAM model (Caramazza, Laudana and Romani 1988), since the present proposal assumes that grammatical words are created and recognized by rule, even if such words are known to the speaker.

The proposal put forth here is that all complex words – with the exception of grammatical words – are listed in the Chinese natural speech lexicon in a form that includes a representation of their morphological structure. Grammatical words – those containing the morphological element G (grammatical affixes: e.g., *-le* 了, *-zhe* 著, *-guo* 过, *-de* 得, *bu-* 不 and *-men* 们) – therefore, are the only complex word type in Chinese that are stored in the lexicon in 'decomposed' fashion: they are posited to be produced and comprehended by on-line use of a productive rule, namely, Rule 2 in (98) (also seen in figure 4). All compound words, bound root words and derived words that are

---

[8] In actuality, Sproat and Shih make this specific claim only for *noun* root compounds (my 'bound roots'). However, there is nothing in their presentation that suggests they would treat other form classes any differently.

[9] Richard Sproat (personal communication).

Table 40   Lexically listed elements in Chinese

investigator	lexically listed complex words	complex words derived by rule
Dai (1992)	bound root words	compound words derived words grammatical words
Hoosain (1992)	none (except through 'familiarity of use')	compound words bound root words derived words grammatical words
Packard (present work)	compound words bound root words derived words (all 'listed' upon first contact)	grammatical words
Sproat and Shih (1996)	those with idiosyncratic meanings (at least)	compound words bound root words derived words grammatical words
Zhang and Peng (1992)	none (?)	'all two-character words'[10]

known to the speaker – including a representation of their morphological structure – are lexically stored, and the relation between those words and the rules that compose them exists in the speaker's grammar in the form of 'lexical redundancy rules' (Jackendoff 1972). The term 'lexical redundancy rule' refers to the knowledge that relates the grammatical structure of the listed word to the rule that produced it, and is also used in the comprehension and coining of new words. In the case of Chinese, these would take the specific form of Rule 1 in (98) (seen also in figure 4). A summary of the differences among investigators regarding what is lexically listed in the Chinese lexicon is presented in table 40.[11]

All morphemes and precompiled words are listed in the lexicon, but only words (precompiled words or free morphemes) are available

---

[10] Zhang and Peng specifically refer to the *orthographic* lexicon.

[11] In table 40 I use my own terminology rather than that of the investigators cited. Also, all investigators would ostensibly assume that all monomorphemic words, and all morphemes, are also lexically listed.

for lexical access and insertion into sentences. Bound morphemes known to the speaker are listed in the speaker's lexicon, but are not available for insertion into syntactic frames. They must be present in the lexicon because they are known by the speaker and must be available for constructing and understanding new words (using the word-formation rules). So, (bound) morphemes and words are differentiated by the fact that words, and not (bound) morphemes, are available for lexical access and insertion into syntactic form class slots.

Why am I proposing that words containing G – grammatical words – are the only type of complex word in Chinese that are stored in the lexicon in 'decomposed' fashion and created on-line by rule? The reason is that the affixation of G in Chinese is completely regular: that is, of the verbs that take G (by far the majority), the phonological forms of G are 100 per cent regular, never undergoing any kind of morphophonological alternation or suppletion. Given that degree of morphological and phonological regularity, it seems reasonable to propose that words affixed with G involve creation by rule rather than proposing a lexical listing of all possible 'word+G' combinations.

This proposal for the structure of the Chinese lexicon is in accord with the model of Chinese word formation proposed in sections 3.4, 4.1, 7.3.1 and 7.3.2. The lexical redundancy rules presented in 5.4 (Rule 1 in (98); and in figure 4) are used by native speakers both to understand and to coin new words. Once a word is coined or understood in conformity with these rules, it is 'listed', in precompiled form, in the lexicon (except for grammatical words). The lexical redundancy rules tell us what words are possible in the language, even though they do not appear as precompiled, 'listed' items. Such non-existent but potential words predicted by rule have been termed 'virtual lexical entries' by Bierwisch and Schreuder (1992: 29). The complex words that are listed in the lexicon therefore may be considered 'actual' rather than 'virtual' lexical entries.[12]

[12] Addressing the possible upper limit on the number of 'actual' lexical entries, C.-C. Cheng (1998) has proposed that the human lexicon has a de facto storage limit of approximately 8,000 lexical elements. If this is so, then it could be that grammatical words are derived and that all other complex words are listed, but only to the extent that they do not exceed the 8,000 limit. As that limit is exceeded, certain of the stored complex words (perhaps those that are less salient or not used for a while) might 'fade' in memory, able to be derived or 'regenerated' when encountered or used once again. Thanks to C.-C. Cheng and Y.-M. Ku for helpful discussion of this interesting issue.

Relating this discussion of lexical listing to our discussion of 'degree of lexicalization' in 6.1.2: when complex forms are lexicalized as words, they become listed as actual, precompiled lexical items along with information about their morphological, phonological, semantic and syntactic properties as discussed in 6.2. As words become 'more lexicalized', it means – following the framework presented in 6.1.2 – that the information on morphology, phonology, semantics, syntax etc. undergoes 'reduction', that is, the representation of that knowledge as part of the lexically listed entry begins to 'fade', thereby making the knowledge become more 'opaque' and less visible to the grammatical processes that operate on and utilize them.

Regarding the relationship between independent words (free morphemes) such as *tú* 图 'picture, chart' and *huà* 画 'picture' and the (compound) words they compose (e.g., *túhuà* 'picture'), the compounds and the free words used to compose them are treated on a par in this model, related by the fact that the free words are available for lexical insertion into syntactic slots and for combination into compounds. When the latter happens, the components often retain their individual meanings and lexical identities (as is the case with the words *tú* and *huà* of *túhuà*). But often the components that have been lexicalized undergo semantic and lexical 'drift' or 'bleaching', as described in chapter 6, with the meanings of those components, over time, 'losing' some of their semantic and lexical identity, as described in the paragraph above. Along with their loss of semantic and lexical identity they may even lose their status as free morphemes (as seen, for example, in (288)), in which case, according to this model, they become X^{-1} elements and are no longer available to the speaker for lexical insertion into syntactic slots.

These proposals on lexical listing yield a model of the Chinese lexicon that has the properties depicted in figure 4. In this model, all (known) morphemes are listed, and all complex words known to the speaker (except grammatical words) are also listed, in precompiled form, along with redundancy rules that account for the structure of all complex words (except grammatical words), and a rule for on-line generation and comprehension of grammatical words.

So in the present proposal, for example, the words *miàndī* 面的 'van taxi' and *wēimiàn* 微面 'minivan' (see (288)) become listed in the lexicon (at the 'word level'; see Zhou and Marslen-Wilson 1994, 1995) as soon as they are used or heard and comprehended by the speaker, and the new word formative *-miàn-* 面 also becomes listed in the

Figure 4 A model of the Chinese lexicon

Chinese lexicon			
listed morphemes	listed (precompiled) complex words (must be known to be speaker)	'redundancy' rules (Rule 1 in example (98))	on-line word-formation rule (Rule 2 in example (98))
all morphemes: $X^{-0}\ X^{-1}\ X^W\ G$	compound words bound root words derived words	$X^{-0} \rightarrow X^{-0,-1,\{W\}}, X^{-0,-1,\{W\}}$	$X^{-0} \rightarrow X^{-0}, G$

lexicon (at the 'morpheme level'; Zhou and Marslen-Wilson 1994, 1995) with its new meaning of 'van', including its morphological status as a bound root (i.e., X^{-1}). This comports with the experimental findings of Zhou and Marslen-Wilson (1994, 1995), who interpret their results as indicating that independent morphemic representations exist for morphemes that are also word components. It is also consistent with the experimental results of Taft and Zhu (1995), who found that independent morphemic representation exists for bound morphemes, as long as their morphemic status has been clearly established (though their results are based upon orthography processing).

Both the structure of Chinese words as proposed in chapters 4 and 5 and the theory of the Chinese lexicon as outlined here and portrayed in figure 4, mesh with the experimental findings of Zhou and Marslen-Wilson (1994, 1995) indicating that the Chinese lexicon possesses both a level of whole-word representation and morpheme representation, and that gestalt words are represented in a way that ensures that the morphological structure of the word is 'marked or bracketed' (1995: 595). The present work fits those criteria, since both morphemes and compiled words are listed, with the 'bracketing' of compiled words corresponding to the form of the rules that generated them.

Thus, a clear answer is proposed to the question 'what is listed?' posed at the beginning of this section. All Chinese morphemes, whether bound or free, are listed in the mental lexicon, but only the free morphemes are available for direct lexical access. All complex words known to the speaker are also listed, in precompiled form, with the exception of grammatical words, which are constructed on-line. In addition, the word-formation rules presented in section 5.4.2 (as seen in figure 4), which represent the knowledge of word structure, are also part of the Chinese speaker's lexicon.

7.5 Chinese characters and the lexicon

Since the visual information processing characteristics of Chinese character orthography have loomed prominently in the Chinese lexical processing literature, in this section we consider the relationship between Chinese characters and the mental lexicon.

7.5.1 Character sound and meaning come from the natural speech lexicon

Perhaps the most important and interesting question to ask about Chinese characters and the mental lexicon is: does Chinese character orthography play a role in the operation of the Chinese spoken language lexicon, with the organization of that lexicon perhaps being affected somehow by the visual information processing characteristics of Chinese characters? The answer, in a word, is *no*. Why? Because the store of lexical items in human language is a natural speech lexicon first and foremost. Natural speech is how the lexical items 'got there' in the first place, and natural speech is normally the medium via which they are extracted. Chinese character orthography could hardly play a role in the organization of this lexicon, except under unusual circumstances involving, for example, speech deficit or deprivation, especially if it were to cooccur with significant exposure to character orthography.

But even though Chinese orthography plays no major role in the operation of the spoken language lexicon, is there still a *relationship* between the two? The answer here clearly is *yes*, there is a very strong and direct relationship between Chinese characters and the natural speech lexicon, and the relationship is this: the visual perception and reading of Chinese character orthography is *completely dependent* upon the Chinese natural speech lexicon for pronunciation and meaning. This is because the properties of sound and meaning that are accessed in reading Chinese characters are precisely those which already exist in the natural speech lexicon, as described in 7.3.1 and 7.3.2.

It is hard to imagine how it could possibly be otherwise. To suppose that character reading is not dependent on the natural speech lexicon, we would have to assume for the reader of Chinese a store of knowledge that contains a representation of the characters including their meaning and sound, with such knowledge completely duplicating the sound–meaning information which already exists – *in toto* – in the natural speech lexicon. Especially given that we know that the characters got their sound and meaning via the sound–meaning relation that is present in preexisting natural speech lexical entries, it would require a stretch of the imagination to posit the existence of two identical sets of sounds–meaning relationship pairs: one for character orthography and one for speech.

Probably the most convincing evidence of this is the simple fact that native speaker knowledge of Chinese words and morphemes exists independently of Chinese character knowledge, as is easily demonstrated in the case of non-literate Chinese speakers. Such speakers are able to make the observation, and will understand when told, that, for example, 'the *shī* (湿 "wet") of *shīdù* (湿度 "humidity") is the same *shī* as in *cháoshī* (潮湿 "damp"), and different from the *shī* (师 "master") in *lǎoshī* (老师 "teacher") or the *shī* (狮 "lion") in *shīzi* (狮子 "lion")'. Although literate speakers might be expected to have a more highly developed sense of 'morpheme awareness' than non-literate speakers (see, e.g., Nagy and Anderson 1999), it is by no means clear that the basic structure of non-literate speakers' lexicons would be different simply because their awareness of morpheme identity is not enhanced by a knowledge of character orthography.

7.5.2 How do characters access the lexicon?

If Chinese character reading is dependent upon the natural speech lexicon, that means in reading, the retrieval of sound and meaning from the lexicon must, by definition, still occur, but that it presumably occurs in a different way from such retrieval in speech production and comprehension. So how do the characters access the lexicon? I propose that it occurs in the following way.

An entry in the lexicon is a relation of sound and meaning (there may be other information, like syntactic subcategorization and form class information, etc. that we set aside for now), as depicted in figure 5. The access of the lexicon by character orthography consists of the visual stimulus of the written character causing activation (i.e., 'retrieval' or 'access') of the lexical entry depicted in figure 5, with either the sound or the meaning potentially being activated, or coming 'on-line' first, depending on the nature of the activity (e.g., silent reading vs. reading aloud, or a lexical decision task vs. a rhyming task,

Figure 5 Relation between lexical entry and orthography

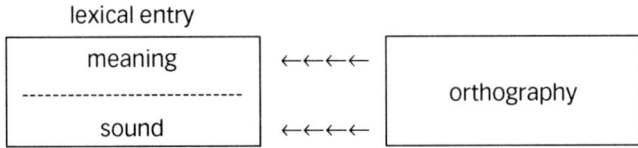

etc.), and perhaps, to some extent, the nature of the character stimulus (e.g., whether it contains a frequent, highly transparent semantic or phonetic component).

This proposed orthographic visual lexical access process is best appreciated by comparing it to lexical access in speech comprehension. Referring to figure 5, when access of a lexical entry occurs in speech comprehension, the input stimulus is necessarily sound (perhaps 'sharpened' by semantic factors; see 7.3.1), thereby activating the 'sound' part of the entry, which then accesses the entire lexical entry by activating a representation of the word's meaning. So we can say (as we did in 7.3.1) that lexical access in speech comprehension is necessarily initiated or 'triggered' by sound.

In the case of visual lexical access, the part of the lexical entry that is activated 'first' may be the meaning part or the sound part. We can think of the visual form as activating or 'calling up' the meaning of the lexical item followed by its sound, or the sound followed by its meaning, or ostensibly even both being activated more or less 'simultaneously'. The point is that according to this model, *either* the sound *or* the meaning of the lexical item can be activated 'first' in visual lexical access. If either the sound or the meaning of a lexical item may come 'on-line' first in Chinese character lexical access, then it is clear that the visual access of a word's meaning may occur without the mediation of sound, and that access of its sound may occur without the mediation of meaning (notice I said *without the mediation of* X, and not *without* X or *independent of* X).

The virtually automatic access of Chinese character sound without the mediation of meaning is a well-documented phenomenon, having been empirically demonstrated in many experimental studies (e.g., Chu-Chang and Loritz 1977, Tzeng, Hung and Wang et al. 1977, Treiman, Baron and Luk 1981, Tan, Hoosain and Peng 1993). The access of a written form's meaning with no significant mediation of sound has also been empirically demonstrated (e.g., Zhou et al.

1999). Furthermore, the sound and meaning of visually retrieved lexical items are dissociable in brain damaged individuals as seen in Chinese readers with deep dyslexia, who are able to retrieve the meaning of a written word despite their inability to retrieve its phonological form (Yin and Butterworth 1992). These kinds of evidence indicate that although lexical items are sound–meaning pairs and the activation of phonology in orthographic lexical access may be a virtually automatic reflex, the activation is nonetheless dissociable in principle from the activation of meaning.

In fact, while activation of either sound or meaning is possible without the mediation of the other, and sound access and meaning access are perhaps equally likely all other things being equal, if we compare different orthographies, it is reasonable to expect a *greater* likelihood in Chinese (as compared with, say, an orthography like English) that the 'meaning' rather than the 'sound' part will be initially activated in reading, for two very cogent reasons. The first is that Chinese character orthography is phonologically opaque (i.e., the relationship between sound and graphic form is quite irregular). The second reason is that the relation between the visual orthographic form and the lexical entry in Chinese is virtually isomorphic, with each visual orthographic form (i.e., character) uniquely identifying one lexical entry (i.e., morpheme; see also discussion in Zhou et al. 1999).

The possibility that *either* the sound *or* the meaning of the lexical item may be activated 'first' in visual lexical access is often downplayed in the literature. Some investigators emphasize the role of *sound* (Perfetti and Zhang 1991, Cheng 1992, Tan, Hoosain and Peng 1993), in some cases claiming that 'reading Chinese requires phonological mediation' (Cheng 1992: 67), or that there is 'no semantics without phonology' (Perfetti and Zhang 1992, Perfetti, Zhang and Berent 1992: 241). Others emphasize the role of *meaning* (Zhou and Marslen-Wilson 1996, Zhou et al. 1999), stating that 'direct, visual access is the predominant way to access information in the mental lexicon', and that 'there is normally no or little phonologically mediated access to lexical semantics in reading Chinese' (Zhou et al. 1999). Proponents of both the sound-dominant view and the meaning-dominant view sometimes defend their claims by positing the existence of an integrated mental lexicon that contains orthographic information in addition to the universally assumed phonological and semantic information (e.g., Zhoux et al. 1999, Tan, Hoosain and Peng 1993).

But even though the mental lexicon must have *connections* to orthography, it is not likely to *contain* orthographic information[13] as suggested by these investigators, because it is – ontogenetically as well as phylogenically – a natural speech lexicon first and foremost. Any connection between the natural speech lexicon and Chinese character orthography is necessarily an add-on function that has been achieved during the process of reading acquisition – a process that exploits the robust sound–meaning connections that already exist in the learner's mental lexicon. To suppose otherwise we would have to assume that the newly acquired orthography – after forming connections to the form–meaning pairs that constitute lexical items – forges new connections to either the meaning half (on the meaning-dominant view) or the sound half (on the sound-dominant view) of the lexical item, that are in some sense more basic and 'direct' than the original connections that existed between the meaning of the lexical item and its sound.[14]

The model of Chinese character lexical access proposed here differs in interesting ways from that proposed by Taft (e.g., Taft and Zhu 1995, 1997). Taft says that S (semantics), P (phonology) and O (orthography) form a tripartite relationship – termed the 'lexical triangle' – with the O part of the triangle serving as a more-or-less coequal partner with S and P, even though the S–P link may be stronger than either S–O or P–O due to earlier and more frequent usage by the learner (personal communication). My position is that S and P are inherently, i.e., 'genetically' more closely related to each other than either is to O, since the S–P link exists not simply as a function of the experience of the organism, but because humans have evolved a specialized language faculty over time, the express function of which has been to relate sound and meaning.

---

[13] I consider the use of localizationist language such as 'contain' and 'in the lexicon' to be merely a heuristically useful spatial metaphor intended to posit a degree of functional relationship rather than localization per se. So in denying that 'the lexicon contains orthographic as well as semantic and phonological information' my intent is to claim a relatively distant functional relation between orthography on the one hand, and sound and/or meaning on the other, as compared with the basic, robust sound–meaning relation that constitutes the lexical entry.

[14] This is an oversimplification of the present state of the field presented for purposes of exposition. The focus nowadays is not so much on which route in the 'dual-route' model – sound or meaning – is 'dominant' in lexical access, but rather on the relative degree of activation of sound and meaning 'prelexically', i.e., ostensibly prior to the access of the sound–meaning gestalt pairs that represent the lexical items.

7.5.3 Is Chinese writing 'ideographic'?

The intuition that Chinese character reading allows visual access of the 'meaning' half of a lexical entry is no doubt what inspired investigators who have insisted that reading Chinese characters provides 'direct access to meaning' or that they are 'ideographic' (the 'ideographic camp'; e.g., Creel 1938, Hansen 1993), contentions that have been vehemently decried by opponents (the 'phonetic camp'; e.g., Boodberg 1940, DeFrancis 1984). A resolution of this conflict becomes apparent when we observe what is correct about each position.

In support of the ideographic camp, direct visual access of a word's meaning is indeed possible and does in fact occur, simply because it is possible – in reading *any* of the world's written languages – for a word's meaning to be activated 'before' its sound (even if only at the level of milliseconds), 'directly' upon apprehending it as a visual stimulus. Furthermore – for reasons having to do with phonological opacity and character–morpheme isomorphism stated in the previous section – Chinese orthography may be more likely than other orthographies to stimulate activation of the 'meaning' part of a lexical item before its 'sound' part.

But in support of the phonetic camp's position, such direct visual access of a word's meaning does not happen independently of spoken language, since it is after all via the spoken language lexicon that a word gets its meaning (as discussed in 7.5.1). When such 'direct access' of a word's meaning occurs, the word's sound is also physiologically activated as a virtual reflex of the lexical access process (a phenomenon termed 'phonetic recoding').

Thus, a resolution of the ideographic–phonetic controversy critically hinges on the meaning of 'ideographic': if the term 'ideographic' is intended to imply that the meaning of a lexical item exists in a mental lexicon dissociated from and independent of the sound of that lexical item, and that such meaning (or 'ideas') can be accessed in reading independently of and without activating the entire lexical item, then the characters cannot be considered ideographic. If, on the other hand, the definition of 'ideographic' is meant to imply only the possibility of relatively direct or 'early' access of the 'meaning' part of the sound–meaning pair that necessarily constitutes a lexical item, then the characters could indeed be considered ideographic.

8 | Chinese words: conclusions

8.1 What have we discovered about words?

In this work we have uncovered scores of generalizations that apply to Chinese words. A reasonable working hypothesis would be that some of these generalizations are also relevant to the formation and use of words in other languages. While it remains to be seen which of the generalizations will be found to apply universally, let us for now take a brief look at what Chinese has told us.

We discussed the fact that, from the perspective of Chinese, the concept of the *word* may not be as intuitive a notion as it is in other languages, for a number of reasons. After considering the various possible definitions of 'word', we found that there is a considerable degree of overlap among the criteria used to define the word, with the definition that offers the most convergence being that of the word as a minimal free syntactic atom.

A framework was offered that describes the internal characteristics of Chinese words by identifying the form classes of the word components. This was related to the fact that normally the word itself also has a form class identity, and that there exists an intimate relationship between the form class identity of the word and that of its constituents. We found that the form class identity of morphemes within words is largely word-driven, with the identity of the gestalt word playing a major role in determining constituent identity. This, it was noted, is different from the situation in syntax, where the 'identity-conferring' power occurs in the 'opposite' direction, with head identity said to determine rather than be determined by the identity of the 'higher' structural node. We observed that the notion of word 'head' can mean different things, and that concepts of 'virtual', 'canonical', 'semantic' and 'structural' head are all relevant to our understanding of Chinese words.

We found that the overwhelming majority of Chinese complex words contain a structural head, with that head occurring on the left in the case of verbs and on the right in the case of nouns. That characteristic was posited to be a language-specific constraint on Chinese word formation which was termed the Headedness Principle. Exceptions to the Headedness Principle were discussed, with one exception being that in words containing a word-forming affix (i.e., derived words), that affix determines the form class of the word. Other exceptions to the Headedness Principle were considered to be possible, albeit 'marked', word forms in the language that were shown to be treated exceptionally by grammatical processes that make reference to word structure.

We found that the form class identity approach to words and their components is usefully augmented by a framework that is based on the [±free] and [±content] status of word components. The resulting properties of the components were characterized in terms of a set of morphological primitives (X^{-0}, X^{-1}, X^W, G), whose formal properties account for both the structures of complex words in Chinese (and English) and the differences in productivity between morphology and syntax. I argued that the concept *affix* universally includes the properties *boundness* ([−free]) and *grammatical function* ([−content]), but does not necessarily include the agreement phenomena, paradigmaticity and morphophonemic alternation that are often associated with affixes in other languages.

It was proposed that in addition to the language-specific Headedness Principle, forms of Chinese words are also constrained by their conformity to the rules in (98), which are manifestations of Selkirk's universal rule in (63). The rules in (98) were found to take precedence over the Chinese-specific Headedness Principle, generating the potential Chinese word structures in table 22. Both universal and language specific rules were found to have less relevance to word structure with increasing lexicalization, so that the more lexicalized a word is, the less it is subject to the word-forming rules and the Headedness Principle.

Following the assumption that the syntax and the lexicon are separate components, I argued that the rules and primitives of syntax and those of the lexicon are distinct, with differences in productivity between morphology and syntax achieved by allowing only one morphological system primitive – viz., X^{-0} – to generate complex, branching morphological stuctures. It was demonstrated that V–O forms in Chinese may belong either to the lexicon or to the syntax, but that once they have been lexicalized, their basic underlying identity is as *words* that may undergo temporary syntacticization. I argued that the indeterminacy often claimed between V–O phrases and V–O words is only apparent, and that although there are different *potential* interpretations of V–O forms as words or phrases, at any given moment in the state of the language processor, there is a singular identity of a V–O form as *either* a word *or* phrase based upon the real-time use of the form. Any perceived ambiguity, it was argued, is illusory and ephemeral, and occurs only upon reflection or analysis.

Most new words in Chinese, it was found, are formed by the combination of content morphemes into complex words, whose constituents then often undergo reanalysis to change their semantic and form class identities, as well as giving up their status as free morphemes. The maxim 'today's morphology is yesterday's syntax' (Givón 1971: 413) was found to apply beautifully in Chinese, since many of today's Chinese word structures involve lexicalizations of syntactic structure. In the case of V–O compounds, lexicalization results in the theta marking property of the verb head no longer being satisfied by the word-internal object element, requiring the verb to reach outside the lexicalized V–O word for theta satisfaction. The development of V_1–V_2 complex resultative verb words in Chinese is also due to lexicalization – followed by the grammaticalization of the V_2 ending – causing that ending to lose its ability to extend theta marking properties outside the boundaries of the complex word. We saw that the lexicalization of syntactic structures gives rise to many exceptions to the Headedness Principle.

It was argued that the basic unit of lexical retrieval from the mental lexicon in Chinese natural speech production and comprehension is the *word*, and that individual morpheme access for complex words in Chinese natural speech processing is unlikely. I proposed that in Chinese, complex words and the rules for their construction and comprehension are listed – redundantly – in the lexicon, for all but the most productive forms, i.e., grammatical words. I argued that Chinese characters receive their pronunciation and meaning values from natural speech lexical entries, but otherwise they are only indirectly related to the mental lexicon, despite the fact that the Chinese character has a less ambiguous morphemic status than the spoken form it represents. Although lexical retrieval in reading may visually access the morpheme or word somewhat independently of its sound, I argued that Chinese characters are virtually irrelevant to lexical retrieval in Chinese speech production and comprehension.

The Chinese data yield a number of findings that point in the same general direction because they are based upon a consistent underlying theory which, I believe, is generally correct, and may help to account for word-formation phenomena in other languages. The theory is that there is a small, fixed set of word-forming primitives that combine in a limited number of ways and have only limited capacity to generate embedded structures. The lexical component or 'lexicon' is a specialized linguistic module where all bound and free morphemes and all complex words known to the speaker (except for words containing grammatical affixes) reside, and where the creation and comprehension of novel words takes place. Over time, the constituents of complex words in the lexicon may lose their individual identities, making them increasingly opaque to the grammatical processes that would refer to them. One cause of the evolution of morpheme and word forms over time is precisely those identity changes that occur due to increasing lexicalization (which may include grammaticalization), another cause is grammaticalization (which may involve lexicalization).

As we saw in 6.3, grammaticalization occurs when morphemes lose their referential 'content' properties and become more 'grammatical'. Linguists describe this 'content > function' relationship in natural language using the concept of the *cline*. Synchronically, the cline is a continuum, at one end of which are located the more 'lexical' forms, and at the opposite end the more 'grammatical' forms. Diachronically, the cline represents the evolution of forms over time from the 'lexical' end of the continuum toward the 'grammatical' end (Hopper and Traugott 1993: 6–7).

Hopper and Traugott term the cline posited by grammaticalization theory the 'cline of grammaticality', and it is depicted in (289) (Hopper and Traugott 1993: 7).

(289) cline of grammaticality (Hopper and Traugott 1993: 7)
content item > grammatical word > clitic> inflectional affix

Note that in this grammaticality cline, not only do forms become more grammatical, in general they also become more bound. This increase in boundness is also a characteristic of the 'cline of lexicality' cited by Hopper and Traugott (1993: 7), as seen in their example of derivational affixes evolving from content words in English: full > cupful > hopeful. Hopper and Traugott do not explicitly characterize the nature of the grammaticality and lexicality clines as moving from less to more bound, but the implication from their examples is clear. Harris and Campbell (1995: 63–4) in their discussion of reanalysis also imply that linguistic forms tend toward becoming more bound. They refer to the boundness of a linguistic form as *cohesion*, defined as 'the status of a linguistic sequence as a fully independent word, a clitic, an affix or an unanalysable part of a larger unit'. This definition, and their examples, imply a directionality from free to bound, since they cite no instances of cohesion whereby a form becomes less, rather than more, bound.

The tendency for morphemes to become bound as implied by the grammaticality and lexicality clines and the concept of cohesion is supported by the Chinese word-formation data. As discussed in 6.4.3.1, Chinese morphemes generally appear to be moving in the direction of free > bound, because free content words (X^0) have a tendency to become bound roots (X^{-1}) as they are used in increasing numbers of new complex words. Also, most word-forming (X^W) and grammatical (G) affixes have evolved from bound roots (X^{-1}) and root words (X^0). And there is no tendency to move in the opposite direction: we tend not to see bound roots becoming content words, affixes becoming bound roots, or – much less – affixes becoming content words. The unidirectionality of the lexicality cline as suggested by the Chinese word-formation data therefore would be as depicted in (290).

(290) lexicality cline (Chinese)
content word > bound root > word-forming affix > grammatical affix

Note that, while the evolution of Chinese morphemes may not follow the path shown in (290) in a strictly linear fashion (e.g., a content word is not restricted to becoming only a bound root, and grammatical affixes do not derive exclusively from word-forming affixes), its unidirectional character is nonetheless clear: forms evolve in a rightward rather than leftward direction along the cline. The implication is that the unidirectionality that is posited in the case of the grammaticality cline is a characteristic of the lexicality cline as well, with the one-way evolution of 'free > bound' in the lexicality cline paralleling the one-way evolution of 'content > function' in the grammaticality cline. Since the predominant characteristic of the grammaticality cline is for forms to become more grammatical, and the predominant characteristic of the lexicality cline is for forms to become more bound, the grammaticality and lexicality clines might be recast in simplified form as in (291) and (292) respectively, interacting to make morphemes more bound and more grammatical.

(291) grammaticality cline
content > function

(292) lexicality cline
free > bound

The Chinese word-formation data support the generalization that in natural language, morphemes over time tend to become more bound and more grammatical. This appears to be a valid generalization, since there are relatively few instances in the languages of the world of bound forms becoming free and grammatical forms becoming content forms (though a non-trivial amount of counterevidence to this 'unidirectionality hypothesis' has been presented; see discussion in Heath 1998: 751).[1] Such a generalization might be taken to imply that languages by now should all have evolved into agglutinative or inflectional languages with words that contain a plethora of bound, grammatical, morphemes. The reason why this is not a necessary implication is that presumably one stage in such an evolutionary process would be for such morphemes to achieve the status of what Harris and Campbell term 'an unanalysable part of a larger unit' (1995: 63–4), in which such morphemes end up disappearing into larger, 'isolated' free forms, allowing for the eventual concatenation or 'compounding' of those forms. This recalls the developmental pathway suggested by some linguists in the posited evolution of language types from isolating languages to agglutinative languages and on to inflectional languages, as cited in Harris and Campbell (1995: 18).

The disappearance of morphemes into isolated free forms discussed by Harris and Campbell is seen in contemporary Chinese, with the

---

[1] There are of course interesting counterexamples to the unidirectionality hypothesis. One example is the preposition *up* (a function, and therefore grammatical, word) becoming a lexical verb as in *to up the ante* (Hopper and Traugott 1993: 127). Another example is the verb *dis* currently used in American English slang as a verb meaning 'to show *dis*respect or say bad things about'; e.g., 'Don't *dis* my music'. We don't know if this verb will become a more permanent and widely accepted member of the American English lexicon, but for now it is a perfect example of a bound, grammatical element (*dis-* is usually a word-forming affix X^W) becoming less bound and grammatical, i.e., a full lexical verb X^0.

reduction and disappearance of complex Chinese word parts occurring via the semantic, grammatical and phonological reduction processes that accompany lexicalization described in 6.1. This hypothesized sequence may also have occurred in the historical development of Chinese, when the posited inflectional characteristics of the Sino-Tibetan protolanguage (see, e.g., Bodman 1980, Mei 1989, Baxter and Sagart 1997) disappeared due to phonological and semantic reduction, leading to the large-scale compounding of isolated free words beginning during the Han dynasty (206 BC–AD 220) in order to disambiguate homophonous single-syllable words (Peyraube 1996: 197; Feng 1997).

The lexicon, therefore, may be both the birth place and the graveyard of morphemes: morphemes are created there when old morphemes take on new identities as they occur in newly coined words, and they disappear there when they lose their individual identities under the dominating influence of the gestalt word.

8.2 The reality of the 'word'

I feel this study stands as evidence that the *word* constitutes a real rather than epiphenomenal construct, because upon examining Chinese and English morphological data we found that two languages so different on the surface clearly have properties in common at a more abstract level. These commonalities reduce the likelihood that the *word* is epiphenomenal and suggest that there are true universals at work. Our working hypothesis has been that there are word properties that are real and shared across natural language, and that we should be able to see these shared properties by conducting careful cross-linguistic investigation.

Anderson (1985b: 150–1) suggests that intuitions supporting the existence of words might be merely illusions, based upon knowledge of languages such as English which lend particular credence to the illusion. If word existence is an illusion, it may be on a par with the illusory nature of our on-line 'stream of consciousness' (Dennett 1991). Dennett argues that although there is a clear sensation of a real-time, punctual, stream of consciousness, it may be merely an epiphenomenal illusion comprising the confluence of inputs from multiple sensory and cognitive components, and that there is actually no punctual cognitive or neural event that corresponds to the introspectively real sensation of a 'here and now' moment of consciousness.

On this view, the *word* may comprise the confluence of phonological, morphological, syntactic, semantic and other inputs, resulting in wordlike entities that are mere illusory constructs, though no less 'real' in the minds of speakers than the stream of consciousness. That confluence of information provides a strong intuition of 'word' for some of us, but for all of us it operates implicitly to structure word acquisition and use. Just as the non-linguistic mind reaches out and tries to make sense of the world using preordained conceptual and perceptual categories, so too does the linguistic mind try to make sense of linguistic data using such preordained categories. I believe that the construct 'word' is just such a category, and that it possesses properties that are shared by the languages of the world.

A glance at the history of science reveals that even in the hardest of hard sciences, our conceptions of what is 'real' change over time. Levels of analysis and properties of matter (like phlogiston, electron shells, the wave status of light rays, etc.) once thought to be incontestable, were subsequently found to be little more than heuristically convenient abstractions. So too it may end up being for the reality of the *word* in natural language. In the end it may also turn out to have been merely a convenient abstraction, but for now, the existence of the *word* is about as real as it gets.

References

American Heritage Dictionary of the English Language (1992). New York: Houghton Mifflin. Electronic version licensed from InfoSoft International.

Anderson, S.R. (1985a). Typological distinctions in word formation, in Shopen (1985), 3–56.

(1985b). Inflectional morphology, in Shopen, 150–201.

(1992). *A-Morphous Morphology*. Cambridge: Cambridge University Press.

Armstrong, B.J. (1997). Good Riddance (Time of your life). WB Music Corporation and Green Daze Music.

Aronoff, M. (ed.) (1980). *Juncture*. Saratoga, CA: Anma Libri.

(1992). *Morphology Now*. Albany, NY: State University of New York Press.

Barale, C. (1982). A quantitative analysis of the loss of final consonants in Beijing Mandarin. Ph.D. dissertation, University of Pennsylvania.

Barker, C. (1998). Episodic -ee in English: a thematic role constraint on new word formation. *Language* 74(4), 695–727.

Bauer, L. (1990). Be-heading the word. *Journal of Linguistics* 26, 1–31.

Baxter, W. and Sagart, L. (1997). Word formation in Old Chinese, in Packard (1997a), 35–76.

Beard, R. (1981). *The Indo-European Lexicon*. Amsterdam: North-Holland.

Bierwisch, M. and Schreuder, R. (1992). From concepts to lexical items. *Cognition* 42, 23–60. Reprinted in Levelt (1993), 23–60.

Bodman, N.C. (1980). Proto-Chinese and Sino-Tibetan: data toward establishing the nature of the relationship, in van Coetsem, F., and Waugh, L. (eds.), *Contributions to Historical Linguistics: Issues and Materials*. Leiden: E.J. Brill, 34–199.

Boltz, W. (1994). *The Origin and Early Development of the Chinese Writing System*. American Oriental Series, vol. 78. New Haven, CT: American Oriental Society.

Boodberg, P. (1940). Ideography or iconolatry? *T'oung Pao* 35, 266–88.

Boyd, R., Casper, P., and Trout, J.D. (eds.) (1991). *The Philosophy of Science*. Cambridge, MA: MIT Press.

Bridgman, P. (1927). *The Logic of Modern Physics*. New York: MacMillan. Chapter 2 'Broad Points of View' reprinted as The operational character of scientific concepts, in Boyd, Casper and Trout (1991), 57–69.

Butterworth, B. (1983). Lexical representation, in B. Butterworth (ed.), *Language Production*, vol. 2. New York: Academic.

Bybee, J. (1985). *Morphology: a Study of the Relation between Meaning and Form*. Amsterdam: Benjamins.

(1995). Semantic aspects of morphological typology. Unpublished paper, University of New Mexico.
Bybee, J., Perkins, R., and Pagliuca, W. (1994). *The Evolution of Grammar*. Chicago and London: University of Chicago Press.
Caramazza, A., Laudanna, A., and Romani, C. (1988). Lexical access and inflectional morphology. *Cognition* 28, 297–332.
Chang, C.H.-H. (1989). Compounds in Mandarin Chinese: with special emphasis on resultative verb compounds. University of Hawaii Linguistics Department Working Papers 20, 59–84.
   (1997). V–V compounds in Mandarin Chinese, in Packard (1997a), 77–101.
Chao, Y.R. (1947). *Mandarin Primer*. Berkeley: University of California Press.
   (1968). *A Grammar of Spoken Chinese*. Berkeley: University of California Press.
Chen, C., He, G., and Xu, Y. (陈晨, 贺国伟, 徐玉明) (eds.) (1986). *Concise Chinese Reverse-Order Dictionary* (简明汉语逆序词典). Beijing: Commercial Press.
Chen, H.-C. (1992). Reading comprehension in Chinese: implications from character reading times, in Chen and Tzeng, 175–205.
   (ed.) (1997). *Cognitive Processing of Chinese and Related Asian Languages*. Hong Kong: Chinese University Press.
Chen, H.-C., and Tzeng, O.J.L. (eds.) (1992). *Language Processing in Chinese*. Amsterdam: North-Holland and Elsevier.
Chen, M.Y. (1975). An areal study of nasalization in Chinese. *Journal of Chinese Linguistics* 3, 16–59.
Chen, S.-Q. (1998). *The Automatic Identification and Recovery of Chinese Acronyms*, in Cheng, Packard and Yoon.
Cheng, C.-C. (郑锦全) (1998). Quantification for understanding language cognition (从计量理解语言认知), in Ts'ou, B.K., Lai, T.B.Y., Chan, S.W.K., and Wang, W.S.-Y. (eds.), *Quantitative and Computational Studies on the Chinese Language*. Hong Kong: Language Information Sciences Research Center, City University of Hong Kong.
Cheng, C.-C., Packard, J., and Yoon, J. (eds.) (1998). *Studies in the Linguistic Sciences* 26: 1/2 (Spring/Fall 1998): *Studies in Chinese Linguistics*. University of Illinois Department of Linguistics Publications in the Linguistic Sciences.
Cheng, C.-M. (1992). Lexical access in Chinese: evidence from automatic activation of phonological information, in Chen and Tzeng, 67–91.
Cheng, X. (程湘清) (1981a). *Research in Pre-Qin Chinese Language* (先秦汉语研究). Jinan, China: Shandong Educational Publishing (济南：山东教育出版公司).
   (1981b). Research in pre-Qin bisyllabic words (先秦双音词研究), in Cheng 1981a, 44–112.
Chi, T.R. (1985). *A Lexical Analysis of Verb–Noun Compounds in Mandarin Chinese*. Taipei: Crane.

Chiang, W.-Y. (江文瑜) (1995). Grammatical constraints on compound abbreviation in Taiwan Mandarin (國語中複合縮簡之文法限制). *Bulletin of the College of Liberal Arts* 43 (文史哲學報第四十三期). Taipei: National Taiwan University, 259–84.

Chinese Academy of Social Sciences, Dictionary Editing Group (1986). *Reverse Order Modern Chinese Dictionary* (倒序現代汉语词典). Beijing: Commercial Press.

  (1988). *Modern Chinese Dictionary* (现代汉语词典). Beijing: Commercial Press.

  (1992). *Modern Chinese Dictionary, Supplementary Edition* (现代汉语词典补编). Beijing: Commercial Press.

Chinese Phonetic Writing Group (ed.) (1985). *Collected Papers on Chinese Phonetic Orthography* (汉语拼音正词法论文选). Beijing: Writing Reform (北京：文字改革出版社).

Chomsky, N. and Halle, M. (1968). *The Sound Pattern of English.* New York: Harper and Row.

Chu-Chang, M., and Loritz, D.J. (1977). Phonological encoding of Chinese ideographs in short-term memory. *Language Learning* 27, 341–52.

Coltheart, M. (1985). In defence of dual-route models of reading. *Brain and Behavioral Sciences* 8, 709–10.

Commercial Press (1988). *New China Dictionary* (新华字典). Beijing.

Committee on Chinese Phonetic Orthography (汉语拼音正词法委员会) (1985). Basic rules of Chinese phonetic writing orthography (汉语拼音正词法基本规定), in Chinese Phonetic Writing Group, 1–16.

Craig, C. (1997). Ways to go in Rama, in Traugott and Heine (1997a). Vol. II, 455–92.

Creel, H.G. (1938). On the ideographic element in Ancient Chinese. *T'oung Pao* 34, 265–94.

Cruse, A.A., Hundsnurscher, F., Job, M., and Lutzeier, P. (forthcoming). *Lexikologie – Lexicology.* Berlin: de Gruyter.

Dai, J.X.-L. (1992). Chinese morphology and its interface with the syntax. Ph.D. dissertation, Ohio State University.

  (1997). Syntactic, morphological and phonological words in Chinese, in Packard (1997a), 103–34.

DeFrancis, J. (1984). *The Chinese Language: Fact and Fantasy.* Honolulu: University of Hawaii Press.

Dennett, D.C. (1991). *Consciousness Explained.* Boston: Little Brown.

Di Sciullo, A. and Williams, E. (1987). *On the Definition of Word.* Cambridge, MA: MIT Press.

Dowty, D.R., Wall, R.E., and Peters, S. (1981). *Introduction to Montague Semantics.* Dordrecht: Reidel.

Drigo, M. (1983). Per una teoria dei composti. Ph.D. dissertation, University of Venice.

Duanmu, S. (1997). Wordhood in Chinese, in Packard (1997a), 135–96.
Feng, S. (1997). Prosodic structure and compound words in classical Chinese, in Packard (1997a), 197–260.
Fodor, J. (1983). *The Modularity of Mind*. Cambridge, MA: MIT Press.
Garrett, M.F. (1988). Processes in language production, in Newmeyer, 69–96.
Givón, T. (1971). Historical syntax and synchronic morphology: an archaeologist's field trip. *Chicago Linguistic Society* 7, 394–415.
  (1979). *On Understanding Grammar*. New York: Academic.
  (1992). Serial verbs and the mental reality of 'event': grammatical vs. cognitive packaging, in Traugott and Heine, vol. I, 81–127.
Hammond, M., and Noonan, M. (eds.) (1988). *Theoretical Morphology*. New York: Academic.
Hankamer, J. (1989). Morphological parsing and the lexicon, in Marslen-Wilson, W. (1989a), 392–408.
Hansen, C. (1993). Chinese ideographs and Western ideas. *Journal of Asian Studies* 52, 373–99.
Hargus, S., and Kaisse, E. (eds.) (1993). *Studies in Lexical Phonology*, vol. IV: *Phonetics and phonology*. New York: Academic.
Harris, A.C., and Campbell, L. (1995). *Historical Syntax in Cross-linguistic Perspective*. Cambridge: Cambridge University Press.
Haspelmath, M. (1992). *Grammaticization Theory and Heads in Morphology*, in Aronoff, 69–82.
Heath, J. (1998). Hermit crabs: formal renewal of morphology by phonologically mediated affix substitution. *Language* 74(4), 728–59.
Heine, B., Claudi, U., and Hünnemeyer, F. (1991a). *Grammaticalization: a Conceptual Framework*. Chicago and London: University of Chicago Press.
  (1991b). From cognition to grammar – evidence from African languages, in Traugott and Heine vol. I, 149–87.
Henderson, L. (1989). On mental representation of morphology and its diagnosis by measures of visual access speed, in Marslen-Wilson (1989a), 357–91.
Hockett, C. (1968). *A Course in Modern Linguistics*. New York: Macmillan.
Hoosain, R. (1992). Psychological reality of the word in Chinese, in Chen and Tzeng, 111–30.
Hopper, P., and Traugott, E. (1993). *Grammaticalization*. Cambridge: Cambridge University Press.
Hu, S. (1985). Certain problems in Chinese phonetic writing, in Chinese Phonetic Writing Group (ed.), 67–77.
Huang, J.C.-T. (1982). Logical relations in Chinese and the theory of grammar. Ph.D. dissertation, Massachusetts Institute of Technology.
  (1984). Phrase structure, lexical integrity, and Chinese compounds. *Journal of the Chinese Language Teachers Association* 19(2), 53–78.

Huang, J.C.-T., and Li, A.Y.-H. (1996). *New Horizons in Chinese Linguistics*. Dordrecht and Boston: Kluwer Academic.

Huang, S. (1997). Chinese as a headless language in compounding morphology, in Packard (1997a), 261–83.

Hue, C.-W. (1992). Recognition processes in character naming, in Chen and Tzeng, 93–107.

Inhoff, A., Wang, J., and Chen, H.-C. (eds.) (1999). *Reading Chinese Script: a cognitive analysis*. NJ: Erlbaum.

Inkelas, S. (1989). Prosodic constituency in the lexicon. Ph.D. dissertation, Stanford University.

(1993). Deriving cyclicity, in Hargus, S. and Kaisse, E.M. (eds.), *Phonetics and Phonology: Studies in Lexical Phonology*. New York: Academic.

Jackendoff, R. (1972). *Semantic Interpretation in Generative Grammar*. Cambridge, MA: MIT Press.

Jiang, S. (蔣紹愚) (1989). *Outline of Old Chinese Lexicology* (古汉语词汇纲要). Beijing: Peking University Press (北京：北京大学出版社).

Kawamoto, A.H. (1993). Nonlinear dynamics in the resolution of lexical ambiguity: a parallel distributed processing account. *Journal of Memory and Language* 33, 474–516.

Kiparsky, P. (1982). Lexical morphology and phonology, in Yang, I.S. (ed.), *Linguistics in the Morning Calm*. Seoul: Hanshin, 3–91.

Kuhn, Thomas (1962). The nature and necessity of scientific revolutions, from chapter 9, 92–110, *The Structure of Scientific Revolutions*. Chicago: University of Chicago Press. Reprinted in Boyd, Casper and Trout (1991), 48–157.

Levelt, W.J.M. (1989). *Speaking: from intention to articulation*. Cambridge, MA: MIT Press.

(1992). Accessing words in speech production. *Cognition* 42, 1–22. Reprinted in Levelt (1993), 1–22.

(ed.) (1993). *Lexical Access in Speech Production*. Cambridge, MA: Blackwell.

Lexicon Group, Committee on Script Reform (ed.) (1964). *A Chinese Pinyin Lexicon* (汉语拼音词汇). Beijing: Script Reform (北京：文字改革出版社).

Li, A. (1990). *Order and Constituency in Mandarin Chinese*. Dordrecht: Kluwer Academic.

Li, C.N., and Thompson, S.A. (1981). *Mandarin Chinese: a functional reference grammar*. Berkeley: University of California Press.

Li, C.N., and Shi, Y.-Z. (1997). On the evolution of aspect markers in Chinese. *Zhongguo Yuwen* 1997(2), 82–96.

Li, P., Bates, E., Liu, H., and MacWhinney, B. (1992). Cues as functional constraints on sentence processing in Chinese, in Chen and Tzeng, 207–34.

Li, Y. (1990). On V–V compounds in Chinese. *Natural Language and Linguistic Theory* 8, 177–207.

(1997). Chinese resultative constructions and the Uniformity of Theta Assignment Hypothesis, in Packard (1997a), 285–310.
Li, Y.-C. (1971). *An Investigation of Case in Chinese Grammar*. South Orange, NJ: Seton Hall University Press.
Liang, S.-C. (梁實秋)(ed.) (1992). *Far East Chinese–English Dictionary* (遠東漢英大辭典). Taipei: Far East.
Liao, S. (廖庶謙) (1946). *Oral Grammar* (口語文法) [cited in Pan, Yip and Han 1993: 39, no further citation given.]
Liberman, M., and Sproat, R. (1992). The stress and structure of modified noun phrases in English, in Sag, I., and Szabolcsi, A. (eds.), *Lexical Matters*. CSLI Lecture Notes 24. Stanford, CA: Center for the Study of Language and Information, Stanford University, 131–81.
Lipka, L. (1990). *An Outline of English Lexicology: Lexical structure, word semantics, and word-formation*. Tübingen: Niemeyer.
Liu, Y., and Peng, D.-L. (1997). Meaning access of Chinese compounds and its time course, in Chen, 219–32.
Longenecker, Y.-C.J. (1995). On the semantic head of [N–N] nominal compounds. Unpublished paper, University of Illinois.
Lu, J.H.-T. (1977). Resultative verb compounds vs. directional verb compounds in Mandarin. *Journal of Chinese Linguistics* 5, 276–313.
Lu, Z. (陆志韦) (1964). *Word Formation in Chinese* (汉语的构词法). Beijing: Scientific (北京：科学出版社).
Marslen-Wilson, W. (ed.) (1989a). *Lexical Representation and Process*. Cambridge, MA: MIT Press.
(1989b). Access and integration: projecting sound onto meaning, in Marslen-Wilson (1989a), 3–24.
Matthews, P.H. (1991). *Morphology*. Cambridge: Cambridge University Press.
McCarthy, J., and Prince, A. (1993). Prosodic morphology I: constraint interaction and satisfaction. Unpublished manuscript, University of Massachusetts and Rutgers University.
Mei, T.-L. (1989). The causative and denominative functions of the *S-prefix in Old Chinese. *Proceedings on the Second International Conference on Sinology*. Taipei: Academia Sinica.
Mohanan, K.P. (1986). *The Theory of Lexical Phonology*. Dordrecht: Reidel.
Murrell, G.A., and Morton, J. (1974). Word recognition and morphemic structure. *Journal of Experimental Psychology* 102, 963–8.
Nagy, W.E., and Anderson, R. C. (1999). Metalinguistic awareness and literacy acquisition in different languages, in Wagner, D., Venezky, R., and Street, B. (eds.), *Literacy: an international handbook*. Boulder, CO: Westview, 155–60.
Nespor, M., and Vogel, I. (1982). Prosodic domains of external sandhi rules, in van der Hulst and Smith, 225–55.
(1986). *Prosodic Phonology*. Dordrecht: Foris.

Newmeyer, F.J. (ed.) (1988). *Linguistics: the Cambridge survey*, vol. III: *Psychological and biological aspects*. Cambridge: Cambridge University Press.

Nunberg, G., Sag, I., and Wasow, T. (1994). Idioms. *Language* 70(3), 491–538.

Paap, K.R., and Noel, R.W. (1991). Dual route models of print to sound: still a good horse race. *Psychological Research* 53, 13–24.

Packard, J. (1990). A lexical morphology approach to word formation in Mandarin. *Yearbook of Morphology* 3, 21–37.

(1995). Word-internal process in Chinese lexical change, in Camacho, J., and Choueiri, L. (eds.), *Proceedings of the Sixth North American Conference on Chinese Linguistics*. Los Angeles: GSIL, University of Southern California, 144–9.

(1996). Chinese evidence against inflection-derivation as a universal distinction, in Cheng, T.-F., Li, Y., and Zhang, H. (eds.), *Proceedings of ICCL-4/ NACCL-7*, vol. II. Los Angeles: GSIL, University of Southern California, 253–73.

(ed.) (1997a). *New Approaches to Chinese Word Formation: Morphology, phonology and the lexicon in modern and ancient Chinese*. Trends in Linguistics Studies and Monographs 105. Berlin and New York: Mouton de Gruyter.

(1997b). Introduction, in Packard (1997a), 1–34.

(1997c). A lexical phonology of Mandarin Chinese, in Packard (1997a), 311–27.

(1999). Lexical access in Chinese speech comprehension and production. *Brain and Language* 68, 89–94.

Pan, Wenguo, Yip, P.-C., and Han, Y.S. (潘文國, 葉步青, 韓洋) (1993). *Studies of Chinese Word Formation, 1898–1990* (漢語的構詞法研究 1898–1990). Taipei: Student Book Co.

Perfetti, C.A., and Zhang, S. (1991). Phonological processes in reading Chinese characters. *Journal of Experimental Psychology: Learning, Memory and Cognition* 17(4), 633–43.

(1992). In reading Chinese there is no semantics without phonology. Paper presented at the 33rd annual meeting of the Psychonomic Society, St. Louis, MO.

Perfetti, C.A., Zhang, S., and Berent, I. (1992). Reading in English and Chinese: evidence for a 'universal' phonological principle, in Front, R., and Katz, L. (eds.) *Orthography, Phonology, Morphology and Meaning*. Amsterdam: Elsevier, 227–48.

Peyraube, A. (1996). Recent issues in Chinese historical syntax, in Huang and Li, 161–213.

(forthcoming) Historical change in Chinese grammar. *International Review of Chinese Linguistics* 2. Amsterdam: Benjamins.

Pinker, S. (1997). *How the Mind Works*. New York: W.W. Norton.

Rice, K. (1993). The structure of the Slave verb, in Hargus and Kaisse, 145–71.
Ross, C. (1990). Resultative verb compounds. *Journal of the Chinese Language Teacher's Association* 25(3), 61–83.
  (1997). Cognate objects and the realization of thematic structure in Mandarin Chinese, in Packard (1997a), 329–46.
Sadock, J.M. (1988). The autolexical classification of lexemes, in Hammond and Noonan, 271–90.
  (1991). *Autolexical Syntax*. Chicago: University of Chicago Press.
Sapir, E. (1921/1949). *Language*. New York: Harcourt Brace Jovanovich.
Sawer, M. (1995). Handling neologisms in teaching and learning modern Standard Chinese. *Australian Review of Applied Linguistics, Series S.* 12, 203–28.
Scalise, S. (1984). *Generative Morphology*. Dordrecht: Foris.
  (1988). The notion of 'head' in morphology, in Booij, G., and van Marle, J. (eds.), *Yearbook of Morphology*, Dordrecht: Foris, 229–45.
Schussler, A. (1976). *Affixes in Proto-Chinese*. Wiesbaden: Franz Steiner Verlag GMBH.
Selkirk, E. (1980). Prosodic domains in phonology: Sanskrit revisited, in Aronoff (1980), 107–29.
  (1982). *The Syntax of Words*. Cambridge, MA: MIT Press.
Shopen, T. (ed.) (1985). *Language Typology and Syntactic Description*, vol. III: *Grammatical categories and the lexicon*. Cambridge: Cambridge University Press.
Siegel, D. (1974). Morphological investigations. Ph.D. dissertation, Massachusetts Institute of Technology.
Snodgrass, J.G., and Jarvella, R.J. (1972). Some linguistic determinants of word classification times. *Psychonomic Science* 27, 220–2.
Spencer, A. (1991). *Morphological Theory*. Oxford, UK, and Cambridge, MA: Basil Blackwell.
Sproat, R., and Shih, C. (1993). Why Mandarin morphology is not stratum-ordered. *Yearbook of Morphology 1993*, 185–217.
  (1996). A corpus-based analysis of Mandarin nominal root compound. *Journal of East Asian Linguistics* 5, 49–71.
Starosta, S., Kuiper, K., Wu, Z., and Ng, S. (1997). On defining the Chinese compound word: headedness in Chinese compounding and Chinese V–R compounds, in Packard (1997a), 347–70.
Stemberger, J.P., and MacWhinney, B. (1988). Are inflected forms stored in the lexicon?, in Hammond and Noonan, 101–16.
Sun, C. (1996). *Word Order Change and Grammaticalization in the History of Chinese*. Stanford, CA: Stanford University Press.
Taft, M., and Chen, H.-C. (1992). Judging homophony in Chinese: the influence of tones, in Chen and Tzeng, 151–72.

Taft, M., and Forster, K. I. (1975). Lexical storage and retrieval of prefixed words. *Journal of Verbal Learning and Verbal Behavior* 14, 638–47.

Taft, M. and Zhu, X. (1995). The representation of bound morphemes in the lexicon: a Chinese study, in Feldman, L.B. (ed.) *Morphological Aspects of Language Processing*. New Jersey: Erlbaum, 293–316.

  (1997). Using masked priming to examine lexical storage of Chinese compound words, in Chen, 233–41.

Talmy, L. (1985). Lexicalization patterns: semantic structure in lexical forms, in Shopen, 57–149.

Tan, L.H., Hoosain, R., and Peng, D.-L. (1993). The role of early presemantic phonological code in Chinese character identification. Conference on Chinese Language Processing, Taipei.

Tang, T.-C. (1993). The relation between word-syntax and sentence-syntax in Chinese: a case study in compound verbs. Second International Conference on Chinese Linguistics, Paris, June 23–5.

  (1995). More on the relation between word-syntax and sentence syntax in Chinese: case study in compound nouns, in Camacho, J., and Choueiri, L. (eds.), *Proceedings of the Sixth North American Conference on Chinese Linguistics*. Los Angeles: GSIL, University of Southern California, 195–248.

Thompson, S. (1973). Resultative verb compounds in Mandarin Chinese: a case for lexical rules. *Language* 49(2), 361–79.

Traugott, E.C. (forthcoming). Lexicalization and grammaticalization, in Cruse, Hundsnurscher and Lutzeier, 1–10 (pre-publication draft).

Traugott, E.C. and Heine, B. (eds.) (1991). *Approaches to Grammaticalization*, vols. I and II. Amsterdam and Philadelphia: John Benjamins.

Treiman, R.A., Baron, J., and Luk, K. (1981). Speech recoding in silent reading: a comparison of Chinese and English. *Journal of Chinese Linguistics* 9, 116–25.

Tzeng, O.J.L., Hung, D.L., and Wang, W.S.-W. (1977). Speech recoding in Chinese characters. *Journal of Experimental Psychology: Human Memory and Learning* 3, 621–30.

van der Hulst, H., and Smith, N. (eds.) (1982). *The Structure of Phonological Representations*. Dordrecht: Foris.

Wang, L. (王力)(1953). Problems with the boundary between words and word groups (词和仂语的界限问题). *Zhongguo Yuwen, September*, 3–8.

Wu, J. (吴景荣) (ed.) (1988). *A Chinese–English Dictionary* (现代汉语词典). Beijing: Commercial Press.

Xia, M. (1946). Methods of composing two-character words (雙字詞語的構成方式). [cited in Pan, Yip, and Han 1993: 37, no further citation given.]

Xu, T. (徐通鏘) (1997). *On Language* (语言论). Changchun: Hebei Normal University Publishing.

Yin, W., and Butterworth, B. (1992). Deep and surface dyslexia in Chinese, in Chen, and Tzeng (eds.), 349–66.

Yu, Genyuan (于根元) (ed.) (1993). *New Words in Chinese for 1992* (1992 汉语新词语). Beijing: Beijing Language Institute Publishing.
   (ed.) (1994). *Contemporary Chinese New Word Dictionary* (现代汉语新词词典). Beijing: Beijing Language Institute Publishing.
Zhang, B., and Peng, D. (1992). Decomposed storage in the Chinese lexicon, in Chen, and Tzeng (eds.), 131–49.
Zhang, L., and Lu, F. (张立茂, 陆福庆) (eds.) (1986). *Reverse Order Verb Dictionary* (动词逆序词典). Fuzhou: Fuzhou People's Publishing.
Zhang, S. (张寿康) (1985). On some problems with Chinese phonetic writing orthography (谈汉语拼音正词法的几个问题), in Chinese Phonetic Writing Group, 61–6.
Zhang, X., and Sang, Y. (张辛欣, 桑晔) (1986). *Chinese Profiles* (北京人). Shanghai: Shanghai Literature and Art Publishing.
Zhou, S. (周生亚) (1982). Problem of disyllabic words in "Shi Shuo Xin Yu" (《世说新语》中的复音词问题). *Jilin University Journal, Social Sciences* 2(1982) (吉林大学社会科学学报), 81–8.
Zhou, X., and Marslen-Wilson, W. (1994). Words, morphemes and syllables in the Chinese mental lexicon. *Language and Cognitive Processes* 9, 393–422.
   (1995). Morphological structure in the Chinese mental lexicon. *Language and Cognitive Processes* 10, 545–600.
   (1996). Direct visual access is the only way to access the Chinese mental lexicon, in Cottrel, G.W. (ed.), *Proceedings of the 18th Annual Conference of the Cognitive Science Society*. Mahwah, NJ: Erbaum, 714–19.
Zhou, X., Shu, H., Bi, Y., and Shi, D. (1999). Is there a phonologically mediated access to lexical semantics on reading Chinese?, in Inhoff, Wang and Chen, 135–72.
Zwicky, A. (1985). Heads. *Journal of Linguistics* 21, 1–30.

Index

AAM (Augmented Addressed Morphology), 297, 299
'A-not-A' operation, 227–9
abbreviation, 267, 268–70, *271–2*
ablative case, 131
accent, loss of, 238
accusative case, 131
'acronyms,' 270
affixes
    defined, 69, *74*, 76, 311
    in Di Sciullo and Williams's application, 149
    as internal word components, 246–9, *247–8*
    in Selkirk's application (X^{AFF} or Y^{AFF}), 138, 142, 151, 154–6
    types of, 70–1, *74*
    as word components, 76–7
    see also grammatical affixes; word-forming affixes
agrammatical lexicalization, 221–2, 233, 234, 236–7
Ancient Chinese language, paradigmatic alternation in, 130 n.27
Anderson, S.R., 11, 19, 217, 245, 316
asemantic lexicalization, 221
aspect markers
    lexicalization of, 118 n.18
    modification of V–O verbs by, 118–19
    see also -*guò* (verbal aspect marker); -*le* (verbal aspect marker); -*zhe* (verbal aspect marker)
'attainment' resultative verbs, 98–9, 102, 250, 254–5
Augmented Addressed Morphology (AAM), 297, 299
Autolexical Syntax, 144

bǎ (direct object marker), 262
Basic Rules of Chinese Phonetic Writing Orthography, 16
Baxter, W., 9, 10
Bierwisch, M., 301
bisyllabic words
    development of, 11, 265–7, 283, 315–16
    formation of, 78
    structures of, 126, *127*, 160
    see also compound words; Compounding Rule
'bleaching,' 217
borrowing, 267, 268
    see also phonetic loan words

'bound' morphemes
    as case markers, 131
    classifiers as, 75
    defined, 67–9, 166–7
    lexicalization of, 118, 123, 314–16
    and metalinguistic judgments, 18
    numerals as, 75
    positionally, 132–3
    in V–O compound words, 107–8, 118, 123, 125
    'wordness' (*cíxìng*) of, 50–7
bound root words
    defined, 80–1, *81*, 167
    in lexicon, 163
    nouns in, 83–4
    in resultative verbs, 102
    Selkirk's treatment of, 141, 153–6, 157
    as V–O compounds, 125
    verbs in, 90–2
bound roots (X^{-1})
    compared to word-forming affixes, 71–3
    creation of, 280–3, *281–2*
    defined, 69, *74*, 165, 166, 196, 197–8, *198*
    lexicalization of, 78
    location morphemes as, 75–6
    numerals as, 75
    prevalence of, 2, 50, 77, 130, 164
    as word components, 77–8, 163
boundness, 76
branching structures
    defined, 173–5
    embedded, 192–3
    multiple, 174, 177–92
    single, 175–7
-*bu*- (resultative potential marker), 174

Campbell, L., 216, 314, 315
'canonical head,' 194–5
Caramazza, A., 297
case markers, 76 n.17
'cause-effect' morphemes (word components), 21–2
Chang, C.H.-H., 255
Chao, Yuen Ren
    on coordinate construction, 31
    on defining compound words, 78 n.19
    on 'phase' resultative verbs, 255
    on phonological words, 10

INDEX 329

on positionally free or bound morphemes, 132–3
on productivity, 132
on sociological words, 8, 14
on syntactic description, 27
on V–O compound words, 109–11, 116, 120, 238
Chen, S.-Q., 270
Cheng, C.-C., 301 n.12
Chi, T.R., 109, 112–13, 114–15, 229, 238
Chiang, W.-Y., 270
Chinese characters (*zì*)
  as ideographic, 309
  and lexicon, 304–9
  as morphemes, 3, 8, 14–15, 19, 287
  orthography of, 284
  primacy of, 1, 14, 15
  relationship to words, 3
  as sociological words, 14–15
Chinese dialects
  and bound-free status of morphemes, 17
  see also Mandarin dialect
Chinese languages
  definition of 'word' (*cí*) in, 1, 2, 3, 14–20, 316–17
  modern lexicalization of, 267–75
  morphology of, 1
  syntax of, 1, 3
  word structure information in, 2
Chinese morphology, reasons for investigating, 1–3
Chinese orthography (pinyin), 3, 16
  see also orthographic words
Chinese speech communication, relationship to written language, 3, 304–5
  see also speech comprehension; speech production
Chinese writing, 16, 309
cí ('word'), 15–16, 18
classical Chinese language
  bound *vs.* free morphemes in, 67–8
  and definition of 'word,' 17
  -zhī- ('to know/knowledge') in, 60
classifiers, 74–5
'cline of grammaticality,' 313–15
'cline of lexicality,' 219 n.2, 313–15
cliticization, 146, 151
cohesion, defined, 216, 314
cohort lexical retrieval model, 287–8, 291
combination ('compounding'), 267, 268–75, 273, 274–5
complementation, degrees of, 145
complete lexicalization, 222–3, 231, 237
component metaphorical lexicalization, 220
compound words
  bound roots in, 78
  defined, 80–1, *81*, 167

evolution of, 2–3, 265–7, 283, 315–16
nouns in, 82–3
relations in N_1-N_2 words, 85–9
relations in V_1-V_2 words, 93–5
verbs in, 90
see also bisyllabic words
Compounding Rule, 158–60, 162
content (*shí*, 'real') morphemes, 69, 73, 166
conventional lexicalization, 219–20
coordinate constructions, 31
coverbs, 131
Craig, C., 263

dà ('big'), as verb in bound morphemes, 65–6
Dai, J.X.-L., 10, 11–12, 163, 298
dǎtiě ('to abolish the system of guaranteed jobs'), 268–9, 276, 280
dative case, 131
-de (verb suffix), 262
-de- (resultative potential marker), 174
-de-/-bu- ('able to'/'not able to')
  potential affix, 95, 96–7, 98, 99, 100–1, 102
'degenerate' resultative verbs, 255–8, 262
derivational affixation, 77
  in English, 196
  in Selkirk's theory, 139–40, 142, 143, 155–6
derived words
  defined, 80–1, *81*
  form class identity of, 65 n.9
  nouns in, 84–5
  verbs in, 92–3
determiners, 74–5
Di Sciullo, A.
  on lexical syntactic objects, 9
  on listemes, 8, 13 n.3
  on morphological words, 11
  on syntactic atoms, 13
  on X-bar analysis, 149
diàn ('electricity, television'), 283
diāo ('carve'), as noun in bound morphemes, 50–6, 65, 235
'directional' resultative verbs, 98, 102, 250, 253–4
dìtiě ('subway'), 276, 280
dogs, derivation of, 146–7
Duanmu, S., 10
dúshū ('to study; to read [books]'), as V–O compound, *121*, 123

-ed (English past tense morpheme), 199
embedding
  multiple, 192–3
  restrictions on, 164
'end-free'/'end-bound' morphemes, 132–3
endocentricity, 112, 195
exocentricity, 112–13, 195, 221–2

Feng, S., 11
FLH (Full Listing Hypothesis), 297, 299
form classes
  criteria for determining, 64–7
  defined, 34–6
  description of word components based on, 32–4
  of gestalt words, 129
  identity of morphemes based on, 36–67, 150, 278–9
  prevalence of nouns and verbs, 125–9
'free' morphemes
  defined, 67–9, 166–7
  determiners as, 75
  and metalinguistic judgments, 18
  positionally, 132–3
  in resultative verbs, 96, 101–4
  'wordness' (*cíxìng*) of, 50
  see also root ('free') words
fù ('double; repeat'), polysemy of, 106
Full Listing Hypothesis (FLH), 297, 299
function (*xū*, 'empty') morphemes, 69, 73, 166
function words, defined, 69, 74
functional unity, degree of, 125 n.23

Garrett, M.F., 293–4
generative capacity
  strong *vs.* weak, 160
  in word formation, 150
genitive case, 131
gestalt words
  form class identity of, 129
  and induced constituent reanalysis, 235–6
  and lexicalization, 220–1, 268
  opacity of meaning and grammar of, 239
  primacy of, 136
  types of, 80–1, *81*
  of [VN] structure, 128
gestalts
  and whole-word processing, 294–6
  words as, 18, 80
Givón, T., 218
gōng ('labour, art, industry, work, job'), bound *vs.* free status of, 68
gōngtuō ('public daycare centre'), 268, 278
grammatical affixes (G)
  defined, 70, 71, 74, 77, 165, 166, 196, 197, 199–200
  in lexicon, 299, 301
  in Mandarin, 174
  in resultative verbs, 102
grammatical agreement, 76, 130
grammatical functions, 76, 130–1
grammatical words
  defined, 80–1, *81*
  nouns in, 85
  verbs in, 93

grammaticalization
  of content morphemes, 69
  defined, 262, 313
  and lexicalization, 218, 262–5
  of location morphemes, 76 n.17
guănfēng ('style of management'), 268
guāngnăo ('photon computer'), 276–7
guāngxiān ('fibre optic'), 277
-guo (verbal aspect suffix), 174, 262, 263
guò ('to pass, cross'), 263

Han, Y.S., 196
hángpíng ('profession appraisal'), 278–9
Harris, A.C., 216, 314, 315
Haspelmath, M., 194, 262 n.21
Headedness Principle
  defined, 39, 63, 66, 126, 127, 169, 170–1, 311
  examples of, 42, 46, 60, 82, 90
  exceptions to, 46, 56, 57, 62–3, 66, 95, 221–2, 225–37, 311
  reliability of, 127
  test of, 125–9
  see also heads
headlessness, 127 n.24, 195, 196
heads
  'canonical head,' 194–5
  defined, 149, 194, 310
  and lexicalization, 260
  'semantic head,' 25, 95, 195–6
  'structural head,' 95, 195–6, 310–11
  'virtual head,' 57, 194–5
  see also Headedness Principle
Henderson, L., 13
'hierarchical' modification structure defined, 22, 23–4
  of N₁–N₂ words, 85–8
  of V₁–V₂ words, 93, 94–5
homophony, 282–3
Hoosain, R., 17–18, 297–8
Hopper, P., 69, 238, 313
Hu, S., 13 n.3
huà ('draw, paint, picture, drawing')
  form class identity of, 42–6, *43*–5, 64
  in verb derived words, 92 n.5
Huang, J.C.-T., 229
  refutation of, 115, 116–17
  on V–O compound words, 109, 112–14
Huang, S., 127 n.24, 226
huŏchē ('train'), 288–91

idiomatic phrases
  development of, 30
  listedness of, 9
indeterminacy, 161
induced constituent reanalysis, 235–6

inflectional affixation, 77
  in Sadock's theory, 146
  in Selkirk's theory, 143, 155–6, 157
instrumental case, 131
internally affixed words, 246–9, *247–8*

Jarvella, R.J., 292 n.6
-jiàn ('view/see')
  as noun in bound morphemes, 66
  as resultative ending, 102–4
jìnkǒu ('entrance; to import'), lexical ambiguity of, 128

kàndào ('see'), 255, 256–7
Kawamoto, A.H., 125
kinship/hypercoristic reduplication, 249
kǒuàn ('harbour'), 195

language-elements (*yǔsù*), 15 n.5
láobǎo ('labour insurance'), 278
láogǎi ('reform through work'), 278
"Latinate prefixes," 167
Laudana, A., 297
-le ('completed action' verbal aspect suffix), 174, 229, 262, 263
left-branching structures
  Chinese examples, 183–92
  English examples, 207–14
left-modified verbs, 233–4
lemma, 293
Levelt, W.J.M., 293–4
lexemes
  defined, 70 n.14
  formation of, 70
Lexical Integrity Hypothesis (LIH), 31, 98, 112, 117
Lexical Phonology and Morphology, theory of, 225 n.4
lexical primitives, 4
lexical redundancy rules, 300, 301
lexical strata, 223–5, *224*
lexical triangle (S–P–O), 308
lexical units
  in speech comprehension, 287–92
  in speech production, 292–4
lexical words, defined, 8–9, 265
lexicalization
  of bound roots, 78
  categories of, 219–25, *222*
  criteria for determining, 118–25
  defined, 216–17
  degree of, 31, 216–17, 219, 223, 302
  and form class identity, 66
  gradient continuum of, 124, 217–18, 237
  and grammaticalization, 218, 262–5
  history of, 265–7
  impact of, 215

  in modern Chinese, 267–75
  and theta role transparency, 99
  of V–O compound words, 115–25
  word formation by, 28, 33
  and word-internal information, 237–61
lexicon
  and Chinese characters, 304–9
  defined, 8–9, 284–5
  and lexical access, 285–96, 305–8
  limits on, 301 n.12
  listings in, 156–7, 286, 296–303, *300*, 312–13
  Sadock's formulation of, 144–8
  'virtual lexical entries' in, 301
Li, A., 76 n.17
Li, C.N., 27, 109, 111–12, 217–18, 222, 255, 263
Li, Y., 100, 252
-lǐ ('one in charge; manager'), as noun in bound morphemes, 56, 65, 235
Liao, S., 27
Liberman, M., 218
LIH (Lexical Integrity Hypothesis), 31, 98, 112, 117
listed syntactic objects, 9
listeme, 8, 13 n.3
Liu, Y., 295, 296
location morphemes, 75–6
locative case, 131
Longenecker, Y.-C.J., 25
Lu, J.H.-T., 97
Lu, Z., 27, 32

Mandarin dialect, 4
  bound *vs.* free morphemes in, 67–8
  grammatical affixes (G) in, 174
  Headedness Principle in, 169
  modification structure of, 25
  morpheme-syllable coextension in, 129–30
  word formation in, 118, 170–2
  word-forming affixes (Xw) in, 174, *174*
  X-bar morphology of, 163–93
Marslen-Wilson, W., 287, 295, 296, 303
'meaning limiting' morphemes (word components), 21
-men (human plural marker), 174
metalinguistic judgment, 17–18
metaphorical lexicalization, 220–1, 261
miàn ('van'), 277–8, 302–3
modality-neutral lexicon, 286, 287
modification structures, 22–5
  of Mandarin dialect, 25
'modificational' morphemes (word components), 21
monomorphemic (full) words, 150, 154
monosyllabic words, formation of, 267
morphemes
  Chinese characters (*zì*) as, 3, 8, 14–15
  classification of, 67–9

creation of, 275–83
disappearance of, 315–16
distinguished from words, 17–18
form class identity of, 36–67
morphological analysis of, 67–76
as syllables, 129–30
types of, 67, 69–76, *74*
versatile *vs.* restricted, 132
see also 'bound' morphemes; 'free' morphemes; word components
morphological paradigms, 76
morphological primitives, 137, 145, 150, 311
    classification of, 165–7
Morphological Rule 1, 147
morphological words, defined, 11–12, 175
morphology, and lexicalization, 245–50
morphophonemic alternation, 76, 130
Morton, J., 292 n.6
mù ('tree, wood; numb')
    bound *vs.* free status of, 68
    polysemy of, 105–6, 279
multiple-branching structures, 177–93
Murrell, G.A., 292 n.6

Nagy, Bill, 130
'native' *vs.* 'non-native' compound words, 140–2
natural speech lexicon, 304–5
Necker cube, 124
neologisms, 231–3, 269, 275
neutral-toned words, 238–44, *240–3*
nominative (agentive) case, 131
nouns
    form class identity of, 125–9
    relations in N_1-N_2 words, 85–9
    types of, 82, 82–5
numerals, 74–5
numerical formulae, creating, 267–8
Nunberg, G., 218

Open class, 284
'oppositional' morphemes (word components), 21
orthographic lexicon, 298
orthographic rules, 16
orthographic words
    defined, 7–8
    as formal words (*cí*), 16
orthography, 284

p*ái* ('arrange, row discharge, push, platoon, perform/rehearse'), form class identity of, 42, 46–50, *47–9*
Pan, Wenguo, 196
paradigmatic alternation, 130
'parallel' ('juxtapositional') modification structure

defined, 22–3
of N_1–N_2 words, 85, 88–9
of V_1–V_2 words, 93–4
parts of speech. *see* form classes
pauses, potential: and phonological words, 10
Peng, D.-L., 295, 296, 298
'phase' ('degenerate') resultative verbs, 255–8, 262
phonetic loan words, 230–1
phonological rules, application of, 10
phonological words, defined, 10–11
phonology, and lexicalization, 238–45, 266–7
phrasal idioms, 218
Phrase Structure Condition (PSC), 113–14, 118
phrases (*duǎnyǔ, lèyǔ*), 15
polysemy
    of 'free' *vs.* 'bound' morphemes, 68
    and grammaticalization, 262–3
    of morphemes in resultative verbs, 105
    of new morphemes, 279
prefixes, 133
productivity
    defined, 132
    limitations on, 168–9
    of syntax, 134
    of word-forming affixes, 73
prosodic words, defined, 10, 11, *11*
PSC (Phrase Structure Condition), 113–14, 118
psycholinguistic research, 287
psychological words, 13 n.3
psycholinguistic words, defined, 13–14

q*ìchē* ('automobile'), 195
qīngbǎo ('protection of juveniles'), 270

-*r* ('nominalizing' suffix), 246–9
Rama (SOV language, Nicaragua), 263–4
recognition points, 288, 289, 290
recursiveness
    restrictions on, 164, 167, 168
    in syntax, 134–5, 150, 167
    in word formation, 137, 150, 164, 167
redundancy, of monomorphemic words, 150, 154
reduplication, 249–50
restricted morphemes. *see* versatile-restricted continuum (morphemes)
resultative verb compounds (V–V compounds)
    argument structures of, 97, 98, 99–100
    'cause-effect' relations in, 22
    defined, 95–8, 101–6
    lexical resultatives *vs.* syntactic extent resultatives, 100–1, 250–8, 312
    types of, 98–100, *103–4*
right-branching structures
    Chinese examples, 177–83
    English examples, 202–7

Romani, C., 297
root ('free') words
  defined, 69, 74, 165–6
  in Packard's application (X⁻⁰), 163–93 passim
  in Sadock's application (X⁻⁰), 145
  in Selkirk's application (X⁻¹), 138, 150–1, 152, 153–6
  in V–O compound words, 107
  as word components, 78
  see also 'free' morphemes
Ross, C., 97, 98, 109

-s (English plural marker), 143, 199
-s (English third person singular marker), 199
Sadock, Jerrold M.
  on 'heads,' 194
  morphology based on X-bar syntactic theory of, 13, 144–8, 149
  word-formation rules of, 150, 164
Sag, I., 218
Sagart, L., 9, 10
sàichē ('race-car; to race cars'), lexical ambiguity of, 128–9
Sapir, E., 9
Sawer, M., 267, 268
Scalise, S., 142 n.4, 148–9
Schreuder, R., 301
Selkirk, Elizabeth O.
  morphology based on X-bar syntactic theory of, 13, 136–43, 311
  refutation of, 149–57, 164
  Scalise's critique of, 142 n.4, 148–9
Selkirk's principle, 136
'semantic head,' 25, 95, 195–6
semantic words, defined, 9–10
semantics
  and lexicalization, 260–1
  word component description based on, 25–7
shāngfēng ('catch cold'), as V–O compound, 120
Shi, Y.-Z., 263
-shí ('rock, stone'), as unambiguous noun, 50–6, 51–3, 56
shifting, 267, 268
Shih, C., 132, 163, 299
shuìjiào ('sleep'), as V–O compound, 119–20
single-branching structures
  Chinese examples, 175–7
  English examples, 200–2
Snodgrass, J.G., 292 n.6
sociological words
  Chinese characters as, 14–15
  defined, 8
speech comprehension, 285–6, 287–92, 306
speech production, 285–6, 292–4
Sproat, Richard, 130 n.28, 132, 163, 218, 299
'start-free'/'start-bound' morphemes, 132–3

'stative' resultative verbs, 98, 102, 250, 252–3
Stem Rule, 158–9
stems
  in Di Sciullo and Williams's application, 149
  in Sadock's application (X⁻⁰), 145, 148, 150–1
  in Selkirk's application, 151
  in Tang's application ('X), 158, 161–2
stress, loss of, 238
'structural head,' 95, 195–6, 310–11
'subject-predicate' words, 27–9, 31
suffixes
  as heads, 149
  and inflectional affixes, 157
  and morphemes, 133
Sun, C., 263
superwords (X⁻²), 151
syllables, morphemes as, 129–30
synonymy
  of N_1–N_2 words, 88–9
  of V_1–V_2 words, 93
syntactic island, 160
syntactic words (Xo)
  defined, 8, 12–13, 18–20, 31, 138, 285
  form class identity of, 33–4
syntactical primitives, 150
syntax
  of Chinese languages, 1, 80 n.1
  and lexicalization, 250–60
  and meaning, 19
  productivity in, 134
  recursiveness in, 134–5, 150

Taft, M., 295–6, 299, 303, 308
Talmy, L., 216
Tang, Ting-chi Charles, 68, 158–63
thematic grids, 251
theoretical words, 16
theta roles
  defined, 250–1
  identification of, 100, 253, 254
  and lexicalization, 250–60
  percolation of, 98, 256, 259
  transparency of, 99
third tone sandhi rule, 244
Thompson, S.A., 27, 99, 109, 111–12, 217–18, 222, 255
3–3→2–3 tone sandhi rule, 244–5, 249
tīnghòu ('to wait for'), 195
tone, loss of, 238
-tou ('nominalizing' suffix), 246–9
tóuzī ('investment; to invest'), lexical ambiguity of, 128–9
Traugott, E., 69, 238, 250, 313
true compounds, defined, 78
tuō ('entrust'), as noun in bound morphemes, 236
two-syllable words. see bisyllabic words

unidirectionality hypothesis, 315
unitary concept, 9
universal principles, 169

verb–object (V–O) compound words
   either-or (word *vs.* phrase) status of, 123–5
   lexical identity of, 115–25, 311–12
   and lexicalization, 238, 258–60
   previous analyses of, 109–15
   and syntax, 28
   types of, 120, *121–2*
   word-phrase indeterminacy of, 106–9, 123–5
verbs
   form class identity of, 125–9
   and lexicalization, 250–60
   relations in V_1–V_2 words, 93–5
   types of, 89–3, *90*
   see also resultative verb compounds;
      verb–object (V–O) compound words
versatile-restricted continuum (morphemes), 132
'virtual head,' 57, 194–5
[VN] word structure, form class ambiguity of, 127–8

Wasow, T., 218
whole-word processing, 294–6
Williams, E.
   on lexical syntactic objects, 9
   on listemes, 8, 13 n.3
   on morphological words, 11
   on syntactic atoms, 13
   on X-bar analysis, 149
word boundaries, native speakers' agreement on, 18–19
word component reduction, 217–18
word components
   affixes as, 76–7
   bound roots as, 77–8
   form class description of, 32–4
   form class identity of, 36–67
   modification structure description of, 22–5, 32–3
   morphological analysis of, 67–6
   relational description of, 21–2, 22, 32
   root ('free') words as, 78
   semantic description of, 25–7, 33
   syntactic description of, 27–32, *28*, 33
   see also morphemes
word-elements (*císù*), 15 n.5
word-formation rules
   application of, 11–12
   application to English, 196–214
   generative and recursive nature of, 150
   by Packard, 168, *170*, 170–93, 197, 311
   restrictions on, 137
   by Sadock, 144–8, 149–50

   by Selkirk, 138–43, 149–50, 168, 174, 197
   see also compounding; lexicalization;
      neologisms; productivity; versatile-restricted continuum (morphemes)
word-forming affixes (Xw)
   classifiers as, 75
   compared to bound roots, 71–3
   defined, 70–1, *74*, 165, 166, 196, 197–200, *199*
   form class identity of, 70
   in Mandarin, 174, *174*
   productivity of, 73
word groups (*cízǔ*), 15
word-internal affixation, 246–9, *247–8*
word-internal information
   defined, 237–8
   morphological, 245–50
   phonological, 238–45
   semantic, 260–1
   syntactic, 250–60
word metaphorical lexicalization, 220–1
word-morpheme boundary, fluidity of, 17
wordhood, of V–O compound words
   indeterminacy of, 106–9
   lexical criteria for determining, 115–25
   previously proposed criteria for determining, 109–15
'wordness' (*cíxìng*), 36–7, 50
words
   Chinese definition of, 1, 2, 3, 14–20, 285, 310–16
   components of. *see* word components
   determiners as, 75
   in Di Sciullo and Williams's application (X^0), 149
   form class identity of, 34–6, 65, 310
   as gestalts, 18, 80
   in Packard's application (X^{-0}), 163–93, 196–200
   as real cognitive constructs, 4
   reality of, 316–17
   in Sadock's application (X^{-1}), 145–6, 151–2
   in Selkirk's application (X^{-0}), 138, 151–3
   special properties of Chinese words, 129–32
   in Tang's application, 161
   types of, 7–14, 80–1, *81*
   see also Chinese languages, definition of 'word' (*cí*) in

X-bar syntactic theory
   alternative application of, 163–93
   applied to Chinese words, 157–63
   applied to words, 135–6
   basic properties of, 134–5
   Di Sciullo and Williams's application of, 149
   expectations about, 135–6
   Scalise's application of, 148–9
   Selkirk's application of, 136–43, 149–57
   Sproat and Shih's application of, 163
   Tang's application of, 158–63

Xia, M., 21, 27
xiǎobiàn ('to urinate'), as verb in bound morphemes, 66
xuémáng ('one who is unable to study without a teacher'), 269

yá ('tooth, ivory'), 280
yán ('speak, speech'), as bound morpheme, 67–8
yǐng ('shadow, movie'), 280
Yip, P.-C., 196
yōumò ('humour; tease')
  in V–O compounds, 116, 118
  as verb in bound morphemes, 66
Yu, Genyuan, 268
-*yuán* ('person'), as bound root, 71–3, 72
yúncǎi ('cloud'), 195

Zero derivation, defined, 46, 234
zero-derived complex nouns, 234

Zhang, B., 298
-*zhě* ('one who does/is X'), as word-forming affix, 71–3, 72
-*zhe* (verbal aspect suffix), 174, 262
-*zhèng-* ('to prove/proof'), form class identity of, 57–60, 58–9, 64
zhǐ ('paper'), as noun, 37, 38–39
-*zhī-* ('to know/knowledge'), form class identity of, 57, 60–3, 61–2
Zhou, X., 295, 296, 303
Zhu, X., 295–6, 299, 303
-*zhù* ('to help')
  as noun in bound morphemes, 50, 54–5, 56–7, 65, 236
  as resultative ending, 104, 105
zhuājǐn ('to grasp tightly'), 255, 257–8
zì. see Chinese characters (*zì*)
-*zi* ('nominalizing' suffix), 246–9
zǒu ('walk, go'), as verb, 37, 39, 40–1
Zwicky, A., 196

Lightning Source UK Ltd.
Milton Keynes UK
21 May 2010
154522UK00001B/25/A